TROPES OF TRANSPORT

TROPES OF TRANSPORT

Hegel and Emotion

Katrin Pahl

Northwestern University Press
Evanston, Illinois

Northwestern University Press
www.nupress.northwestern.edu

Printed in the United States of America

10 9 8 7 6 5 4 3 2 1

Library of Congress Cataloging-in-Publication data are available from the Library of Congress.

Contents

Acknowledgments

This book has formed in many layers of learning, teaching, reading, and thinking together. I would like to thank my teachers Hélène Cixous, Judith Butler, Winfried Kudszus, Ann Smock, and Trinh Minh-ha. Each one of you not only taught me a specific approach to literary and philosophical texts but also taught me to dare. I want to thank the students in my Hegel seminars at Johns Hopkins University—in particular Florentina Costache, Malte Wessels, and Markus Wilczek—for the great discussions, thoughtful feedback, and intelligent objections. I cherish the vibrant intellectual milieu at Johns Hopkins and am grateful to my colleagues and mentors Amanda Anderson, Jane Bennett, Rüdiger Campe, Bill Connolly, Jennifer Culbert, Bill Egginton, Frances Ferguson, Dean Moyar, Mary Ryan, and Rochelle Tobias for discussing various parts and versions of this book with me. Without the support, encouragement, and critique of many colleagues whom I admire, this book would not have appeared: Gabriele Brandstetter, Anne-Lise François, Christine Hentschel, Simon Jarvis, Catherine Malabou, John McCumber, Christoph Menke, Terry Pinkard, Eva von Redecker, Denise Riley, Art Strum, Rei Terada, and Karen Tongson deserve more than my most sincere thanks. The book has profited from my fellowship as a visiting professor at the Cluster of Excellence "Languages of Emotion" at the Freie Universität, Berlin. I have shared versions of chapters at various colloquia and am grateful for the intense discussions and the feedback I received there, in particular at the Institut für Germanistik, Vergleichende Literatur- und Kulturwissenschaft of the University of Bonn (thanks to Christian Moser for inviting me), the Kolloquium für Sozialphilosophie at the Humboldt University (thanks to Rahel Jaeggi for the invitation), the Literaturwissenschaftliches Kolloquium of the University of Erfurt (thanks to Bettine Menke and Martin Schäfer for inviting me), the Deutsche Haus of New York University (thanks to Paul North for the invitation), and the Doreen B. Townsend Center for the Humanities at UC Berkeley (where I held a fellowship). I have fond memories of the Marxist philosophy group at the University of Bonn, in particular Leander Scholz, because we discovered Hegel together. Currently, I find intellectual kinship in the newly formed multidisciplinary research group "Material Lives of Emotionality" at Johns Hopkins University and thank them for discovering uncharted sites of emotionality with me.

I want to wholeheartedly thank the two anonymous readers for their very detailed and substantive comments on the manuscript. Henry Carrigan Jr., senior editor and assistant director of Northwestern University Press, stands out because of his superb editorial work and because he infected others (including me) with his excitement about this project. I was truly fortunate that Jane Bennett, Rebecca Brown, Jennifer Culbert, and Lisa O'Connell read drafts at a moment's notice, and I thank them for their inspiration, encouragement, patience, and sociability. John Tinkler showed a great faculty of plasticity when he paid attention to both detail and the overall argument while editing an earlier version of this book. I thank Karen Tongson and Jennifer Culbert for eliminating unwanted remnants of German syntax in my English, Christina Hinz for her assistance in preparing the manuscript, Paul Mendelson for preventing me from going too crazy with last-minute changes during the copyediting process, and Martijn Buijs for expertly preparing the index. A part of chapter 7 is adapted from my article "The Way of Despair," published in *Hegel and the Infinite,* edited by Slavoj Žižek, Clayton Crockett, and Creston Davis, © 2011 Columbia University Press. A part of chapter 5 has previously appeared as "A Reading of Love in Hölderlin's *Andenken,*" in *The German Quarterly* 78, no. 2, © 2005 American Association of Teachers of German. I thank Columbia University Press and the American Association of Teachers of German for granting the one-time non-exclusive rights to use these publications here.

It was a special treat that my friend Jordan Tierney agreed to create the cover art for this book. Jordan read parts of the text and related them to aspects of her rich, intelligent, material-responsive, and chance-embracing work in sculpture and collage. I offered bits of readings of some of her pieces that particularly speak to my concerns. I love the result for what it is and for what it reminds me of, namely, the process of relating complex thoughts to the complex materiality of her art. I thank Jordan for these conversations and for the artwork that lends such a thick and yet translucent, fluid and yet parched, torn and yet exuberant face to the text.

Greetings to Maxine Fredericksen, the heart and free spirit of the Rhetoric Department at UC Berkeley, who is retiring this year after nearly twenty years of service as graduate student affairs officer. She importantly contributed to the great experience that Berkeley was for me. So did Rob Miotke, Will Bishop, and the working group in Critical Feminist

Inquiry at the Doreen B. Townsend Center for the Humanities. I am grateful to Stanford University for a postdoctoral fellowship, and I want to thank the University of Southern California, in particular Alice Gambrell and Peggy Kamuf, for giving me the opportunity to spend a year in Los Angeles. Finally, I want to express my appreciation for German at Hopkins, where I received a wonderful introduction to the assistant professor experience.

TROPES OF TRANSPORT

Introduction

Hegel is not a very agreeable philosopher—that much can probably be agreed upon. From Schelling and Kierkegaard to Derrida, his name has come to stand for the imperialism of an all-appropriating spirit, cold magisterialism, and Prussian state control. Yet, his work does not always agree with this reception. Some of the more interesting recent readers of Hegel today find in his philosophy a transformative thought in progress, a restless openness to contingency, and an ecstatic vulnerability.[1] The incompatibility of these two strands of Hegel's reception goes to prove that what we refer to with the one name "Hegel" still moves.

It is widely accepted that Hegel introduced philosophy to a dynamic notion of truth. *Tropes of Transport: Hegel and Emotion* locates the tropes that render truth dynamic in the emotional register. Focusing primarily on the *Phenomenology of Spirit,* I read his work—using the tools of literary and rhetorical analysis—in dialogue with literary texts contemporary to Hegel or to us.[2] The latter constellation serves to explore how Hegel resonates with some of our concerns today. In my reading, I trace how emotionality (dis)organizes the logical, quasi-existential, and narrative unfolding of Hegel's text. Emotions transport consciousness, the protagonist of the *Phenomenology,* across its various stages of self-reflection, and draw the reader into that process of self-reflection. I call this (dis)organizing force the "emotional syntax" of Hegel's text. Through a thorough analysis of the emotional syntax of Hegel's philosophy, *Tropes of Transport* contributes both to the recently begun reevaluation of Hegel's philosophy, and to the burgeoning interdisciplinary studies of affect and emotion.

Emotionality clearly forms a primary, albeit much neglected concern in the explication of Hegelian philosophy. With its account of emotional temporality, *Tropes of Transport* elucidates the cross-vectored temporality of Hegel's text. It describes Hegel's speculative logic as a logic of sympathy that undoes the dichotomy of rationality and emotionality by drawing on emotion to propel self-reflection and on self-distance to thicken the experience of emotion.

Intervening in the multidisciplinary study of affect and emotion, *Tropes of Transport* illustrates that a fresh analysis of Hegel's philosophy offers an important resource for a cutting-edge theory of emotionality.[3]

In particular, it explores how Hegel's thought and textual practice of mediation, plural subjectivity, impersonal subjectivity, and sympathy advances such a theory.

Mediation

> If the form is said to be in parity with the essence, then it is for that very reason a bald misunderstanding to suppose that cognition can be content with . . . the essence, but can do without the form.
>
> —Hegel, *Phenomenology of Spirit*, § 19

If it is usually assumed that the force of intensities and the sincerity of emotions depend on their immediacy, I explore to what extent mediation—and therefore a certain degree of fabrication and manipulation—is constitutive of emotionality. Hegel serves as a particularly helpful interlocutor for such an exploration not only because he offers a sophisticated analysis of mediation, but also because the notion that feelings are immediate and therefore non-reflective dates from the Enlightenment era, and Hegel, as this book shows, is one of its earliest critics.

The idea of mediation plays such an important role in the long and complex history of the Marxist reception of Hegel that it might be confusing to encounter the term here, in the context of a discussion of transports. Indeed, I am not concerned with the concrete forms of mediation—between man and nature or between classes—that Marxist theorists have foregrounded. Capital, the media, or labor are not my primary interests here (although my irritation at the fact that the discipline of philosophy is interested in the emotions only when they labor in the service of epistemology or morality, and the fact that this emotional labor is unevenly divided across gender lines, was an important motivation for this work). Instead, I draw on the structural notion of mediation in Hegel, according to which the immediate appears as simple, straightforward, and unrelated to other things, whereas the mediated is complex, indirect, related to other things, and resultant. Hegelian thought shows that every certainty that seems immediately evident and fresh to a particular consciousness proves, from a different perspective, indeed socially and historically mediated. Hegel relentlessly criticizes the idea that we have immediate access to the truth, or rather that there is such a thing as a simple truth independent of our practices of reflection.

I apply to the context of feeling this wide meaning of mediation that we know mainly from the epistemological context in Hegel. Modern philosophical, literary, and everyday discourses of emotion are highly charged with anxiety about the authenticity of feelings and the sincerity of their expression.[4] But if, as I argue, emotions are—in the most pared-down description—modes of relationality, they cannot be simple, pure, whole, consistent, and "at one with themselves." Thus, emotionality is inherently ambivalent, contaminated, disrupted, confused, and incongruous with itself—or, in one word, inauthentic—and we necessarily have a hard time experiencing emotions fully and expressing them sincerely. Both pleasurable and painful at the same time, they never quite fit the categories elaborated by centuries of classificatory impulse (they shift between love and hate, fear and desire, grief and relief—to name but a few of the more obvious examples of emotional ambiguity). In addition, they are split between the singular and the common: an emotion feels both urgent in that it concerns me in my singularity, and banal in its commonality. The experience of grief, joy, and so on is possible to the extent that I share it with another (this other could be myself), which means that I never "fully" experience these transports (even if the other I share them with is myself). For all these reasons, we need to attend to the double modality of emotionality: that, on the one hand, emotions are real and, on the other hand, they are manipulations, performances, or cultivations of the real. Hegel's structural notion of mediation helps us to get into view both the mediatedness and the immediacy of emotion.

This has several implications—epistemic, critical, and ethical. The fact that emotionality is inherently ambivalent, confused, and incongruous does not mean that it is irrational. Conversely, we will observe in Hegel that attention to the forms of reflection and self-reflection inherent in emotionality changes the rules of rationality. The idea that feelings should be purely immediate leads to more or less willful denials of mediation, which in turn make it only easier for external manipulations to take hold.[5] Attention to the social and historical mediation of feeling can serve as a first step toward criticizing the economic and political capture of affect, but it also implies that feeling cannot and should not be immune to critique. Finally, and most importantly for the current study, Hegel offers conceptual tools and analyses that make it possible to shift from an ethics of truthfulness to an ethics of sympathy. A single individual without interpersonal interactions, without recourse to the imagination of interpersonality, or without the ability to relate to herself as another, would have no emotions. Hegelian transport is always shared; that is to say, it creates a texture of sympathy.

Plural Subjectivity

By "transport" I mean an emotion—strong or slight—that carries one out of oneself and to a different self. The self-reflection of spirit, which Hegel traces in the *Phenomenology of Spirit,* relies on such transports.[6] Hegel describes the logic of transports as one of "determinate negations." This logic—which Hegel famously characterizes by exploiting the multivalence of the German term for "negating," *Aufhebung*—suggests that there is an overlap between negation and affirmation. Hegelian subjectivity is the capacity to self-negate without self-destroying, to generate new selves out of the contradictions of former selves. What Hegel abstractly calls "negativity," this book renders more concretely with descriptions of emotional processes. Hegelian negativity manifests, for example, as tremble, brokenness, laughter, or release. While these transports enable the emergence of different selves, they also expose and breach the boundaries of the self-sufficient subject. *Aufhebung,* since it preserves what it negates, divides the subject. In the transition from one subject to the next, the former subject does not simply disappear. The new self encompasses and is forced to relate to the remains of its former manifestations. As modes of self-relation, transports thus project new selves and remember old selves. The history of cumulative *Aufhebungen* multiplies internal differences and makes the subject more emotional with each step.

This brings me to an important challenge of Hegel's quasi-literary text: its temporality.[7] While philosophical texts traditionally make atemporal truth claims, the *Phenomenology*'s conceit—that we are accompanying the self-assessment of exemplary worldviews or epistemes—not only temporalizes truth but does so by creating a complex temporal plasticity. The *Phenomenology* has often been read as a narrative, more specifically as a bildungsroman.[8] I argue rather that the text intertwines the temporalities of the three major literary genres: the syncopating measures of poetic rhythm, the virtual present of theatrical enactment, and the folded sequence of narrative. This intertwinement of different, in themselves disrupted and complex, times contributes to the emotionality of the Hegelian text.

The subject of the *Phenomenology of Spirit* is the path of spirit's self-reflection or of its coming-to-know-itself. Hegel defines spirit as a plural subject: "the 'I' that is 'We' and the 'We' that is 'I.'" The double genitive of the title indicates that spirit serves as both the agent of the phenomenological inquiry and its subject matter. This means that the subject of the *Phenomenology* is divided between spirit in the form of the protagonist and spirit in the form of the phenomenologist. In other words, the book has two characters who manifest and propel spirit's self-reflection:

the phenomenologist and the protagonist, called "consciousness." Hegel refers to the phenomenologist in the first-person plural ("we"), indicating that the author and the reader share in the plural subjectivity of the phenomenologist and reinforcing the slippage between author, reader, and spirit. The protagonist is also a plural subject. Indeed, I argue throughout this book that the *Phenomenology* does not trace the linear development of one consciousness, but presents the constellation of many figures or shapes of consciousness. Therefore I will sometimes speak of protagonists in the plural. Strictly speaking, the protagonist is neither singular nor plural because the many figures of consciousness all have their own identities and are also versions of one another. It is thus possible to refer to the constellation of different figures of consciousness as the protagonists or as the protagonist (then understood as manifoldly divided within).

Trembling—one of the tropes this book explores—literalizes or materializes the back-and-forth movement of the self between its various shapes. The self trembles with fear before the transition to a new self and such tremble propels the transition, yet the new self is also shuddered through by the old selves. The trembling movement blurs the shape of each self. Indeed, it blurs the border between intra- and intersubjectivity. Another trope that jumbles the prefixes intra- and inter- is "acknowledging," which renders thinking, cognition, and recognition as always again incipient movements toward an other self and also toward the practice of thinking and knowing itself. Hegel's speculative logic demands considerable plasticity in casting the self-relationality that emotionality essentially is in at times intra-, at times intersubjective modes. Thus, rhythm emerges as an important characteristic of emotionality that this book explores. Emotional subjectivity is plural subjectivity in the sense that it moves to multiple, incongruent beats and incessantly combines dynamic and complex shifts between self-reference and external reference.

Impersonal Subjectivity

Hegel's notion of "objective spirit" offers an effective tool for an account of emotional processes going on outside the heart or the mind. Since Hegel does not think of subjectivity as the exclusive attribute of persons, the emotional relations that oscillate or tremble between the intra- and the intersubjective are often transpersonal or entirely impersonal in character. The still-pervasive habit of attributing emotion exclusively to human subjects requires a critical analysis. Terada has developed a deconstructionist theory of emotion based on the insight that a unified subject as traditionally conceived could not possibly experience emotion (Terada 2001). Riley locates emotion at the interstices of the human, in particular in language, where she observes "impersonal passions" that don't quite coincide with the felt emotions of individual speakers (Riley 2005). Despite these and other advances in thinking emotion as impersonal or anonymous, we still tend to project a person who "has" or "expresses" the emotion whenever we speak of emotion (as different from affect). This book follows a different approach and explores, especially in its second part, the impersonality and exteriority of emotion. I am aware of the fact that it is quite counterintuitive to think of emotion as not primarily human, especially since humanity is often regarded as synonymous with the capacity to have feelings. Still, my point here is not to extend the faculty of emotion to non-human animals, as Nussbaum does (Nussbaum 2001, 89–138). I am not concerned with emotions as stable attributes that animals or other organisms might "have."[9] Nor do I agree with Nussbaum when she argues that emotions "always involve thought of an object" even if "this doesn't necessarily include reflexive awareness" (Nussbaum 2001, 23). Rather, I submit that emotions always include reflexive awareness but that this reflection does not require a human self. I consider emotions as dynamic self-relations of emotionality to itself. That is to say, I subjectivize non-human sites of emotionality. To adjust to this counterintuitive idea, it helps to anthropomorphize emotionality. Broadcast on the right wavelengths, "emotionality" sounds like a proper name, and there is reason to appreciate the agency and subject status that the proper name confers upon the phenomenon. Of course, I recommend such anthropomorphizing with a winking eye and only as a strategy to relativize the strained anthropomorphizing of humans that we practice every day. As much as possible, I push toward exploring emotionality in its own right and not merely as experiences or expressions of human actants.

Sympathy

Hegel's textual practice generates an almost inadvertent sympathy with the protagonist/s in the reader, just as Hegel's logic demands sympathy of the thinker with the subject of her thought. Sympathy poses a threat to the idea of autonomy.[10] The "free agent" in the classical sense—whether inner-directed or tradition-directed (to fall back on Riesman's influential but dated terminology)—knows who he is and can tell right from wrong; he is at one with himself, single-minded, and calm. Pinkard argues that such self-sufficiency might be a beautiful idea, but it "cannot survive its confrontation with other putatively self-sufficient agents—unless the agents in question are gods" (Pinkard 2007, 15). Pinkard refers to Hegel's discussion of the dialectic of mastery and servitude as evidence for the problems with conceiving freedom as self-sufficiency. A less divine but more workable notion of freedom values the emotional turmoil of challenging ourselves and others, of adopting a negative, reflective, or ironic stance toward our own and others' beliefs and feelings. It appreciates the wounds and the tears (*Zerrissenheit*) through which others enter the self.[11] And it embraces the notion of a plural self enacting many roles. This freedom—which, I argue, is Hegel's notion of freedom—demands that we reconcile ourselves to emotionality—not that we repair what is torn.

Hegel sees this model of freedom exemplified in the "self-alienated spirit" of *Rameau's Nephew*. The nephew abandons individual selfhood to become all the voices of existence. He

> "piled up and mixed together some thirty airs, Italian, French, tragic, comic, of all sorts of character; now, with a deep bass, he descended into the depths of hell, then, contracting his throat, with a falsetto he tore apart the vaults of the skies, alternately raging and then being placated, imperious and then derisive." (§ 521)[12]

The "inverted and inverting, disrupted" performance of the nephew proves contagious; it infects the philosopher-judge with an inadvertent sympathy (§ 653). The calm and sincere consciousness (Diderot's "*Moi*")—who usually "in all honesty composes [*setzt*] the melody of the good and the true in . . . *one* note"—is not quite sure what to think of the nephew's performance (§ 521, trans. modified). He remains torn in his judgment of the nephew and, thus torn, ends up imitating or *nachempfinden* the entire gamut of emotions that the nephew just performed:

> For the motionless [*ruhig*] consciousness . . . this speech appears as a "blather of wisdom and folly, a medley consisting of as much skill as it did of baseness, of as many right as of false ideas, of such a complete inversion [*Verkehrtheit*] of sentiment, of such consummate disgracefulness as well as of such entire candor and truth. [The supposedly motionless consciousness] *will be unable to refrain from going into all these tones* [*in alle diese Töne einzugehen*], and from running up and down the entire scale

> of feeling, of moving from the deepest contempt and depravity to the highest admiration and stirring emotion." (§ 521, trans. modified, italics: my emphasis)[13]

The honest consciousness turns into a reiteration of the disrupted consciousness. Such contagion or inadvertent sympathy shows that the model of subjectivity that is bound up with emotionality and freedom, as Hegel sees them, does not emphasize individuality and does not clearly distinguish between the singular and the plural. Even the consciousness whose honesty consists in sticking to one note inadvertently becomes several.

Hegel's notion of freedom and his analysis of contagion imply an ethics of sympathy.[14] By "ethics," I don't mean a substantive definition of goodness, or a procedural definition of right action.[15] What I consider "ethical" lies at the intersection of ethics, aesthetics, and philology.[16] It is the practice of paying close attention to subtle complexities, acknowledging alterity, and appreciating the confused and often messy process of juggling contrary pulls and negotiating differences. Sympathizing with the unfamiliar while retaining a gait of one's own, adjusting to another rhythm without losing one's beat: these are the domains of emotionality. To avoid such negotiations by reducing, denying, or stabilizing differences seems to me unethical. But to engage in these negotiations requires the willingness to temporarily be wrong, do wrong, be done wrong, and allow for forgiveness. It is an ethics beyond good and evil, if that is possible. This emotional ethics is obviously too large and complex a topic to be dealt with adequately here, but I can isolate two aspects of it that are relevant to the book: emotional ethics demands a practice of sympathizing with (one's) other selves (including impersonal selves) and an extreme plasticity of the self (or a practice of self-figuration).

Trilling observes that, around the time when sincerity emerges as both a value and a problem (with the increase in social mobility beginning in the sixteenth century), interest in "the villain" rises. Originally, a "villain" is simply a man at the lowest scale of feudal society, but "the villain of plays and novels is characteristically a person who seeks to rise above the station to which he was born," and thus becomes morally villainized.[17] He is not what he is, in the double sense of denying his given social identity and playacting (using flattery and deceit) in order to get ahead. Not only is Rameau's nephew a villain in this sense, but all the shapes of consciousness and formations of spirit that the *Phenomenology* presents, its protagonist/s in general and even its phenomenologist/s, must come across as villains. Consciousness makes its way through the phenomenological narrative by relentlessly rising above its presupposed identity. At the same time, the narrative cannot advance without the villainous or insincere involvement of the phenomenologist/s. The phenomenologist/s must be what they are not, must play the role of "natural consciousness" and sympathize with the protagonist/s in order for the text to unfold. Spirit is multiply divided, and each of its personae acts in the double consciousness of being both the hero and the villain of this story. The syntax of Hegel's text reflects this singularly plural subjectivity of emotionality: it articulates—that is, it separates and joins—the different formations of spirit and the various shapes of consciousness in such a way that it is impossible to decide whether the text has one protagonist (who appears in many incarnations) or many protagonists (who tend to get collapsed into one by the conventions of the developmental narrative). Rameau's nephew thus exemplifies the structural alienation of emotional subjectivity that is at work in each and every instantiation of the phenomenological subject. He models the plasticity of shifting freely between the singular and the plural—the plasticity that I have described as one aspect of emotional ethics.[18]

Hegel uses a philosophical version of free indirect discourse—a narrative technique that blurs the distinction between the voice of the narrator and the voice of a character. Hegel presents the theories (or "certainties") and insights of his protagonist/s by oscillating often imperceptibly between the protagonist's voice and the phenomenologist's voice. In doing so he creates a plastic syntax of emotionality in the *Phenomenology*. Throughout this book, I call attention to Hegel's use of this literary device and analyze its various effects. They range from allowing for intimate knowledge of highly problematic and thus commonly dismissed positions, to creating the reflective distance necessary for emotion to register, to generating perspectival shifts within and between the protagonist/s themselves. As already noted, Hegel thoroughly abandons the idea of the strictly in-dividual subject—all subjects of the *Phenomenology* are divisible and internally divided without completely falling apart or losing all coherence. Free indirect discourse presents the difference between internal and external differences and exchanges as hard to pin down and the distinction as impossible to maintain. Overall, free indirect discourse enhances the plasticity of emotionality and facilitates an ethics of sympathy.

Chapter Overview

The present study falls into two parts. The first part ("Emotional Subjects") focuses on Hegel's thematic accounts of emotionality and the second part ("Emotional Syntax") on his performative accounts of it. With literary and rhetorical analyses of the Hegelian text I hope to reveal, in the first part, some of the shortcomings of straightforward readings of Hegel's explicit thematizations of emotion. To read the *Phenomenology of Spirit* at face value is to miss some significant challenges of this quasi-literary text. The fact that the *Phenomenology* has a protagonist ("consciousness") and a first-person plural narrator ("we"—the phenomenologist/s) demands that the reader attend to the differences between the perspective of the author, the perspective of the narrator, and the perspective of the protagonist. That is to say, when Hegel discusses "feeling" or "pathos," he doesn't develop his theory of emotion. Instead, he offers a critical analysis of the assumptions at work when one conceives of emotion as feeling or as pathos.

The book opens with a chapter on the trope of the "Heart." It addresses Hegel's response to schools of thought that give matters of the heart a philosophical value (eighteenth-century sentimentalism and philosophical mysticism). Hegel derides this celebration of feeling. He describes feeling as an inefficient way of relating to the world, one that indulges in nebulous idealizations because it lacks the "strength" to take a clear stance in words and actions. Reading Hegel on "the feeling heart," one wonders whether Hegel values the significance of emotion.[19] In this introductory chapter, I remind readers that Hegel does not disparage feeling as such, but criticizes only the sentimental and mystic understanding of feeling. I argue that he does so for two reasons. First, the sentimental and mystic preference of feeling over reason reproduces the dichotomy between rationality and emotionality. Second, the figure of the heart relegates feeling to interiority. Thus, this introductory chapter familiarizes the reader of *Tropes of Transport* with two important demands of Hegel's philosophy of emotion: first, that reason and emotion be mutually implicated, and second, that thoughtful "transports" or emotional thoughts call into question the construction of interiority.

This brings me to the second thematic figure of emotion, namely "Pathos," which plays a crucial role in Hegel's theory of the tragic. Hegel defines pathos as an absolute commitment to a particular ethical calling. Pathos has two advantages over the figure of the heart: because it calls for action, it escapes Hegel's critique of mere interiority, and in that it takes a clear stance, it integrates emotionality with rationality. Nevertheless, it cannot properly be described as a trope of transport, since the passionate stance absorbs the person so fully that she is absolutely congruent with her ethical commitment. Far from effecting a transformation, pathos leads to the tragic annihilation of the individual who is under the sway of this trope—it quite literally comes to a dead end. For this reason, I contend, Hegel grows rather disenchanted with philosophical investments in passionate characters and instead shifts to an analysis of how the theatricality of tragedy affects the trope of absolute sincerity, which is pathos. I argue that Hegel's preoccupation with theatricality importantly informs the composition of the *Phenomenology*. The theatrics of the *Phenomenology* builds ambivalence into the structure of the emotional subject by dividing the subject of the *Phenomenology* into a protagonist and a phenomenologist. I argue that the different roles of this plural subject both invigorate and break one another. Yet, they also serve as remainders of one another, so that there is never any complete destruction of the subject in the *Phenomenology*.

The analysis of Hegel's critique of heart and pathos enables me to identify *ex negativo* three main points of his own conception of emotion: (1) that reason and emotion implicate one another; (2) that thoughtful "transports" or emotional thoughts foil any clean-cut separation between, or hierarchical organization of, interiority and exteriority; and (3) that transport generates a plural subject, spoiling any desire for coherence and unification.

At the end of this first part—on "Emotional Subjects"—it becomes evident that where emotion is the explicit subject of analysis, the account inadvertently unifies and stabilizes the emotional subject. In order to reach an affirmative view of the non-unified subject and of emotion as a vehicle for self-transformation, we need to turn to non-reifying, that is, performative presentations of emotion as transports. We need to analyze what emotions do in Hegel's text, how they carry the self-reflection of spirit. Thus, in the second part of *Tropes of Transport* I explore how the syntax, not the subject matter, of Hegel's speculative logic moves thought.

Most discussions of Hegel make the assumption that the promise or threat (depending on the discussants' taste for grand narratives) of Hegel's philosophy is to overcome divisions. This book challenges that assumption. The second part—"Emotional Syntax"—explores how the emotional syntax of Hegel's *Phenomenology* both creates a plural or manifoldly divided subject, and connects the different parts of this plural subject (the series of figures of consciousness that make up the protagonist, as well as the author and the readers who share in the subjectivity of the phenomenologist) in a moving, mutually informing and deforming synthesis.

The emotional syntax of the *Phenomenology* features specific tropes of emotionality, such as "release," "juggle," "acknowledging," "tremble," and "broken." I have organized each chapter of "Emotional Syntax" around one of these figures, which are key words from Hegel's *Phenomenology of Spirit.* These key words involve a tropic dislocation in the sense that they are used not quite according to common sense. The most common meaning of "trembling," for example, in the context of a study of emotion, would be the shaking movement of a human body affected with great fear. *Tropes of Transport* employs the term in a defamiliarized way to describe the shaking movement of the Hegelian text, arguing that Hegel's text trembles.

"Emotional Syntax" opens with a chapter, titled "Release," that discusses the ending of the *Phenomenology of Spirit.* Rather than in absolute knowledge, the text ends in a tear: a dash, from which two lines of Schiller's poem "Friendship" drop. The supposedly grandiose narrative of the *Phenomenology* "releases" its grasp of the subject and its grip on the reader by speaking in another's voice. Yet no one remains intact here. This chapter demonstrates that numerous shapes of consciousness have been ruined, that the Hegelian text falls short of coherence and closure, and that Hegel alters the verses he cites. Chapter 3 argues that the mutual syncopation and disintegration of self and other are requirements for the experience of emotion. It is thus an act of friendship when Hegel alters Schiller's lines and when he allows his own text to be interrupted and torn open to future readers. At the beginning of the second part of the book, this argument demonstrates the appropriateness of my own method of reading, which is to remain true to the Hegelian text by transforming it.

Building on the argument developed in the preceding chapter—that emotionality is an effect of dissonances—chapter 4, "Juggle," shows that Hegel's language is not one with itself. The chapter analyzes what Hegel means when he contends that the phenomenological exposition must juggle the rationalistic syntax of predicative propositions and the dynamic syntax of the Hegelian "speculative judgment." Arguing that Hegel rhythmically interweaves the two different functions of the phenomenologist (author and reader) by mutually syncopating authorial will and reader expectation, I propose a Hegelian ethics of sympathy. When Hegel asks his readers to identify with consciousness on its path, he demands of them to do what he does in his writing, namely, to march to the beat of (at least) two drums at a time.

Via a linguistic and poetic analysis of *Anerkennen,* the next chapter, titled "Acknowledging," explores the non-closed or unending temporality of knowledge as well as the plural subjectivity of consciousness. Bringing passages from Hegel's *Phenomenology* into dialogue with Hölderlin's poem "Remembrance" and Goethe's poem "Reunion," chapter 5 questions Hegelian claims to completion and perfection. I show how Hegel tries to perpetuate the ecstasy of love by repeatedly changing the subject. While Goethe's poem establishes self-sufficiency as the ideal, I read Hölderlin's poem as chiefly concerned with the question of how con/versing can foster an always transient mutuality. And I argue that Hegel understands recognition as a mutual acknowledging of transports (of one's ceaselessly becoming someone else). Translating *Anerkennen* as acknowledging, rather than recognition, I highlight the constitutive sociality and incipience of knowledge.

Analyzing Hegel's brief but stunning passage on "absolute fear" in the dialectic of mastery and servitude, chapter 6 makes two arguments about the trope "Tremble." First, it shows that no individual consciousness in the *Phenomenology* ever actually experiences absolute fear. If by "individuals" we mean undivided, self-identical beings, then individuals cannot experience transports. Only tremulous subjects, moving from one figure of themselves to another, riddled with intervals that intertwine exteriority and interiority, are transported with fear. That said, chapter 6 makes a second argument. It shows that the syntactical arrangement of the different shapes of consciousness produces absolute fear. Specifically, the transitions between the chapters of the *Phenomenology* are moments of absolute fear. They are intervals of trembling: a back-and-forth movement that breaks with the linearity of any narrative of progress the *Phenomenology* might construe or be construed as. These transitions are not irrational or alogical but rather constitutive of the emotional syntax of Hegel's speculative logic.

The twentieth century has read the *Phenomenology* as a triumphant story of progress. The seventh chapter of *Tropes of Transport* tells the story of spirit's consumption and dismemberment. "Broken" notes that *Bildung* is experienced as torture because it repeatedly shatters self-certainty. The chapter argues in favor of an ethics of emotionality that calls for a reconciliation with disruptedness rather than of the disrupted. After exploring Hegel's description of the *Phenomenology* as a path of despair, I proceed with a discussion of two exemplary moments of breaking spirit: the breaking of the phrenologist's judgment and the breaking of the "hard heart." This chapter concludes my analysis of the *Phenomenology*'s emotional syntax by demonstrating again the overlap of emotionality and rationality in Hegel: I argue that the analytic activity of the understanding fractures the phenomenological text and thus enhances its emotionality while the self-reflecting emotionality of despair emerges as a lighthearted transport.

In the epilogue, "Against Emotional Violence," I modulate the tropes of transport addressed in this study for a final argument against approaches and paradigms in affect and emotion studies that amplify their vehement, passionate, or violent force. Instead, I foreground the incongruence and plasticity of emotional subjectivity and offer tools to attend to dispersed feelings and fleeting emotions that give a texture of the provisional to experience—opening onto an ironic and even lighthearted kind of sentimentality.

Part 1

Emotional Subjects

1

Heart

From its inception Western philosophy has produced, sustained, and reproduced a fierce antagonism between rationality and emotionality. To expel emotion from the sphere of reason must be considered one of the foundational gestures of philosophy as a discipline. In the eighteenth century, this antagonism is attenuated somewhat as sentimentalism and philosophical mysticism give matters of the heart a philosophical value. Hegel derides this new celebration of feeling. He describes feeling as an inefficient way of relating to the world, one that indulges in nebulous notions and edifying idealizations because it lacks the strength to take a clear stance and to do the work of the concept. Reading Hegel on the feeling heart, one wonders to what extent Hegel really recognizes the epistemic significance of emotion.

Yet I argue in this chapter that Hegel does not disparage emotionality per se. Rather, he targets the specific conception of emotionality that is encapsulated in the sentimental and mystic trope of the feeling heart. His critique of this trope brings into view two important concerns of his philosophy: the reconciliation of rationality and emotionality, and the dismantlement of interiority.[1] In regard to the first concern, Hegel critiques the sentimentalists and philosophical mystics for valuing feeling over analysis without resolving the dichotomy between rationality and emotionality. In regard to the second, he denounces the figure of the heart for relegating feeling to interiority. Rather than locate emotions inside, Hegel offers a performative account of emotionality as moving one outside and beyond oneself; that is to say, he considers emotions as transports. In sum, this first chapter introduces two demands of Hegel's philosophy of emotion: that reason and emotion be mutually implicated, and that thoughtful transports (that is, emotional thoughts) call into question the construction of interiority.

Hegel spends a good part of the preface to the *Phenomenology of Spirit* defending what he calls a scientific philosophy against the philosophy of feeling (*Gefühlsphilosophie*) advanced by many of his contemporaries. He chiefly attacks Schleiermacher—who claims that "the essence of religion lies neither in thought nor in practice, but in intuition and feeling"—but also Jacobi, Görres, and Eschenmayer, who all in some way or another argue for an extrasensory or inner intuition as the faculty that distinguishes reason (*Vernunft*—derived from *vernehmen*, "to hear") from the understanding (*Verstand*).[2] Hegel charges this kind of philosophy of feeling with (a) excluding rational approaches in favor of pure feeling, and (b) withdrawing from the outside world into inwardness. According to Hegel, these limitations are the result of a misguided insistence on the sacred and metaphysical quality of the absolute and thus of a failure to understand that spirit is manifest in physical reality.[3]

As if anticipating Nietzsche—who of course included Hegel in the list of German veil-makers (*Schleiermacher*)—Hegel seems to pun on Schleiermacher's name when he underscores how the philosophers of feeling revel in obscurantism and nebulous ideas.[4] Even though he is critical of what he calls "abstract" rationality or *Reflexionsphilosophie*—because he associates it with fixity rather than fluidity—Hegel does not endorse the move to the other extreme, that is, to a philosophy that renounces rationality altogether.[5] In the preface to the *Phenomenology of Spirit*, he instead famously praises the work of analysis as the power of the understanding. Clearly, a philosophy to his taste must combine a unifying perspective with analytic acumen. The latter is quite familiar to the discipline of philosophy; we know that "the activity of parting [*Scheiden*] is the force and labor of the *understanding*" (§ 32, trans. modified). But do we properly understand philosophy's emotional capacities when we relegate the unifying perspective to feeling, and when we oppose intuitive feeling to the understanding by conceiving of feeling as an immediate sense for the whole or as an overwhelming sense for the immediate? Hegel does not think so.

While recognizing the politically progressive aims of the philosophy of feeling, he also worries about the dangers of its being co-opted by established political powers.[6] He charges the philosophers of feeling with retreating into interiority all the while promoting change and transformation. He chides them for having abandoned the reality principle, as it were, and for having instead indulged in fantasy and wish-fulfillment dreams:

> When the proponents of that view abandon themselves to the unbounded fermentation of the substance, they suppose that, by throwing a blanket over self-consciousness and by surrendering all understanding, they are *God's very own,* that they are those to whom God imparts wisdom in their sleep. What they in fact receive and what they give birth to in their sleep are also for that reason merely dreams. (§ 10)

Hegel combines his denunciation of religious experience (especially of the pietistic flavor, because of pietism's testimonies to the ineffability of the sacred) with an attack against aesthetic experience when he ridicules both as "the shapeless roar of the pealing of bells, or that of a warm vapor filling a space [*eine warme Nebelerfüllung*], or that of a musical thought which does not get to the concept [*das nicht zum Begriffe . . . kommt*]" (§ 217, trans. modified). Attacking the "powerless beauty" of the beautiful soul's moral sentiment because it "detests the understanding," he also critiques Kant's aesthetic experience for its self-centeredness (§ 32). While the "beautiful soul" is by definition naive, that is, unaffected by rational judgment, aesthetic pleasure lies in suspending the judgment of knowledge about the object, in not forming a concept of the intuition (*nicht zum Begriffe . . . kommt*), but in reflecting on the subjective state of the subject instead. Likewise, the inner intuition of the sacred might be uplifting—so Hegel—but the pleasure it affords remains a private sensation: "Instead of grabbing hold of the essence [*statt das Wesen zu ergreifen*], consciousness merely *feels* and has thus fallen back into itself" (§ 217, trans. modified). In all these observations, Hegel's point of contention is that the feeling heart feels only itself and does not reach the other.

When Hegel disparages his contemporaries because, according to them, "the absolute is not supposed to be conceptually grasped [*begriffen*] but rather to be felt and intuited [, and] it is not the concept but the feeling and intuition of the absolute which are supposed to govern what is said of it [*das Wort führen*]," he is concerned not only with a relation to the absolute that is different from theirs, but also with a way to articulate this relation (§ 6). Whenever intuitive feeling has the say (*das Wort führen*), it has literally a (i.e., one) word; that is to say, it doesn't use discursive language but puts forward single words that are supposed to be fraught with significance: "The beautiful, the holy, the eternal, religion, and love are the bait demanded to awaken the craving to bite," Hegel mocks (§ 7, trans. modified).[7] It is Hegel's position that these words do not signify anything unless they unfold or divide into predicative propositions. That is to say, Hegel considers propositional statements as the self-analyses of words or the self-diremptions of the concept. He generally holds that spirit manifests itself physically, and he thinks of language as one mode of this physical manifestation. Because any physical manifestation is necessarily finite it must call forth a multiplicity of manifestations in view of giving existence to the whole of infinite spirit. For the realm of propositional language, this means that each word generates many sentences, that each subject can be predicated in various ways, and that spirit tends to manifest itself therefore in discursive language. We discuss Hegel's critique of predicative propositions in chapter 4, when we take a closer look at his idea of the "speculative proposition," but in this context it is important to note that Hegel welcomes the analysis of the name into propositions before he can dance with them to the rhythm of speculative logic. While this dance—Hegel's "bacchanalian revel"—might remind one of the "ferment of enthusiasm" (*gährende Begeisterung*) with which he charges the philosophers of feeling, Hegel nevertheless claims that his revel embraces "the cold forward march of the necessity of the subject matter [*die kalt fortschreitende Nothwendigkeit der Sache*]" and its discursive analysis (§ 7, trans. modified). Hegelian Bacchantes reel and wobble because they understand and grasp themselves.

This is not to say that Hegel ignores the significance of emotion. On the contrary, we will see throughout this book what an important role—both thematically and syntactically—emotionality plays in his thought. Nevertheless, because much of his philosophy hinges on transports that not only function as mediating but also emerge as mediated, Hegel does argue against a philosophy that considers feeling to be immediate and uncomplex. For fear of killing the feeling with words, the feeling heart might try to preserve the integrity of its intuition in single-word expressions, but Hegel believes such simplicity to be illusory. His philosophy brings to the fore the analytic, self-differentiating, self-disrupting—even self-lacerating—and self-reflecting quality of emotion.

Heartthrob of Law

The *Phenomenology*'s section on the "law of the heart" explores some of the philosophical tenets of eighteenth-century sentimentalism, in particular Rousseau's *culte du coeur* and its reliance on the idea of natural law. With his *culte du coeur,* Rousseau celebrates feeling as free from being corrupted by the vicissitudes of reflection. Since he cannot completely deny the self-reflective aspect of feeling, Rousseau tends to construct binary differences within the field of emotion: between natural feeling and decadent passion or between *amour de soi* and amour propre. He then idealizes the side that is less mediated by culture, reflection, or imagination, and condemns the other. Rousseau thus establishes the dichotomy between nature and culture as the most fundamental difference, with good, virtuous, pure—in short, authentic—feeling falling on the side of nature, while culture opens the realm of reflection and therefore alienation.[8] Rousseau naturalizes feeling and vigilantly protects the authenticity of "natural feeling" against the elements of simulation and theatricality that inevitably come with reflection, mediation, or representation.

From today's point of view, two reasons might justify Rousseau's relentless worry about the possible insincerity of emotions. The first is the emancipatory role that emotion plays for the emerging bourgeoisie. In the eighteenth century, countering birthright with emotional alliances and defining the emerging bourgeoisie via a culture of emotionality against the calculated esprit of the nobility were driving forces in the emancipation from the Old Regime. The propagation of love, care, and natural virtue as characteristics of the new, bourgeois family, set against the economic and political self-interests (or amours propres to use Rousseau's term) of the first estate, made the early members of the bourgeoisie feel morally superior to the aristocracy (see Kontje 1998, 4). As one of the most important assets of this new class, emotions had to be protected against inflation. In this light, the modern concern with authenticity in matters of the heart makes good sense. But this concern does not apply to today's context anymore, since the once emerging class has established itself quite thoroughly at this point, and the emancipatory thrust of emotion is largely lost. Unfortunately, we have now an all too thorough knowledge of the suppressive character of the bourgeois ideology of emotion. Emotionality was only briefly embraced by the paterfamilias and then quickly relegated again to the private and passive sphere of women and children where it served patriarchal control rather than emancipation. Today, the more we move beyond the public-private, active-passive, and male-female or masculine-feminine divide, the more reactionary and manipulative the gesture of celebrating immediate, pure, and genuine feeling must appear. Therefore the opposition of true versus false emotion will lose its appeal to contemporary theories of emotion. This chapter will show that Hegel was one of the earliest critics of authenticity and its inherent violence.

The second reason for Rousseau's urge to protect sentiment from the intrusion of reflection lies in the disorienting skepticism introduced by enlightened rationality. This reason still persists today or has been renewed by deconstruction's assaults on what has passed for too long as "common sense." The current investment of cognitive philosophy in emotions as providers of salience in decision-making processes is surely a reaction to such assaults.[9] With the confession by the Savoyard vicar in *Emile* and later in *Les reveries du promeneur solitaire,* Rousseau portrays "the frightening inner life of the doubter" and shows how an individual could become engulfed by a personal skeptical crisis (Popkin 1992, 290). The emotional charge of this crisis of rationality is indisputable, and yet Rousseau proposes that feeling offers protection from such fright. Rousseau and a host of followers seek remedy against the analytic frenzy that preys on their mind by "listening to the Voice of Nature in the most hidden part . . . of [their] intimacy" (Olaso 1988, 56). Olaso's phrasing here bespeaks an important new requirement. In order to provide a reliable reference point in this disorientation created by the pervasive skepticism of rationality, feeling has to be thought of as interior. It has to be constructed as hidden away in the deepest intimacy of the heart so as to protect it from analytic negation and from the indifference of objective universality.[10] In this light, the preoccupation with interiority, which is still widespread today, appears as a protection mechanism. While such desire for protection deserves attention, I think that the harm done by a strong investment in the interiority of emotion outweighs its benefits. Hegel helps us see some of the important benefits of exposure and of thinking emotionality as an experience of exposure.[11]

With the section on the "law of the heart," Hegel offers a critique of the Rousseauian dichotomy of natural and naive feeling versus pretentious and self-reflective feeling by staging the internal tensions of Rousseau's position and by placing the entire discussion within the chapter on "Reason." He thereby suggests that the sensibility of the figure of the "law of the heart" might be cultivated as a counterweight to rationality, but it is fundamentally part of and in line with reason. "Reason" in Hegel refers not to a mental faculty or a psychological process, but to a particular worldview. From the abstract "I" to objective reality extends the sphere and age of reason. The subjective and the objective dimension of the concept mutually penetrate and embrace one another in reason—but it is abstraction that buys the universality here.[12] The relation of the pure "I" to the world is animated by two interrelated yet contradicting premises, that of rational reality and that of interiority. It is by definition reasonable to consider the real to be rational and the rational to be real.[13] The rational "I" therefore seeks to find its mental and moral organization (the categories that determine its thoughts and its actions) in all other minds, all social institutions, and all of nature—that is to say, in objective reality in general. Short of being able to mirror itself in everything and everyone out there, it takes comfort in the idea that reason surely is behind it all, that the inner essence of everything and everyone is rational, and that reason is at the heart of all external reality. It thus comes dangerously close to saying that rational reality is a merely inner ideal rather than a fact. In an attempt to bind interiority to exteriority, the sphere of reason therefore "creates the law that says *that the outer is the expression of the inner*" (§ 262).

With the figure of the "law of the heart," Hegel shows how the culture of sensibility and the philosophy of natural law build on each other. In his description, the promoters of sensibility strive to lift the pressure placed on the individual by the laws of convention and the decrees of the powerful, which together form a "violent order of the world" (§ 369). They worry about people being subject to laws they don't identify with and to laws that the inner nature of their heart doesn't resonate with. That is why they develop the idea of natural law or of the "law of the heart."[14]

The phrase "law of the heart" couples universality with individuality: on the one hand, laws are by definition binding for everyone subject to them, a principle which in this case applies without restriction, since natural law claims universal validity; on the other hand, the heart functions as the figure for the inner nature and personal self-feeling of the individual. Sentimentalism believes in the inalienable right of all people to follow the voice of their heart to their fullest potential and to live in harmony with their own nature. It views alienation as cruelty, and self-realization as a normative value. This self-realization is obviously not to be taken in the frivolous sense of looking to satisfy every whim—that was the subject of the previous section, "Pleasure and Necessity"—but in the grand sense and "seriousness [*Ernsthaftigkeit*] of a high purpose, which seeks its pleasure in the exhibition of its own *admirably excellent* essence [*Darstellung ihres vortrefflichen eigenen Wesens*] and in bringing about the *welfare of mankind* [*Hervorbringung des Wohls der Menschheit*]" (§ 370).[15]

The tension between universality and individuality at work in the phrase "law of the heart" could generate speculative transports. The incongruity at the center of this figure of reason could make the heart throb across difference; it could open the heart for transport and trans-subjective figuration and for the transformation of worlds. But the peculiar seriousness of the sentimentalist resists such emotionality. Instead, sentimentalism tries to regulate the fraught link between the universal and the singular via the normative ideal of organic self-expression. It thus naturalizes feeling instead of spiritualizing it or rendering it speculative.

Hegel agrees with one part of the normative thrust of the "law of the heart," namely, that it is not enough that the welfare of mankind and the excellence of the individual's own nature exist as ideals somewhere in the imagination. They need to be brought about (*Hervorbringung*) and exhibited (*Darstellung*).[16] Only the real is indeed rational. But he doesn't agree with sentimentalism's condemnation of alienation. Instead, he conceptualizes realization—or what he calls "actualization"—as a form of alienation, of ironic reversal and of self-emptying rather than fulfillment.[17] He critiques the naturalizing conception of feeling and its expression because—as we will see in a moment—this naturalizing conception actually makes the realization of feeling impossible. When the advocates of the "law of the heart" link the universal purpose of promoting the welfare of mankind with the particular purpose of displaying the excellence of their own nature, they claim organicity: the promotion of the welfare of mankind is supposed to naturally grow out of one's character just as the achievements of such promotion are supposed to reflect back on that character, evincing its excellence. One is the expression of the other. The ideal of expression demands the organic unfolding of the singular inner core or heart into a universally recognizable external reality. It follows a logic of integrity, in the double sense of uninterruptedness or wholeness, and of moral incorruptibility or honesty.[18] "Expression" as an ideal leaves no room for the irony, the alienation, or even the indirectness of spirit's model of self-realization.

In addition to not endorsing this organicism of the "law of the heart," Hegel demonstrates that sentimentalism, itself, is not as sincere as it claims in its valuing of organic expression. Despite supporting reason's claim that the inner mental world and the outer material world fundamentally cohere, sentimentalism establishes and upholds a firm opposition between the public sphere of external reality and the privacy of the heart. Across this firm opposition the values of singularity and universality switch sides, but they never actually come together. The all-too-admirably sensible individual starts out by claiming the heart's universality against the particularity of the positive laws, but then—once it has established its law—feels frustrated to have lost its singularity and self-feeling to the alienating objectivity and heartlessness of the public sphere.[19] As soon as the values of the heart are exhibited and put forth as statutes, the individual can't feel its own heart beating in them anymore.

It is the paradox of self-realization "that the individual in *putting forward* [*aufstellt*] *his own* order no longer finds it to be his own" (§ 372). While Hegel embraces this kind of self-alienation, the sentimental individual resists it and insists that his heart be his possession. This resistance to alienation evinces for Hegel that the sentimentalist neither feels much nor actually thinks, since Hegel regards acknowledging the alien within the self as a constitutive part of emotional and conceptual transport. Thus, for Hegel, the sentimentalist doesn't so much conceive (*denkt*), but rather conceits (*dünkelt*). "The heart-throb for the welfare of mankind" (*das Herzklopfen für das Wohl der Menschheit*) has turned into *Eigendünkel* or self-conceit, a cold arrogance that dehumanizes large parts of humanity: "the individual . . . now . . . finds that the hearts of people are opposed to his admirable intentions, and that they are thus . . . to be loathed" (§ 377; § 373). The naturalizing efforts of the theory of natural law end up denaturalizing all those who do not have the face of the excellent (*vortrefflich*) individual. Hegel offers here an important critique of sentimentalism, exposing its (more or less inadvertent) backing of social and political injustice.[20] He shows that sentimentality's universalist rhetoric of recognition based on true feeling proves rather limited in scope.

Only the cultivated soul that has achieved a certain degree of emotional self-mastery enjoys this recognition—everyone else gets dehumanized as heartless rebel. The section on the "law of the heart" has been read as an allusion to the Karl Moor character in Schiller's *The Robbers*.[21] Schiller depicts Karl Moor as the avenger of the disappointed and maltreated and the judge of tyrants and exploiters, but his conversion back into normative society at the end of the play is largely driven by his newfound conviction that the people he led in his sentimentalist battle fall short of sentimental excellence: that they are nothing but robbers and murderers.[22] From the perspective of the subaltern, this change of heart from compassion to disdain effectively reinforces the violence against humanity that the sentimentalist originally condemned.

Overly protective of his precious possession (his heart), the well-meaning sentimentalist is clearly not ready to "entrust" (*anvertraut*) his inner life to the alienating forces of mean reality (§ 374). Having just been on the verge of losing its beat, the sentimentalist's heart now pounds in a fury for self-preservation: "The heart-throb for the welfare of mankind . . . passes over into the bluster of a mad self-conceit [*verrückten Eigendünkels*]. It passes over into the rage of a consciousness which preserves itself from destruction" (§ 377). Hegel helps us understand why the sentimentalist turns on his initial goal to fight for human welfare, why he begins to shun the political in favor of what Berlant calls the "juxtapolitical"—that is to say, why, rather than act in the pursuit of political transformation, the sentimentalist now prefers to share his critique with a public that feels intimate (thus pitching his critique in the register of complaint).[23] The sentimentalist has found that his heart stops beating once he begins to enact the law of his heart. It is therefore self-preservation—the desire of the heartthrob to continue the heartthrob—that motivates his withdrawal from the pursuit of actual change. The heartthrob for the welfare of mankind turns from a motivation for action into a goal in itself: the cultivation of feelings for the sake of feeling, be it that of self-pity. The result is a psychic paralysis that Hegel calls mad.[24]

Pitting the private interior against the public exterior, the culture of sensibility has created a double and mutually exclusive imperative. On the one hand, the values of the heart must be realized. On the other, their private or "originary" character must be preserved and their peculiarity must not be abandoned (*preisgeben*) to the alienating forces of the public (§ 311).[25] Despite or rather because of the idealized demand for expression, the heart remains the inner and private locus of the self. And the treasure of the self's innermost nature remains locked in the heart when the sentimentalists—ventriloquized by Hegel—claim that, "through its actualization, the law of the heart precisely ceases to be a law of the *heart*" (*das Gesetz des Herzens hört eben durch seine Verwirklichung auf, Gesetz des Herzens zu sein,* § 372).

This verdict echoes the second line of Schiller's distich on "Language," "When the soul *speaks,* alas, it is no longer the *soul* that speaks" (Spricht *die Seele, so spricht ach! schon die* Seele *nicht mehr*).[26] Both statements suggest that language defiles the beauty of inner life—to use language for self-expression is like getting embroiled with a band of robbers. Stylistically, the two propositions are very similar. Both repeat the same phrase (Hegel: "Gesetz des Herzens," Schiller: "spricht die Seele") but shift the stress from the first to the last word of the phrase in order to make their point. Their arguments thus rely on nonverbal elements of speech, such as intonation and emphasis. And the more or less discursive style both use requires that prosodic elements be signaled by typographic styling—both use italics to emphasize *Seele* or *Herz* in the second iteration.[27] Hegel, I wish to argue, parodies the literature and philosophy of sensibility epitomized in Schiller's line—in particular its demonstrative use of paralinguistic elements to communicate the subjective intensity of inner life that is supposedly lost in language. His mimicry shows that while the nonverbal elements make the argument (that language defiles inner beauty and gets it embroiled in a band of robbers), they also undercut that very argument (since language actually acts rather successfully here). Both Schiller's and Hegel's lines are concerned with the appearance of spirit in the so-called real world. According to the model that we find epitomized in Schiller's distich, matters of the heart, the soul, or the living spirit cannot, or rather must not, take shape in time and space. But while Schiller asks—or, indeed, declares and prescribes—why the living spirit fails to appear ("*Warum kann der lebendige Geist dem Geist nicht erscheinen?*"), one of the main interventions of Hegel's philosophy is to argue that spirit does indeed appear, that is to say, that it does take shape in space and time.

Text versus Expression

Hegel argues that spirit takes shape in space and time, but he does not think of this actualization or manifestation along the lines of expression.[28] The law of expression or self-expression that many recent readers of Hegel take to be the heartland of Hegelian philosophy in general is in fact the particular province of reason.[29] Spirit, on the other hand, puts itself in a textual relation to itself.[30]

Expression is supposed to refer back to an inner truth. It makes manifest for myself and others an inner nature, voice, or impulse that was previously hidden or latent.[31] Two models of expression concern us here: the outward display of an inner character, state, or agitation through facial, vocal, gestural, linguistic, or artistic means; and the organic unfolding of an inner core, understood along the lines of Aristotelian entelechy. Hegel's "reason" vaguely combines both notions of expression, that of ostensibly immediate communication and that of inner teleology. A figural organicism—idealizing organic development in the cultural sphere of representation—drives the conception of linguistic, artistic, and physical expression at work in the realm of reason.[32] For example, the "rational" ideal of a life path feels organic because such a life follows an inner logic that rules out contingency and disaster. The organicism of the sphere of reason is strongly invested in continuity, coherence, and integrity.

But spirit welcomes alienation (*Entfremdung*),[33] externalization or self-emptying (*Entäußerung*),[34] and—as I will argue throughout this book—disruption. Hegel sees language use and active conduct not as expressions but as utterances (*Äußerungen*) or exposures.[35]

> Speech and labor are utterances [*Äußerungen*] in which the individual in himself no longer retains and possesses himself; rather, he lets the inner move wholly outside of him and he thus abandons it to the other. For that reason, we can just as well say that these utterances [*Äußerungen*] express [*ausdrücken*] the inner too much as we can say that they express it too little. *Too much*—because the inner itself breaks out in these expressions, no opposition remains between them and the inner; they do not merely provide an *expression* [*Ausdruck*] of the inner, they immediately provide the inner itself. *Too little*—because in speech and action the inner makes itself into an other and thereby abandons itself [*sich preisgibt*] to the mercy of the element of transformation, which twists the spoken word and the accomplished deed and makes something else out of them than what they, as the actions of this determinate individual, are in and for themselves. (§ 312, trans. modified)

Utterances always express both more and less than they are supposed to. That makes them emotional, and yet their very emotionality, when registered and embraced, has already converted the expression into a text. Unlike Schiller, Hegel does not blame the medium for the inadequacy of expressions, but rather blames the user for insisting on adequacy and for conceptualizing self-realization as expression in the first place. The expressive individual considers his inner life to be the measure, the proper essence, and the proprietor of the external marks of expression. The external marks are supposed to be expressions "in which the individual . . . retains and possesses himself [*worin das Individuum . . . sich behält und besitzt*]." Yet, by the same token, he just as often ends up feeling restrained and possessed by his own inwardness. If they are measured against the expressive ideal of continuity between inner and outer, utterances always "express too little," in the sense that the individual can't recognize itself in them. It cannot find in external reality what it meant to express and, thus, it remains locked in the heart.

Hegel's alternative to the model of expression consists in a textual notion of utterances (in the broadest sense, which includes actions) that serve as escape routes from the prison of interiority.[36] Across the vast interval between Bataille's sovereign destruction and Hegel's dogged labor of the negative, Hegel's utterances, where "the inner itself breaks out [*ausbricht*]," resonate with Nancy's version of Bataille's "unleashing of passions" (Nancy 1991, 32).[37] Nancy de-dramatizes Bataille's "passion," and Nancy's version of "unleashing" is related to Hegel's unusual celebration of alienation as the double of self-realization. Nancy's version understands "unleashing" or *ausbrechen* (lit.: "to break out") as "not the free doing of a subjectivity" (be it Bataille's sovereign individual or the rational expressionists who actively, even though in the latter case with considerable agony, press through the walls of their cages), but as the uncontainable effect of communication understood as contagion (ibid.). Passion, then, is never mine to begin with, nothing inside me to be expressed, but "always already" out there, unleashed, passing through.

The slight shift in the terminology of Hegel's passage, from *Ausdruck* (expression) to *Äußerung* (utterance), makes all the difference. While *Ausdruck* refers back to an inner authority and remains solipsistic in scope, *Äußerung* exposes to others. It is thus synonymous with *Entäußerung*—and I am indeed tempted to translate both words as "exposure." Such utterances or exposures "do not merely provide an *expression* of the inner, they immediately provide the inner itself [*sie geben nicht nur einen Ausdruck des Innern, sondern es unmittelbar*]." Nothing is held back for future excuses. Hegel abandons the idea that the essential is left inside while the outside manifestation is simply a representation, a portrait so to speak, that more or less resembles the original. Nancy's reading of Hegel crystallizes for us that there is no agent or knowing subject beyond, behind, or before the utterance for Hegel: "Manifestation surges up out of nothing, into nothing. The manifested is something, and every thing is manifested. But there is no 'manifester' that would be yet another thing than manifestation itself. Nor is there a spectator to manifestation" who would be exempt from manifestation (Nancy 2002, 33). While manifestation surges up out of nothing, it is always in the plural since the acts of witnessing and reading the manifested themselves manifest what is manifest. "Manifestation is therefore of itself"—and thus divided within or plural—"it is of itself as much as it is of nothing" (ibid.). It is not that an individual's deed gives an indication of her real internal character, but "the deed *is* this, and its being is not merely a sign, it is the thing itself [*die Sache selbst*]. The deed *is* this, and the individual person *is* what the deed *is*" (§ 322). Hegel's almost obsessive repetition of the verb "*is*" hammers home the point that, instead of a hierarchical opposition between material existence and ideal meaning, he proposes the unranked and interwoven multiplication of reflexive instances of being. As in the speculative proposition, where the subject is dragged into the predicate, here the inside is drawn to the outside.[38] In that sense, what used to be called "inner" has already become other; it is alienated in a good sense.

Expression is beholden to subjective intention—or to put it slightly differently, in the model of expression the individual is beholden to itself. But in Hegel's textual model of self-realization, the subject relinquishes, exposes, even carries to the market and puts a price on (*sich preisgibt*) its insides, without therefore being caught in an economy of possession or sacrifice. "Manifestation *makes a return* and is nothing but this return. But, because this return does not come to a presupposed substance, it is return to nothing—or it is not a return, and it only comes back in throwing itself forth . . .—being thrown out of self as self, *being* this throw itself, and thereby its *own* passage into the other" (Nancy 2002, 39). The text—made of words or acts—sends forth and carries on. Rather than being the result of my intention (*mein Meinen*), its being (*Sein*) is its own (*sein*): the text is a self-reflective subject in its own right. The self-reflection of the text's materiality or being (*Sein*) in its possessive pronoun (*sein*) introduces a slight discrepancy between the mirror images (here in the form of an upper- and a lowercase *s*) that makes the text restless. This restlessness is its capacity for transport or self-transformation, for "its *own* passage into the other." Through exposures, exertions, utterances, the individual "abandons itself to the mercy of the element of transformation, which twists [*verkehrt*] the spoken word and the accomplished deed." While such negativity—the capacity for self-affectation, emotional self-reflection, and transport—would have been locked into interiority in the model of expression, in Hegel's textual model of emotionality, this inner difference manifests as outer difference. "Unrepresentable by any individual sign, emotion is represented by traces in a differential network. Textuality offers an alternative to expression and indication" (Terada 2001, 45). The *Phenomenology of Spirit,* as textual manifestation of spirit's textual relation to itself across its various shapes, puts to work what Terada describes as "a concept of emotion as the phenomenology of the textual difference between ideality and substance" (ibid.). According to Terada, emotion registers textual difference. In Hegel, we see that the textual difference within spirit (between ideality and substance or, as Hegel would say, between for-itself and in-itself) transports spirit from one manifestation of itself to another. That which exists transforms—"continues on his own to grow [*es wächst für sich fort*]" (§ 372)—that is to say, it enjoys its own spirituality, emotionality, and subjectivity.[39]

An utterance made is always duplicitous: "The act as an accomplished piece of work has the double and opposite significance of being either the *inner* individuality and *not* its *expression;* or, as external, to be an actuality *free-standing* from the inner [*vom Innern freie Wirklichkeit*], which is something entirely different from the inner" (§ 312). The individual is beside itself with manifestation, and, as such, it has become another. Any such "being-of-itself-outside-itself-in-the-other" is already double if not triple (Nancy 2002, 35). The singular exists only in the plural. No spectator of manifestation or reader of text can be outside of manifestation and textuality; therefore every view will itself be another manifestation and every reading another text. These texts will reflect one another and get embroiled in one another without therefore being the same. The text model of self-realization interrupts the focus on the individual. It unbinds or dislocates the self, and unleashes "the *passion* of singularity as such" (Nancy 1991, 32). Every utterance passes. Passes into an other. We can describe this with Nancy as "the sharing of singularities in movement" (Nancy 2002, 78) or with Hegel as the entangling of one in the other: "through the actualization . . . he gets himself entangled [*sich zu verwickeln*]" (§ 372).

When Hegel argues that "the force of spirit is only as great as its exertion [*Äußerung*], and its depth goes only as deep as it trusts itself to disperse and lose itself in its display and interpretation [*in seiner Auslegung sich auszubreiten und sich zu verlieren getraut*] of itself" (§ 10, trans. modified), he doesn't refer to an organic unfolding of an inner core, but describes a self-loss and discontinuity—an *Auslegung,* like the display of unrelated goods in a discount store or like the hermeneutic process that adds one interpretation to the other without necessarily digesting all previous interpretations. "The self is what does not possess itself" (Nancy 2002, 36). Hegel suggests not that the subject gets to realize its own integrity, but that it gets entangled in others.

Manifestation is necessarily finite, and "finite being always presents itself 'together,' hence severally" (Nancy 1991, 28). Hegel describes spirit therefore as "the *I* that is *we* and the *we* that is *I*" (§ 177).[40] The sphere of reason, on the other hand, does not yet have a sense for plural and palpable difference. It has in a rather rash and undifferentiated way sublated singularity into universality and therefore doesn't have much of a conception of community. Its notion of self-realization as self-expression is tortuously focused on the individual. This focus leaves its heart frustratingly empty—"an empty depth" (§ 10).

Why does the sphere of reason produce solipsistic individuals? So far we have shown that this is so because of its peculiar notion of emotionality. The sphere of reason is more concerned with the true expression of somehow preexisting feelings than with transports (which are textual and performative generations of and identifications across radically different worlds and life forms of spirit). Therefore it produces abstract individuals and abstract universals. But how was it possible for this abstract notion of emotionality to gain traction? How is it possible for reason to completely elide the plural? In order to address this question we need to examine the birth of reason. While, so far, we have analyzed a particular figure of reason (the sentimentalist and his law of the heart) and compared the worldview of reason in general with the worldview of spirit in general, I will now go back in the phenomenological narrative to offer a genealogy of reason.

Hegel's chapter on reason in the *Phenomenology* opens once the "unhappy consciousness" has abandoned all agency, self-knowledge, and satisfaction, that is, once it has effectively renounced personal freedom and has turned itself into a thing. Through what is easily identified as the customs and rituals of the Catholic Church—the centrality of the priest, the purchasing of sin-forgiveness with the abdication of the will, and the blind following of uncomprehended rites, in particular the liturgy performed in the foreign language of Latin—self-consciousness has, after a long process of halfhearted attempts, eventually succeeded in "having in truth emptied itself of its *I* [*seines Ich sich entäußert*], and . . . having made its immediate self-consciousness into a *thing,* into an objective being" (§ 229). At this point, the unhappy consciousness truly bows to its lord, that is, to its own conception of an unchanging truth.

The pleasure gained from this masochistic performance comes in the form of the "certainty for this consciousness that, in its individuality, it . . . is all reality [*Gewißheit des Bewußtseins, in seiner Einzelnheit . . . alle Realität zu sein*]" (§ 230, trans. modified). By making itself into an object of knowledge, the "unhappy consciousness" has posited that consciousness is not the agent of the ongoing epistemological endeavor, but rather is subjected to the phenomenological drive of a bigger subject—what Hegel calls spirit. In the transition to reason, consciousness learns to be an object, not for itself but for others—a "being for an other," as Hegel puts it (*Sein für anderes,* § 351). To be precise, since others in the plural (*andere*) have at this point not yet entered consciousness's horizon of experience, all that the protagonist has learned (advancing in baby steps throughout) is to subject itself to a singular and neutral other (*anderes*)—its lord or its conception of truth as unchanging. By thus rendering itself the object of a knowledge that operates with the truth criterion of inalterability, this consciousness refuses to get a sense for the self-humbling, self-emptying, and self-transforming of spirit. It misses its chance to recognize that absolute knowledge is not a positive knowledge, but a regulative principle, as it were, that gives individual manifestations of spirit the freedom to break away from their certainty or "naturalness," as Hegel would put it, and thus generate a multiplicity of different manifestations.[41] Instead, consciousness is quick to identify with its lord. In the blink of a transition, it has already installed itself in the position of certainty again and has reduced all difference to its own identity: it is a "certainty for this consciousness that, in its individuality, it . . . is all reality" (§ 230). But certainty of course differs from truth; it is truth only "for consciousness," not "in and for itself." Since certainty as such is thus insufficiently mediated, consciousness in the position of certainty has something abstract, immediate, or "merely natural" to it.

The sphere of reason immediately unites universality ("all reality") and individuality in the abstract "I," without attending to the differences among the many. From a later, more mediated perspective we can see that this kind of abstraction is enabled by the textuality of spirit. Hegel's retrospective description of the transition from self-consciousness to reason reads: "The unhappy self-consciousness emptied itself of its self-sufficiency [*entäußerte sich seiner Selbstständigkeit*] and agonizingly rendered its *being-for-itself* into a thing [*und rang sein Fürsichsein zum Dinge heraus*]. As a result, it returned from self-consciousness into consciousness" (§ 344, trans. modified). Textual difference is legibly at work here. The passage offers a typical example of Hegel's easy shifts in perspective—part and parcel of his use, as I argue, of free indirect discourse throughout the *Phenomenology*. The extra-linguistic referent for the personal pronoun "it" in the second sentence is not the same as the referent for the subject of the first sentence (the unhappy consciousness). Rather, "it" refers to the new figure of consciousness—"observing reason"—which indeed behaves as consciousness relating to the world. The unhappy consciousness does not relate to the world since it has (that was the point) renounced its subject status. Nevertheless, according to syntactic conventions, "it" refers to the subject of the previous sentence. This passage thus shows beautifully how Hegel treats the different shapes of the protagonist as figuring one another—that is, as able to stand in for each other and therefore as both different and identical. Thematic reference and syntactic reference differ but imperceptibly slide into one another. Hegel continues, "However, this, which is thing, is self-consciousness . . . the *immediate* unity of *being* [*des Seins*] and *what is its own* [*des Seinen*]" (§ 344, trans. modified). Here he synthesizes both references, reminding us that what is now the object of "observing reason" used to be the subject of the first sentence—a self-consciousness unhappily trying to escape from its self. As the result of an itinerary that is, in good Hegelian fashion, preserved in the outcome, the world being observed, which presents itself as thinghood in its sheer material being (*Sein*), thus carries with it its prehistory as a subject and thus retains the power to reflect on itself and to possess itself (*Seinen*). The slippages in reference, drawing the memory of one into the other, transform the dejected self not just into a physical thing, but into a physical thing with self-awareness: "Self-consciousness found the thing as itself and itself as a thing; i.e., *it is for self-consciousness* that it is *in itself* objective actuality" (§ 347). Despite the finitude of its embodiment, despite its individuality, this self-conscious thing enjoys the pleasure of knowing that it is "*in itself* objective actuality" or "*all* reality." Its happiness comes courtesy of the easy shifts in reference. These shifts have allowed consciousness to identify or confuse itself with the supreme other (*anderes*)—the position of objectivity and stable truth—and, in doing so, they have elided the existence of others in the plural, of other rational things, with whom this rational thing might have had to share reality and to whom it might have had to expose itself. This is to say that the felicity of the sphere of reason (which, as we know, will soon give way to a feeling of emptiness that will battle with heart-throb madness) is sponsored by the textuality of spirit.[42] Textual difference underlies expressivity.

Force of Interiority

We will now explore the textual emotionality of spirit from a different angle by focusing on how Hegel's work dismantles the construction of interiority and entangles rationality with emotionality. Once again, we will pursue a genealogical approach: this time we will trace the emergence of interiority in the *Phenomenology*.

Interiority makes its first appearance in the *Phenomenology of Spirit* in the chapter on "Force and the Understanding"—not as the inner life of human subjects, but as "the *inner* of things [*Innres der Dinge*]" (§ 136). I'd like to take seriously the fact that Hegel presents inwardness as primarily not human. It is the first step in dismantling the sentimental construction of interiority as the touchstone of true humanity.

The focus on "the inner of things" also allows us to take a closer look at the understanding's analytic mode of thinking, which I have bracketed with the worldview of reason under the category of rationality. To those who like to follow the linear development of the *Phenomenology* chronologically, I have to send out a warning. It may seem strange to relate the much earlier and (within the chapter on "Consciousness") relatively small configuration of the understanding to the later chapter and much larger sphere of reason. But there is a Hegelian reason for this: reason unites consciousness and self-consciousness, and the understanding is the figure of transition from consciousness to self-consciousness. Once the temporal distinction between consciousness and self-consciousness is "relieved" in reason, the understanding actually functions as the mode of thought internal to the worldview of reason that bridges the moments of consciousness and self-consciousness. I will, however, also make a further leap and draw on Hegel's extra-narratival remarks in the preface while analyzing the specific figure of consciousness that is the understanding. In the preface, Hegel describes the understanding as a specifically analytic mode of thought that not only severs the inseparable, but fixes, stabilizes, or reifies what it has thus severed.

The figure of consciousness that Hegel calls "the understanding" has lost faith in perception and sense-certainty. It considers what nature presents to the senses as mere appearance—an appearance that lies and deceives—and imagines that there must be "a *supersensible* world as the *true* world" behind the veil of appearance (§ 144). The understanding imagines that truth must be hidden in the "inner of things."[43] Why does it come up with this strange idea that vacillates between the politically progressive (finding agency and interiority in non-human beings and thus challenging the modern apotheosis of human being) and the paranoidally metaphysical (suspecting that things lie when they present themselves)? Because the object has dissolved in front of its eyes, as it were, into a play of forces. Rather than offering up for perception more or less substantial things, the objective world presents itself to the suspicious understanding as an anchorless and unpoised (*haltungslos*) web of forces that disappear as soon as they appear: "The *force as actual* exists purely and simply in the *exertion* [*Äußerung*], which at the same time is nothing but a self-negation [*ein sich selbst Aufheben*]" (§ 141, trans. modified). While the understanding can isolate and identify particular forces, it quickly realizes that a force doesn't exist as isolated, but only in a precarious and dynamic dependence on its opposite force: "These two forces exist as essences existing for themselves; but their existence lies in the kind of movement of each against the other so that their *being* is even more a pure *being-posited through an other,* which is to say, that the pure meaning of their being is even more that of *vanishing*" (§ 141). Upon close consideration, the object has thus revealed itself as a dynamic interplay of transient forces.

With the discovery of this interplay, the understanding has found infinity within the realm of finite physical existence. This infinity—which Hegel defines as the trembling "sameness of the non-same as the non-same [*Gleichsein des Ungleichen als Ungleichen*]" (§ 160) and at the same time as the tension-producing "repulsion of the homonymous, as the homonymous, from itself [*Abstoßen des Gleichnamigen als Gleichnamigen von sich selbst*]" (ibid., trans. modified)—brings with it a great deal of restlessness, especially since the movements of self-division and self-unification have themselves ceased to function as stable opposites ("the distinctions [within and between] *estrangement* [*Entzweiung*] and *coming-to-be-in-parity-with-itself* [*Sichselbstgleichwerden*] are likewise only *this movement of self-sublation* [*diese Bewegung des sich Aufhebens*]" (§ 162). Hegel indeed describes infinity as the "absolute restlessness [*absolute Unruhe*] of pure self-movement" (ibid.).

Now, one could say that the understanding projects an inner space of truth and calm because it doesn't like all this agitation. That would be a relatively familiar critical move—exposing the affect (in this case irritation, suspicion, paranoia) that motivates the ostensibly rational stance. One could add that the understanding remains too "natural" or dense a shape of consciousness to be comfortable with this kind of transient self-overcoming of the spirited world. Yet Hegel proposes something slightly different and much more unsettling. According to his account, the understanding manages to dissociate emotionality from rationality by splitting the "inner of things" off from the interplay of forces. It posits the interplay of forces as the restless, moody, and self-negating outer appearance of things that is opposed to the perfectly rational and stable inner truth of those things. In doing so, the understanding simply does what it is supposed to do as understanding: it separates the inseparable. Yet in this rather matter-of-fact pursuit of its business, the understanding *is* one dimension of restless infinity—the activity of "dividing . . . what is undivided" [*Unterscheiden des Ununterschiedenen*]"—and therein lies its contribution to the emotionality of spirit (§164, trans. modified).

Rationality has emotional qualities in Hegel's account, while the emotionality at work in his philosophy has rational qualities. In the world of spirit, emotionality and rationality are entangled. As I have proposed earlier, emotionality is analytic and self-reflective in that it registers and thus reinforces self-incongruity. At the same time, rational analysis generates tears (*Zerrissenheit*) that are emotional.[44] It is therefore no accident that, when Hegel enlists the analytic capacities of the understanding in the service of spirit, he turns up with something very much akin to psychic work:

> Spirit is this power not as the positive that avoids looking at the negative, as is the case when we say of something that it is nothing or that it is false, and then, being done with it, go off on our own way on to something else. No, spirit is this power only when it looks the negative in the face and lingers with it. (§ 32, trans. modified)

The understanding performs a kind of "working-through," where the rational and the emotional cannot be separated from one another.

It is true that the understanding, by itself, is unable to supply the unity of estrangement and self-sameness, which is the other dimension of restless infinity. It *is* the restless "dividing of what is undivided," but it cannot register what it is doing as emotional—both because it doesn't hold together what it severs (it is the figure that will bring us self-consciousness, but it isn't quite self-conscious yet), and because the activity of separating the inseparable is precisely what defines the understanding and in this activity the understanding is thus actually not incongruous with itself (§ 164). This self-consistency is the reason why the understanding identifies with the calm rationality of the supersensible world—"raised above perception, consciousness exhibits itself as merged with the supersensible world by virtue of the middle term of appearance [*durch die Mitte der Erscheinung*] through which it gazes into this background"—and thus transitions to self-consciousness (§ 165).

I sense an irony in Hegel's predication of self-consciousness as "raised above perception [*erhoben über die Wahrnehmung*]." The protagonist's identification with calm rationality here in effect solidifies infinity; it thus produces not so much a consciousness that has attained higher wisdom as a consciousness that proves unspirited and aloof. While Hegel has a fluid notion of infinity—which he describes as the "absolute restlessness of pure self-movement"—and while the understanding deserves credit for being the first figure of consciousness to discover the spiritual notion of infinity, this fluidity gets lost in the Platonic ideas of the understanding (§ 163). The understanding is the power of fixation; it turns even infinity into a fixed idea by isolating it from finite existence and assigning it the virtual space of interiority.[45] This kind of stable infinity is surely just as bad an infinity (*schlechte Unendlichkeit*) as the one that is posited by the Romantics as unattainable, which Hegel disparages. It doesn't register spirit's emotionality.

While the understanding hopes in this way to have anchored the play of vanishing forces, we will see shortly that it has dropped its anchor into nothingness. At the end of the chapter on the understanding, during the transition to self-consciousness, it becomes clear that the inner is indeed empty, that the veil of appearance hides nothing: "It turns out that behind the so-called curtain, which is supposed to hide what is inner, there is nothing to be seen unless *we* ourselves go behind it, just as much so that there be somebody who does the seeing as so that there be something behind the curtain that can be seen" (§ 165, trans. modified). The phenomenality of the vanishing forces is indeed infinitely richer than this virginal space of interiority that the understanding has cracked open—and yet consciousness is drawn to this empty space.

Even when consciousness fills the room behind the veil to look at itself, there is nothing to see. Consciousness has no content other than the objective world at this point. After having gone through the dialectics of sense-certainty, perception, and the understanding, consciousness knows nothing about itself as such. The textual itinerary has not given us any information about what consciousness might be, apart from its perspective on the world out there. Now that consciousness wants to be exclusively "for-itself," it has nothing to show for itself but empty ideality. Nancy reminds us that "the self reveals itself to be nothing other than *negativity for itself*. But negativity for itself is not a thing . . . 'Self' is nothing that preexists 'for itself'" (Nancy 2002, 36–37). In the subsequent struggle for life and death, self-consciousness will become embodied and gain a sense for its precarious life. Then it will slowly create more and more threads of attachment and thus shape a more and more concrete identity. But at this point, we encounter the unreal (perhaps awesome) self-reflection of pure interiority without any exteriority: "the gazing of the inner into the inner" (§ 165)—the gazing of nothing into nothingness. Out of nothing, the magic of the understanding, we know, will create something. But in this moment—when the "inner of the thing" and the inner self stare at each other and into each other's void—a sense "surges up," as Nancy would say, that "'being for itself' is to be 'for' this absolute non-preexistence" (Nancy 2002, 37).[46]

The transition from the understanding to self-consciousness demonstrates in an exemplary fashion how the phenomenologist/s are affected by the mindset of the protagonist/s they observe. Or rather—since this formulation still presumes the independent preexistence of sophisticated phenomenologist/s who might or might not fall for the naïveté of their subject—I should say that this passage shows how the phenomenologist/s develop together with the protagonist/s. The pronoun "we," in the phrase "there is nothing to be seen unless *we* ourselves go behind it," includes the protagonist/s as much as the phenomenologist/s.

The evidence for this identification lies in the specific meaning of two terms used in this passage: "free" and "concept." When the phenomenologist/s claim that "this infinity is, to be sure, already the soul of all that came before, but it was in the *inner* that it itself first freely emerged [*frei hervorgetreten*]," they don't use "free" in the full-fledged Hegelian sense of being able to act in full acknowledgment of the self-alienating dynamic of action and of one's interdependence with others in a sociality, but in the simple sense of free from, meaning in this case that infinity is isolated and no longer obscured by finitude (§ 163). Similarly, when the phenomenologist/s state that "what is an object in sensuous covering [*in sinnlicher Hülle*] for the understanding is now there for us in its essential shape as pure concept," they don't use "concept" in the full-fledged Hegelian sense of the self-differentiating unity of self-reflecting materiality and self-actualizing ideality, but in the more common sense of an intellectual notion, a mental entity that is fundamentally different from and supposedly superior to its material instantiation or sensuous covering (§ 164, trans. modified). Clearly, the narrator of the *Phenomenology*, or the phenomenologist/s, use the terms "free" and "concept" here in the sense in which the understanding uses them.

The fact that the protagonist and the phenomenologist co-develop their terminology and thus their interpretations of the world says something important about Hegel's notion of "absolute knowing." While it is the common reception of Hegel that the phenomenologist has "absolute knowledge" from the beginning, it takes perhaps a literary reading—one that eschews the typically philosophical (even though not Hegelian) habit of abstracting from the temporal dimension of the argument and instead attends to strategies of narrative development—to bring into view that this is indeed not the case. On the verge of becoming self-conscious, the protagonist identifies with those who observe it—that is, the phenomenologist/s—not because they know more, but because this shift in perspective opens the gap that allows "natural consciousness" to negate its naturalness and to construct a second nature. The identification between protagonist and phenomenologist/s is mutual: the phenomenologist/s (readers and narrator) identify with the protagonist in order to gain experiential insight into one of the life forms of spirit, and the protagonist identifies with the phenomenologist/s in order to gain self-consciousness. In this mutual identification, the phenomenologist/s have precisely nothing to offer. There is no hidden treasure of superior knowledge that lies at the heart of inwardness. The immaterial, supersensible "inner of things" is an empty abstraction, and neither the protagonist/s nor the phenomenologist/s can fill it with given knowledge about the future of spirit. Hegel does not think of spirit as some kind of sack, inside which one might find something positive—a knowledge, a feeling, or "all sorts of faculties, inclinations, and passions."[47] If it is anything, interiority is the space of negativity; it can perhaps best be described as the reified gap within the subject. A fully saturated phenomenality would be a world without transport—but the understanding's rational analysis has cracked phenomenality and has therefore introduced emotionality. The space of interiority, which is opened by the understanding, gives us the sense of self-incongruence that transports the subject beyond any "natural" or given figuration.

The fact that interiority has made its first entrance on the scene of phenomenology as the interiority of the thing shows that it is an abstraction from, and a derivative of, exteriority. The "inner" is not to be taken as something positive, neither at the beginning of the protagonist's path nor at the end. The "inner" cannot be felt, nor rationally determined, nor "unfolded," nor attained—as if it were some thing. Its role is to unbind the rich web of attachments and determinations characteristic of the empirical world. With its abstract analysis, the understanding cracked open the phenomenal world. This crack both allows for self-reflection and prevents the mirror images from coinciding. It is the negativity or incongruity that sets thought into motion and unsettles (or makes emotional) nature and mind at every stage of their passage.

The expression model of self-realization is of no use for Hegel because it treats spirit as a sack—it presupposes that there is something positive inside the individual that can or should subsequently be expressed. In Hegel's text model, outside and inside leap simultaneously "out of nothing, into nothing" (Nancy 2002, 33). Negativity is at work in the outside world; "the 'phenomenon' is not appearance: it is the lively transport of self and the leap into manifest existence" (ibid.). But the understanding isolates this work, abstracts it from the phenomenal world, reifies it and arranges the space of interiority for it. It internalizes the sense of nothingness and tends thereby to lose it. Instead of allowing all determinations to pass, the understanding holds on to a representation of negativity, to the image of an interior space—like a pit, as we will see in the next section—carved into a stony body.

The Pit

In the "Psychology" chapter of the *Encyclopedia of the Philosophical Sciences*, Hegel describes human intelligence as a pit, shaft, or mine (*Schacht*). This pit is obviously another figure for interiority, and this time we have to take it at face value, since the *Encyclopedia* is a fairly straightforward philosophical text with no protagonist or narrator who could allow the author to assume an ironic distance from the thought figures under discussion.[48] Hegel's discussion of this figure of interiority is again bound up with a discussion of language. We will see once more that Hegel's conception of language is quite different from the expressive language that the sphere of reason is so fond of. Also, the vector of his discussion here is different. While the proponent of the "law of the heart" was concerned with expression, with giving an external reality to what is harbored inside the heart, Hegel here analyzes the inverse movement: how do external things get inside, into our minds.

He conducts this analysis under the heading of *Erinnerung*. The word usually means recollection, but Hegel uses the term in the literal sense of "inwardizing." In Hegel's account, perceived objects are inwardized (*erinnert*), or their images are transferred from outer intuition into the pit of intelligence, where—quite surprisingly—they are not deposited but disappear. It is grossly naive, according to Hegel, to think of this pit of intelligence as a physical space, where ideas are deposited in "special fibres and areas [*besonderen Fibern und Plätzen*]."[49] The space of the inner pit is not divided like empirical space, but has its own indivisible spatiality. In the process of inwardizing (*Erinnerung*), the intuitions thus lose the spatiotemporal coordinates that are a given in the outside world. Hegel uses another metaphor to hint at this utter lack of empirical coordinates, describing the pit of interiority as "nocturnal" (*nächtlicher;* Hegel 1971a, § 453, *Zusatz*). Across and beyond these imperfect metaphors, the "inner" has to be thought of as rigorously immaterial, ideational, and indeterminate. But in Hegel's philosophical world indeterminacy means lack of reality. It is in this sense that the images disappear in the pit of intelligence like in a black hole or an abyss.

One particular kind of image is the written word. (Hegel actually prefers the term "name" rather than "word.") In addition to, let's say, the dagger as object, we can look at the script *dagger* and we can transfer this image into the nocturnal pit of our intelligence. Nevertheless, Hegel insists that the image of the script is special. Unlike other sensual images, the script image is for him the result of a history and an archive of layers of mediation.[50] The written name or word is, strictly speaking, a sign for a sign for the recollection of an inwardized intuition or, rather, for repeated recollections of repeated intuitions. Therefore the script is not simply internalized the way immediate sensory images are. In this case, Hegel does not speak of inwardizing (*Erinnerung*) but of memory (*Gedächtnis*). The script is an external interiority: the material memory of previous acts of inwardizing and externalizing.

Here is the kind of history that is archived in the external memory that is the script: after the original literal "inwardizing" (*Er-innerung*) of the intuition of a dagger and its disappearance in the interiority of the nocturnal pit, repeated vanishing acts of the same kind have slowly built up the affective and cognitive energy that then surged up again as a recollection (now *Erinnerung* in the common sense—"sogenannte Erinnerung"—as opposed to literal inwardizing) out of the nothingness of the immaterial pit (Hegel 1971a, § 454). The immateriality or negativity of the black hole of interiority has received further density from the recurring counter-vectored movements of recollecting and inwardizing. This proto-linguistic texture has generated a somewhat external internal space—the "inner workshop [*innere Werkstätte*]," where the "imagination which creates signs [*Zeichen machende Phantasie*]" then has produced a sign for this complex event: the name *dagger* (Hegel 1971a, § 457, *Zusatz*, trans. modified). The name was produced first in the form of a spoken word. The written word, *dagger*, Hegel insists, is a sign of the second order. It stands not for the meaning of the word dagger but for the spoken signifier "dagger." This relative distance of the script from the dagger facilitates the dislocation of signifier and signified that Hegel generally postulates when he insists on the arbitrary character of signs.

We know, especially since Derrida's analysis of Hegel's semiology, that Hegel differentiates between sign and symbol and that this distinction is based on the arbitrary character of the sign as opposed to the motivated character of the symbol. The symbol illustrates its meaning. Signs, on the other hand, are apt to transport meaning without bringing it into view.[51]

As a matter of principle for Hegel, Western languages consist of signs. That is also why he prefers to speak of "names" rather than of words—names are "externalities which of themselves have no sense, and only get meaning as signs" (Hegel 1971a, § 459, *Zusatz*, trans. modified). Yet he calls attention to the fact—and draws considerable capital from it—that, as proficient readers, we tend to treat written words like hieroglyphs.[52] We forget that they are written signs for spoken signs. Without having to vocalize the words while reading we know immediately what is meant, or rather—and this is taking it one step further—we don't even bring to mind the meaning of the word, but mechanically string together words that we know inside out. Reading is like thinking in this: both reach their characteristic speed precisely because they do not have to take a detour via the pronunciation of the words, or the representation of their meaning in the mind, let alone the visualization of the objects in the imagination. Hegel refers to this economy of thought when he claims that "we *think* in names" (Hegel 1971a, § 462, *Zusatz*).

Proficiency in reading and thinking not only undoes Hegel's distinction between sign and symbol, it also undermines the proper working of both. While he had originally defined names as signs and hieroglyphs as symbols, reading and thinking now turn out to operate by way of symbols, but of symbols that do not symbolize: they don't bring meaning into view. This absence of meaning in turn shows that signs have also ceased to properly signify. The mechanical stringing together of words that we know inside out, as it were, brings to the fore the more than radical arbitrariness of signs: their fundamental insignificance and impropriety. Signs gain a peculiar kind of literality or materiality in this display of their catachrestic character. The written word now becomes the thing itself, without referring back to a putatively antecedent reality: "The name is thus the thing as it . . . counts in the realm of representation [*die Sache, wie sie im Reiche der Vorstellung Gültigkeit hat*]" (Hegel 1971a, § 462). The mechanical "memory which retains names [*Namen behaltende Gedächtniß*]" thus not only establishes a strangely externalized space within interiority, but it completely turns the pit of intelligence inside out, it magically creates being out of nothingness: "This supreme inwardizing [*höchste Erinnerung*] of representation is the supreme self-emptying of intelligence [*höchste Entäußerung*], in which it renders itself the mere *being*, the universal space of names as such, i.e. of meaningless words" (Hegel 1971a, § 461/ § 463, trans. modified). Signs are in view without meaning. Such is their monstrosity. It overlaps with the monstrosity of Hegel calling intelligence an "unconscious pit" (*bewußtloser Schacht;* Hegel 1971a, § 453, *Zusatz;* trans. modified).

With his semiology Hegel "relieves" the clean-cut divisions between inside and outside, subjectivity and objectivity, ideality and materiality and turns them into textual (i.e., self-differential) differences. He even tackles the distinction between signification and insignificance: "Memory [*Gedächtniß*] is in this manner the passage into the activity of *thought*, which no longer has a *meaning* [*Bedeutung*], i.e. the subjective is no longer severed from its objectivity, and its inwardness is existing in itself [*an ihr selbst seyend*]" (Hegel 1971a, § 464, trans. modified). Thought doesn't mean; it *is*. That is to say, the activity of thinking creates reality, and it does so without any return to meaning, which, in fact, has no effective reality (*Wirksamkeit*). A meaning (*Bedeutung*) beyond this reality of thinking and reading would be a *Meinung* (opinion) or a mere *Gemeintes* (intention), that is to say a mere subjectivity without objectivity, an inner without an outer, or a narcissism that expires without making a change: "The inwardness, which is supposed to be the true, is the 'ownness' [*Eigenheit*] of the intention and the individuality of being-for-itself. Both are the spirit which is *aimed at* [*der gemeinte Geist*]," or my (*mein*) spirit, but not actual spirit (§ 320). Only the insignificance of thought—the fact that it "no longer has a *meaning*"—makes thought real.[53] Real thought is, thus, impersonal thought: it is a thinking that exists and develops independently of the individual mind. It is the thing itself, which, for Hegel—unlike the noumenon for Kant—is available for (broken) experience.[54]

By literalizing *Erinnerung* Hegel specularizes it, as it were. The inwardizing he describes results in a more radical exteriorizing than that of recollection, which dredges things up from the recesses of the mind into the strangely reified space of interiority, but not into actual exteriority. Hegel thus uses *Erinnerung* as a speculative word, that is, a word that means one thing and its opposite. In Hegel, it denotes both the inward and the outward movement.[55] In speculative *Erinnerung* or in the meaningless thoughtness of *Gedächtnis,* objects vanish repeatedly: layering traces that reflect each other and thus building the affective and cognitive textuality of the interior, they im-materialize into names, which are things in themselves, that can be perceived, and inwardized, and so turn into other names, which in turn reflect on and thereby enhance the emotional and mental textuality of the pit. Language thus functions not as expression, but as a self-constructing texture that traverses materiality and immateriality, entangles exteriority and interiority and reflexively enhances impersonally emotional and rational life.

Hard Heart

The last version of the figure of the heart in the *Phenomenology* is not a figure of interiority anymore. It presents the limit case of the conception and practice of feeling. I am referring to the "hard heart" and its double, the "beautiful soul." The epithet of "beautiful soul" usually—and most explicitly in Schiller's taxonomy—stands and falls with the naïveté of the person. Her or his purity depends on ignorance, on not knowing how beautiful, true, and good s/he really is.[56] Hegel offers a different account of naïveté. The hyper-conscientious beautiful soul enjoys an extreme purity not because its feelings are pre-reflective, but because they are completely transparent to it and others. It harbors no secret; it claims no *Meinung* that differs from outer display; it has abandoned all inwardness. This excessively self-conscious purity spells the death of natural feeling, and, as I will discuss in more detail in chapter 7, it is the beginning of an emotionality without drama: a lighthearted transport.

The beautiful soul speaks beautifully. What it says is crystal clear, its language is "completely transparent" (*das vollkommen Durchsichtige,*

§ 658). Its speech is an immaculate expression of its spirituality. "The absolute self-certainty of itself is immediately converted into a . . . sound" (*schlägt ihr unmittelbar in ein Austönen um,* § 658). The beautiful soul thus consummates the ideal of expression developed in the sphere of reason: its speech "is the pure form of translating" from the interior to the exterior, without distortion (§ 396). It is perfectly satisfied when it hears itself: everything it says represents it properly.

In this flawless self-expression the outer is bound to the inner and the inner bound to the outer to the point that the two collapse into the extensionless point of the "I" with its voiceless voice and shapeless shape. What the beautiful soul puts forth it retains as its own: the echo of its voice returns only to itself.[57] Nobody else hears it. Its words are "a dying sound" (*Austönen,* § 658). It is as if they never made a sound. When the beautiful soul speaks, it is a "quiet coalescence of the pithless essentialities of [its] evaporated life" (*stille Zusammenfließen der marklosen Wesenheiten des verflüchtigten Lebens,* § 659, trans. modified). It might just as well say nothing. Its "activity alters nothing and opposes nothing" (§ 396). It "has the appearance of the movement of a circle, which within itself set itself into motion and moves freely in the void, and which, as unimpeded now enlarges now contracts and is fully satisfied in playing such a game within itself and with its self" (§ 396, trans. modified). The heart of the beautiful soul expands and contracts in a rhythm that is regular and undisturbed because the beautiful soul speaks only to its kind. It has surrounded itself ad infinitum with equally beautiful souls and thus knows no other who would resist it. But the satisfaction it gains from being recognized by the likes of it leaves a flat aftertaste: "The spirit and the substance of their bond is thus the reciprocal assurance of both their mutual conscientiousness and their good intentions; it is the rejoicing over this reciprocal purity, the refreshment received from the glory of knowing, articulating, fostering and cherishing such excellence" (§ 656). The communion is perfect and the recognition is vapid. The beautiful soul finds no other to thrust its heart against. It goes against no one and doesn't touch anybody. Thus floating alone in infinite space (even though it is surrounded by like-minded souls), the beautiful soul longs for real friends.[58] "Its activity is a yearning" (§ 658). Like the "unhappy consciousness," who in its attempt to rise to God has "fallen back into itself" (§ 217), the beautiful soul, in its gesture to communicate with friends, merely "falls back on itself, [and] merely finds itself as lost" (*zurück zu sich fallend sich nur als Verlornes findet;* § 658). Together with its words, "its own fire consumes it and dies out, and the beautiful soul vanishes like a shapeless vapor dissolving into thin air" (§ 658, trans. modified).

The (self-)transparency of the beautiful soul comes at the expense of difference; it really amounts to a refusal of emotionality.[59] In its ethereal existence, the beautiful soul has lost its voice before it begins to speak. It understands language as the universal and transparent medium of the universal self, and it sees universality and singularity, like the pure and the stained, as mutually exclusive.[60] By embracing universality, it opts against "the *natural* consciousness, i.e. impulses and inclinations [*Triebe und Neigungen*]" and turns into the hard heart (§ 643).[61] Its untainted self-expression remains empty: "the hollow object which it generates to itself thus now fills it with the consciousness of emptiness" (§ 658). For its language to gain significance it would have to be saturated with "the so-called sensuousness" (*sogenannte Sinnlichkeit*) that the beautiful soul despises—with "the caprice [*Willkür*] of the individual, and the contingency of his unconscious natural being" (§ 643, trans. modified). Such "sensuousness" is only "so-called"; it cannot be named appropriately because, according to the idea of language harbored by the beautiful soul, the sensual is supposed to exist only prior to language, before it is subjected to the universality of a generic concept.

With the notion of an absolutely transparent and therefore empty language, the beautiful soul is at odds with Hegel's own conception of language. For Hegel, language has its own "sense-nature" in the materiality of the signifier. It has its own "impulses and inclinations" and emotionality in the self-incongruity of "the self-moving permeation [*sich bewegende Durchdringung*] of the universal . . . and individuality" (§ 394). With the *Phenomenology*, Hegel famously constructs the concept (*Begriff*) as at the same time reaching through (*durchgreift*) and embracing (*umgreift*) both universality and individuality. The last figure of consciousness in the *Phenomenology* has driven to the extreme the abstract notion of language as universal that was the insight of the first figure of consciousness. While "sense certainty," the first figure of consciousness, loses its sensuous self in the universal dimension of language, the hard heart loses the sensuous dimension of language in its universal self. The materiality and inner life of language, the impulses and inclinations of words, the self-reflexive density and subjectivity of the medium are lost on the hard heart, whose ethereal transparency has congealed into an unexpectedly unnatural solid—a heart of glass.

At the extreme of perfect self-expression, feeling is exhausted. In order to explain what I mean by this, I need to expound a little bit upon the Kantian background of the figure of the beautiful soul. The beautiful soul avoids impulses and inclinations (*Triebe and Neigungen*). Operating on minimal affectivity, it only allows for two pure kinds of feeling: on the one hand, the pure self-feeling of the transcendental synthesis of apperception (the extensionless "I") and, on the other hand, the feeling of disinterested pleasure in the aesthetic experience of beauty. The first kind of feeling is posited as a universal or natural ground of all cognition, and the second kind is naturalized through the procedure of taste. The postulate of universal communicability (*allgemeine Mitteilbarkeit*), which motivates the individual to impute (*ansinnen*) its aesthetic judgment to virtually everyone, naturalizes feeling along the lines of: "you would all feel this pleasure if only you had taste." Both kinds of feeling evince the non-propositional status of "feeling," and support the Romantic idea that feelings are not appropriately expressed in discursive form. The "I think" that must be able to accompany all of my thoughts and representations is a unified and unifying feeling that needs no articulation. Aesthetic pleasure is a feeling voiced for others, but voiced without voice because those "others" have no resistance to offer: they are themselves but extensionless extensions of the self. If the source of aesthetic pleasure lies in the harmony of the faculties *within* the mind (*Gemüt*), this concord perpetuates, strengthens, and reproduces itself in the conformity of judgment among "all" minds.[62]

At the same time, this idea of natural, authentic, substantive, and self-harmonizing "feeling" brings us to the verge of the conception of "emotionality"—as the negative, supplemental, and hollow feeling of self-discord.[63] Kant's other aesthetic experience, the sublime, indicates and performatively reinforces the ineffability and unrepresentability of the most precious and infinite faculty of the mind—reason—and thus offers the theoretical groundwork for the hard heart's refusal to externalize its inner beauty—its refusal to expose it to real difference, that is, and not just to a community of taste. The sublime also presents the traumatic destruction of the integrity of feeling—the breaking of the hard heart.

Thomas Pfau argues that, with his aesthetics of the sublime, Kant profoundly alters the essential bond between interiority and expression. Pfau describes the sublime as the shock of the absence of the feeling of pleasure and the fabrication of the quasi-feeling of "respect" (for the supersensible quality of reason) to fill in the void. This procedure "transforms the entire conception of 'feeling' from an inward authentic event into something essentially notional and figural in kind"—something fabricated or fictional—and "throws into relief the strictly 'virtual' character of all feeling, including that of the beautiful, to begin with" (Pfau 2005, 42/43).[64] The (non-)experience of the sublime means the death of natural feeling. From hence on, the duplicity of the hard heart will undo the naive simplicity of the beautiful soul, and self-reflexive emotionality will not ground cognition, as "feeling" did, but transport concepts from one figuration to the next.

With the hard heart, the beauty of naturalized or "organic" feeling is exhausted and the trope of interiority breaks. Even though spirit is spirit only when it actualizes or realizes itself (its values and beliefs), we have traced in this chapter how "we"—or spirit through us—come to discover that the trope of the heart (figuring interiority) actually makes this self-realization impossible. We have seen that the sentimentalist prefers feeling the mad throbbing of his heart to losing heart in the alienating endeavor to bring about actual political change. It has become clear that the logic of expression leads to a frustrating double imperative to withhold what is to be communicated (epitomized in Schiller's sigh of the soul). We have followed this double imperative to the figure of the beautiful soul, who carries the logic of interiority to extremes by downright refusing to expose any part of its precious interiority to an alienating exteriority, so that not only the expression but even the experience of feeling becomes impossible.

In between, we have explored Hegel's alternatives to the logics of expression, purity of feeling, and interiority. We have seen that spirit has a textual rather than an expressive relation to itself. We have discussed one of Hegel's strategies to imbricate rationality and emotionality. Rather than dismiss intellectual analysis for interfering with, perhaps even threatening, the holistic intuition of feeling—as the philosophers of feeling do—Hegel proposes that the analytic activity of the understanding actually produces and furthers emotionality. As a strategy to dismantle the construction of interiority, we have analyzed how Hegel twists together the counter-vectored movements of internalizing and recollecting by literalizing *Erinnerung*, and thereby undoes the inner-outer opposition.

In the end, the beautiful soul has led us to the verge of a radically new conception of emotionality, where authenticity depends on fabrication. The beautiful soul's duplicity (be it within the hard heart or between the figures of the hard heart and the ironist into which the beautiful soul splits) will in a later chapter (chapter 7) provide a prime example for the broken syntax of emotional thought and thoughtful emotionality in the *Phenomenology*. But before we address the syntax of emotionality in more detail in the second part of this book, we will turn to another important thematic account of emotionality in Hegel, that of "pathos." Pathos is less severely criticized by Hegel, because—even though it tends to come across as another naturalizing figure of emotionality—it is less unambiguously stuck in that naturalizing register than feeling is. In fact, we will see that the *Phenomenology* offers a naturalizing and a theatrical account of pathos. It thus builds on the lesson of the sublime that, in the absence of feeling inside, pathos must be fabricated and exhibited on stage—including the stage that is the world.

2

Pathos

Hegel sometimes distinguishes *Pathos* (pathos) from *Leidenschaft* (passion) and at other times he uses them as synonyms. When one term stands in for the other, Hegel usually wants to confer the ethical prestige of tragic "pathos" upon "passion" in order to argue against the rationalist (Kantian and Socratic) tendency to view passions as by definition irrational and immoral. When the two terms are differentiated, *Leidenschaft* refers to an intense but temporally circumscribed and ultimately selfish motivation to act, whereas *Pathos* is described as a temporally unlimited or categorical identification with an ethical cause.

Pathos clearly has two advantages over the figure of the heart: because it calls for action, it escapes Hegel's critique of mere interiority; and in that it takes a clear position, it integrates emotionality with rationality. Yet the intractability of pathos—the fact that the passionate stance absorbs the person completely, defines his entire life, and leaves no room for ambivalence—leads to the tragic annihilation of the individual who is under the sway of this trope. Because of this obduracy, I contend, Hegel grows rather disenchanted with pathos and shifts to an analysis of how the theatricality of tragedy affects this trope of absolute sincerity.

Nietzsche exposed the difference between a character-defining passion and a passing passion as one not of essence but of perspective. In retrospect, he points out, we might realize that a passion that seemed absolute to us in the moment was indeed relative and has passed.[1] Analyzing Hegel's account of tragedy in the first section of this chapter, I argue that Hegel, like Nietzsche, reveals the difference between pathos and passion (*Leidenschaft*) as merely one of perspective. I thereby arrive at two different accounts of pathos: the naturalizing or dramatic account from the in-the-moment subjective perspective, and the theatrical or lighthearted account that draws on reflective and ironic distance. My dramatic account of pathos attends to the fact that the dramatic character sincerely believes in the absolute, universal, and ethical quality of his pathos, but my description of this account as "naturalizing" already suggests that the dramatic character produces or constructs his pathos by aggressively gating out other perspectives. My theatrical account of pathos addresses the fact that Hegel merges two realms of reference—real life and theater—in his discussion of the pathos of "ethical life"

(*Sittlichkeit*). This account attends to the oscillation between these two realms, which renders the passionate character ontologically ecstatic and therefore lighthearted.

Both accounts can be applied to the textual pathos of the *Phenomenology*. Read dramatically, the pathos of the *Phenomenology* consists in consciousness having to suffer for knowledge—this is the pathos of experience. Wahl has best articulated the self-dramatizing economy of Hegelian dialectic, arguing that each contradiction has to be sharpened into a tragic collision before the phenomenology can move to the next form of spirit.[2] Yet I will show that experience, understood as a dramatic pathos, cannot effect a transformation of self—it cannot move someone to become a different person or move consciousness to become a different "shape of consciousness." Instead it leads (quite literally) to a dead end. To transport consciousness to another version of consciousness requires the doubling and duplicity provided by theatricality.

The last section of this chapter introduces "acknowledging" as the *Phenomenology*'s preferred mode of learning. This mode of knowledge is able to transport the protagonist. "Acknowledging" develops out of the pathos of experience and carries its suffering, but it is also the lighthearted passion that drives the movement of the *Phenomenology*. This section gives an account of *Aufhebung* as lifting the weight off of pathos and offers a preview of what I mean by "transport"—something that I will develop more extensively in the second part of the book.[3] I contend that, in the composition and syntax of the *Phenomenology*, Hegel draws more on his analysis of the theatricality of tragedy than on his theory of the tragic conflict. The *Phenomenology*'s theatrics build plasticity and ambivalence into the structure of the subject. It constructs the subject of the *Phenomenology* as a subject to transport by dividing it into a protagonist and a phenomenologist. I argue that the different roles of this plural subject affect, undo, and transform one another, but that they also serve as remainders of one another, so that there is never a complete destruction of the subject in the *Phenomenology*.

While throughout this book I maintain that the quasi-literary text of the *Phenomenology* intertwines three different literary spatio-temporalities (complex narrative, theatrical enactment, and poetic rhythm), this chapter focuses on theatrical enactment. The peculiar reality of the theater, which combines the authenticity of present-tense embodiment, feeling, and insight with the self-reflective supplement of an internal spectatorship, doubles the meaning not only of acting, but also of feeling and of thinking. If Hegel's philosophy is fundamentally a philosophy of *Bildung*, which maintains that spirit must negate or shape itself into forms of nature and second nature, and nature must negate or educate itself into the ideality of spirit, then the theater seems to offer the right combination of reality and virtuality, or nature and spirit, to host such a philosophy. This idea of *Bildung* had one of its earlier champions in Schiller who, in assessments like this one, offered the basic premise behind Hegel's idea that spirit needs to appear to itself: Man "does not stop short at what Nature herself made of him, but has the power of retracing by means of Reason the steps she took on his behalf, of transforming the work of blind compulsion into a work of free choice, and of elevating physical necessity into moral necessity" (Schiller 1982, 11). If Schiller inspired Hegel, he did so not incidentally by talking about theater.

Ethical Drama

Hegel draws upon Aristotle to develop his rather unusual—I would say Nietzschean—understanding of pathos. Even though he discusses pathos in the context of his analysis of tragedy it is not primarily Aristotle's *Poetics* that he consults, nor the *Rhetoric*, in which Aristotle discusses the different *páthe* of concern for the orator. Instead, Hegel turns to a work that Aristotle wrote around the same time as the *Rhetoric* and the *Poetics*, namely the *Magna Moralia*. For Hegel, passion does not—and here he agrees with the author of the *Magna Moralia*—hinder ethical life, but furthers it.[4] In his *Lectures on the History of Philosophy*, Hegel quotes and comments on Aristotle's critique of Socrates' intellectualist notion of virtue:[5]

> Concerning Aristotle's criticism of the principle of Socrates, we should note here that he says, Socrates placed virtue exclusively in logos, in knowing. . . . "He made virtue a matter of insight. So Socrates does away with the alogical [*allogike*] aspect of the soul, to which belong pathos and ethical custom" [Aristotle, *Magna Moralia* 1.1.1182a.15–23]. . . . This is a good clarification of virtue. Although virtue consists in self-determination according to universal purposes rather than private ends, it is not only insight or consciousness but also involves the agent's identifying "heart and soul" [*das Herz, das Gemüt*] with the insight, and this is what Aristotle calls the alogical aspect of being. (Hegel 2006, 139)

For Aristotle, in order to determine what is good, one needs not only knowledge, but also *ethos* or character, and *páthos* or passion. Hegel agrees with Aristotle's critique of Socrates when he argues that the good is "not mere thought, but a defining and effective presence" (Hegel 2006, 139). In Socrates' philosophy "the good as such [with an eye to human actions] still remained indeterminate"; it is "only a universal maxim" (Hegel 2006, 138). The good as universal principle (*Maxime*)—Hegel contends with obvious allusion to Kantian moral philosophy—lacks the force that drives concrete individuals to take it to heart.

In chapter 1, I discussed Hegel's rather severe critique of the age of sensibility and its overappreciation of "the law of the heart." Against this background, the analogy he draws here between pathos and the heart—"We see that what Aristotle misses in Socrates' determination of virtue, the aspect of subjective reality, is what we today call 'heart'"—strikes one as imprecise (Hegel 1986, 473, my translation).[6] Given that we are dealing with lecture notes here, I think that we can attribute this imprecision to Hegel's pedagogical impetus to illustrate the relevance of Aristotle's position with a contemporary reference. It is certainly true that the ethics of sensibility presents a critique of the intellectualism of Kantian moral philosophy just as Aristotle critiques here the intellectualism of Socratic moral philosophy. Like the sentimentalists, Hegel critiques Kant's moral rationalism, but the pathos model of emotionality serves him better than the sensibility model, because pathos desires action and externalization, whereas feeling remains locked in the interiority of the heart.

Like Aristotle, who speaks of virtuous passion, Hegel underscores the ethical value of passion and defines pathos as passion for a cause. Passion, or pathos, in this specific sense, drives a person to put into action what he thinks is good and right. For Hegel, then, pathos has two advantages over the figure of the heart. By "identifying heart and soul with insight," it reconciles rationality with emotionality and, because it propels action, it escapes the critique of mere interiority.

In a world of pathos, the sphere of the good and the true is not to be located in the inaccessible interiority of the heart, nor in some metaphysical heaven—situated "who knows where" (a typical Hegelian phrase when it comes to exposing some so-called truth as merely imagined). The good and the true find their reality, effectiveness, and presence in the customs of a people and in the passions and thus actions of its heroes: "The individual presence of the universal good [*das allgemeine Gute am Einzelnen als solchen*] is 'pathos,' the universal that drives the individual" (Hegel 1986, 474, my translation). The various universal goods or causes that can drive an individual are imagined as divine forces, but not as metaphysical ones. The Greek gods move among the mortals and participate in their activities. More precisely, the gods drive the mortals to action and the mortals actualize the values that the gods represent:

> Regarding their substance, the gods are abstractly universal—this universal is actualized in the act; this actualization belongs to human activity, the activity of subjective individuality. This subjective individuality has as its substantial content the divine matter [*Stoff*], the *pathe*. They are the interests of the human agents, the powers that drive them. (Hegel 1998, 98, my translation)

While each Greek god presents a particular passion to the imagination, Hegel underscores that the gods are part of the human tissue and find their objective realization in the acts of the mortals.

As subjective motivations and as objective gods, the *páthe* constitute accepted reasons for the way things are done. In precisely this sense (of accepted reasons), they are, thus, rational. "Pathos is the power in general [*überhaupt*] insofar as it moves the human heart and soul, and it should be considered an aspect of the rational and free will," Hegel contends (Hegel 2005, 96, my translation). While, from a modern perspective, we might feel compelled to find rational only the political pathos of Creon, whereas Antigone, who is driven by the "unwritten laws" of family allegiance, might seem irrational to some of us, Hegel insists that their tragedy develops precisely because they are both motivated by different but equally rational and ethical causes.

As the third characteristic of pathos (in addition to its external reality and its rationality) we need to mention its intransigence: "The individual is what it is; it acts out of this character, this pathos, and it is character because it is precisely this. This is the strength of the ancient characters: that they don't choose, but are what they do. . . . The figures are this and eternally this, and that is their greatness" (Hegel 1998, 305, my translation). Passionate characters are heroes because pathos leaves no room for ambivalence or critical self-reflection. Without wavering or second-guessing, the hero is absolutely firm in his commitment. Pathos thus refers to an innate character disposition, not a temporary upheaval of passion.

The fact that Hegel uses pathos to refer to the character or ethical calling of an individual who is embedded in the social customs of his community shows once again that Hegel draws upon the *Magna Moralia*, rather than other, perhaps more familiar, works by Aristotle. In the *Rhetoric*, for example, Aristotle discusses various character types (*ethe*) that the orator might encounter in the audience he is trying to convince; these character types are determined by social factors (such as age, class, and fortune) and thus remain relatively constant. *Páthe,* on the other hand, such as anger, pity, or jealousy, can be spontaneously created; the skilled orator can arouse affects in the audience (in order to influence their judgment) by displaying the signs of the desired affect, that is, by first arousing the affect in himself. Meanwhile Aristotle underscores the importance of the orator's credibility. To protect his credibility, his speech and his affect must be in line with his character or *ethos*. *Ethos,* in this case, means honesty and trustworthiness. Hegel's notion of pathos, on the other hand, does not allow for the possibility of auto- or hetero-affection, that is, of the conscious and artful manipulation of pathos. For Hegel, pathos is unchanging. The ancient characters are "eternally this." Their heroism consists in being uncompromising and steadfastly true to their character. Pathos is Hegel's figure for the authenticity of emotion and for the saturation of a person with substance: "The substance appears *with* individuality [*an der Individualität*] as his *pathos,* and individuality appears as what brings substance to life. . . . Ethical individuality is immediately and in itself at one with its universal; it has existence only within it" (§ 470, trans. modified). The complete congruence of the hero with his cause certainly suggests honesty and trustworthiness. Hegel thus uses pathos as virtually synonymous with character or *ethos* in the sense of Aristotle's *Rhetoric.*

The earlier-quoted passage from the *Lectures on the History of Philosophy* (where Hegel comments on Aristotle's critique of Socrates) continues by citing "love, ambition, thirst for glory" as examples of virtuous pathos.[7] Here, it is thus taken for granted that even such morally ambiguous passions as thirst for glory, ambition, or love inevitably (through the infamous "cunning of Reason," one would assume) serve the good. But Hegel's discussion of pathos in the *Phenomenology of Spirit* is embedded in an analysis of ethics played out not in a providential, but in a tragic world. Here, even the righteous passion brings about disaster.[8]

So far we have analyzed the different characteristics of pathos (virtuous, reasonable, intransigent, and driving) from the meta-theoretical perspective of Hegel's critique of rationalist morality in the *Lectures on the History of Philosophy.* Now we turn to Hegel's discussion of pathos in the *Phenomenology.* In the tragic world of ethical action, two different but equally ethical values collide. The two heroes, each of whom ardently serves his own cause but offends the god who impassions the other, both behave ethically and unethically to equal degrees. But such ambiguity doesn't fit the heroic sense of self. From the hero's point of view, things are clear. He sees his own passion as righteous pathos—he genuinely serves an ethical cause—whereas the other's behavior seems to him an insincere and unnecessary production of pathos—at best a private end posing as a universal purpose. Tragedy ensues from the refusal to recognize the pathos of the other.

The phenomenological approach adds an existential aspect to the discussion of pathos that will promptly introduce a certain amount of theatricality. In general, the *Phenomenology* enacts the various figurations of consciousness and allows us to identify with them—the phenomenological presentation as such has, thus, something theatrical about it. In addition, the particular figure of consciousness we are analyzing now—ethical passion—is best known from ancient Greek theater. Hegel calls attention to this intertwining of the theatrical and the ethical realms by using the word *Handlung* (action, act, plot) rather than *Tat* or *Tun* ("deed," or "doing") to describe the activities of the passionate individual. He thereby suggests that pathos—his trope for absolute emotional sincerity—has indeed something staged about it.

The theatricality of ethical action gives rise to suspicions about the true value of pathos. The need emerges for a line to be drawn between virtuous, substantial, genuine, and right passions on the one hand, and self-serving, insubstantial, phony, and wrong passions on the other. Hegel begins to mark the difference by reserving the word *Pathos* for the former and *Leidenschaft* or *Leidenschaftlichkeit* for the latter. The part of the *Phenomenology* that deals with the realm of ethics from the point of view of religion, for example, states that merely subjective and arbitrary interests are "not the pathos [*Pathos*] of the hero; they have in the hero's eyes descended to the level of being his passions [*Leidenschaft*]—that is, they have sunken to the level of accidental essenceless moments, . . . which are neither capable of constituting the character of heroes nor of being expressed and revered by them as their essence" (§ 741).[9] The protagonist of the section on "the ethical order" in the "Spirit" chapter draws the line around himself. As the drama of the ethical action unfurls, the heroic perspective multiplies by two.[10] This duplication allows each hero to project the theatricality that has infected pathos onto the other: to experience his own passion as genuine pathos and the other's as mere *Leidenschaftlichkeit.*

In the remainder of this section, I will discuss how Hegel treats the collapse of the distinction (which is not only problematic but also rather precarious) between *Leidenschaft* as unethical passion, and *Pathos* as virtuous passion. It is the hero's own action that will precipitate this collapse.

The ethical world knows a plurality of causes or ethical authorities that are personified by different gods. They usually exist peacefully side by side and can be honored as equally valid. Under certain and indeed necessarily occurring conditions, two of these values come to a head in a tragic collision that produces severe physical suffering:[11]

> There are different ethical authorities [*sittliche Mächte*]. In a state of calm, they form the circle of the gods and are in harmony with one

> another. But it must also happen that they are offended and, thus, called to the scene to act [*zur erscheinenden Tätigkeit aufgerufen*]; individuals thus appear as the pathos, as the actualization of an ethical power. (Hegel 1998, 302, my translation)

The god appears on the scene as the pathos of an individual. The passionate character fully identifies with his pathos and thus lends reality to only one of the many ethical authorities. The other gods are offended by this exclusivity that defines pathos. The intransigence of pathos then precipitates the tragic collision: "Because . . . ethical life consists essentially in this immediate *decisiveness* [*unmittelbaren Entschiedenheit*], and for that reason only *one* law is the essence for consciousness, . . . the ethical powers . . . acquire the significance of *excluding* each other and being *opposed* to each other" (§ 465). The many ethical authorities are thus reduced to two: "Because it has *decided* [*entschieden*] for one of them, ethical consciousness is essentially *character*. . . . It sees right only on its own side and sees only wrong on the other" (§ 465). Pathos, by Hegel's definition, determines a person's character and thus behaves like *Ethos* as defined by Aristotle's *Rhetoric* in that it cannot be manipulated and does not change easily. This resolute character of passion spurs tragedies.

Clearly, the passionate acts that constitute the tragic world of ethics intertwine activity and passivity. The hero suffers his agency. He lives in the service of a higher ethical authority, god, or spirit. He receives his high standing from the fact that he personifies this ethical authority, but he also gives his life, his full existence as an individual, to this one cause. In this sense, his passion for the cause spells suffering.

> The existence of the pure concept . . . is an individual which spirit elects to be the vessel for its sorrow. Spirit exists in this individual as his universal and as his power, from which he suffers violence—as his pathos, to which he has surrendered himself, so that his self-consciousness loses its freedom. (§ 704, trans. modified)

The cause drives the individual to action and determines his character. It moves the individual at his core, and yet it enters from the outside:

> [The *páthe*] are the agents' interests, their driving forces. On the one hand, they determine the subjectivity of man; on the other, they are independent determinations existing in and for themselves. As far as they belong to the human being, and are man's genuine character, and drive him, the conflict arises that the same determinations can be represented as self-sufficient individualities over and against man [for

example as gods], and thus collide with human freedom. (Hegel 1998, 98–99, my translation)

Against common assumption—including the hero's self-image—Hegel shows the heroic subject to be not fully autonomous, but heteronomous to the extent that the law that rules his character is imagined to have an independent existence in the form of a particular god: "Man in passion is in a pathos, a god has overpowered him, he is not a free subject anymore, he is beside himself [*außer sich*]" (Hegel 1998, 103, my translation).

In the pathos model of emotionality, inside and outside overlap to the extent that gods and heroes mutually penetrate and actualize one another. The mortals, with their actions, turn divine ideality into concrete external reality. Meanwhile, the gods are the personifications of *páthe;* the gods are men's emotionality in exterior form: "The outward appearance must at the same time show something of man's inwardness. . . . Since the gods are in the heart and soul, even if they exist to a certain extent outside. In Homer, this constantly moves to and fro [*geht dies stets herüber und hinüber*]" (Hegel 1998, 99–100, my translation).

Pathos, as Hegel understands it, is always interior and exterior at the same time. Structurally, pathos trembles between inside and outside; it oscillates between the literal and the figurative, the staged and the genuine. This flutter blurs the difference between the opposites; each side briefly but repeatedly appears as the other. The inside appears as the outside; the genuine as staged; the figurative as literal. This is to say that pathos renders the passionate character ontologically ecstatic. In an almost literal sense, the passionate is beside himself with passion. With this account of the ek-stasy of passion, Hegel offers a critique of interiority. He shows that it is more productive to understand emotion as pathos than as feeling locked into the interiority of the heart.[12]

This same ecstasy of passion—the flutter between inside and outside, between activity and suffering, or between the genuine and the staged—suggests another interpretation of pathos—one that attends to its lightheartedness. Naturalizing pathos in his discussion of Greek ethical life as the first—that is to say, the most natural—shape of spirit, Hegel explicitly excludes from the context of tragedy the interpretation of pathos as theatrical and lighthearted. Nevertheless, by superimposing aesthetic and existential concerns in this discussion, he implicitly draws attention to the problems of a naturalizing account of pathos. I think that the problem with the pathos model of emotion is that it feeds on a misguided desire for authenticity and drama. By drama, I mean not theatricality but emotional and existential weight.[13] Driven by his desire for real drama, the passionate character ignores that pathos itself trembles—lest this flutter introduce an air of self-irony. Instead, he reinforces the impression of complete inner coherence, which, as we have seen, leads to intransigence and thus to tragedy.[14] The passionate character insists that "there is neither arbitrary choice nor is there struggle or indecision. . . . Instead, in its eyes, the ethical essentiality is the immediate, the unwavering, what is free of contradiction" (§ 464). Dramatic pathos creates tragedy and tragedy generates dramatic pathos.

So far, we have established that Hegel considers the pathos model more useful than the sensibility model of emotion (with its trope of the feeling heart). At this point, we will turn to the problems—indeed the tragic pitfalls—that the intransigence of pathos poses.[15] Hegel shows that the totalizing gesture of pathos is based on ignorance or, rather, on disavowal:[16] "Now, because . . . ethical life consists essentially in this immediate *decisiveness,* and for that reason only *one* law is the essence for consciousness, . . . thereby arises in consciousness the opposition between the *known* and the *not known*" (§ 465–66). If he were aware of his trembling, the dramatic character might be able to suspend (*aufheben*) his resolve (*Entschiedenheit*) and see that there are gods on the other side as well. Such suspension would open a space for lightheartedness in the midst of pathos. But Hegel presents awareness of the constitutive trembling of pathos, of its movement "to and fro," as a purely aesthetic concern (Hegel 1998, 100). He discusses the phenomenon in his lectures on the philosophy of art as well as in the section on "Religion in the Form of Art" of the *Phenomenology,* but not in the section on the "Ethical Order"—as if such flutter had no room in the practical world of ethical decisions.[17] Apparently, the person passionately caught up in the action cannot or should not be aware of his trembling between the literal and the figural. The effects are tragic, we know. The dramatic character doesn't realize that the position of his antagonist is as justified, as reasonable, and as ethical as his own: "He takes his purpose from his character and knows it as the ethical essentiality; however, by virtue of the determinateness of his character, he knows merely the *one* power of substance, and, for him, the other power is concealed" (§ 737). He doesn't see that the other also acts out of passion for a good cause.

Only after the fact, after his pathos has driven him to act, will the dramatic character experience his agency as a suffering, and will he have to acknowledge that the other's position was always as valid as his own:

> The accomplished deed turns the point of view of ethical consciousness topsy-turvy. What the *accomplishment* itself articulates is that the *ethical* must be *actual,* for the *actuality* of the purpose is the purpose of acting.

> Acting directly articulates the *unity* of *actuality* and *substance.* It says that actuality is not accidental to essence, but rather that, in league with essence, actuality is not granted to anything that is not a true right. On account of this actuality and on account of its deed, ethical consciousness must recognize its opposite as its own. It must acknowledge its guilt:
> *Because we suffer, we acknowledge that we have erred.* [*Weil wir leiden, anerkennen wir, daß wir gefehlt.*] (§ 469, trans. modified)[18]

By acting upon his beliefs, the passionate character shows that external, tangible reality is important to him. He is not satisfied with knowing what is right; he needs to see it realized. He feels justified in altering the given reality in the service of his pathos, and his ability to do so only proves to him the truth and righteousness of his position. Yet, because his antagonist was also able to alter the given and to establish the reality of his pathos and law through action, the other's action must have ethical validity as well. Because the passionate character believes that "actuality is not accidental to essence," and that it "is not granted to anything that is not a true right," he will have to acknowledge his adversary's act as righteous. We can see more clearly now what I touched upon earlier when I introduced the flutter of pathos, namely how the act alienates the passionate character to a certain extent from his position. Hegel insists that this shift appears only in retrospect. It first requires that the passionate character act authentically, that is, that he fully identify with the knowledge of what is to be done. And yet "action itself is this inversion [*Verkehrung*] of *what was known* into its *contrary,* into *what is* (§ 738). The act that fully expresses the agent's commitment also shows that the agent didn't fully understand what his commitment truly was. Hegel explicitly values the fact that pathos calls to action and that action turns the character inside out. What he less explicitly thematizes in the phenomenological account is that such an "inversion" (or rather: "eversion") introduces an incongruity into the character (between the self before the act and the self after the act) that renders him ek-static. We will see in section 3 of this chapter ("Theatrical Lightheartedness") that this ecstasy of pathos importantly structures the *Phenomenology*'s mode of presentation. What emerges for our context here, in this section on the dramatic account of pathos, is that the tragic character, because he comes "outside of himself" in his passage to the act, is thus forced to "acknowledge" the relevance of alterity.

The suffering of the tragic hero is his physical experience of the other's reality. Since the tragic hero's insight into the other's relevance is born of suffering, his mode of understanding here is not one of mastery, but one of acknowledgment (*Anerkennung*): "Because we suffer we acknowledge [*anerkennen*] that we erred."[19] At first, the dramatic character considers all other positions as unjustified, unethical, unreasonable, and emotional without substance. "Since it sees right only on its own side and sees only wrong on the other, . . . consciousness . . . beholds in the other side [either] the violence of human caprice [*menschliche zufällige Gewalttätigkeit*] . . . [or] the obstinacy . . . of inward being-for-itself [*Eigensinn des innerlichen Fürsichseins*]" (§ 465, trans. modified). Whatever the other party says or does the passionate hero deems it as not driven by *Pathos*—since *Pathos* is inherently righteous—but as mere *Leidenschaft* or emotionality without substance. The other is seen as acting out of a temper (*menschliche zufällige Gewalttätigkeit*) or out of narcissistic oversensitivity (*Eigensinn des innerlichen Fürsichseins*), but not out of passion for a just cause. After his passage to the act, the dramatic character is forced not only to recognize the relevance, justification, and righteousness of the other's passion, but also to acknowledge the subjectivity and arbitrary bias of his own pathos: "The right of the ethical, namely, that actuality is nothing *in itself* in opposition to the absolute law, learns [*erfährt*] from experience that its knowledge is one-sided, that its law is only a law of its character, and that it has grasped merely the one power of substance" (§ 738). What he took to be universal law turns out to be more like a personal passion: his law is only the law of his own character. What is more, his conviction that the given "is in itself nothing" and that reality should be actively transformed according to the laws of ethics doesn't allow him to simply accept his character as a natural given. He has to acknowledge that he made a choice among a multiplicity of valid causes and that this choice was, in the final analysis, arbitrary.

In the section on the "Ethical Order," Hegel reduces the multiplicity of possible *páthe* (evidenced in the multiplicity of gods) to two: a female and a male. This reduction—which is an effect of the tragic collision—lends an air of necessity to these specific alignments of gender and pathos (woman's pathos: the family, man's pathos: the polis). In my view, Hegel's discussion of ethical tragedy offers a critique of naturalized gender and gendered pathos. He shows that the passionate character, who takes the genderedness of his pathos to be natural, is actually mistaken in treating his pathos as a given, rather than as a subjective construction that can be constructed otherwise.

Here we see that the distinction between merely subjective *Leidenschaftlichkeit* and substantial *Pathos* breaks down. The terminological difference does not index a difference in the phenomenon, but a difference in perspective. That is to say, the emotional phenomenon we call *Leiden-*

schaft is not inherently evil or irrational and the emotional phenomenon we call *Pathos* is not inherently good or rational, but the terms we use betray our attitudes toward emotion:

> These [universal powers], when they are in men, and are active in them, they are what the ancients called *pathos*. Our "passion" [*Leidenschaft*] isn't exactly the right term for this; "passion" carries the connotation of something that should be subjugated, something base. . . . Pathos is the power in general, insofar as it moves the human heart and soul, and it should be considered an aspect of the rational and free will. (Hegel 2005, 96, my translation)

Pathos is used to express the rational and righteous quality of passions, whereas *Leidenschaft* is used to reject passions as immoral and irrational.[20] Love, for example, can be regarded both as a danger to virtuous life and would then be called a *Leidenschaft*, or as a force that compels one to virtuous action, that is to say, a *Pathos*.

The hero's passage to the act reveals that righteous pathos and arbitrary temper or sensitivity always overlap. Whenever a person acts emotionally, one can safely assume—without risking life and limb in a tragic crisis—that there is some substance behind it. But we also have good reason to be skeptical about any show of pathos that inflates a personal issue into a "just cause." Pathos thus loses its nimbus of righteousness, while temper and sensitivity can be recognized as integral to pathos. That is to say, temper and sensitivity no longer need to be projected to the side of the other, but can be acknowledged—in the self and in the other—as displaying the overlap of agency and suffering that constitutes passion.

Tragic Recurrence

With this lesson learned, the world of drama and of tragic pathos has seen its day. Hegel pronounces the death of the gods, thus figuring the end of tragic pathos.[21] *Pathos* was defined over and against *Leidenschaft* (passion) as rational, ethical, universal, and firm. Now that it has become obvious that the dramatic character trembles between the pretense of resolute greatness and the reality of unpredictable suffering, tragic pathos is effectively dead. At least it has no future as a life form of spirit on its journey toward self-awareness, that is to say, as a subject of the *Phenomenology*.

And yet, as usually in the *Phenomenology*, the subject undergoing the experience does not learn the lesson. The same kind of tragedy will therefore repeat itself in different figurations. Spirit will continue to produce figures who are completely certain that truth is on their side, and who are utterly assured of their own righteousness. Let me first explain why the protagonist doesn't embrace the theatricality of pathos, before I briefly discuss how dramatic pathos repeatedly resurfaces in the *Phenomenology* and thus can be said to structure the phenomenological text. In the next section, we will then discuss the importance of theatrical or lighthearted pathos for the structure of the *Phenomenology*.

Tragedy teaches the spectator and the self-reflective agent that there are just and justified norms other than the one he subscribes to. Rather than a knowledge that is power, or a knowledge in the mode of mastery, tragedy produces a humble kind of knowing that is best described as acknowledging (*Anerkennen*).[22] The other person, whose actions seemed so irrational and unjustified, indeed acted according to his own pathos, that is, to a different, but equally justified, ethical commitment. This experience relativizes pathos. It retroactively introduces negativity—the question mark of self-reflection—into the full and completely positive identification of the passionate individual with his cause.

But—and this is an important qualification—it does so not for the hero. Pathos cannot properly be described as a trope of transport since, far from effecting a transformation, it quite literally comes to a dead end. The tragic hero suffers without learning from his mistakes. He disavows his trembling and the theatricality of pathos because he defines himself as absorbed by pathos and intransigent in his complete identification with it. Therefore his suffering takes the form of complete annihilation: the substance "is a pathos which is at the same time his character. Ethical individuality is immediately and in itself at one with its universal; it has existence only within it and is incapable of surviving the downfall [*Untergang*] that this ethical power suffers at the hands of its opposite" (§ 470). For the dramatic character, to acknowledge the other's reality is to have his own reality destroyed. If every fiber of my being is seized by a particular pathos, then there is no fiber left to recognize the other's pathos and to integrate the insight. This is the problem with the desire for authenticity. Tragic heroes do not cultivate the elastic self-negativity that, according to Hegel, constitutes subjectivity. Their fate is that "they do not discern themselves [in the negative power] but rather . . . sink and vanish" in it (§ 742).[23] What is more, the hero would rather kill himself than acknowledge that the temper or oversensitivity that he projected onto the other is actually also his own; he would rather kill himself than recognize the other within him and thereby acknowledge his constitutive *ekstasis.* The heroic passage to the act takes the self-alienating or ek-static structure of action to the suicidal extreme.[24]

With his suicide the tragic hero restores the order he disturbed. The reconciliation of the conflict between the two ethical authorities thus remains, as Pinkard points out, a quasi-natural one: Greek justice follows a homeostatic principle of fighting any disturbance by reestablishing the initial calm.[25] Pinkard thus agrees that the shape of spirit that naturalizes pathos learns no lesson—crises will naturally reoccur just as they will naturally be balanced out. Resolution takes place in the mode of forgetting rather than in the mode of acknowledging:

> The reconciliation of the opposition with itself is the *Lethe* of the *underworld* in death—or the *Lethe* of the upper world in the form of absolution [*Freisprechung*]. . . . Both are *forgetfulness,* the disappearance of actuality and of the activities on the part of the powers of substance, of their individualities and . . . of the abstract thought of good and evil. (§740, trans. modified)

With this vanishing act, Hegel's text transitions to a new shape of religious worldview, one that doesn't abstractly oppose good to evil. But the passionate character has learned no lesson. Out of the oblivion to his passage to the act will rise a new dramatic character and a new tragedy like Phoenix from the ashes.

Hegel conceives of the tragic conflict as a collision between individuals, not as a rift within one subject. The interpretation of emotion as natural, which characterizes the pathos model, doesn't allow for difference within; it only knows difference between (and it casts this difference as one between righteous *Pathos* and impulsive *Leidenschaft*). This means that despite all its advantages, namely its exteriority and its integration of emotionality and rationality, the pathos model—in its naturalizing or dramatizing version—lacks what Hegelian philosophy finds most important: the negativity of the subject. For Hegel, the foremost characteristic of the subject is its power to negate itself and to endure or survive this negation. We will see in the next section that the theatrical account of pathos integrates negativity, but here it is important to note that the dramatic subject doesn't know that power. The hero is so identified with his pathos that he either literally dies or—if he indeed manages to acknowledge the other's passion—becomes unheroic and thus irrelevant. Feeding on the individual's misguided notion of authenticity and on the world's tendency to forget inconsistencies, tragic drama will therefore reemerge in endless repetition.

This brings us to the question of how naturalized pathos structures the *Phenomenology of Spirit.* Hegel's dialectic is often read as an economy of drama: conflicts are brought to a head in order to provoke a solution; to the parties involved in the conflict, the "solution" inevitably comes in the form of death, perishing (*Zugrundegehen*), or utter oblivion; after that, it is a new day and a new shape of consciousness presents itself.[26] As we have seen, this economy of drama—steeped in the Hegelian understanding of tragic pathos—creates suffering without learning.

The *Phenomenology of Spirit* sets as its goal to generate spirit's self-awareness. Telling the story of a representative of spirit—so-called natural consciousness—and of its successive reincarnations, the book models the path to achieving this goal. I argue that the text superimposes three different literary modes: a narrative of *Bildung,* theatrical enactments of the various life forms of spirit, and the lyric poetry of the speculative proposition that syncopates the trembling rhythm of this text. In this chapter, I focus on theatrical enactment. Spirit is the subject, the object and the observer of the various acts and actions that the *Phenomenology of Spirit* presents; it is the author, the actor, and the spectator of its own drama. In its subject function, spirit is at times compared with God.[27] In its object function, it takes the stage as "natural consciousness." The observer role is played by us, the readers of the *Phenomenology,* in conjunction with Hegel, the author of the *Phenomenology.* Through us—who are struggling to comprehend the text—spirit gains an awareness of itself.[28] In all three instances, spirit suffers its agency and therefore—because it suffers—is supposed to acknowledge that it erred. Such an acknowledgment would be one step further on the path toward self-awareness. But to what extent does this acknowledgment really happen? To what extent are lessons learned and is *Bildung* accomplished?

Consciousness's *Bildung* consists in a series of painful experiences, in the repeated breaking of consciousness's certainty and existence. It can be more properly described as a *Brechung* than as a *Bildung,* as the breaking and the refraction, rather than as the formation, of an identity.[29] Each chapter and each dialectic shows the same pattern, namely, that consciousness's initial axiom is untenable. Consciousness is forced to acknowledge that it erred. It has a chance to gain this insight only by fully identifying with its epistemological core assumption and acting accordingly. Each figure of consciousness in the *Phenomenology* is a dramatic character who realizes its (epistemological) pathos. Its mode of learning and knowing would be that of experience and humble acknowledgment (of actively suffering each and every insight)—if only consciousness were able to learn. Instead, each figure of consciousness—like the tragic hero—"dies" from its self-contradictions. A new figure emerges—

another character in the drama of the *Phenomenology of Spirit*—who in turn will, after having exposed its pathos to the ironic negativity of reality, nevertheless cling to this pathos and thus become irrelevant. This scenario of experience without benefit is repeated with each chapter of the book.[30]

You might wonder: how does this fit with our image of Hegel? Well, it doesn't, because our image of Hegel is largely skewed by our desire for dramatic pathos. You will answer: it is the phenomenologist who learns from consciousness's experience; the author and the reader are able to integrate the insights that kill the protagonists. To a certain extent, that is true; yet Hegel warns emphatically of the danger of staying above the action, of avoiding the passage to the act in order to preserve intellectual superiority and control. I am happy to concede that most of Hegel's lectures evince the detrimental effects of dialectical mastery, of knowing in advance where the dialectical three-step will lead.[31] But in the *Phenomenology,* things are still fresh, and Hegel still struggles with confusion. Precisely because it acts out spirit's *Bildung,* the *Phenomenology* has an air of unpredictability to it. It takes place here and now while I read it; we don't know what is going to happen because the next step is contingent upon the current one. This event character of the *Phenomenology* depends on the reader's willingness to abandon herself to the action and suspend disbelief, as it were. We are called to identify with the protagonist and to let ourselves be absorbed by the action. As readers, we are asked to make "the effort to give up this freedom, and, instead of being the arbitrary principle moving the content, . . . to immerse this freedom into the content [*diese Freiheit in ihn zu versenken*]" (§ 58, trans. modified). Hegel's textual practice is designed to draw the reader in.[32] In order to avoid mere *Erbaulichkeit* (edification, playing it safe), the *Phenomenology* bets on identification and absorption. It thereby risks that the reader will get lost in the pathos of the protagonist. Indeed, its readers often consider the position of a particular figure of consciousness to be the author's position; this means that Hegel's strategy "worked," that these readers have actually submerged their freedom in the content to the point that they are unable to tell play from philosophy. They have identified with the epistemological pathos of one figure of consciousness—only to "die" with it at the end of the chapter or to save themselves by repudiating it as "false" and to throw in their lot with another figure.[33] Encouraged by Hegel's textual practice, these are mistaken readings: passages to the readerly act, if you will, without guarantee that the reader will learn from the experience.

Hegel even forces God—or spirit as the self-revealing agent of the phenomenological process—into passionate earnestness:[34] "The life of

God and divine cognition might thus be articulated as a game love plays with itself, this Idea will be downgraded into edification [*Erbaulichkeit*], even into triteness, if it lacks the seriousness, the suffering, the patience, and the labor of the negative (§ 19). For Hegel, it doesn't make sense to conceive of spirit as a transcendent being that is all-powerful. Instead, he locates spirit in the political institutions, the laws, the arts, the philosophical systems, the religious and cultural practices, and the minds (to the extent that they are socially constructed) of the people of this world. In such this-worldly form spirit suffers from alienation. Yet Hegel insists that self-awareness, or being-in-and-for-itself—cannot be gained without being serious about self-abandonment:

> *In itself* that life is indeed an unalloyed parity and unity with itself, since in such a life there is nothing serious in otherness and alienation nor in overcoming this alienation. However, this *in-itself* is abstract universality, in which . . . its nature, which is *to be for itself* . . . [is] left out of view. (§ 19)

Hegel rejects the idea of a transcendent spirit that rests assured of itself and engages in reality only for play, secure in the knowledge of a positive outcome. He thus addresses the fear of "divine comedy" that Žižek reformulates in "The Act and Its Vicissitudes":

> When [Christ] was dying on the cross, did he know about his Resurrection-to-come? If yes, it was all a game, the supreme divine comedy, since Christ knew his suffering was just a spectacle with a guaranteed good outcome—in short, Christ was FAKING despair in his "Father, why did you forsake me?" (Žižek 2005)

In response to this anxiety, Hegel insists on earnest pathos and fulminates against irony.[35] Yet, if we buy into his repudiation of irony, the question arises: how is spirit able to attain self-awareness if it identifies completely with its pathos of self-revelation and is dead serious about abandoning itself to the alienating forces of the real? According to Hegel's analysis of dramatic pathos, it simply wouldn't be able to gain self-knowledge: the passion of spirit will impede rather than enable it to learn from experience.

I hope to have shown that while it is very possible—even quite attractive—to read the *Phenomenology of Spirit* as organized by an economy of drama, such a reading, by itself, prevents the *Phenomenology* from reaching its goal. It makes the protagonist/s, the reader/s, and the author/s suffer without offering an epistemic gain in return. We will now turn to an alternative reading, which—Hegel's rage against irony notwithstanding—attends to the text's ironic distance from its content, and to the theatricality of its composition.

Theatrical Lightheartedness

While pathos as a thematic life form of spirit becomes irrelevant and the passionate character dies, the mode of knowledge produced by the pathos model of emotionality will remain central for Hegel's philosophy. With his translation of Antigone's line, *weil wir leiden, anerkennen wir, daß wir gefehlt* (because we suffer we acknowledge that we erred), Hegel offers an epiphonema, a summarizing pithy sentence, for the epistemological pathos of experience that structures the *Phenomenology of Spirit.* Experience is, then, a second-degree pathos (a pathos that governs the syntax of the *Phenomenology* rather than determining a particular figure in the *Phenomenology*). Like first-degree pathos, one can understand experience in two different ways—dramatically or theatrically. A naturalizing version of the pathos of experience produces an eternal recurrence of drama, a continuous revival of emotionally intense, passionate figures, and a *Handlung* or story line of suffering without learning. Since a series of experiences without accumulating experience does not conform to the prevalent image of Hegel, this scheme is usually complemented by the logic of *Aufhebung* in such a way that this repetition of experience can be read as progress. I take issue with both components of traditional Hegel interpretations—the dramatic notion of experience and the idea that *Aufhebung* purchases progress—and will argue instead that the logic of *Aufhebung* works to dislocate emotionality from itself and to produce not drama, but lightheartedness.

We will now explore what exactly the theatrical account of pathos entails. I will argue that registering the theatricality of pathos doesn't curtail but rather enables the existential feel of pathos. Only he who "watches himself act" (*sich selbst spielen sieht*) can feel genuine passion *and* understand or negate pathos without himself being annihilated by this procedure (§ 747, trans. modified). By contrast, we have seen that naturalized pathos lacks the negativity that Hegel describes as constitutive of subjectivity—the ability to survive its own self-negation. Read in the spirit of the self-reflective version of the pathos of experience, the *Phenomenology* offers an education in acknowledging theatricality and in developing the lighthearted humility necessary for the mode of knowledge that is "acknowledging." Many have claimed that Hegel's exploration of tragedy inspires his philosophy in a fundamental way. They see in the tragic conflict and its resolution a model for Hegelian dialectics.[36] In the remainder of this chapter, I will argue that Hegel's analysis of the theatricality of tragic pathos even more importantly than his theory of tragic conflict informs his composition of the *Phenomenology* and his philosophy in general.

The production of dramatic conflicts, the constant need to bring differences to a head and to sharpen them into a collision, already reveals the theatricality inherent in the dramatic model of dialectics. Drama needs to be produced; thus, it is to a certain extent staged. The second part of Hegel's section on "The Ethical Order" is titled "Die sittliche Handlung" ("The Ethical Act"). The choice of the word *Handlung* is striking in that it means "deed" but also "plot" and thus explicitly refers the deed to the realm of fiction.[37] From the very beginning, starting with the title, and throughout his analysis of the ethical order, Hegel plays the double register of ethics and theatrics.

Hegel's language shifts back and forth between real life and theater to make a fundamental argument about the theatricality of life. For example, with a subtle reference to acting—"self-consciousness has not yet come on the scene [*ist noch nicht aufgetreten*] . . . *as yet, no deed* has been committed"—he suggests that the individual has to produce his pathos theatrically—that is, as a deed that is performed in front of spectators—in order to be able to reach an awareness not only of what he has done, but of what his pathos (his motivation and intention) really was (§ 463, trans. modified). The agent has no epistemic access to his pathos as a "given," and self-consciousness can only be attained after the fact, that is to say, after having appeared on stage.

Discussing Hegel's engagements of tragic, comic, and confessional literature in the *Phenomenology*, Speight has offered a strong and convincing argument for the retrospectivity and theatricality of agency. Taking Hegel's reading of *Antigone* as exemplary for an account of agency in general, he observes that "the desire or intention [the proper term for the tragic context would be "pathos"] relevant for [Antigone's] understanding [of] her deed is not to be found in prior deliberation, but is rather *embodied* in the deed itself and read off of it retrospectively" (Speight 2001, 59,). Since such a self-understanding must be refracted through the eyes of the spectators, it drives home the "socially mediated or 'theatrical' character" of pathos (Speight 2001, 70). Speight's formulation "read off" bespeaks his sense that the deed doubles as a plot or *Handlung* that demands to be read like a text. After what has emerged in the first section of this chapter, we need to add to Speight's account of retrospectivity that Hegel proposes not only that we come to recognize the specifics of our motivating pathos after the fact, but that we must in the same breath acknowledge the ruin of *Pathos* proper in its overlap with *Leidenschaft*. The hypocrisy (of inflating a personal cause into a universal one) that the tragic hero had projected onto the other, whom he therefore accused of mere show and scene-making, in fact characterizes the tragic hero himself. Hegel contends that passionate individuals are driven to show their character and to act out their beliefs. He demonstrates that their deeds alienate them from their pathos when their activity turns into suffering. Because of its inherent link to agency and because of the overlap of ethical pathos and narcissistic passion (temper and oversensitivity), even this suffering has something of an act to it. In the final analysis, Hegel thus argues that pathos compels the person to make a scene.

Uneasy with theatricality's potential for pretense and hypocrisy, while nevertheless embracing the social mediation that theatricality affords, Speight draws on one of Pinkard's stipulations for free agency—that one needs to identify with one's action as one's own—to argue that theatricality is sublated in the forgiveness plot at the end of the spirit chapter.[38] Whether or not this argument is convincing, I see no need to sublate the threatening dimension of theatricality, especially because the theater is itself the paradigmatic scene of *Aufhebung*. On stage, action is make-belief and genuine reality at the same time: reality is sublated in make-belief and illusion is sublated in the physical reality of the actors' bodies. Let us therefore further examine the theatricality of pathos that Hegel presents.

As passionately as the heroic individuals identify with their pathos, their cause also exceeds them (it is universal—they are individual, it is divine—they are mortal). It exists before and beyond them: the dramatic characters enact a script—be it written or unwritten.[39] The hero plays a role in the double sense of the phrase. On the one hand, he draws courage from the half-avowed fact that he can rely on a safety net of customs and rules while acting out his role within a canonical plot: "self-consciousness's action rests on a secure trust [*Vertrauen*] in the whole" (§ 467).[40] On the other hand, the tragic hero differs from the epic one in that he "steps forth" to deliver his lines himself. He is "the artist himself" and exposes himself in front of an audience. This standing out and standing apart of the tragic hero is another sense of the ek-stasy of pathos that has emerged earlier. It is time now to examine more closely the trembling between inside and outside, between the literal or existential and the figural or theatrical that I have briefly touched on earlier. Doing so, we will get a better sense of the lighthearted version of pathos.

When the passionate character steps forth and feels himself stand out, he—if perhaps only imperceptibly—begins to tremble. He fears that which drives him: he fears his pathos. The sense that he, as an individual, exposes himself to bear the consequences of acting out his pathos while his god remains whole and his cause remains holy (at least in his eyes) positions him as slightly apart from his pathos: "That of which human beings can truly be afraid is an ethical power, the power of their own bosom. This power is eternal and unalterable . . . ; it stands above the individual, and in comparison with it the individual vanishes" (Hegel 2005, 250, my translation). This slight but fearful distance from one's own pathos might turn into self-pity or into respect—not only for one's pathos, but for oneself as driven by this pathos. In any case, the self-difference that trembling opens calls forth an affective embrace of or a sym-pathy for one's ek-stasy: "Compassion or sympathy can have two objects: sympathy with distress, . . . with the negative. . . . The other one is sympathy with the affirmative force in the subject. This affirmative is the brave, ethical, and truthful in individuals; this kind of sympathy also needs to exist, the fear of this ethical power" (ibid., my translation). Apart from lifting Aristotle's very physical *páthe phobos* and *eleos* on the high horse of the moral sublime, Hegel suggests here that there exists a difference within the dramatic character—even an, if ever so slight, dislocation within the structure of pathos itself.[41] As if watching himself act, man pities himself and fears himself as a passionate character. Such sympathy or awe for the self implies the doubling of the emotional subject into one who is overcome by pathos and immersed in the action on the one hand, and one who has reservations about his pathos or embraces and reinforces it on the other. This duplicity introduces an air of pretense into the structure of pathos. When we foreground the theatricality of pathos, we find that the resoluteness and intransigence that defines dramatic pathos becomes unsettled by the interference of such second-degree emotions as self-pity and self-respect. This interference creates emotional plasticity.

Pathos is both reinforced and ruined by the conflicting second-degree emotions layered on top, as it were. If we apply this insight into the theatricality of pathos to the textual pathos that structures the *Phenomenology of Spirit*, we can see that the ecstasy I have earlier defined as the ontological condition of "being beside oneself" is better described as a hovering above oneself. It turns out, then, that the logic of *Aufhebung* has a spatial more than a temporal bent. The subject of the *Phenomenology* is moved and negated by passion, and at the same time it hovers above the scene of its negation. This kind of *Aufhebung* creates the undramatic and lighthearted pathos of the text. The subject perishes in its passionate passage to the act and, at the same time, it persists and integrates the lesson of the experience, which, in turn, relativizes the passion. To think *Aufhebung* spatially means to consider negation and preservation as simultaneous movements, and to not distribute them onto different figures who relieve one another in time (in the sense that one figure of consciousness disappears in order for the next more integrative figure to emerge).[42]

As I mentioned earlier, the subject of the *Phenomenology* is divided within: spirit is the author, the actor, and the spectator of its own drama. The text contains numerous moments of parabasis, where the spectator is explicitly involved in the scene. The endings and beginnings of chapters are preferred times for parabasis.[43] Here, the phenomenologist comes to the fore and uses the first-person plural to communicate something the protagonist does not understand. The spatial movement of parabasis differentiates between an actor in character who participates in the action and an actor who steps out of character to reflect on the situation. At the same time, the phenomenological "we" is also the "we" of spirit (of "the *I* that is *we* and the *we* that is *I*" [§ 177]). The first-person plural thus mediates between the divisions within spirit: a protagonist becomes phenomenologist and rises above the scene (or steps onto the proscenium) in order not only to communicate directly with the spectators (who share in the phenomenological "we") but also to indeed become one of the spectators and reflect on the action. Such parabasis can be described as a self-reflection of spirit that is more immediate than the self-reflection via the actions of the protagonist only in the sense that the experience of the protagonist is precisely the material and the result of its self-reflection: protagonist and phenomenologist are only different versions of the same subject. The divisions are far from clean-cut.

The functioning of the *Phenomenology* depends on cross-identifications among its subjects, its objects, and its observers. The different aspects or moments (*Momente*) of spirit are both different from and identical with one another.[44] Each refers to the others in an elastic web of differentiation yet cohesion. Spirit, who is this web, can die and survive at the same time, as can each one of its figurations or shapes of consciousness. Every protagonist and every phenomenologist has the ability to self-negate, that is to say, to die and survive at the same time. This is the negativity that so famously defines the subject in Hegel. This negativity is, in my view, fundamentally emotional because it is the ability to acknowledge and negotiate inner difference. Such emotionality is plastic and theatrical rather than linear and dramatic, because there is always a remainder of the subject in action that hovers above the scene and reflects it. At the same time, the subject is existentially enwrapped in the passionate act. Malabou's term of "plasticity" helps to bring out the very real exposure and physical commitment that is part of theatrical embodiment, when she points out that "while certainly in opposition to 'rigid,' 'fixed' and 'ossified,' [the adjective 'plastic'] is not to be confused with 'polymorphous.' Things that are plastic preserve their shape" (Malabou 2004, 8f)—that is to say, they take shape and commit to a shape rather than hovering eternally aloof in a noncommittal version of irony. The genuineness of the *Phenomenology*'s theatrically emotional subject consists in the humility of abandoning itself to the alienating force of the real, rather than in the arrogance of dramatic pathos.

The lightheartedness of theatrical pathos permeates the *Phenomenology*. At each instant, the text combines the gravitas of pathos with the levity of irony. If the thematic discussions of pathos—in the section on the ethical order, and in the section on religion as a work of art—both end with tragedy turning into comedy, the book as a whole is suspended at the tipping point of tragedy into comedy or—since the suspension ruins linearity—of comedy into tragedy. Therefore, if I make a case here for the lightheartedness and theatricality of the *Phenomenology*'s pathos, I do not want to simply exchange pathos for irony, or tragedy for comedy. The *Phenomenology*'s emotional syntax is characterized by the oscillation between the two; I will describe it as a syntax of trembling back and forth, and as a syntax of bouncing up and down.[45]

We could say that the *Phenomenology*'s lightheartedness imitates the bouncy joyousness and serenity (*Heiterkeit*) of the Greek gods that Hegel—according to Hotho's notes—described in his lecture on the philosophy of art: "The gods must remain eternally serene. . . . To pursue a particular aim with rigor and single-mindedness and to perish going to the bottom of it [*darin zugrundegehen*], this cannot happen to the gods" (Hegel 1998, 98, my translation). Even though the Greeks knew many gods and each one had therefore a finite character, their life was indeed infinite and divine suffering thus never took the form of natural death. As immortals, the gods do not take the pathos they personify all too seriously—they do rage or love in earnest, but they also rise above the action for a break: "They interfere here and there, but just as well they abandon their business and amble up [*wandeln empor*] to the Olympus" (ibid.). I read this *Emporwandeln* as a form of *Aufhebung*. Breaking with and taking a break from natural existence is the Greek gods' mode of negativity or of self-reflection. Hegel indeed describes it as a form of irony, as "the irony that is spread over the Homeric gods" (ibid.). The Greek gods are swathed in an irony less abstract than the one Hegel in other contexts harshly critiques. Hegel usually attacks irony for its arrogance and lack of commitment, its tendency to dissolve into wit everything but the superiority of the self. Such self-aggrandizing is not part of divine irony. The Greek gods tremble. They personify the trembling of pathos when they move back and forth between negating their Olympic existence to participate in finite life and withdrawing from human reality to the Olympus. They even die (as we have seen at the beginning of the last section). As tragic pathos, the Greek gods die, but, we will see now, they return in comic levity. Their irony covers both ethereal and earthly existence.

While the gods of the Homeric epics assume an ironic distance from their actions, the noble humans of the tragedies are left to suffer and perish. The tragic hero sticks to his dramatic pathos; he remains faithful to his god even when the god has abandoned him to take a break. Since the gods are figures for *páthe,* Hegel's comment about the gods taking off in mid-fight, as it were, suggests that pathos is less unambivalently substantial than originally defined. As Aristophanes' comedy suggests to Hegel, the gods "are clouds, a disappearing vapor" (§ 746). Divine passions control the atmosphere but, in this capacity, they are anything but firm. To us who are concerned with a theory of emotionality, Hegel here offers a most interesting account of emotion as not without self-negating irony. Tragedy ensues from the hero's not understanding this reflexivity and lightheartedness of emotion and instead essentializing or naturalizing pathos, that is, considering his pathos an unchangeable given. The tragic hero is stubbornly attached to his pathos even when the feeling has dissipated and the god who moved him has dissolved into thin air. With the substance of passion gone, the firmness of character becomes a selfish vanity because it is stripped of content.

The tipping point, when virtuous pathos inevitably turns into self-serving pretense, is relentlessly exposed, mimicked, and mocked by the "eternal," that is to say, the uncontainable and immortal or divine "irony" of the feminine (§ 474). Under the direction of "the feminine" (I propose to include women, comedians, and Hegelian phenomenologists in this category), the (male) youth gives performances in which "the posturing of the universal essentiality is betrayed" (§ 744).[46] On the stage staffed by womankind and youth, the gods appear naked ("those essentialities still have . . . merely the nakedness [*Nacktheit*] of their immediate existence," § 746) and the privileged members of the polis make fools of themselves:

> That *demos,* the universal social sphere, which knows itself to be master and regent as well as being the understanding and insight which are to be respected . . . exhibits the laughable contrast between its own opinion of itself and its immediate existence, between its necessity and contingency, its universality and its ordinariness [*Gemeinheit*]. (§ 745, trans. modified)

By embracing the lightheartedness of emotion, "the feminine" threatens the ethical order with "the consciousness of the dialectic which these [pathetic] maxims and laws have in themselves and . . . thereby [with] the consciousness of the disappearance of the absolute validity in which they had previously appeared" (§ 746). What the dramatic character tried to repress, the secret that he labored to keep (from himself)—to the point that he would rather die than watch his claim to unconditional validity dissolve—is revealed.

The theater of womankind and youth features self-ironic subjects who come to know and divulge their secrets. The self-ironic subjects act and watch themselves act passionately. They experience and learn from their experiences (i.e., negate their experience); they can do both because they are agent, actor, and spectator at the same time, in an elastic identity of differences:[47]

> The self, which comes on the scene here in its significance of being actual, plays with the mask which it once puts on in order to be its "persona."—However, it just as quickly makes itself come out from this illusion and once again come forward in its own nakedness and ordinariness, which it shows not to be distinct from the literal self [*eigentlichen Selbst*], from the actor, nor from the spectator. (§ 744, trans. modified)

In parabases and asides to itself, the self-ironically passionate subject reveals its secret lightheartedness by slipping in unsettling ways between "significance" and "ordinariness." It shifts from putting on the mask of the protagonist to putting on the mask of the actor to putting on the mask of the spectator. Meanwhile all of the identities are acting as genuine or "literal" selves. And so tragedy turns into comedy:

> The pure thoughts of the beautiful and the good thus give a comic spectacle: emancipated from opinion [*Meinung*]—which provides their determinateness as content and also provides their absolute determinateness in that consciousness resolutely clings to this content [i.e., the intransigence of pathos]—they become empty, and precisely as a result, turn into a game played by the opinion and the caprice of contingent individuality. (§ 476, trans. modified)

The negation of opinion (*Meinung*), which always carries the overtone of the first-person possessive pronoun *mein* in Hegel, allows the subjective to bounce back and play with the objective. This circularity of self-negativity gives grief to some; others take pleasure in it. The ethical order used to provide security: the dramatic character could trust in the righteousness of his cause. But his own action has broken the promise; it has refracted the ethical order in the ironic lightheartedness of self-negating emotion, and has thrown the crestfallen hero, who used to occupy the center of the ethical world, into an uneasy eccentricity: "Since its trust is therefore broken, and since the substance of the people is therefore shattered [*in sich geknickt*], spirit, which was the mediating term . . . henceforth now stands out as the extreme [*in das Extrem herausgetreten*]" (§ 701). This is the ecstasy of "spirit . . . which mourns over the loss of its world" (ibid.). Others enjoy the fact that the naturalized order is not set in stone: "Actual self-consciousness, . . . in employing what is natural for its adornment [*Putz*] . . . , shows itself to be the fate to which the secret is betrayed, namely the truth about the self-essentiality of nature" (§ 745, trans. modified). The secret is betrayed. The gods the heroes worshipped, the passions they considered natural are now taken as whimsical properties of the subject, rather than authorities that require subjection. "The subject is . . . elevated above that sort of [abstract] moment as it would be elevated above an individual property [the God as universal moment or the pathos as abstract substance], and, wearing this mask, the subject articulates [*spricht aus*] the irony of something that wants to be something on his own" (§ 744). With a light heart, womankind turns the gravity of moral pathos into frivolous ornaments and adornments (*Putz* and *Schmuck*): "The feminine—the polity's eternal irony—changes the . . . universal purpose into a private purpose, transforms . . . universal activity into this determinate individual's work, and . . . inverts . . . universal property into the family's possession and ornament [*Putz*]" (§ 474).

This passage from the Spirit chapter has often been read as decrying womankind's resentment and petty egotism: because they are weak, women have to erode all greatness.[48] Apart from the fact that Hegel attributes a similarly strong resentment to older men (they engage in fraud and deception because they are "preoccupied [with] and anxiety-ridden [by] . . . the individual details of life"), it is fundamentally unclear that this should be the straight sense of the uncontainable irony at work here (§ 746).[49] I therefore want to propose a different sense: the eternal irony, when it "transforms" and "inverts" pathos, actually compels pathos to "come forward in its own nakedness" (§ 474; 744). While dramatic pathos, in its naturalizing thrust, interpellates mortals into bearing the fate of the reversal of their acts, this irony turns the tables of fate on pathos. It reveals that pathos, which cloaks itself in the mantle of *ethos* (of a substantial cause with a claim to universality), has always also an aspect of private passion or *Leidenschaft,* of self-serving individuality to it. This irony means that pathos "lets the mask [of gravity] drop" and that subjectivity floats with comic levity (§ 744):

> The consummation of ethical life in free self-consciousness and the fate of the ethical world is therefore . . . the absolute lightheartedness [*Leichtsinn*] of ethical spirit which has dissolved within itself all the fixed distinctions of its stable existence and the social spheres of its organic structure, and, being perfectly sure of itself, has achieved a boundless joyfulness [*schrankenlose Freudigkeit*] and the freest enjoyment of itself [*Genusse seiner selbst*]. (§ 701, trans. modified)

This apparent victory of subjectivity has nothing in common with the idea of the supremacy of any one human subject, or of a group of human subjects (let's say women) or even of the human subject, in general. What has emerged here is what I referred to in the introduction as the non-human subjectivity or impersonal subject status of emotionality. Pathos has become reflexive; it behaves like a self-relating, self-dividing, and self-negating entity and in that sense it acts as a subject. The tragicomedy of pathos might involve human beings, but, if so, then always in the plural, that is to say, always as inwardly divided and ontologically dependent on others. Human subjects or characters might come on the scene, play a part, show up for an act, but they are neither a sufficient nor even a necessary requirement for emotionality.

Subjects to Syntax

Impersonal emotion, emotion as self-reflective subject indifferent to the human subject, is to be found on the level of textual performance. With the second part of this book, we will move away from an analysis of the different models of emotionality that Hegel discusses (heartfelt feeling, dramatic pathos), which tie emotion to the human subject, and embark on the analysis of Hegel's emotional textuality. It has emerged from our discussion of the theatricality of pathos that passionate individuals are indeed texts—self-differential entities—who as such, and only as such, can tremble and be emotional. In the next part of the book, we will move beyond the compulsion to attribute emotions to humans and instead explore the emotionality of texts. We will be concerned with the syntax of Hegel's philosophical moves and with the emotional tropes that shape this syntax. I will describe these tropes as "transports" because they divide and connect the different moments and figures of Hegel's text, transporting spirit from one to the other by way of an emotional mode of registering and negotiating incongruity.

The composition of the *Phenomenology of Spirit* reflects Hegel's critical analysis of dramatic pathos and it remedies the shortcomings of the dramatic model, namely its lack of ambivalence, irony, and reflexivity. The theory of tragedy has often been thought of as constituting the core of Hegel's philosophy, because the tragic conflict and its resolution are seen as a model for Hegelian dialectics. I contend that his philosophy in general, and his composition of the *Phenomenology* in particular, are more deeply informed by his analysis of the theatricality of tragic pathos than by the drama of the tragic conflict. The theatrics of the *Phenomenology* builds ambivalence, irony, and self-reflection into the subject structure of emotionality. It does so by elastically dividing the subject of the *Phenomenology* (spirit) into a circle of protagonists and a virtual assemblage of phenomenologists, all of whom are singular and plural at the same time. Their connection is maintained and forged by the fact that they all serve as (emotionally and intellectually involved) spectators of one another: they all read one another, identify with one another, and, in doing so, figure one another.

At the end of this chapter I compared the structural pathos of the *Phenomenology* to the Greek gods moving up and down between the ether and the earth. Against the common reading of the Hegelian narrative as progressively elevating (*Aufhebung*) consciousness from one shape to the next and thus perfecting its education (*Bildung*), the text turns out to repeatedly negate (*aufheben*) the ethereal moment of spirit, bringing it back down to earth, and recurrently form (*bilden*), embody, and actualize spirit. Dramatic pathos—as we have discussed in the second section of this chapter—thwarts the teleology of education because its naturalizing mode of negation doesn't allow for learning. But theatrical pathos—with its spatialized and virtualizing mode of *Aufhebung*—doesn't do any better in serving such a presumed teleology. In this case, the development does not advance because linear time has been ruined, and because the trembling between ether and earth takes place within each formation of consciousness/spirit. Such movement in stasis or trembling within bends the series of shapes (*Gestalten*) of consciousness, which we usually imagine as organized into a progressive line, not back into the circle of internal teleology, but into the circle of the Greek gods, that is to say, a relatively loose group of figures. Each shape has its own epistemological pathos and plays the part of a particular god. In the moments of transition, though—from one pathos to another, one shape of consciousness to another, one truth paradigm to another—the relativity of pathos becomes particularly palpable. Here, in this in-between space, pathos is seen to be as much private and fickle passion (*Leidenschaft*) as it is *ethos* or absolute firmness of character. Nietzsche has pointed out that this ambivalence of pathos can come into view only after the fact:

> While we are living each phase of our lives we rarely recognize its true pathos, but always see it as the only state that is now possible for us and reasonable and—to use some words and a distinction of the Greeks—thoroughly an *ethos* and not a *pathos*. (Nietzsche 2001, § 317)

With his theatrical composition of the *Phenomenology* and its elastically self-differentiated subject, Hegel anticipates the Nietzschean deflation of exalted values through genealogy. Above all, he contests the value of sober and unchanging, objective, and timeless truth.

Like Nietzsche, Hegel needs both: irony *and* sincerity, tragedy and comedy. While the experience of relativity generates lightheartedness, it also (re-)creates the danger that the subject may collapse into the complete unity of self-identity, that one may be absolutely at home in appearance, and that Spirit may lose its restlessness and find repose in well-being.[50] Again, it is the structure of the text that safeguards against this collapse. The different personae of the *Phenomenology*'s plural subject trouble and undo, transport and shape one another. They serve as supplements and remainders of one another, so that no one shape, character, or moment is ever fully one with itself or ever completely eliminated.

Most interpretations of the *Phenomenology* see only one side of the supplemental relation between "natural consciousness" and "phenomenologist." When one of the heroes of the *Phenomenology* perishes, received wisdom has it that Hegel meant for the trembling afterimage of its pathos to ascend to the memory of the phenomenologist. I find it rather impossible to decide who resides on the Olympus in this text: the phenomenologist or the protagonist. Who suffers his pathos dramatically and who has the serenity and lightheartedness not to get too attached? Does the cunningly ironic world spirit ascend to the heavens dropping shape after shape of consciousness into the pit of memory?[51] Or does the protagonist blissfully amble from incarnation to incarnation only to leave the phenomenologist ruminating on each and every crisis? Any reading of the *Phenomenology of Spirit* that wants to get a sense for the particular emotionality of this text needs to retain this fundamental ambivalence. The self-dividing and self-relating negativity of the *Phenomenology*'s textuality creates both earnest pathos and lightheartedness.

Our analysis of the theatricality of Hegel's composition has brought into view the transport model of emotion that we will explore in further detail in the second part of this book. A transport can be strong or slight, but it lifts one out of oneself. Because transports move one beyond oneself and render one ek-static in a rather matter-of-fact way, they cannot be located inside the self as parts of an inner life. Transports thus differ from heartfelt feelings. They unsettle the distinction between inside and outside as much as that between within and between. Transports generate a subject that is transient and multiply divided. In contrast to dramatic pathos, the transport model shows that ambivalence, reflexivity, and irony are constitutive of emotion itself. Following Hutcheon, who wants us to see the affective dimension of irony, I am foregrounding the ironic dimension of emotionality.[52] In keeping with her argument against an irony that cynically evades all affective engagement, I don't want irony to be confused with evasiveness and lack of commitment. Instead, I insist on taking seriously irony's ambivalence, that is, the fact that despite all her self-negations the ironist does take a stance. And if she manages a "generous irony," this stance will transport her across the region where sympathy and distance overlap.[53]

Transports produce instances of acknowledging (*Anerkennen*) as their particular kind of rationality. Acknowledgments are movements toward knowledge or cognition that involve a certain amount of passivity or suffering, and that are constitutively incipient or underway, never definitive or complete. Highlighting the overlap of rationality and emotionality, the transport model brings into view a syntax of emotion over and against the prevalent focus on pre-linguistic affect.

Part 2

Emotional Syntax

3

Release

> This release of itself from the form of its own self is the highest freedom.
>
> —*Phenomenology*, § 806

I will begin with the end. This first chapter on emotional syntax analyzes how Hegel's *Phenomenology* ends, in order to clear the way for a new beginning in the reading of this Hegelian text. Against the expectation raised by the title of the last chapter of the *Phenomenology* and by the common view that this text is a teleological narrative, the *Phenomenology* ends not in the presence and plenitude of absolute knowledge, but in release. With his final chapter, Hegel abandons any imperialist project of knowledge that he or his readers might have pursued over the course of the text.

Rather than provide a positive result, which one might be able to identify as "absolute knowledge," the final chapter of the *Phenomenology of Spirit* keeps circling. Rather than close the circle of spirit's self-exploration once and for all, it finds more and more ways to indicate openings. On the fifteen or so pages of the chapter entitled "Absolute Knowledge," the words *entäußern* or *Entäußerung* (self-emptying) appear twenty-eight times. This is the highest concentration of the word in any chapter of the *Phenomenology*. As if this wasn't enough, the signifiers of release proliferate—among them, one finds *Entlassen* (release § 806), *Ablassen* (giving-up, § 796), *Verzichttun* (relinquishing, § 796), *aufopfern/Aufopferung* (sacrifice, § 807), *offenbaren/Offenbarung/Offenbarkeit* (note the double signifier of exposure: *offen* [open] and *baren* [to bare]), *sich hinausstellen* (put itself forth, § 792, trans. modified), *herauskehren* (put on view, § 803), and *aussprechen* ("articulate," nine times). The chapter on "absolute knowledge" not only thematizes release, but the very end of this last chapter also performs release. The last sentence of the *Phenomenology of Spirit* is perhaps not exactly grammatically incorrect, but it is certainly grammatically incoherent and thus performs non-closure.

In addition, the text resists coherence by breaking off with a dash, from which two lines of poetry dangle.

In the course of a close analysis of the ending of the *Phenomenology of Spirit,* I will introduce in this chapter the juggle of poetry and philosophy, which I will further pursue in the next chapter. This opening to another (here, the opening of philosophical syntax to the syntax of poetry) allows me to address the question of whether one needs others in order to become emotional. Attending to the example of grief, this chapter examines to what extent and how mediation is constitutive of emotionality in general.

I will also contend in this chapter that it is an act of friendship when Hegel alters the verses he cites. This claim anticipates the argument, more thoroughly developed in chapter 5, that "mutual acknowledging" is an interaction among self-reflexive parties, in which no one remains intact. But my claim about the nature of friendship also reveals the double bind of my own practice of reading: I derive my method of transformative reading—in good hermeneutic fashion—from the text's own economy, so that (paradoxically) I remain true to the Hegelian text by transforming it. As a result, no matter how much I alter the text, my reading will still be Hegelian—but hopefully I will have been a good friend and will have introduced a shift in the meaning of "Hegelian."

For the line of inquiry about mediation as a constitutive element of emotionality, I will rely on Terada's philosophy of emotion in *Feeling in Theory* and on the work of Hélène Cixous, who, particularly in her book *Déluge,* her play *L'histoire qu'on ne connaîtra jamais,* and in several of the essays assembled in English under the title *Stigmata,* explores the affinity between sorrow and theatricality. Terada argues that "people can feel emotions only through intermediate representations" (Terada 2001, 18).[1] Cixous holds that humans need theater (in the most extended sense) to be able to cry. For what seem to me clearly strategic reasons, Cixous maintains that "the universe of emotion" is human and not gendered.[2] The desire for melodrama—the desire to cry in the theater, at the movies, or while reading a book—is nothing specifically feminine, she would say. Yet the theatrical, fictional, or figurative structure of emotionality—which allows, even necessitates one to have emotions by proxy or as a proxy—makes possible a division of labor in emotional affairs. This division is still mostly organized along gender lines. Women still do emotional work for others while this work goes unrecognized and is disapproved of. For strategic reasons that are different from Cixous', then, I point out that, with their tears, women clean the house of the self and wash men's dirty underwear. Against this backdrop, a challenge arises that I am unable to ignore: can I make Hegel cry?

Hegel's *Phenomenology of Spirit* doesn't appear to shed a tear. The individual figures of consciousness are of interest only as long as their self-contradictions aren't exhausted. Once understood, they are discarded and the text invests in a new figure of consciousness. Each shape of consciousness dies a death without pain, without grief, without burial, a death that doesn't haunt. As Butler has it: "There is little time for grief in the *Phenomenology* because renewal is always so close at hand" (Butler 1999, 21). Only when the text is about to end is it able to gesture toward the skeletons in its closet. At its limit, the *Phenomenology* acknowledges its finitude, conjures up a friend, and dissolves in tears.

Hegel's Tears

The title of the *Phenomenology*'s last chapter seems to suggest the final supersession of all non-knowledge (ignorance, error, opinion, madness, etc.) in "absolute knowledge." The final word of the chapter, *seine Unendlichkeit* (its infinity), would then present the grandiose culminating point of a narrative of progressive self-awareness. Yet, upon close examination, this apparent closure of the *Phenomenology of Spirit* looks more like a release and an abortion of the project of self-knowledge. Lacoue-Labarthe had the inkling that "the closure [of the speculative system] can scarcely contain the pressure under which it has perhaps already succumbed without anyone's becoming aware of it" (Lacoue-Labarthe 1989, 224). Perhaps it is time to take notice.

The very last lines of the *Phenomenology* are preceded by fifteen or so pages of an almost unintelligible whirl of sentences that McCumber has called a "stew of words" (McCumber 1993, 21). Spirit has been cooked and recooked for a long time now. In the last chapter more than anywhere, the *Phenomenology* reads itself and, to borrow a phrase from Agamben, "bend[s] the prose of philosophy into a ring" turning upon itself and returning to itself, round and around (Agamben 1991, 78).[3] The pressure mounts. Finally, this concoction froths over:

Out of the chalice of this realm of spirits	*aus dem Kelche dieses Geisterreiches*
Foams forth to it its infinity.	*schäumt ihm seine Unendlichkeit.*
(§ 808, trans. modified)	

This ending might be read as an ejaculation. The *Phenomenology*'s cum shot, where spirit finally gets to see its own sperm. Instead of losing the seeds of its wisdom again and again in the chalice of phenomenological inquiry, recognition foams back out of the abyss of experience—and spirit succeeds in knowing itself. Schiller's "Ode to Joy," a poem that is kindred in its acclamation for friendship to the one Hegel quotes here (Schiller's poem "Friendship"), celebrates such male homosocial and autoerotic exuberance:

Joy in foaming beakers creams:—	*Freude sprudelt in Pokalen,*
Influenced by the golden vine,	*In der Traube goldnem Blut*
Civilized the savage seems,	*Trinken Sanftmuth Kannibalen,*
Timid hearts with valour shine.	*Die Verzweiflung Heldenmuth—*
Let the generous flagon pass;	*Brüder, fliegt von euren Sitzen,*
Brethren, in your sites rise,	*Wenn der volle Römer kreist,*
To good fortune drain a glass,	*Laßt den Schaum zum Himmel spritzen:*
Effervescing to the skies!	*Dieses Glas dem guten Geist!*
("To Joy," trans. Arnold-Forster; Schiller 1902, 63–64)	(Schiller 1983, "An die Freude," stanza 7)

The brothers used to be at each other's throats and feeding upon each other like cannibals. But they are assuaged now, and in this round they feel like heroes (they drink *Heldenmut*). In a carousal that has orgiastic overtones, they encourage each other to aim for the stars with their ejaculates (*Laßt den Schaum zum Himmel spritzen*): even the good heavenly spirit might be impressed by that!

Yet this intertextual reference also reveals the despair (*die Verzweiflung*) that underlies such self-aggrandizing exuberance. One can read the line that features *Verzweiflung* as a parallel structure to "*trinken Sanftmuth Kannibalen,*" thus translating it into something like "courageous heroes imbibe despair."[4] In chapter 7, I will elaborate on the fractures and ruptures that are the physical manifestations of despair. Here, we must at least notice that the triumphant ending to the book-length self-reflection of spirit is sapped by an uncanny word choice. Let's look at the full passage of Hegel's ending:

> The goal, absolute knowledge, that is, spirit knowing itself as spirit, has for its path the recollection [*Erinnerung*] of spirits as they are in themselves and as they achieve the organization of their realm. Their preservation [*Aufbewahrung*] in terms of their free existence appearing in the form of contingency is history, but in terms of their conceptually grasped organization, it is the *science* of *phenomenal knowledge.* Both together are conceptually grasped history; they form the recollection [*Erinnerung*] and the skull place [*Schädelstätte*] of absolute spirit, the actuality, the truth, the certainty of its throne, without which [*ohne den*] it would be lifeless and alone; only—

Out of the chalice of this realm of spirits
Foams forth to it its infinity. (§ 808, trans. modified)[5]

Das Ziel, *das absolute Wissen, oder der sich als Geist wissende Geist hat zu seinem Wege die Erinnerung der Geister, wie sie an ihnen selbst sind und die Organisation ihres Reiches vollbringen. Ihre Aufbewahrung nach der Seite ihres freien in der Form der Zufälligkeit erscheinenden Daseins ist die Geschichte, nach der Seite ihrer begriffenen Organisation aber die* Wissenschaft des erscheinenden Wissens; *beide zusammen, die begriffene Geschichte, bilden die Erinnerung und Schädelstätte des absoluten Geistes, die Wirklichkeit, Wahrheit und Gewißheit seines Throns, ohne den er nur das leblose Einsame wäre; nur —*
aus dem Kelche dieses Geisterreiches
schäumt ihm seine Unendlichkeit.

What kind of fluid is it, after all, that foams back at spirit? The text doesn't name the liquid, but circumscribes it as "infinity." Earlier in the *Phenomenology*, at the end of the chapter on the understanding, infinity is described as the "universal blood" (*das allgemeine Blut*, § 162). Does absolute spirit drink blood? There is certainly something vampiric about the constant need for *Aufhebung*. I can almost see spirit frothing at the mouth from a mad desire for the life essence of its manifestations. Infinity, the last word of the *Phenomenology*, suddenly seems less than the triumphant culminating point of a narrative of progress. And the glorious chord of "the actuality, the truth, the certainty" that buttresses absolute spirit's throne is slowly and creepingly drowned out by the ghastly overtone of the word *Schädelstätte* (literally: "skull site").

Certainly, with a little bit of effort, *Schädelstätte* can be read as communicating a sense of sovereignty. The Latin *caput* combines the meaning of skull with that of "head" or "chief," and *Schädel* can profit metonymically from its Latin counterpart. Of course *Schädelstätte* can also easily be translated into Calvary or Golgotha, and will receive from the Christian context the absolution that a swift elevation to heaven affords. But *Schädelstätte* reinscribes what the Latin-derived *Kalvarienberg* (Calvary) or the Aramaic-derived *Golgatha* (Golgotha) covers over: a lingering sense of death.[6] *Schädelstätte* means "skull site" or "place for skulls" (as do Calvary and Golgotha for those who know Latin and Aramaic). Some say that the hill by Jerusalem got its name from its skull-like shape.[7] Legend has it that the skull of Adam was buried there, and the belief is that Jesus sacrificed himself there to expiate Adam and reverse man's death.[8] These stories are attempts to soften the drastic ring of the word *Schädelstätte* by reducing the numerous skulls to one, which then can more easily be turned into n-one. Yet *Schädelstätte* has the very profane meaning of mass grave: a place where a large number of skulls come to lie either at once (due to war) or as accumulated over time.[9] Golgotha was Jerusalem's place for executions; it is a site of serial killings. Jesus died on a heap of bones; he simply added one to the numberless skulls that were already amassed there. He was one among many. Similarly dies "absolute knowledge."

Absolute spirit has erected its throne on a pile of bones. The message of these last lines is very clear: without the death of many, absolute spirit would be lifeless. Its life is the result of the path of suffering that is the *Phenomenology* and the death of many figures of consciousness that went down in the annals of history. In a footnote to the word *Schädelstätte,* Nancy notes the obvious, namely that "history is also a vast and pain-ridden ossuary, a place where suffering and death are preserved" (Nancy 1997, 143, my translation). The *Phenomenology of Spirit* reads the bones of history and re-stashes them in an orderly fashion. The book preserves the various forms of spirit and organizes them according to the rules of "the *science* of *phenomenal knowledge.*" Yet from the depth of the mountain of skulls, a putrid liquid wells up and muddles things. It foams forth to remind absolute spirit that it is made of death and thus subject to death. The infinity of knowledge is not unlimited. Its reign (*Reich*) doesn't hold. Hegel's last words don't give us absolute knowledge once and for all. They also do not implement the neat organization (according to the rules of "the *science* of *phenomenal knowledge*") that they assert. Instead they veer into confusion. Like the fifteen or so pages leading up to it, the last sentence teeters at the edge of intelligibility. It does so not because it ventures out into unknown zones of knowledge, but because it circles back and back again, refusing to come to the point. Hegel's last words don't tell us what absolute knowledge consists of. Thank God!—one might say. We have learned not to ask. Absolute knowledge is nothing but the path toward absolute knowledge ("the truth is the whole[;] however, the whole is only the essence completing itself through its own development"), and so the request to state what spirit knows when it has come to know itself would launch us back into the entire development again (§ 20). Hegel's last sentence doesn't give us absolute knowledge. Rather, as if the author was distracted at the very apex of the phenomenological development, it oddly shifts referents and slips into an incoherence so slight that it would have almost remained unperceived.

Note the relative pronoun in the phrase *ohne den.* Grammatically it is not incorrect—it can refer to the throne (both are masculine in German)—but it certainly interrupts the parallel structure of this convoluted sentence: "*beide zusammen, die begriffene Geschichte, bilden die Erinnerung und Schädelstätte des absoluten Geistes, die Wirklichkeit, Wahrheit und Gewißheit seines Throns, ohne den er nur das leblose Einsame wäre*" (one expects *ohne die—die Wirklichkeit, Wahrheit und Gewißheit*). The final sentence folds back on the one before it. The penultimate sentence bravely—with "a hero's courage [*Heldenmuth*]," we could say—pronounces the goal (*das Ziel*) right away, then names it as "absolute knowledge," then defines it as "spirit knowing itself as spirit," and then continues its regress by describing the path toward absolute knowledge rather than telling us what this knowledge actually consists of. The final sentence repeats, with some additional clarifications, what the penultimate sentence already stated. "Their preservation" in the final sentence repeats "the recollection of spirits" in the penultimate. Similarly, "in terms of their free existence. . ." repeats "as they are in themselves" from before. And again, "in terms of their conceptually grasped organization" repeats "as they achieve the organization of their realm." Then comes another summary ("both together") and we arrive back at the beginning: "recollection." This is "the actuality, the truth, the certainty" of "spirit knowing itself as spirit," without which spirit would be lifeless and alone. Without what? Without the actuality of the realm of spirits, or without the recollection of spirits? Either one would make sense, but *Wirklichkeit, Erinnerung, Aufbewahrung*—all the words that would offer up a coherent meaning—are feminine. *Den* must refer to the throne—but it is incoherent with the rest of Hegel's philosophy to say that spirit be lifeless without its throne. Absolute knowledge does not need to prop up its power with such a dead symbol. The sentence makes more sense if we consider another, more remote, possibility: if we take *den* to refer to "absolute spirit." The gender alignment works (*Geist* is also masculine). It would be more Hegelian to say that the throne would be lifeless without absolute spirit. Yet, apart from the syntactical stretch of this version (*den* is too far away from *des absoluten Geistes* to sustain the reference), we are also not able to meaningfully relate the proposition's remaining attributes to the throne (should the throne be *das Einsame* and the thing that drinks infinity out of the chalice?).

The significance of this pronoun, I'd like to propose, is something other than its semantic referent. *Ohne den* marks a qualitative shift in the syntax of the sentence, which both consolidates the confusion and interrupts it. Mieszkowski has argued that the figure of anacoluthon (a change of grammatical structure within one sentence) shows up language's emotionality, that is to say, its incapability of creating a truly monolithic organizing schema (Mieszkowski 2009, 648–65). While the strange, almost imperceptible shift that *ohne den* initiates can perhaps not be qualified as an anacoluthon in the strict sense, it certainly marks the fact that this sentence relates to itself as to something other than what it presents itself to be. This sentence is not at peace with itself, but emotional. Even if *ohne den* is nothing but a small mistake, it breaks with the endless repetition of recollection. With it, the structuring of spirit's "realm" (*Reich*) comes undone, and absolute knowledge begins to dissolve. *Ohne den* is the tear in absolute knowledge. Because of it, the throne totters. In despite of it, the stew bubbles over. And absolute spirit breaks into tears.

Make a Scene

How to experience the moment of grief that takes spirit by surprise and that it loses immediately as the text breaks off? On the way toward answering a similar question, Cixous notices in the human psyche an infinite desire to shed tears. Puzzled by the observation that we enjoy sad stories, she asks, "Why do we read books that make us weep?" Her response is, "undoubtedly because we never have, in reality, enough to lament" (Cixous 1998, 42). With this statement Cixous certainly does not mean to deny real experiences of suffering. Instead, she points to the problematic relationship between reality and emotionality.

"In reality," we never have "enough to lament," not because the lamentable isn't real or there is not enough of it in real life, but because we need something in addition to the real in order to be able to lament. Affects—in Deleuze and Guattari's sense of the non-conscious and non-linguistic experience of intensity—have an immediate quality to them that gives us no means to lament. Physical pain might be one of the most-discussed examples of such intensity. Scarry notes that pain is difficult to describe because it destroys language.[10] "Pain has an element of blank," writes Emily Dickinson.[11] Pain subjects us to its absolute presence since "it cannot recollect / When it began" and "It has no future but itself" (Dickinson 1891). For the body in pain, circumscribing, that is, re-presenting pain through recollecting and anticipating its limits are impossible operations because they require an (if ever so slight) distance from the present, a slight gap or lag—precisely that which pain eliminates in its absolute rule. Without this interval, no lament, no language of pain is possible. "In reality, we never have enough [distance] to lament."[12]

Against the idea of immediate affect and dumb pain, Hegel contends that subjectivity requires the pain of (self-)negation. Self-reflection and pain are thus intertwined for Hegel. He considers pain as a form of mediation: pain is mediated and reflects itself, and self-reflection or subjectivity involves pain. The subject needs to show "that there is nothing on hand in it itself which could not be a vanishing moment for it" (§ 187). Yet, it is obviously a paradoxical demand on the subject-to-become that self-negation be constitutive of subject formation. One can enjoy self-negation only as long as one survives it. This is the lesson of the *Phenomenology*'s "struggle for life and death." "We need to mourn for ourselves. And yet to stay alive," notes Cixous (Cixous 1998, 42). She admires Siegfried's swan song in the *Nibelungenlied*: his extraordinary capacity for transport. Siegfried is able to lament his own death because he anticipates it and because he identifies with those surviving him:

> In former times, the husband of Kriemhild collapsed among the flowers in stanza 988, one saw the blood pouring from his wound. . . . Sigfrid didn't want to die without having said everything he thought. Dying, he spoke by turns to his friends and to his traitors, and to everybody he said, fatally wounded, what he had to say. In stanza 999 the flowers all around were drenched in blood. At the end, the dying Sigfrid still bothered to suffer vicariously for [*à la place de*] his father, his mother, and his barons. When he had no more strength to speak he still exhaled at the end one terrible stanza. He had such a furious pity for those who awaited his return for long. It was the agony of those who waited for him in vain that he wanted to lament before he died. (Cixous 1992, 15, my translation)

Siegfried gives the best proof of his subjectivity when, rather than getting swallowed by the mute reality of sheer pain and death, he finds the intervals of negativity (anticipating his death and putting himself in the position of those around him) that allow his feelings to resonate. Of course, that was "in former times," and we are no Siegfried. That is why we need books that make us weep. Because in reality we don't have Siegfried's sublime ability to invite self-difference, we need fiction, metaphor, or theater to create the interval that makes emotion resonate and allows us to experience it in the first place. The sheer "reality" of pain is not an emotion; the lament is the true emotional experience. Emotion is, thus, a manner of speaking.[13]

Our ability to feel emotion is, then, a matter of understanding emotionality. I mean this in the double sense. Emotionality is a mode of understanding, or, as Terada puts it, "emotions are an interpretive act that involves representation and mediation" (Terada 2001, 17). But we also need the right understanding of emotionality—we need to understand emotionality as self-reflective—if we want to feel emotions. If we think that the authenticity of emotion lies in its immediacy, we will have a hard time experiencing emotion. On the other hand, the fiction that opens a gap within emotion takes nothing away from the truth of emotion. On the contrary, the idea of affective clarity and integrity emerges as a disavowed fiction when Terada describes it as the white mythology of emotion, which wants emotions to be "affective cognitions with none of the disadvantages of affects" (Terada 2001, 31). In the first chapter of *Déluge*, entitled "C'était l'entre deux," Cixous stresses our disappearing ability to live in-between. For her, "the emotion is born *at the angle* of one state with another state" (Cixous 1998, 26). The self-identical facticity of brute loss, for example, doesn't resonate emotionally. One feels numb about it until one makes a scene of it. "I need imagination to 'excite' sorrow even at a loss of my own" (Terada 2001, 38). I need to find that distance to myself—to my own loss—that allows me to lament it. "Making a scene" thus involves reflecting and refracting the loss across various figurations of loss, self, and presence.

This turns emotion into transport, into a traveling across states that figure one another and that by this very figuration get condensed. For example, a weeping act can be understood as a chant that echoes past and future losses. With one's tears one repeats the loss that one anticipates. At times the reflection takes place externally; sometimes a figure of the in-between hits one from outside—as it happened to the "old friend" Cixous remembers, "who had just lost her husband. . . . And she said to me, with an utterly surprised air: you know, at the corner of *boulevard Jourdan* and *rue Deutsch de la Meurthe,* all of a sudden, I started to cry. Well, that is the point: it takes place quite exactly at the corner, at the angle" (Cixous 1997, 42). But it takes understanding for grief to take place; it takes an understanding of emotionality as transport; it takes the suppleness to comprehend (to penetrate and embrace) and identify with different figures and states across intervals (without eliminating the differences) to experience grief or any other transport.

Emotional transport involves time travel (past and future losses), spatial constellations (tears at the corner), interpersonal identifications (Siegfried and his entourage), or intrapersonal identifications (I'll come to this in a moment). Yet what I have distinguished here—time and space, inter- and intrapersonal relations—indeed overlaps, because emotionality cuts across the distinction and separation between inside and outside. The idea of emotion as a mental content (to be expressed) illustrates well how the wrong conception of emotion generates only numbness and leaves us feeling empty. "Emotions appear to be exemplary inner contents . . . *because* the history of thought about emotion has invested in theories of expression" (Terada 2001, 28). But emotions are never fully inside or fully outside; they travel across and in-between. The expressive hypothesis can be confirmed by experience only when it has gone through deconstruction, and when expression is understood in the rather uncommon way Mark Taylor understands "secret(ion)s":

"Secretions, it seems, are always *entre-deux.* While a secret is an outside that is inside, a secretion is an inside that is outside" (Taylor 1990, 190). There is no inner plenitude that can be perfectly put into language or other forms of expressions; rather, the inner is already alienated from itself when the uncanny fluid wells up and the shedding of tears or other secretions makes one feel the tears (*Zerrissenheit*) within.

This brings me to the somewhat counterintuitive notion of intrapersonal identification. "We feel not to the extent that experience seems immediate, but to the extent that it doesn't; not to the extent that other people's experiences remind us of our own, but to the extent that our own seem like somebody else's" (Terada 2001, 22). Terada notes here something very important, namely, that the cross-identification required for emotion does not simply aggrandize the self by appropriating the other, but estranges the self as well. We feel to the extent that our own experiences seem like somebody else's. Our self-feeling paradoxically turns us into objects for ourselves. "A situation that Wittgenstein considers too absurd seriously to contemplate—in which people can feel emotions only through intermediate representations, which he likens to 'inanimate things' or 'dolls'—is the case even when the intermediary is oneself" (Terada 2001, 18). Even self-feeling turns us into things: dense and inanimate objects—dolls, for example, or dummies or skull bones—things that are not entirely transparent to us. It is to Hegel's great credit that he embraces this kind of self-alienation. There is no absolute knowledge without spirit acknowledging "that the being of the I is a thing" (§ 790).

We can lament only when we relate to ourselves as something else. I remarked earlier that emotion is a way of speaking; now we can specify that emotion is an indirect way of speaking. Only by way of indirection can we communicate (even to ourselves) what we truly feel. "The ventriloquist spills his or her guts by speaking from the belly. . . . Ventriloquists, of course, do not speak directly. They speak indirectly by speaking through an other who cannot speak and who is, therefore, a dummy" (Taylor 1990, 190). Only by relating to ourselves as dummies or things can we find that interval that allows us to cry.

Yet the assumption that the doll or the skull bone is a dummy who cannot speak still belongs to what Terada identifies as the "ideology of emotion" (Terada 2001, 3). This ideology is based on the idea that feeling distinguishes humanity from inhumanity. Hegel, on the other hand, allows us to register the fact that the "dummy" does speak and does experience transports at least to the same extent that human subjects do—that "the thing is I" and I can only echo this thing (§ 791). Emotionality, then, comes always in multiple voices that mix and mingle, that affirm and negate, that interrupt one another and inaccurately echo one another. As

Cixous puts it, "I live of living and dying interwoven into a sonata. I don't want the world by one eye and just one dimension, no, our life is not cut and dry, but at least five times varied, awry, contorted" (Cixous 1992, 16, my translation). Emotionality, thus, has a sense for complexity, and furthers ethical relationalities where each party imitates other tongues without simply translating them into one unified voice that it claims as its own.[14]

Joys of Grief

The interval that generates emotionality also affects individual emotions. Self-distance opens a gap within emotions and gives them an ironic character: emotions are experienced not as clear and simple, but as oscillating between different, often opposite flavors. There is, for example, an overtone of pleasure in the experience of grief. With his speculative logic—which elastically captures the unity of opposites and the difference within identity—Hegel offers an excellent tool for attending to this ambivalence of emotionality. The speculative quality of tears—the fact that these secretions nourish—is not lost on Cixous, either. "Pouring out and taking in," we drink our tears, she notes (Cixous 1998, 47). "It is salted milk" that suits the taste of adults (Cixous 1997, 44).[15] If spirit breaks into tears at the very end of the *Phenomenology*, Hegel's thoughts on infinity and alienation enable absolute spirit to drink its tears from the chalice of spirits.

The need for a metaphoric distance from pain is bound up with the theatricality of grief. The staging of grief proves necessary for the feeling of grief to be registered at all, and it also mixes grief with pleasure: the "happiness in tears . . . is connected to the theater, to representation, to the fact that there are witnesses" (Cixous 1998, 47). Only shared grief allows full pleasure. This explains Hegel's theatrical paroxysm at the end of the *Phenomenology of Spirit*. With the final lines of the book he suddenly slips into the language of poetry and into the character of a friend. Hegel thematically and performatively conjures up friends who can introduce the self-difference necessary for the joyful experience of grief. Only the echo of another's voice allows the *Phenomenology* to dissolve into tears. This other is easily identified as Schiller, the end of whose poem "Die Freundschaft" ("Friendship") Hegel cites here. Another other called to the scene is poetry, the ambivalent friend of philosophical discourse.

When Hegel mimics poetry by unfaithfully reciting Schiller's poem "Friendship," an unexperienced grief unexpectedly interrupts this ostensibly triumphant phase of "absolute knowledge." In the indirect presence of a friend, Hegel is able to abandon the imperialist gesture of systematic knowledge. He has reached his limit. If there is any content to "absolute knowledge," it can only be the reflexive claim that for knowledge "to know its limit [i.e., to know itself] means to know that it is to sacrifice itself" (§ 807). In keeping with the unending regress of his final chapter, Hegel at first seems to circle back to the empirical material that phenomenology processes: "This sacrifice is the self-emptying within which spirit exhibits its coming-to-be spirit in the form of a *free contingent event*" (ibid). In its function as a chalice or container, the book holds and organizes the sacrificial manifestations of spirit. But at the end of the *Phenomenology* this containment finds its limit. Self-emptying takes the form of a shedding of tears. The spirits bubble over the rim of this chalice that is the *Phenomenology* and systematic discourse breaks into song. With his ventriloquism (of Schiller), Hegel spills his guts: he empties himself. He abandons control over the book. But to him—who argues that the "release of itself from the form of its own self is the highest freedom"—such surrender of control is a freedom more meaningful than the problematic notions of intention, agency, and free will (§ 806).

Of course, Hegel does not release his book without hoping that he might get a response—that in some way or another the liquid he spills might come back to nourish him. Ten years earlier he had mused about the speculative reversal of natural force. On vacation in the Alps in 1796, Hegel has the opportunity to observe that liquid—even a liquid that is not bound in an organism—does not submit to the law of linear progression. Even water that falls off the mountain (i.e., water that is propelled with considerable force in one direction) will change direction and come back up. He commits his pleasure at this speculative reversal to a travel log. While mountains and glaciers interest him little, Hegel describes in detail three different waterfalls (the falls of the Staubbach, the Reichenbach, and the Aar). He doesn't tire of specifying again and again how the water dust, produced by the water foaming back, dances in the sun and wets his face, clothes, and body. One waterfall is accessible via a footbridge: "The Aar makes a few glorious waterfalls that plunge down with terrible force. One of these is spanned by an audacious bridge, on which one gets completely wet from the dust" (Hegel 1986a, 1:616, my translation). Another one is not so easy to reach, but as soon as Hegel and his friends spy it, their excitement gets them wet: "Suddenly the upper part of the Reichenbach fall now presented itself to us . . . and we approached it merrily through wet meadows. On the green hill opposite the fall, the water dust—that the wind caused by the fall chased toward us—soaked us completely" (Hegel 1986a, 1:615, my translation). Lingering near the "brink of the abyss," Hegel meticulously describes the play of the falling waves in their course through the air and over the rocks (ibid.). Here the surprising return of the river appears most poignantly. After the falling water is already out of sight, it miraculously comes out of the abyss back to life: "After the waves thus . . . plunge into the abyss where the gaze cannot follow them . . . one perceives smoke surging out of a crevasse. This smoke one recognizes as the foam that shoots up from the fall" (ibid.). About ten years later, Hegel conjures up a similar image with the final lines of the *Phenomenology*: "out of the chalice of this realm of spirits / foams forth to it its infinity." He does so surely in part to reassure himself that the thoughts he just put forward and the words he just spilled will not be lost in dank darkness, but will freely come back to him with increased liveliness. But, at the same time—across the Alpine hikes—he is now in the position of someone who submits to the fluid as something strange, of someone who runs through the meadow to be wetted by a liquid that comes from someplace else. The act of release presents a conscious gesture of exposing his work to alteration and dispersal. Like the waters of the Reichenbach, the *Phenomenology* will return "not unified into *one* substance" but "ever dissolving and leaping apart" (Hegel 1986a, 1:614, my translation).

Readers and Friends

Quoting is an act of friendship—not only because Hegel allows Schiller to take the floor before he has finished his sentence to give his own book closure, but also because he borrows Schiller's lines not without transforming them.[16] The friendship of philosophy and poetry consists in the fact that neither of them speaks alone here—each gains voice through the other and each twists the other's words. Hegel moves what he quotes and changes what he reads. By that I mean not only that the lines of Schiller's poem receive a new meaning in the very different context of the *Phenomenology*, but that Hegel actually modifies almost every word in this "quotation." Schiller's original reads:

Friendless was the great master of the worlds,
Felt a *want*—so he created spirits,
Blessed mirrors of *his* blessedness!—
Found the highest Being not his like,
From the chalice of the entire realm of souls
Foams forth to *him*—infinity.
(my translation)

Freundlos war der grosse Weltenmeister,
Fühlte Mangel—*darum schuf er Geister,*
Sel'ge Spiegel seiner *Seligkeit!*—
Fand das höchste Wesen schon kein Gleiches,
Aus dem Kelch des ganzen Seelenreiches
Schäumt ihm—*die Unendlichkeit.*
(Schiller, "Die Freundschaft," last stanza)

In a careful analysis of the discrepancies between Schiller's and Hegel's versions, McCumber argues convincingly that Hegel's alterations take the form of "a series of dereifications, in which all references to anything unconditioned or atemporal . . . are replaced in favor of various kinds of situated (local and passing) phenomena" (McCumber 2000, 49).[17] While Schiller's lyrical "I" mirrors itself in "the great master of the worlds" when it sings its hymn to friendship, Hegel's "absolute spirit" does not lay claim to mastery.[18] As I have discussed in chapter 1 (drawing upon Nancy's work), Hegel doesn't accept the idea of a creator who is above and beyond the world; similarly, he doesn't propose that spirit be the author or independent and masterful creator of its story. Rather, "manifestation surges up out of nothing, into nothing. The manifested is something, and every thing is manifested. But there is no 'manifester' that would be yet another thing than manifestation itself" (Nancy 2002, 33). Similarly, just as there is no creator beyond manifestation, there can be no knowledge outside of manifestation. The knowledge that the last chapter of the *Phenomenology* provides is not absolute in the sense that it can stand on its own as a categorical, timeless truth. "Absolute knowledge" does not supersede all the errors that led us here, but it is part of the erroneous path. Or, as McCumber puts it, "the universal—the goal of the whole process—is now, like all other stages of the book, nothing more than its position in the whole" (McCumber 2000, 56). Absolute knowledge is self-reflective, but it doesn't close the system, since the system—because of its strict immanence—must logically be an open or unfinished system. Spirit that knows itself knows that it cannot lay claim to totality, and so Hegel changes Schiller's *Aus dem Kelch des* ganzen *Seelenreiches / Schäumt ihm*—die *Unendlichkeit* (From the chalice of the *entire* realm of souls / Foams forth to *him*—infinity) into *aus dem Kelche* dieses *Geisterreiches / schäumt ihm* seine *Unendlichkeit* (Out of the chalice of *this* realm of spirits / Foams forth to it *its* infinity)—thus effectively situating "absolute knowledge."

In the circular structure of its self-referentiality, "spirit knowing itself as spirit" is infinite. Yet its infinity is local and temporal and therefore finite. Spirit can gain knowledge of itself only as *this* spirit. Across the specific narrative of this book, this spirit gains self-awareness—not as the only possible formation of spirit, but as this spirit that has gained this shape across this history. McCumber explains the surprisingly frequent use of demonstrative pronouns in the last chapter of the *Phenomenology*, arguing that "the universal . . . the truth which was to be written down . . . thus dies away in its separate being and becomes nothing more than the knowledge of *this* sequence of shapes of consciousness" (McCumber 2000, 56).[19] Universal truth dies away. The kind of truth that can be written down because it will be the same tomorrow as it was today, this notion of truth as categorical and unchangeable, which was the operative notion of truth for the protagonist throughout the *Phenomenology*, finally dies here, at the very end of the book.

While we might want to rejoice over the death of the problematic and often repressive ideology of timeless truth, this is also, perhaps more than ever, the moment to ask whether the *Phenomenology* can mourn its dead. Is there finally time for grief here, at the end of the book, where we don't have to hasten to the next step on the ladder of *Aufhebung*? Where, for once, renewal is not at hand? Can the protagonist of the *Phenomenology* shed tears over the loss of an idea, in which it had invested for its whole life? Not if the book (and our interest in the protagonist) comes to a definite end. This is why this last chapter keeps circling—so as to protract the reader's being done with it. Acknowledging "the necessity of interval," Hegel finally stages an interruption and allows for tears (Blanchot 1993, 75).[20] He lets poetry and philosophy interrupt themselves and one another—but not just in order to (let) speak, but rather, in order also to render possible the worklessness or *désoevrement* of tears (pronounced both ways).[21] Breaking into verse, the text sheds tears not only for the countless "skulls" that litter the path toward absolute knowing, but also for the idea of an unchanging and eternal truth, which has animated all the shapes of consciousness and formations of spirit.

The last word authored by Hegel alone is *nur* (only). It is a lonely word and a sad word—a signifier of restriction, disappointment, and finitude. Isolated by a semicolon on its left side and a dash on its right, *nur* stands between two discourses (Hegel's and Schiller's, philosophy and poetry) and works on both.[22] *Nur* reverses the gesture of Schiller's poem. Schiller's "great master of the worlds" has a master's appetite (*Begierde*) and needs the entirety of creation to provide him with a sense of infinity, which means that Schiller envisions this master's self-knowledge in the form of a universal and eternal truth. Meanwhile, the subject of Hegel's version of Schiller's lines drinks its infinity "only" from a specific chalice and its truth is therefore circumscribed. But this "only" also applies to what precedes it and thus it affects our way of reading the Hegelian text, as well. Across the word *nur* Schiller's poetry and Hegel's philosophy syncopate each other. The verses bend the linear movement of philosophical prose while *nur* functions as the pivot.[23] Looking back at the Hegelian text from the vantage point of the two verses at the end, we come to understand that the truth of absolute knowledge is not the kind of truth that can be simply written down. Rather, it is like the truth that we encountered at the very beginning of the book—in the chapter on "sense certainty"—the truth that was lost by writing it down.[24] Absolute knowledge is "only" the kind of truth that one cannot hold onto by preserving it unchanged. Or better—and this would be reading his text backward from the end—absolute knowledge acknowledges that its truth changes with every utterance. It knows itself to be the kind of truth that is altered by being written down and altered by being read.

This is the point where the *Phenomenology* sets the reader free, and that is why I began my discussion of emotional syntax here, at the end. In the end, the spirit of this *Phenomenology* surrenders to the uncontrollable effects of place and time and gives itself over to the future that will come to it from its readers.[25] Readers from other places and other times now arrive to interrupt this way of "writing down (up) the truth." Some might do so by moving and transforming the text—as is done among friends. Others might consider the *Phenomenology* to be dated and not worthy of being reworked, as Hegel did when he wrote in 1831: "peculiar early work, not to be reworked—related to the time of its composition" (quoted in McCumber 2000, 57). The latter attitude takes the book's meaning to be like sense certainty's truth: only a *Meinen* (mere opinion). At any rate, with its last lines, the *Phenomenology* releases the grip it had on its reader, from whom it had demanded extraordinary suppleness and complete devotion. Now, the *Phenomenology* abandons itself to its own *Aufhebung*—to being altered and turned from the vantage point of another perspective.

In my proximity to Hegel—a mediated and self-referential proximity that leaves enough room for the syncopating rhythms of mutual acknowledgment to resonate and that can serve as an echo chamber for the tears, the trembling, and the brokenness of Hegel's text—with my supple yet firm hand on the small of his back, I have just led him into a slight turn in an unexpected direction.

4

Juggle

> This conflict between the form of a proposition per se and the unity of the concept which destroys that form is similar to what occurs in the rhythm between meter and accent. Rhythm results from the juggle and unification of both. In that way, in the philosophical proposition, the identity of subject and predicate does not abolish their difference.
>
> —*Phenomenology*, § 61

For Hegel, rhythm affects logic. What is more, logical necessity is constituted by the rhythm of the concept's movement: "It is in this nature of what is to be its concept in its being that *logical necessity* in general consists. This alone is the rational and the rhythm of the organic whole . . . —that is, it is this alone which is the *speculative*" (§ 56, trans. modified). Yet, the rhythm of the concept is far from steady and predictable. It is a constant juggle. There is no preexisting concept of the rhythm of the concept; rather, its rhythm emerges contemporaneously with its fumbling steps of self-comprehension. Each phenomenological scenario compels the concept to (re-)create its rhythm in communication with its context. Because the "rhythm of the organic whole" thus changes constantly, it is quite difficult, if not impossible, to identify speculative rhythm. "When you think you have it, it evaporates and returns as a new rhythm" (Trinh 1999, 14). The situatedness of knowledge—even of absolute knowledge—that we discussed in the previous chapter returns here as the incessantly changing rhythm of the whole.

We will discover in this chapter that speculative rhythm emerges from the divided method of philosophical science, which juggles contrary demands. This method is grounded in sympathy understood as a sharing of non-identity, a sharing that itself is shared. Every articulation of a new insight thus alters the rhythm of the whole. Like someone who dances to her own heartbeat. Every move she makes with her arms, her legs, or her torso to accompany her heartbeat changes the rhythm of that beat, which in turn has an effect on her dance moves.[1]

Echolalia

Speculative rhythm has often been constructed as a regular three-step. In that case, dialectics becomes a rocking movement that feels soothing. It assures that individual concepts come and go, and that thought departs and returns, while nothing is lost and nothing imposes itself forever. But Hegel's analogy between logic and rhythm suggests something more disturbing. Hegel's rhythm has an element of chaos. It is reminiscent of the description of rhythm by Deleuze and Guattari, who specify that "what chaos and rhythm have in common is the in-between" (Deleuze and Guattari 1987, 313). Oscillating between different notions of the concept, between judgment and speculative proposition, and between philosophy and poetry, speculative rhythm introduces chaos and contingency into the realm of logic—and that can be a quite troubling thought. The elements of the two different logics of Hegel's divided methodology do not join under the rule of a common beat. Not one of these dancers leads. Instead, they bring different rhythms to bear on one another, forming "a zone in which dissonant, differently tuned voices, discordant voices out of tune with themselves and with the times, may be heard echoing through one another" (to use a formulation of Michael Levine 1997, 111). Yet the different logics "unexpectedly click in, come apart, meet halfway, and so on; in other words, . . . they do and undo one another in their diversified movements" (Trinh 1999, 261).

The self-actualizing activity of Hegelian concepts cuts across the clear-cut distinctions that traditional logic tries to enforce. For Hegel, language, thought, and reality overlap and are inseparable. Thoughtful statements are acts that alter reality. The "form of writing" must therefore be of great concern for Hegel when he embarks on the project of the *Phenomenology*, that is, of presenting spirit as it appears to itself (Hegel 2002, 251). It comes as no surprise, therefore, that he devotes an important part of the *Phenomenology*'s preface to his thoughts on the form of philosophical exposition (§ 56–66).[2]

Spirit appears (*phainesthai*) to itself in the logic and syntax of its language (*logos*). The *Phenomenology of Spirit* mediates spirit with itself through writing. Nevertheless, as we have seen in the previous chapter, Hegel is much attuned to the fact that a dynamic truth cannot simply be written down. In response to this fact, the language of Hegel's *Phenomenology* divides itself between the language of traditional logic and the language of the speculative. Hegel describes the relation between the two forms of writing as a juggle, a tremulous harmony in motion, and as a rhythm that comes to life through the syncopated ensemble playing of two ways of thinking. This moving incongruence of the phenomenological text makes it emotional.

The always subtly changing rhythm of speculative writing resists quick understanding, and refuses the smooth supersession of the signifier "with a view to the concept" (Derrida 1986, 9a). The "magisterial coldness" and unemotional, "imperturbable seriousness" of Hegel's *Geist* is "semantically infallible" solely "for those who have read him a little—but only a little" (Derrida 1986, 1a); that is, for those who have read him only in one direction.[3] In the following, I will traverse Hegel's text back and forth in an attempt to bring its body to life again and again as a warm body. Then we might notice that, rather than the motionless flight of the eagle in the very high cold regions of the sky, the *Phenomenology* performs an eagle dance—the imitation of the afterfeeling of the eagle on the ground. Close to the ground, "very lowly, low down, close to the earth," the dancers respond to a multitude of at times contradictory calls: they save yet lose themselves curling up into a tight ball or crossing the road slowly with hundreds of swift little steps (Derrida 1991, 234). For German ears, the "eagle"—this emblem of Prussian authoritarianism, and this word that is already the translation of another echolalia: of the French echo of Hegel's name (*aigle*)—turns into an *Igel:* one of poetry's names.[4] Poetry sets the eagle on its feet.[5] There, on the ground, in an unfamiliar element, the eagle looks quite awkward and vulnerable.

The complex rhythm of Hegel's philosophical language restores thought to its body. Poetic language brings to the fore a general characteristic of texts, namely that they survive their physical vanishing in the uptake of information. Unable to decide where best to place the stress, we read over and over again and thus remain attached to the materiality of words. We keep the bodies of words company (or allow them to keep us company).[6] Doing so, we begin to notice that words communicate with one another, that they echo one another even where the grammar of meaning prevents such associations.[7] Lyric poetry, says Hegel, "allows particular ideas to subsist alongside one another without being related, whereas thinking demands and produces dependence of things on one another, reciprocal relations, logical judgments, syllogisms, etc."[8] By juggling logical judgments and syllogisms, Hegel invites some of the chaos of this lyric "alongside" in an effort to counteract dependence, oppression, and the hierarchical understanding of *Aufhebung*.

This chapter interrogates logic, that is, rules of intelligibility, in order to show not only that emotion is a mode of thought, but also that emotionality calls for and produces a different logic. The argument that emotions function like judgments, because they are intentional in that they have an object or aim, is rather problematic in my view.[9] The syntax of judgment demands the existence of a subject and an object, their separation, and their hierarchical organization. The established rules for logical judgments force us to think in hierarchical subject-object relations. And while Nussbaum, for example, is at pains to prove the intentionality of emotions and their status as "forms of judgment," she misses an opportunity to interrogate the very rules of intelligibility that separate emotionality from rationality in the first place (Nussbaum 1997, 234).[10] Hegel suggests that there is something to be gained from bringing together the two contradictory logics of traditional argumentation and speculative sympathy while allowing them to syncopate each other and to exchange their steps. The discord and confusion that is thereby introduced into the rigidly ruled discourse of conventional logic urges thought to move in more than one direction. A self-difference has opened up within logic to construct the emotional syntax of philosophical language. It creates resonances within that cannot close themselves off from resonating with other bodies or even other logics. Emotionality is lodged in the language of the *Phenomenology*, in the tremulous harmony of the "doleful cry of the owl at twilight" (Nancy 2001, 38).

Emotional Concepts

Hegel radically redefines the notions of concept and proposition used in traditional logic generally and, more specifically (and closer to Hegel's concerns), in Kant's transcendental philosophy. Traditionally, the definition of concepts as abstract, self-identical, and timeless terms has served to shield the rules of thought from empirical and emotional interference. Hegel's phenomenological approach counteracts this aversion against experiential knowledge. It undoes the traditional separation between logic and empiricism by insisting that a concept realizes itself and that reality comprehends itself. For Kant, concepts are general and abstract terms, empty containers or, as Hegel puts it, "inert receptacles" that need to be filled with the concrete material of experience (*gleichgültige Behälter;* Hegel 1975a, §162). Kant famously refers to concepts without intuitions as void, thus underlining their status as subjective forms of representation that call for objective content (Kant

1990, B75 and B298–99). Hegel understands the concept (*Begriff*) as reaching through (*durchgreifen*) and undoing such abstract divisions as subject and object, form and matter, or logic and ontology.[11] The concept is no fixed entity distinct from comprehension. Herein consists precisely the novelty of Hegel's notion of the concept: that it is not a term but a movement, the movement of comprehending. But this activity doesn't necessarily require a human agent. Concepts comprehend themselves.

Hegel's phenomenology of spirit thus not only examines how a situated consciousness "applies" certain concepts, but traces how concepts "actualize themselves": how concepts self-differentiate and recollect, embrace themselves and tear themselves to pieces—all the while generating realities that affect and situate consciousness. Concepts thus have a reality somewhat independent from those who "use" them. When Hegel says that it is in the "nature of what is to be its concept in its being," he considers being not just as substance but also as subject (§ 56). Substance is usually understood as self-identical, timeless, and stable: "On account of its simplicity, that is, its parity-with-itself [*Sichselbstgleichheit*], [substance] appears to be fixed and persisting" (§ 55). But this appearance passes: "this parity-with-itself is likewise negativity" (ibid.). Traditional philosophy assumes that such negativity or moving force is exerted upon being by the thinking subject, that is, externally. "However, that [what is] has its otherness in itself and that it is self-moving are contained in that *simplicity* . . . which is the pure *concept*" (§ 55). No human subject is required for the concept to come to differ from itself and to emotionally respond to, negotiate, and juggle this disparity with itself. Hegel's radical contribution to the philosophy of emotionality consists in suggesting that, in their self-tearing and self-embracing dynamic, concepts themselves are emotional (and not just the philosopher). Hegel reinscribes the emotionality that traditional philosophy has severed from conceptual life back into the concept itself.

Kant's demand that "an abstract concept be *made sensuous*" must strike Hegel as redundant because a concept makes itself sensuous (Kant 1990, B299). It differentiates itself and takes the form of an *Ur-teil* ("judgment" or "predicative proposition," literally: "original partition").[12] Of course, Hegel's notion of judgment is as unusual as his notion of the concept. For him judgments are not formal and atemporal assertions, but living bodies ("the judgment of the plant," for example, develops out of the unity of the germ), concrete things ("all things are a judgment"), or conflict-laden propositions (Hegel 1975a, § 166 *Zusatz;* § 167). They change over time and at no time are they one with themselves.

Hegel thus introduces self-dissonance or emotionality into his notion of the concept, into his notion of judgment, and even into his notion of truth. While, according to traditional logic, predicative propositions are either (wholly) true or (wholly) false (depending on whether concepts have been correctly applied), for Hegel they are both true and false because their concept realizes itself in them in a self-contradictory way.[13] If nothing can be "wholly true," as Hegel indeed maintains, the truth comes always mixed with untruth (ignorance, error, opinion, madness, etc.). There is no solid, self-identical, and sober truth, but only a dynamic, precarious, and emotional process of self-reflection that must juggle self-affirmation and self-critique.

Hegel thus defines truth as subjective—not in the sense that it lacks reality, and not only in the sense that it is a reality perceived (a reality for another, as Hegel would say), but in the sense that truth itself constitutes a subject:

> In my view, . . . everything hangs on apprehending and expressing the truth not merely as *substance,* but equally as *subject.* . . . Furthermore, the living substance is the being that is in truth *subject,* or, what amounts to the same thing, it is in truth actual only in so far as it is the movement of self-positing, that is the mediation of itself and its becoming-other-to-itself [*sich anders Werdens*]. (§ 17–18)

The concept's activity of self-positing by way of partially negating and partially affirming itself thus can be apprehended—so Hegel proposes—as the self-reflecting subjectivity of the concept. This self-reflection juggles the conflicting and emotionally charged demands of self-othering and self-collecting; it is an activity that is not reserved for human agents.

All this said, the emotional and material reality of Hegel's concept is easy to overlook because Hegel twists the traditional use of the word "concept" so radically that it is difficult to accept. Most interpretations of the Hegelian text—even the best—have in fact disregarded the concept's materiality and self-dissonance in favor of an understanding of the concept as metaphysical abstraction. Derrida, for example, offers a weak reading of the notion of the concept when he writes that for Hegel "language accomplishes itself [and] thus becomes signifying only by relieving within itself the (sensible, exterior) signifier, traversing it and denying it with a view to the concept" (Derrida 1986, 9a). While tradition justifies the view that "the logic of the concept is the eagle's," Hegel certainly opposes this tradition (Derrida 1986, 55a).

Emotional Judgments

In the preface of the *Phenomenology*, Hegel introduces the rhythm of the speculative judgment as actively critiquing and disarticulating the logical form of philosophical writing that is the predicative judgment (§ 60–66).[14] Predicative judgments are composed of or can be logically reduced to three parts: the subject, the copula, and the predicate.[15] Hegel denounces the predicative judgment as the symptom of a rigid, overly clear-cut and hierarchical thinking. He shows that its claim to simplicity and straightness only superficially covers over the conflicts it actually harbors. In the previous section, I already noted that concepts actualize themselves in judgments in a self-contradictory way. It is now time to specify these contradictions.

According to Hegel's analysis, every judgment presents a discord between what it means and what it says. The judgment means that subject and predicate are identical—*a* is *b*—but in reality it separates them into two different terms—*a* and *b*—and the copula physically stands in between the two, holding them apart. "The meaning seems to be that the difference is denied, although at the same time it appears directly in the proposition" (Hegel 1989, 90, trans. modified). The letter of the judgment is at odds with its spirit; the judgment means to cover over a difference that its body exhibits. In this situation, "clever argumentation [*Räsonnieren*]"—as Hegel calls the formal thinking that produces predicative judgments—solves or, rather, controls, the conflict by establishing a hierarchy (§ 58).[16] The body of the text is rejected once the meaning is retained.

But the judgment contradicts itself in more ways than one. Not only do its meaning and its physical appearance fail to coincide, but it is also of two minds about what it means. While the judgment claims to express the identity of subject and predicate, its own rules of intelligibility prohibit this identity.[17] Good judgment demands that the predicate must not be the same as the subject. Whenever they are indeed identical, the proposition doesn't make any sense; it is, as Hegel observes, commonly rejected as saying nothing: "If, for example, to the question 'What is a plant?' the answer is given 'A plant is—a plant,' the truth of such a statement is at once admitted by the entire company on whom it is tested, and at the same time it is equally unanimously declared that the statement says *nothing*" (Hegel 1989, 415). "A rose is a rose" says nothing. Supposedly. The predicate has to be different from the subject, and difference—logically—is understood as subordination. The subject in its particularity or individuality is supposed to be subjected to the universality of the predicate. Even if subject and predicate are different but equal, the proposition does not constitute a logical judgment because it is impossible to decide which term should govern the "identity" of the two. Does "poetry is a hedgehog" say anything? Can we subsume poetry under hedgehog? The sentence is grammatically correct, but it is no predicative proposition because it contains no predicate. According to good judgment, it gives no answer to the question "what is poetry?" because it joins two terms that are equally particular. In order for the predicate to say anything about (*über*) the subject, it has to be higher, more general, and more significant than the subject which must be lower, more particular, and without the ability to speak for itself.[18]

Again the conflict is managed—or attempted to be managed—by introducing a hierarchy. The order of the terms in the judgment must not be reversed: a (every) rose is a plant, but that does not mean that every plant is a rose. Or, to cast the same in more humanistic—albeit not more human—terms: Socrates is a man, but not every man is a Socrates. The logic of "clever argumentation" here betrays its inherent violence. The Enlightenment holds that all men have reason and understanding. These faculties allow them to make judgments, construe arguments, and engage in public reasoning. If we listen to the logic of the judgment, though, it turns out that only those who subject themselves to Socrates can claim reason (his name functions as shorthand for the canon of Western philosophy). The others teeter precariously at the edge of having their humanity denied. Socrates agrees to sending the flute player away. Her unruly rhythm would only disturb a rational "evening in conversation."[19] The basic idea of the Enlightenment does allow for the contraposition—someone who does not have reason and understanding (or quite unreasonably declines to follow its rules) is not a man.

Together with Hölderlin and Schelling, the early Hegel demands that the style of philosophical conversation be changed. In the "Earliest System-Program of German Idealism" they urge that "the philosopher must possess just as much aesthetic power as the poet" (Hegel, Hölderlin, and Schelling 2002, 111). In order to counteract the discrimination inherent in philosophical discourse, the new philosopher must display the contradictions at work in any assertion, the contradictions that the formal rules of logic so far have worked hard to subdue. The new philosopher must be able to attend to the sensuous qualities of language, register the subtle syncopations between the letter and the spirit or the body and the meaning of a judgment, and develop a philosophical syntax that juggles or rhythmically interweaves both logical and poetic language. "Thus in the end enlightened and unenlightened must clasp hands" and dance, with not one of these dancers leading (ibid.).[20]

Instead of the clear-cut logic of the judgment, which separates enlightened and unenlightened, Hegel proposes the syntax of speculative rhythm. Against the covering-over of conflict through the hierarchical organization of subject and predicate, or matter and meaning, Hegel exposes the conflicts and affirms that "the *non-identical* aspect of subject and predicate is also an essential moment" (Hegel 1989, 91). While "in the judgment this is not expressed," speculative syntax arranges together the different pieces of the whole (that is the truth) in a way that they gesture toward each other, figure one another, and imitate each other's steps across the vast interval of their differences. It creates a complex and moving interplay, a strange—partly monstrous and partly ludicrous, at times powerful and at times heartbreaking—configuration: the dance of the *Igel* with the eagle.

Invitation to Dance

Hegel does not advocate a purity of expression that "rigorously excludes" the logic and grammar of judgment (§ 64). He makes use of predicative propositions even though he considers them inappropriate for speculative philosophy. In the *Science of Logic,* Hegel warns: "We must, at the outset, make this general observation, namely, that the proposition in the *form of the judgment* is not suited [*nicht geschickt ist*] to express speculative truths" (Hegel 1989, 90). According to the (general) principles of his systematic philosophy, judgments have no place in philosophical discourse. And yet he was dealt his cards and he is committed to play them. Tradition has sent (*geschickt*) him a philosophical language that is not suited (*nicht geschickt*) to express speculative truth, and he will not argue with tradition.[21] Neither does he desist from presenting or exposing the speculative. But he is happy to forego the claim of expression with its calls for authenticity and purity.[22]

The *Phenomenology* clarifies what it means to remain faithful to speculative truth: "The exposition [*Darstellung*] which stays true to its insight into the nature of what is speculative must retain the dialectical form and must import nothing into it [*nichts hereinnehmen*] except what is both comprehended and is the concept" (§ 66). Hegel breaks the vow of fidelity by admitting judgments. He hosts the foreign logic in his own system. It is a move that will cause him, his readers, and his text a lot of trouble. It is a move that generates emotionality. Yet this unfaithfulness to his principles allows him to flexibly respond to the historical reality of non-Hegelian philosophical discourse, and ultimately to remain true to his own thinking. Allegiance to the speculative necessitates unfaithfulness to general principles. It would be quite un-Hegelian to abstractly oppose tradition. Instead, Hegel seduces those readers who expect conventional logic by speaking their language. (He knows that, as far as philosophy is concerned, there is no other language.)[23]

Hegel's style is susceptible to its others, including traditional logic. The rhythm of Hegel's moving exposition juggles two ways of philosophically constructing propositions: speculatively and "argumentatively [*räsonnierend*]."[24] Such "commingling" upsets both speculative and argumentative thought since "each of those modes interferes with the other" (§ 64). His writing thus loses in clarity and definition. "It is only the kind of philosophical exposition which rigorously excludes the ordinary relations among the parts of a proposition which would be able to achieve the goal of plasticity" (ibid.). With "plasticity" (*plastisch sein*), Hegel means here that only this kind of exposition would achieve the definition and well-rounded completeness of sculpture. But Hegel happily renounces the well-proportioned tangibility of Greek sculpture in favor of a philosophical elasticity.[25] Hegel has noted that the ideal of Greek self-containment and repose favors an "aloofness from feeling" and turns life quite literally into stone.[26] With the *Phenomenology* he is interested, rather, in the dynamic plasticity of something as unending and difficult to identify as rhythm. Troubled and torn like the "doleful cry of the owl at twilight," speculative rhythm has replaced the "tranquil trait of mourning" that the solitary statues retain (Nancy 2001, 38; Pinkard 2008, fn. 28).

In Hegel's rhythmic exposition, the different modes (argumentative and speculative) take part in one another while taking each other apart. Traditional logic does not persist untouched; it is shaken by speculative rhythm. Similarly, by embracing the very logic that rejects the speculative, Hegel invites trouble into the heart of his philosophy. Yet the emotionality generated by the fact that different grammars mingle is not suppressed by hierarchical sublations of one mode in the other. The dance of the *Igel* crosses the dance of the eagle without crossing it out. Hegel even speaks of a "harmony" between the two, but this harmony, to be sure, amplifies dissonance, interference, and syncopation:

> This conflict between the form of a proposition per se and the unity of the concept which destroys that form is similar to what occurs in the rhythm between meter and accent. Rhythm results from the juggle [*schwebende Mitte*] and unification of both. In that way, in the philosophical proposition, the identity of subject and predicate does not abolish their difference [*Unterschied*], which is expressed in the form of the proposition. Instead, their unity emerges as a harmony. (§ 61, trans. modified)

This passage renders the friction between two possibilities of reading—reading the material form and reading the meaning—as, once again, a conflict between identity and difference. For Hegel, this conflict does not have to be (dis)solved but can be made productive as a harmonic disunity in oscillating motion. Pinkard translates Hegel's complex expression *schwebende Mitte* as "oscillating midpoint," conveying the sense that speculative rhythm finds balance through constant counterbalancing movements. I translate it as "juggle" in order to communicate that unification, for Hegel, is a precarious juggle and not a stable synthesis (no matter how insistently the third step of the dialectical three-step is read as such).[27]

To construct judgments argumentatively is to follow the steady meter of a strict grammatical arrangement: subject, copula, predicate. The "subject constitutes the basis" for the succession of beats, the "solid ground [*feste Boden*]" on which predication advances (*fortlaufen,* § 60). There are two ways of accentuating predicative judgments. The subject can be understood as agent, that is, as privileged over and against its various and passing activities. Then the emphasis lies on the individual. Or the subject can be taken as remaining mute, demure, and (e)motionless while it "passively [*unbewegt*] support[s] the accidents" (§ 60). Without being an agent or having a voice it simply provides substance for judgment. In this case, "the understanding downgrades [the subject] to the status of something lifeless, since it merely predicates it of another existence, and takes no cognizance of the immanent life of this existence" (§ 53, trans. modified). The predicate, on the other hand, then makes a fuss (*macht ein Aufhebens*). It suppresses difference and sublates phenomena into the unity of its abstractly universal concept.[28] Its mode of *aufheben* is again unilateral: it puts an excessive emphasis on universality. Without much art, the proposition's accent thus lies either on the first term, the subject—*one* two three; *a* is b; *god* is being; *poetry* is x—or on the last term, the predicate—one two *three*; a is *b*; god is *being*; poetry is *x*. Either way, it presents a simple cadence.

To construct judgments speculatively is to juggle both of these cadences, to keep them both in play. Of course it is quite difficult to render both cadences at the same time. Therefore, "much has to be read over and over again" (§ 63). First, one might conclude that "*the I is a thing,*" i.e., that the subject as agent is predicated of a lifeless and abstract accident (§ 790). Yet this very emphasis on the subject "compels knowledge to come back to the proposition and now to grasp it in some other way" (§ 63). The correction reads the initial statement in the opposite direction and says "*The thing is I*" (§ 790). The supposedly lifeless accident is in fact an I or a self-reflecting agent. But then how can one categorical statement change into its reverse like that? Clever argumentation feels impelled to reinforce the status of the copula by clarifying "that the *being of the I is a thing*," i.e., that "is" establishes a solid and stable, thing-like or categorical link (§ 790). But it has already been stated that "the thing is I." Thus, the thing (the copula) which is the being of the I is I. The copula itself acts, moves, and reflects upon itself. The self-negating movement of the copula functions as the "oscillating midpoint" that unifies this quasi-syllogism (or speculative syllogism) into which the one judgment has unfolded through multiple readings.

But we have jumped ahead to the final chapter of the *Phenomenology;* let us return to the preface and read again Hegel's account of the emotional syntax of judgment. Speculative thinking raises the prosodic charge of philosophical language. It introduces a disruptive accent that syncopates the pattern of formal logic. The speculative deals a "counterpunch" to the normal accentuation of philosophical language:

> The nature of judgment, that is of the proposition per se which includes the distinction of subject and predicate within itself, is destroyed by the speculative judgment [*spekulativen Satz*], and the identical proposition which the former comes to be contains the counter-punch [*Gegenstoß*] to such relations. (§ 61, trans. modified)

The proposition has doubled: there is "the proposition per se which includes the distinction of subject and predicate within itself" and "the identical proposition" which deals the counterpunch that confounds these distinctions. When the proposition "God is being" is read speculatively, the second term "being" trades the abstract universality of the predicate for the dynamic self-mediation of the subject (in Hegel's emphatic sense), that is, of the self-negating concept. In the movement from the first to the second term, the subject, thus, reappears—as in "Rose is a rose is a rose is a rose." The subject is entangled in the predicate: "thought, instead of getting any farther with the transition from subject to predicate . . . finds the subject also to be immediately present in the predicate" (§ 62).[29] The note of the subject lasts through the beat of what is usually the predicate, and the reader finds the attack on the third count lacking. What now? The reader "feels . . . inhibited [*gehemmt*]." The predicate makes no fuss, *macht kein Aufhebens,* and allows for no stress. The proposition breaks off in the middle of an enjambment and leaves the reader hanging with one foot in the air (§ 62). Trying to figure out where to rest the foot, the reader "is thrown back to the thought of the subject" (§ 62). She pivots on one foot to move through the proposition in the other direction. Yet, turning around in an attempt to regain the subject, she realizes that the accent on the first count is lost, too. "God" has ceased to provide the stable ground on which the movement of thought can rest. Instead, this subject has been tossed in the air: "Here, 'being' is not supposed to be a predicate. It is supposed to be the essence, but, as a result, 'God' seems to cease to be what it was by virtue of its place in the proposition, namely, to be a fixed subject" (§ 62).[30] Speculative reading turns an abstract subject into the self-reflecting concept that tears itself to shreds and recollects itself. Instead of referring to something outside of language, the subject has become a reality that writes itself: "Since the concept is the object's own self, that is, the self which exhibits itself as *the object's coming-to-be* [*sein Werden*], it is not a motionless subject passively supporting the accidents; rather, it is the self-moving concept which takes its determinations back into itself" (§ 60). The subject makes its own sense. Realizing this, the reader has lost her former definition of the subject: "Within this movement the motionless subject itself breaks down [*geht zugrunde*]" (§ 60). Now that "the subject has dropped out of the picture [*verlorengeht*]," the suspended foot is thrown back to the count of the predicate (§ 60). Yet it does not safely land there to resume the course of a measured choreography. With this awkward pirouette, the reader—who has lost her footing on this base that "totters [*schwankt*]" (§ 60)—falls into the arms of the subject now understood as self-reflexive subject-matter: "Thought thus loses its fixed objective basis [*Boden*] which it had in the subject, when, in the predicate, it is thrown back to the subject [*darauf*], and when, in the predicate, it returns not into itself but into the subject of the content" (§ 63, trans. modified).

The clear-cut separations between subject and predicate, as well as between the reading subject and the content or subject matter of the proposition, are unsettled by the fact that the concept reaches through these divisions. Moved by the concept, the reader is unable to dissociate herself from what she reads. Drawn into the dance, she finds that she is not grounded in herself but depends on the other, the one she reads, to hold her. But clever argumentation loathes giving up control. Hegel, thus, exerts a certain kind of violence when he seduces the reader to read the judgment speculatively. His diction betrays this violence. According to his description, the reading subject "suffers from a counter-punch" (§ 60). It "feels . . . inhibited . . . and . . . thrown back" (§ 62). The violence of Hegel's writing style consists in not allowing the reader to translate the conflicts of a proposition into the higher synthesis of a stable meaning. It interferes with the reader's wish to be done with the text.

> However, since that former subject [subject of the proposition] enters into the determinations [accidents] themselves and is their soul, the

> second subject, which is to say, the knowing subject, finds that the former, which it was supposed to be over and done with, which it wants to go beyond in order to return into itself, is still there in the predicate. Instead of being able to be the agent [*das Tuende*] in the movement of predication . . . the subject is still occupied with the self of the content. The subject is not supposed to exist on its own, but it is supposed to exist together [*zusammensein*] with this content. (§ 60, trans. modified)

Hegel frustrates the reader's desire to withdraw as quickly as possible from the contact with the other into the aloof identity and superior authority of the I. Speculative science asks us to "be with [*zusammensein*]" being (apprehended and articulated as subject) to sympathize with its self-disruption without losing our own beat, to join hands with it and dance.

Half-Sympathetic Speech Acts

Let us return once more to the passage quoted at the beginning of this chapter: "It is in this nature of what is to be its concept in its being that *logical necessity* in general consists. This alone is the rational and the rhythm of the organic whole . . .—that is, it is this alone which is the *speculative*" (§ 56). Speculative philosophy does not rely on a set of unchanging rules of logic that it applies equally to all cases. Rather, the speculative philosopher observes—while acknowledging the impact of her own subjectivity on the phenomenological scenario—how being comprehends itself and how this process of self-comprehension (or of being "in its being its own concept") plays itself out in particular situations. The method of speculative philosophy is thus divided between attending to its own rules and attending to the way its subject grasps itself. Speculative thought juggles this self-division: "This nature of scientific method—that partly [*teils*] it is inseparable from the content, and partly [*teils*] it determines its rhythm by way of itself—has . . . its genuine exposition in speculative philosophy" (§ 57, trans. modified). The divided methodology of speculative thought consists partly (*teils*) in dancing to its own beat, and partly (*teils*) in following the lead of its subject matter. Rather than simply applying abstract (i.e., ostensibly objective, timeless, and universal) rules of logic, the speculative thinker needs to attend to the way the particular concept at hand comprehends itself (what criteria it sets for its comprehension). And she needs to do so without losing her own beat. As a matter of fact, she needs to foreground the particularity of her own way of grasping. Only a dance of (at least) two different beings, trying to comprehend themselves and each other by trying to respond to each other's and their own movements, realizes what Hegel calls philosophical science.

Dancing thus to two different measures requires effort and attentiveness. Hegel describes what he calls the "exertion of the concept [*Anstrengung des Begriffs*]" and the "attention to the concept [*Aufmerksamkeit auf den Begriff*]" as emotional labor (§58). It might be intellectually difficult to find the right category for a phenomenon and draw inferences according to the formal rules of logic, but there is no emotional difficulty here. Speculative philosophy, on the other hand, requires emotional labor. It is frustrating for the philosopher to renounce authority over the matter.[31] Hegel notes the emotional difficulty of injured pride. He even suggests that the movement of the concept can produce a feeling of shame—"the kind of shame which supposedly lies in something's having been learned"—since learning implies an acknowledgment of previous mistakes.[32] But the speculative philosopher must be able to bear such shame.[33] Hegel, in fact, asks her to transform vanity and shame into sympathy with what she is trying to comprehend. He demands of the philosopher to "sink [her] freedom into the content [*diese Freiheit in ihn zu versenken*]," that is to say, to refrain from manipulating the content and instead to follow and to imitate the movement of the content's self-reflection (§ 58, trans. modified).[34]

In its proximity to empathy, sympathy is certainly not an uncontentious notion. Scholars today ardently debate whether empathy is appropriate in matters of epistemology and hermeneutics, whether it is politically helpful, and whether it is even possible.[35] Complicating my use of the term here is the fact that it has undergone important changes in meaning between Hegel's time and ours.[36] I don't have room here to thoroughly engage in this debate, but I do want to clarify two aspects of sympathy that are important to me and that differentiate it from similar terms (and from different understandings of the same term). I'd like to understand sympathy strictly as feeling with or feeling together, as sharing feeling, or, in short, as commiseration. That is to say, sympathy has nothing to do with the condescending notion of compassion. In addition to the horizontal relationality of sympathy, I would like to stress its temporal character. I take sympathy to translate the German *Nachempfinden* ("having an afterfeeling" or "imitating a feeling"), as opposed to *Einfühlung* ("feeling into"). The latter reinscribes interiority whereas I appreciate the temporal lag and supplementarity of *Nachempfinden*. The Greek *empathês* simply means "in a state of passion," as opposed to *apathês,* which means "without passion." But this neutrality of the term is lost when, around 1900, Lipps uses *Einfühlung* to initiate an important discussion about the knowledge of other minds that nevertheless suffers from presupposing an all-too-stable notion of the self.[37]

Hegelian sympathy is a resonance between transports, rather than between individuals.[38] Indeed, Hegel finds sympathy possible because he doesn't have an emphatic notion of the singularity of the individual. Instead, he operates with a logic of figuration. The three moments of the concept—individuality, universality, and particularity—figure one another in the sense that they are distinct but that "each distinction is confounded in the very attempt to isolate and fix it" (Hegel 1989, 620). By the same token, individual concepts figure one another. The individual, according to Hegel, tends to isolate and fix distinctions. It conceives of itself as an indivisible monad without openings toward others—as one who excludes and repels other individuals. As such, the individual is an important moment in the movement of the concept (across individuality, universality, and particularity), but it necessarily passes. Unlike Kierkegaard and those who follow his criticism that Hegel lacks regard for singularity, I appreciate this passing of the individual, because it is the condition of the possibility of transport. The logic of figuration makes it possible that one be carried out of oneself and to a different self.[39] Hegel's rhythm of partial sympathy breaks up the integrity of the individual. Rather than unifying to full singularity, divided characters resonate across a distance in a way that might partially confound their distinction.

Nevertheless, as already noted, Hegelian sympathy has little to do with compassion. Rather, having an afterfeeling or imitating another's feeling (*Nachempfinden*) involves the (partial) negation of the other and the self. Juggling identity and difference includes that one speak in another's voice while twisting his words.[40] Rather than compassionately affirming the fullness and sincerity of someone's feeling, Hegelian sympathy moves the other and the self: it transports. We have begun to see in the last chapter, and will discuss it further in this and the remaining chapters, that emotion, for Hegel, is always mediated intersubjectively and across a temporal lag. All emotion, thus, necessarily takes the shape of sympathy in the sense of afterfeeling or *Nachempfinden* (be it a sympathy with oneself). At the same time, *Nachempfinden* (in the sense of "adapting from") opens a future for transports because it calls for further textual enactments (or readings) of emotional judgments.

It becomes clear, then, that the emotional labor Hegel is concerned with has an ethical bent (if a somewhat perverse one). The "attention" and "exertion" that Hegel demands of the speculative philosopher consists in renouncing vanity and instead bearing the shame of risking sympathy (§ 58). The method of speculative philosophy thus shapes the relations between self and other. It helps the emotionally thinking and reading subject to identify with what at first appears as alien.[41]

With his opaque writing, Hegel responds to the violence he registers in conventional reading acts. Hegel specifies that the straightforward meaning that clever argumentation retains by avoiding the difficulty of attending to an unstable rhythm is, in fact, a negative one, or simply the negation of the subject-matter: "clever argumentation conducts itself negatively towards the content apprehended; it knows how to refute it and reduce it to nothing" (§ 59). The argumentative reader has everything already understood; her purely intellectual or formal knowledge, then, negates the otherness of the other by capturing it in a knowledge statement. Or she quickly makes up her mind and says: "*A rose is a rose* means nothing." In both cases, she is able to position herself above the "object" of her thought:

> Instead of entering into the immanent content of the subject-matter, the understanding always surveys [*übersieht*] the whole and stands above the individual existence of which it speaks, or, what amounts to the same thing, it does not see it at all. However, scientific cognition in fact requires that it give itself over to the life of the object. (§ 53, trans. modified)[42]

From the scientific thinker, that is, the speculative reader, Hegel demands sympathy with the life of the subject matter.

Sympathetic reading and sympathetic knowledge partially negate not only the other but also the self. They spring from the acknowledgment of self-difference.[43] Sympathetic "identification," for Hegel, does not consist in the affirmative recognition of the inner contents of other minds. Rather, "what is shared . . . is sharing itself, and consequently everyone's nonidentity, each one's nonidentity to himself and to others" (Nancy 1991, 66). The ethics of Hegelian sympathy thus destroys individual integrity. Rather than trying to preserve the unity of indivisibility, the subject opens to the self-difference and emotionality of the concept and becomes self-dissonant, unsettled, and emotional. Negativity thus plays an important part in Hegel's version of sympathy. "It is death—but if one is permitted to say so, it is not a tragic death . . . it is death as sharing and exposure. It is not murder—it is not death as extermination" (Nancy 1991, 66–67). The loss of self on either side must only be partial if this movement of comprehension is not to end in nothingness. The concept half-exerts itself by dancing to (at least) two different measures.

Reading Hegel's prose resembles reading a poem aloud: one hesitates as to where to put the accent—is it in accordance with the meter, or with the syntax, or with the stress of the meaning? What if all three differ from one another? Where to articulate the beat? When to rest the foot? The reader feels herself checked halfway through the sentence, gets lost, and is forced to go back, to repeat the reading in order to find the subject. Subject and predicate exchange positions. Back and forth. Predicative propositions are by law irreversible, but the speculative judgment breaks this law to construct its rhythm. Rhythm "changes direction," as Deleuze and Guattari have it (Deleuze and Guattari 1987, 313). The speculative philosopher reads propositions backward and forward. Such reading acts transform linearity into textuality and create plasticity.

The *Phenomenology* as a whole is one unendingly plastic—shape-taking—emotional judgment. I read the *Phenomenology* as the meticulous exposition of all the conflicts and contradictions Hegel could detect in the one infinite judgment that is the self-reflection of spirit. The different figures of consciousness in the *Phenomenology* articulate this emotional judgment in progress while consciousness reads itself differently in each of its shapes: consciousness is a consciousness is a consciousness is a consciousness. The *Phenomenology* in its entirety provides the speculative reading of this one judgment: the self-differentiation of spirit, across which spirit appears to itself by negating itself again and again. Speculative reading refuses to reduce the proposition to one single and straight meaning. The union of subject and predicate allows for difference while their absolute difference accepts being articulated as identical: "Rose is a rose is a rose is a rose."[44] While Rose is ceaselessly signifying rose and multiplying particularity without aspiration to the universal, the repetition also articulates her self-differentiality.

This kind of reading undermines the logic of argumentation by refusing to answer the question: "What is a speculative proposition?"[45] Nancy suggests, "We shall not reply to the question: Hegelian discourse nowhere does so. But it is against it, along it or on its edge, that we shall see Hegelian discourse being laid out, used and scattered, to the very extent that it is forced to change its form" (Nancy 2001, 77). "Hegel has already subtracted his text from the logic of argumentation, from the play of the *Gegenreden*" and responses (Nancy 2001, 11). Against and alongside predication, speculative writing prolongs the reading. And as this reading takes shape, moving back and forth in endless repetition, Hegel's discourse transforms, if ever so slightly. It begins to verge on poetry.[46]

Hegel's quasi-verse takes part in conventional logic while taking it apart. Not only does his strategy of seduction entangle the reader in the movement of the speculative, but it also leaves his own writing trapped in the logic of predication. In order to seduce the reader to give up her aloof position and superior authority, to renounce her vanity and to move with the content, Hegel himself has to write with, instead of about and above (*über*), the subject matter. "Speaking nearby or together with certainly differs from speaking for and about" (Trinh 1989, 101). But if he wants to stand a chance of being accepted when asking the reader for a dance, Hegel needs to speak the language of his philosophical audience, the language of judgments and of formal logic. His exposition therefore must be divided within.

Hegel does not invent an idiom that would unambiguously express speculative movements. In order to appear, spirit borrows the form of judgments: "It is worth remembering that the dialectical movement likewise has propositions for its parts or elements. Thus, the highlighted difficulty seems to recur continually" (§ 66). Spirit's self-reflection requires that spirit abandon itself to finite assertions. Whether it will grasp itself across that difference remains an open question.

What is meant as interplay between predicative judgment and speculative judgment can always be read simply as predication. "The philosophical proposition, because it is a proposition [a *Satz*], evokes the common opinion about both the usual relationship between subject and predicate and the customary procedure of knowledge" (§ 63). Hegel conceives of the speculative as a movement, yet every sentence (*Satz*) is set (*gesetzt*) according to grammatical and logical laws (*Gesetze*), which Hegel is not ready to break. Hegel does not invent a language different from the one that can be read as predicative judgment. There is no new speculative language which escapes the spider web of predicative judgments spun by blood-sucking concepts (to invoke Nietzsche). There is no strictly speculative idiom that avoids finite thought and precludes argumentative reading by corresponding only to the speculative movement of the concept. Herein lays the passion of the new science that gives the reader the power to transport the text—despite the often-repeated fact that Hegel's texts feel like mousetraps.

Infinite judgments might best perform the exertion and attentiveness of the concept. In them, difference does not remain locked in or *eingeschlossen,* but gets disclosed or *aufgeschlossen.*[47] The labor of the concept consists in reaching through (*durchgreifen*) and joining what is commonly regarded as incompatible. Infinite judgments posit the incongruous as identical: for example, "the I is a thing," "spirit is a bone," or "poetry is a hedgehog." But these judgments make no sense in the context of traditional logic. For traditional logic—which is bound up with metaphysical ontology—mind and body or body and soul are incompatible.[48] Against the foil of traditional logic, it becomes clear, then, that it is neither mysticism nor metaphoric speech when Hegel describes the concept as a life-giving force. We call it life when spirit gets embodied or when a body is moved by soul. Life—the interpenetration of body and spirit—becomes possible, then, because the concept juggles both.

Yet such life is always haunted by death. "Spirit is a bone" can always be read as a straightforward assertion. It would not even be incorrect, or against speculative logic, to say that spirit is a dead thing, inert and defenselessly exposed to the abstractions of clever argumentation. "Taken just as it stands, that judgment is devoid of spirit, or rather is itself the epitome of what it is to be devoid of spirit. However, in terms of its *concept,* it is in fact the richest in spirit" (§ 790, trans. modified). Speculatively comprehended, this infinite judgment manifests the power of spirit to join the disjointed. It is a precarious power, however—because spirit depends on others to read itself. Precisely because the speculative links the incompatible, the spheres it links can always fall apart.

Traditional logic accepts infinite judgments only in their negative form. Even Hegel mentions only the negatively infinite judgment (with examples like "spirit is not red," "the rose is not an elephant," and "the understanding is not a table") in his *Science of Logic* (Hegel 1989, 642). When the infinite judgment is taken literally (which is always possible), we are in the realm of the negatively infinite judgment, and that means the death of the life of spirit: "Similarly death [is] a negatively infinite judgment . . . in death, as we ordinarily say, body and soul part, i.e., subject and predicate utterly diverge [*auseinanderfallen*]" (Hegel 1975a, §173, *Zusatz*). Death passes through the speculative judgments—and Hegel juggles identity and difference to keep them alive.[49]

The precariousness of speculative unions can provoke violence. Hegel is almost ready to smash the face of anyone who reminds him of this tenuousness: "The retort here would really have to go as far as smashing the skull of the person who makes a statement like that in order to demonstrate to him in a manner as palpable as his wisdom that for a person a bone is nothing in-itself and is even less *his* true actuality" (§ 339). Speculative sympathy includes anger, fear, despair, and grief. *Tropes of Transport* traces these figures of emotionality in the Hegelian text. The source of the text's power and fragility—its emotionality—lies, however, in its divided language that juggles argumentative and speculative syntax. Hegel's speculative thought is infected to the core with the abstract logic of the understanding. Power is shared: "in fact, non-speculative thinking also has its rights, which are valid"; and such power-sharing requires the ceaseless renegotiation of the terms of their disunity, and an incessant mediation and exposure to negativity (§ 65). In short, there is a constant demand for the work of emotionality.

5

Acknowledging

They *acknowledge* themselves as *mutually acknowledging each other.*
—*Phenomenology,* § 184

The title of this chapter translates *Anerkennen*—in Hegel's trope of *gegenseitiges Anerkennen*—as "acknowledging" rather than using the standard translation, which is "recognition." Let me explain this choice. "Recognition" has two meanings in English. The first meaning presupposes a prior knowledge of what or whom one now encounters again. To recognize is to identify again something or somebody one has seen before. This would be *Erkennen* or *Wiedererkennen* in German. Secondly, "to recognize somebody" means to appreciate or to formally confer a status of value onto someone. This second use comes indeed very close to the German *Anerkennung,* but the prefix *re* reinscribes the sense of retrospection and repetition, which is not there in the German. In order to recognize somebody *as* embodying a certain value one needs to have a prior knowledge of this value. We need to have norms in place, against the background of which we can confer or receive recognition. Even in the sense of appreciation or of conferring a status of value onto somebody, recognition thus requires either the prior existence of that which is recognized declaratively, or—if we follow the "constitutive" theory of recognition, which contends that the act of recognition creates the status of the recognized —recognition still requires a prior knowledge of what such a status might entail. In any case, whether performative or constative, both senses of re-cognition match a currently encountered object or situation with a preexisting notion or memory of it.

Gegenseitiges Anerkennen, in Hegel's *Phenomenology,* is not based on previous knowledge. At the beginning of the chapter on self-consciousness—where the account of *Anerkennen* is located—the subject has no preexisting notion of who or what the other might be because it has never encountered another subject before. So far, it has been a consciousness and, as such, has related only to a world of objects. It also has no positive knowledge of itself or of what might constitute self-consciousness, since its very young "self-certainty" has, until now, only consisted in negating the empirical world. It is, thus, a mistake to assume that the parties involved in the movement of acknowledging identify each other *as* something or someone in particular. And if they did, they would have fallen back to the status of consciousness and would treat each other as objects, rather than subjects.[1]

Hegel shows how self-consciousness comes to life in the plural as the movement of mutual acknowledging (*gegenseitiges Anerkennen*). They "*acknowledge* themselves as *mutually acknowledging each other* [*sie anerkennen sich als gegenseitig sich annerkennend*]" (§ 184, trans. modified). Without a preexisting notion of what they might be and without coming to a substantive conclusion about each other, subjects emerge as the movement of self-reflection without any content other than this movement itself. "*An*" signifies a movement-toward without a certain aim, while "re" suggests a doubling back to a preexisting notion or object. This is why I choose the verb "acknowledge" to translate *anerkennen*. It renders the tentativeness as well as the togetherness of *anerkennen* in its prefix "ac" (as in "accord") and thus relates the emergence of a "knowledging along with," as it were.

Such mutual and shared acknowledgment without any substantive notion of subjectivity can obviously not arrive at a judgment, be it a judgment of knowledge (in the modes of *Erkennen* or *Wiedererkennen*), or a value judgment (in the mode of *Anerkennung*).[2] Hegel thus clearly conceives of acknowledging as a movement in progress (not a completed act). Current political and legal discourse on recognition treats recognition as a relatively stable good that can be conferred or received, withheld or demanded. When this discourse takes place in German, it operates with the word *Anerkennung*. The suffix *-ung* points to the stable and regulated character of such an evaluation as well as to its sense of completion. But Hegel does not use the term *Anerkennung* in the *Phenomenology*.[3] He prefers to turn the verb *anerkennen* into a noun—*das Anerkennen*, preferably in the phrase: *die Bewegung des Anerkennens* (the movement of acknowledging)—because he is concerned here with an unfinished movement (§ 178, trans. modified). I render the continuous character of this movement with the gerund. The movement of mutual acknowledging is necessarily shared, but—because of its incompleteness—it does not produce recognition as a good to be exchanged in reciprocity.

Mutual Penetration and Mutual Embrace

In this chapter I will explore and critique the different valences of *Anerkennen*. In order to do so, I will branch out into a discussion of two poems, Goethe's "Wiederfinden," written about ten years after the publication of the *Phenomenology*, and Hölderlin's "Andenken," written just a few years before. *Wiederfinden* relates to *Anerkennen* on the semantic level, whereas *Andenken* participates in a chain of signifiers—from *Andacht* to *Andenken* to *Anerkennen*—that challenges those readings of Hegel that see him making claims to completion and perfection. We will see that Goethe's poem presents an image of perfection and completion while also establishing the world-spiritual three-step that is often attributed to Hegel (naive identity, separation through reflection, reunion on a higher level). While in Goethe's poem truth is static and love hierarchical, Hölderlin's poem (like Hegel's philosophy) pursues the question of how to foster the always transient movement of mutual solicitude and participation.

Before discussing in more detail what Hegel's *Anerkennen* or acknowledging entails, I would like, in this first section, to more firmly establish the contrast between acknowledging and recognizing. We have said that all recognition (appreciation, conferral of status, or identification) involves an element of remembering. The German equivalent that highlights this aspect of recognition would be *Wiedererkennen*, which is also the literal translation of recognition: re (*wieder*) and cognition (*Erkennen*). *Wiederfinden* is another entry in the same semantic field. Translated literally as "re-finding," *wiederfinden* means to recover something or someone and to find this thing or person identical even after a period of separation. Let us turn now to the poem from Goethe's *West-Eastern Divan*:[4]

> ***Wiederfinden***
> *Ist es möglich! Stern der Sterne,*
> *Drück ich wieder dich ans Herz!*
> *Ach, was ist die Nacht der Ferne*
> *Für ein Abgrund, für ein Schmerz.*
> *Ja, du bist es! meiner Freuden*
> *Süßer, lieber Widerpart;*
> *Eingedenk vergangner Leiden,*
> *Schaudr ich vor der Gegenwart.*
>
> *Als die Welt im tiefsten Grunde*
> *Lag an Gottes ewger Brust,*
> *Ordnet' er die erste Stunde*

Mit erhabner Schöpfungslust,
Und er sprach das Wort: Es werde!
Da erklang ein schmerzlich Ach!
Als das All mit Machtgebärde
In die Wirklichkeiten brach.

Auf tat sich das Licht: so trennte
Scheu sich Finsternis von ihm,
Und sogleich die Elemente
Scheidend auseinanderfliehn.
Rasch, in wilden, wüsten Träumen
Jedes nach der Weite rang,
Starr, in ungemeßnen Räumen,
Ohne Sehnsucht, ohne Klang.

Stumm war alles, still und öde,
Einsam Gott zum ersten Mal!
Da erschuf er Morgenröte,
Die erbarmte sich der Qual;
Sie entwickelte dem Trüben
Ein erklingend Farbenspiel,
Und nun konnte wieder lieben,
Was erst auseinanderfiel.

Und mit eiligem Bestreben
Sucht sich, was sich angehört,
Und zu ungemeßnem Leben
Ist Gefühl und Blick gekehrt.
Sei's Ergreifen, sei es Raffen,
Wenn es nur sich faßt und hält!
Allah braucht nicht mehr zu schaffen,
Wir erschaffen seine Welt.

So, mit morgenroten Flügeln,
Riß es mich an deinen Mund,
Und die Nacht mit tausend Siegeln
Kräftigt sternenhell den Bund.
Beide sind wir auf der Erde
Musterhaft in Freud und Qual,
Und ein zweites Wort: Es werde!
Trennt uns nicht zum zweitenmal.
(*West-Östlicher Divan*, 1815)

The first stanza conjures a scene of recognition between two lovers: "O can it be!" (*Ist es möglich!*)—"Yes, it is you" (*Ja, du bist es!*). Beyond this specific encounter, the exclamation that opens the poem—"O can it be!"—ponders the condition of the possibility of recognition in general. The poem's answer lies in the projection of a previous familiarity. The title of the poem is "Wiederfinden." By the second verse, the encounter of the lovers is established as a reprise: "I press you to my heart again!" (*Drück ich wieder dich ans Herz!*). And the fourth stanza postulates the breakup of a previous union as the condition for the possibility of love: "everything that fell apart / Now could fall in love again." Even *Widerpart,* in the sixth line of the first stanza (which means "opponent" or "opposite party," with *wider* spelled without an *e*) phonetically joins the three *wieder* of the poem—especially since *Widerpart* and its rhyme and semantic echo *Gegenwart* (*wider* and *gegen* both mean "against") together bracket and embrace the activity of recalling (*eingedenk*) in the seventh line. For Goethe, to love (*lieben*) means to love again ("*wieder lieben,*" fourth stanza); love must be grounded in a previous union just as knowledge must take the form of re-cognition.

The scene of recognition is repeatedly interrupted by the memory of separation—"chasm is the night" (*Nacht der Ferne*), "far apart, what pain!" (*Abgrund, Schmerz*), "bygone suffering I recall" (*eingedenk vergangner Leiden*)—but this disturbance also intensifies the lovers' reunion. The "shudder" (*schaudr ich vor der Gegenwart*) that allows the lyrical "I" a trembling dis-identification with the "present time" (across the interfering past) could be a true form of emotionality or lighthearted transport in the sense I propose. Yet, it functions here to dramatize and consolidate unification, rather than to emotionalize or destabilize identity.

The most substantial distraction from the present encounter, the drift into the mythical narrative that spans three stanzas, securely establishes in its very first line the preexistence of primordial cosmic love: "When the world lay in the depths / Utmost on God's eternal breast" (*Als die Welt im tiefsten Grunde / Lag an Gottes ewger Brust,* trans. modified). This preexisting love grounds and enables the scene of recognition between the two lovers of the first stanza. The lyrical "I" can recognize the other as its *Widerpart,* its "image, . . . rhyme," as that which "belong[s]" to it (*was* [ihm] *angehört*), because they had lain in each other's arms before. The same applies for the relation between God and world. God has a preconceived notion of his other. Before he creates the world through a constitutive act of recognition—conferring the status of independent being—the world already exists (whether physically laying on God's breast or existing as an idea that is close to his heart). There are, thus, two layers of recognition here: the recognition of the other's separate being ("*Es werde!*") and then the recognition of the other as the lyrical "I"'s "*you*" ("Yes, it is you"). The first recognition performs the first act of analysis and thereby initiates reflection and explicit understanding. Yet this realm of analysis is here staunchly described as lacking love. The second recognition is possible only in love—that is to say, through two layers of remembering: remembering the painful separation and remembering the (even deeper) union. In sum, the poem tells a story of three stages that is rather typical for the early nineteenth century: initial union without freedom and reflection, freedom and reflection through separation, reunion and reconciliation of the two prior stages. The question that interests me here is whether the third stage does indeed afford both a loving reflection that acknowledges the other's freedom, and a self-reflective love that encourages the self's freedom. And what is its conception of freedom?

Hegel describes reflection as an impersonal activity: as the movement of the concept. The concept envelops all and indwells in everything. As "an infinite and creative form, which includes . . . the fullness of all content," it is absolutely comprehensive (Hegel 1975a, § 160, *Zusatz*). And it also acts from within each individual being: "Things are what they are through the action of the concept, immanent in them, and revealing itself in them" (Hegel 1975a, § 163, *Zusatz* 2, trans. modified). The concept's activity consists in mutually self-penetrating and mutually self-embracing. (I apologize for this awkward phrasing, but the distinction between self and other is really not stable when it comes to the movement of the concept.)

On the one hand, the concept generates and embraces totalities—as when Hegel suggests that the concept underwrites the integrity of the *Phenomenology*'s path ("By virtue of the movement of the concept, this path will encompass [*umfassen*] the complete worldliness of consciousness in its necessity," § 34). But this embrace is only one aspect of the concept's movement. The other aspect of its movement is that it empties itself and grants everything an independent existence: it "at the same time releases from itself the fullness of all content" (Hegel 1975a, § 160, *Zusatz*). The totality that is produced by the enveloping activity of the concept is contained and curtailed by the ambiguity of the concept, which always oscillates between comprising and dispersing or appropriation and externalization.

Hegel's discussion of conscience offers a good example for the curtailment of totality. It also very nicely stages what we have discussed in the last chapter as the juggle of the concept. Like a line of poetry that resists a quick reading and calls to be reread with a different intonation, the concept moves from one aspect of its movement to another by rereading itself and placing the accent differently the second time:

> Insofar as the moment of *universality* exists in this knowledge, it is part and parcel of the knowledge of conscientious action that it comprehensively grasp [*umfassen*] the actuality before it in an unrestricted manner and that it thus both precisely know the circumstances of the case and take everything into consideration. However, since it is *acquainted* with universality as a *moment*, this knowledge of these circumstances is thus the kind of knowledge which is fully aware that it does not comprehensively grasp [*umfassen*] them, that is, it is aware that it is not therein conscientious. (§ 642)

The stress on universality allows for a comprehensive embrace, but once a different emphasis has brought into view that such totality is in fact partial (that it is only a "moment"), the totality has de facto disintegrated. The other aspect of the concept's movement thus consists in letting itself be penetrated and separated from itself. Only non-reflective self-naturalizing substantiality "resists all invasion" (*nichts in sich eindringen lassen will;* Hegel 1975a, § 159). The example of "sense certainty"—a form of consciousness that refuses self-reflection and preserves its truth "as a relation remaining in parity with itself [*sich selbst gleichbleibende*] . . . and into which . . . no disparity [*Unterschied*] at all can force its entry [*eindringen*]"—shows *ex negativo* that the concept moves against such selfsame integrity and instead invites division (§ 104). In short, the concept is (self-) totalizing and (self-)fragmenting, infinite and finite, at the same time.

At first take, Goethe's poem seems to suggest a similar dynamic. The third stage of its narrative is characterized by a sense of life as both finite (because individual) and infinite or "measureless" (*ungemeßnem*). It combines the unifying feeling of love with the eye's faculty for discrimination: "Sight and feeling hurtle them / Back to life that's measureless" (*Und zu ungemeßnem Leben / Ist Gefühl und Blick gekehrt*). The word *Ergreifen* (grasp) in the next line echoes Hegel's *Begriff.* Yet the rest of the line is a bit more disturbing. *Raffen* means something like "reap" and carries overtones of obsession and ruthlessness. With the lines, "Grasp or snatch, no matter how, / Take hold they must, if they're to be" (*Sei's Ergreifen, sei es Raffen, / Wenn es nur sich faßt und hält!*), Goethe seems to suggest that the means do not matter as long as the embrace is tight. This begs the question whether the third stage, which is supposed to reconcile love with freedom and understanding, doesn't give freedom a raw deal, and whether it does so perhaps because it overcompensates for the void associated with the second phase.

The second phase is experienced as "stiffened" (*starr*), "void, and mute, and still" (*stumm, . . . still und öde*), and characterized by "solitude" (*einsam*), because of an absence of feeling, especially of love. The only feeling mentioned in those three stanzas is "diffidence" (*Scheu*). We will see in a later section of this chapter that Hegel considers shyness (he uses the word *Scham*) to be a speculative transport that draws lovers together by pulling them apart. For Hölderlin, *Scheue* works similarly. But the love of Goethe's poem is "without longing" (*ohne Sehnsucht*). It doesn't draw together; it only repels in search of independence. The god of this poem repairs the situation with a more instrumental than sublime second act of creation: "then he made the rose of dawn" (*Da erschuf er Morgenröte*). According to Benjamin Hederich's *Gründliches mythologisches Lexikon*—Goethe's preferred source on Greco-Roman mythology—Aurora was punished by Venus with an insatiable desire for love, and her role in this poem's mythical account of genesis is to provide the necessary desire (*Sehnsucht*) to counteract the drive for independence. Goethe thus divides into two different emotions the double pull that characterizes shyness in Hegel and Hölderlin. Of course, we could read "the rose of dawn" as a figure for *Scheu:* the blushing of the morning after, the rosy glow that veils the stark contrast between "light" (*Licht*) and "dark" (*Finsternis*). The rose of dawn invents a game of hues and harmonies to distract from the abyss (*Abgrund*) and to mediate between the elements that "fell apart" (*auseinanderfiel*) and "clove apart" (*auseinanderfliehn*). But as we will see, the fact that the mediation is an aesthetic one—the beautiful semblance of harmony—has an important impact on the experience of love and freedom created by this poem.

The reconciliation through the aesthetics of beauty that the morning-red affords is mirrored by Goethe's poem as a whole. Despite its insistent evocations of pain, separation, and death, the poem ends firmly on the positive note of unassailable unification: "And a second word 'Become!' / Shall not tear us apart again" (*Und ein zweites Wort: Es werde! / Trennt uns nicht zum zweitenmal*). With its six stanzas of equal length and its consistent cross rhyme (ababcdcd), the poem impresses balance and harmony on the ear and the eye. It is a perfectly organized, well-rounded, and unified piece of beauty. And so are its characters: the two lovers are described as "exemplars" (*musterhaft*); they represent the most beautiful of humanity in both joy and pain (*Freud und Qual*). The beloved stands out among the many as "star of stars" (*Stern der Sterne*) and the lyrical "I" reflects itself in the image of God when it tells the mythical story of God's separation from the world. At no point does the evocation of primordial cosmic events become seriously threatening because the two stanzas presenting individual human love (the first and the last stanza) literally bracket and contain the cosmic love and breakup that is dealt with in the middle stanzas. There is pain here, but no excess or ecstasy. Even the sublime delight of God (*mit erhabner Schöpfungslust*) is restrained by human measure, which calibrates the unified into the unique (even though, as we have seen, unification requires repetition) by putting an end to repetition from here on: "*nicht zum zweitenmal.*" At last, the savage and desolate dreams (*wilde, wüste Träume*) of primordial lust and flight are reined in by the beautiful image that shows the cosmic powers (all the stars in the universe) reduced to witnesses to the marriage of these two exemplary individuals: "Starbright with a thousand seals / Night the bond will ratify" (*Und die Nacht mit tausend Siegeln / Kräftigt sternenhell den Bund*).

In such play of mirrors between universality and individuality, the sense for plurality—that is to say, the sense for real differences—gets lost. Everything echoes the exemplary couple. What is more, there is no indication of mutual love within the couple. Just as the play of mirrors between the human and the divine or between individuality and universality establishes a clear hierarchy in favor of the human individual, there is a hierarchy within the couple so strong that we get no sense for the freedom of the beloved. The only time she (the poem does suggest the feminine gender) has an independent existence, this existence is experienced as "void, and mute, and still."

The unification that is realized under the sign of taking hold (*sich faßt und hält*) establishes the singular. If this love allows for freedom, it is the freedom of one, and freedom means self-sufficiency. The tight grip on the other of *fassen* and *halten* affords the one his *Fassung* (composure) and *Haltung* (poise). It realizes an aesthetics of balance and composure that disavows vulnerability, struggle, emotionality, and difference within the couple. Mutuality has no value here; instead, the lyrical "I" loves itself. Satisfied with itself, it has overcome division. Just as the lyrical "I" has no need for an independent lover, this poem does not need the reader. It is perfect in itself. The poem is the image of self-sufficiency. Goethe might offer a specific account of love with "*Wiederfinden*," but he is not looking for love. He has found it already. Hegel's *Phenomenology of Spirit*, on the other hand, needs readers. Only through the reader, in the identificatory journey of reading along the path of spirit, does spirit actually gain an awareness of itself.

Luck of Love

Hegel's style demands a reading of love.[5] It does so in both senses of the phrase. It demands a practice of reading that engages the reader in a—for a philosophical work perhaps unusually sensual—love relationship with the text. And it demands a reading of the trope of love—or, to be more precise, the trope of "mutual acknowledging"—that we find in the text and that also structures the text.[6]

The fact that *The Phenomenology of Spirit* demands love means that it isn't sure of it. In the previous section we discussed a poem where love (between two individuals, between world and God) is presupposed as a given. There, I have also begun to explain that Hegel understands the "concept" as a mutual physical-cum-intellectual penetration and embrace of subject and object, or of self and other, or of different "moments" of the concept, like individuality and universality. Nevertheless, Hegel never presents such interpenetration as a given. Even when he describes interpenetration—as he does in the section on mutual acknowledging—his account is so obviously ideal that it cannot quite produce the impression of present existence. The text asks for love: it asks the reader to acknowledge, that is to say, to join and share the movement of mutual acknowledging, in order to actualize—imperfectly—what the author can only offer as an ideal. The text's call for love is not a desire for recognition.

The *Phenomenology* tries to seduce the reader to join its conceptual movements. It doesn't allow her to remain at a distance, safely withdrawn. It doesn't offer itself to a quick opening of the optical lens. It wants the reader to expose herself to the phenomenological development and to engage with it—to enter the text and to let herself be enveloped by it, but also to take it in and be unsettled and altered by it. It demands a mutual penetration and a mutual embrace of reader and text.

Rather than stringing together thoughts (*Gedanken*), the *Phenomenology* proceeds by way of concepts (*Begriffe*). Hegel wrote in his notebook while working on the *Phenomenology:* "*Thoughts* are not so much the issue anymore. We have enough of them, good and bad, beautiful and bold. Rather, *concepts* are the issue" (Hegel 2002, 251, trans. modified). The difference that he establishes between "thoughts" and "concepts" is one between stasis and movement: he suggests—perhaps counterintuitively, but coherently throughout his work—that "thoughts" denote the end of the activity of thinking, whereas concepts move and motivate one to think. Concepts dynamically realize thought. "Thoughts," on the other hand, are fixed and compact; they can be easily appropriated ("we have enough of them"). Yet, even though they come in all varieties to suit every taste—"good and bad, beautiful and bold"—to possess thoughts doesn't yield much satisfaction for Hegel. Uninterested in ownership, he desires the interaction with a free subject. With the *Phenomenology,* Hegel is looking for love.

Just as they are easily appropriated, "thoughts" are easily exchanged from one person to another. They are universal currency, accepted by everyone because their value is stamped on their face: "thoughts" are "through themselves immediately made valid," Hegel's aphorism continues (ibid.). Similar to Descartes' "intuitions," Hegel's "thoughts" immediately present themselves as common sense. But to have them does not mean to penetrate or to embrace them.

"Concepts," on the other hand, are neither good, nor beautiful, nor bold; they are embarrassing: "But in that thoughts are through themselves immediately made valid, whereas concepts, on the contrary, must be made comprehensible, the form of writing thereby undergoes a change and acquires a form of appearance demanding a perhaps painful and embarrassing [*peinlich*] effort" (Hegel 2002, 251, trans. modified). Concepts do not immediately offer a clear picture of their value. They thus produce embarrassment. Concepts exhibit themselves without presenting a face. They don't represent but come naked (skinless, even) and demand of the readers to similarly denude themselves. This is not a pretty picture. Unlike "representational thinking" (*Vorstellungsdenken*), the concept doesn't provide images that are easily absorbed. Instead, the movement of concepts involves groping, touching, trying and tasting. It seduces the reader to the humiliating labor of *Selbstdenken*, a thinking that engages the embodied, desiring, experiencing subject while exposing it to change: "The last royal road in studying is thinking for oneself [*Selbstdenken*]" (Hegel 2002, 251).

The text of the *Phenomenology* demands a more than cursory penetration from the reader. Thoroughly, not just with one organ from which the mind has withdrawn, but completely naked, with her bare hands, lips, and nose, the reader is asked to open skin after skin until her body reaches fluidity and drinks the slime of the written. Some reject this gift: "They stick their noses straight into the texts—and immediately withdraw them, choking and gasping for air" (McCumber 1986, 641).[7] More than embarrassing, concepts can be repulsive, even painful. Barely having received the gift, some spit out the slimy fluid that isn't easily swallowed. It sticks between the roof of the mouth and the root of the tongue and forms threads in the throat. Like Schelling, they hastily and with clattering chimes retire into their shell, and spit the stuff at Hegel's feet. They refuse to digest what seems indigestible.[8]

Hegel must have been very offended by the fact that Schelling didn't read past the preface of the *Phenomenology*. He could become furious when people—let alone one of his best friends—looked for quick answers in easily digestible bites instead of responding to the embarrassing exposure of the concept by exposing themselves to its movement in return.[9] With an ironic attack he anticipates the scene of injury in the preface to the *Phenomenology,* expressing his indignation at readers who barely touch a book and yet believe they got its main ideas:

> No matter how much a man asks for a royal road to science, no more convenient and comfortable way can be suggested to him than to put his trust in healthy common sense; and then for what else remains, to advance simply with the times and with philosophy and to read reviews of philosophical works, perhaps even go so far as to read the prefaces and the first paragraphs of the works themselves. (§ 70)

One of Hegel's strategies to foil readerly shortcuts is to produce an indigestible preface, one that sticks in the reader's throat and prolongs the contact. For more than fifty pages, Hegel refuses to write a preface. Instead, he argues against summarizing his arguments and forces the reader to turn around in circles without understanding a thing. Slowly, his preface undresses its readers and strips them of everything they know and everything they rightfully expect. It is the foreplay to the lovemaking of concepts.

Promise of Vulnerability

The lovemaking of the concept is a grasping that both penetrates and embraces. It involves mutual exposure and mutual solicitude. Hegel describes acknowledging as a "movement of self-consciousness in its relation to another self-consciousness," that is, as an act of mediation that engenders the self as double or, rather, as plural (§ 182).[10] Common parlance often describes the self-mediating movement of the concept as "self-reflection." Unfortunately, "reflection" comes with the ballast of a visual notion of thought. *Selbstvermittlung,* or self-mediation—the term Hegel actually uses—is indeed not visual. In addition, "mediation" introduces a third element into the dyad—a medium that has its own materiality and subjectivity, as it were, and that thus opens and exposes the closed relation of self-consciousness onto a multiplicity. If we use the term "self-reflection," we need to keep in mind the physical and even sometimes existential valences of penetration and embrace, exposure and care.[11] Hegelian "reflection" loses its critical potential if it is reduced to a *Wiedererkennen* of myself in the other or to a simple mirroring. As we have established in the opening section of this chapter, *Anerkennen* is not "recognition" in the sense of *Wiedererkennen;* it doesn't take place between two already established subjects but generates subjectivity as shared and exposed. This exposure takes concrete material, physical, sometimes even deadly forms.

The movement of self-reflection or self-mediation-with-another (ac-knowledging) introduces an important ambiguity (*Doppelsinnigkeit*) into the structure of the subject/s: "This twofold sense . . . lies in the essence of self-consciousness, which is to be infinite or immediately the opposite of the determinateness in which it is posited" (§ 178, trans. modified). This ambiguity prevents the subject/s from ever fully coinciding with themselves; it is the root of the constitutive emotionality of subjectivity. Hegel characterizes self-differentiality negatively as "negativity" (as self-conscious, I relentlessly question myself) and positively as "infinity" (self-negation moves me beyond any particular identity).

The ambiguity of self-consciousness—the fact that it opposes or negates itself as much as it affirms or identifies itself—creates a plural subject. Subject/s emerge in the plural. The subject/s' doubleness is duplicitous in the sense that they freely, and often imperceptibly to themselves and others, shift between inner dialogue and outward conversation—that they address themselves indirectly by way of addressing one another and are spoken by another when they mean to speak themselves.[12] All this is to say that, theoretically, ac-knowledging cannot be not mutual: "They *acknowledge* themselves as *mutually acknowledging each other*" (§ 184, trans. modified).

Yet the experience is usually quite different. Experience tells us that subjects do not necessarily engage in a reciprocal exchange of recognition. The fact that I gain recognition from you in no way forces me to give it back. On the contrary, if we expect reciprocity, we will most certainly be frustrated. The *Phenomenology* relentlessly paints scenes of failing reciprocity: beginning with the first figure of self-consciousness, whose fall from the ideal of mutual acknowledging ends the struggle for life and death in servitude, and ending with the last figure of spirit, who is provoked to the "highest rebellion" (*höchste Empörung*) by the fact that its admission of wrongdoing remains unilateral (§ 667). If reciprocity happened—and it is uncertain that it ever does—it would be by accident.[13] It cannot be brought about by the force of necessity that we invest in the dialectical process.

Granted, subject/s come to life through mutual acknowledging. That is to say, there is no subject that isn't being acknowledged in some way or another—otherwise, it wouldn't be a subject. "Self-consciousness exists *in* and *for itself* because and by way of its existing in and for itself for an other; i.e., it exists only as an acknowledged being [*als ein Anerkanntes*]" (§ 178, trans. modified). Yet the fact that subject/s come to life as inherently dialogical (and duplicitous in this dialogue) also means that they lose their independence or self-sufficiency (*Selbstständigkeit*) at the very moment that they gain it. It means, to put it in a somewhat different register, that the autonomous subject can legislate itself only when it posits itself as being bound by external forces.[14] Subjects are evidently more dejected by the loss of something they never had (self-sufficiency) than they are elated by the gain of something they cannot do without (a mutual relation). Due to this strong frustration, self-sufficiency becomes the dominant trope in the subject's unending self-mediation; it will be pursued with an obsessive *Begierde* and ruthless hunger that is reminiscent of Goethe's *Raffen* ("Grasp or snatch, no matter how") in "Wiederfinden."[15]

The desire for independence and self-sufficiency (the lost promise of subject formation) translates into a negative relation to the entire realm of alterity—into a need to treat all other subjects as objects and all objects as something to be either destroyed or absorbed into the self. On the phenomenological path, the movement of acknowledging develops out of the movement of *Begierde*. Even though the subject enjoys the power to destroy, it meets the limits of its ability to negate the other in the infinity of its object. No destruction is definitive. For every head it severs, two new ones grow from the wound. Its desire never reaches full and lasting satisfaction, but feeds on its own accomplishments. The desiring consciousness is therefore forced to acknowledge the object of its desire as another subject that is as self-sufficient and ecstatic as itself—one that is infinite in its own right and freely exercises its own negativity, but is also exposed and vulnerable in its relation to alterity. Out of unsatisfied appetite, another self-consciousness is born as inassimilably different from yet fundamentally bound to the first. Hegel's treatment of Faust—Goethe's glorious drama of *Begierde*, which Hegel alludes to in the section on "Pleasure and Necessity" of the chapter on "Reason"—shows the same experience in its temporal aspect. According to Hegel, Faust realizes that he cannot undo what he has done (abandon Gretchen): he realizes that his current self cannot absorb his former self. Because his prior self retains an inassimilable independence, Faust must ac-knowledge his prior actions.

Begierde aims at assimilating all that is external to the form of present consciousness (fantasized as pure self-transparency). Mutual acknowledging, in contrast, affects consciousness with opacity. It opens self-consciousness's pure being-for-self onto an inassimilable beyond, to the touch of an irreducible other. In this encounter with another self-consciousness, "consciousness . . . does indeed get *outside of itself* [*außer sich*]" (§ 184). For a moment only, Hegel's text gives us a taste of mutual acknowledging: it is a precarious movement shared with plural subjects, where each is "out of itself" yet sustained by another, without any one being in control of itself or of the whole movement—unable, for that matter, to guarantee its continuation. The default response of consciousness will be to deny the loss of self-sufficiency and to guard against the precariousness that comes with mutuality. What the trope of mutual acknowledging demands of us, therefore, ethically and politically, is to learn to experience exposure and vulnerability.

Charles Taylor has initiated an important discussion about the "need for recognition."[16] But why do we experience a need for recognition when, as we have seen, acknowledging cannot not be mutual?[17] In Taylor's account, subjects are not only driven by the desire for self-sufficiency, but they also want to be recognized as self-sufficient—as who they really are, as self-made men, or as artists whose most accomplished creations are themselves. All of these options define acknowledging as a re-cognition of preexisting independent identities. But precisely this kind of recognition interrupts mutuality. Taylor contends that our attempts to win positive (celebratory) and substantive recognition (*as* something) can fail. Hegel would say that they must fail, because we do not get to make our identities autonomously. But if substantive recognition is forced into existence—and this can be done through the power of individuals or the power of norms—such recognition fails the mutuality of acknowledging. Subjects emerge together, in a messy entanglement with others from whom they are not even clearly distinguishable. Who we are can only be provisionally determined in action, that is to say, in the interaction with (our) others.[18] Hegel shatters all dreams of complete self-sufficiency. But he also shows that the desire for self-sufficiency remains, and that this desire in turn ruins any utopia of a world without masters or servants.[19]

With the promise of self-sufficiency lost, and the relation within/between subject/s firmly established as a relation of dependency between a master and a servant, *Begierde* thus makes a comeback. Perhaps luckily so—after all, what would a love relation be without appetite! Yet, given the destructive legacy of *Begierde* in Hegel's *Phenomenology, Begierde* affects recognition in the form of a desire to kill the other. At the same time, the master's need for recognition inevitably turns against him. The master's controlling attitude toward recognition would be unnecessary if he didn't in fact have a need for recognition. Thus experiencing his own insufficiency—his need—he desires an other who can sovereignly grant recognition and who can provide him with the self-knowledge he doesn't possess on his own. Yet, the other of the master is not a self-sufficient subject. Rather, the other of the master embodies the fundamental condition of self-consciousness to be bound to an unassimilable other: he is the servant. The master thus finds his own recognition dependent on another who is vulnerable and not in control. The servant's vulnerability spurs the master's desire to kill him. The master needs to get this image of dependency out of his sight. He needs to put an end to the precarious movement of acknowledging. The threat of death, on the other hand, binds the servant only more securely to the master, and they both find themselves deeper and deeper mired in the catch-22 of their mutual dependency.

And yet there is an ethical side to the death wish. It is part of the subject/s' freedom. Mutual acknowledging depends on the desire to kill the other and the desire to kill the self. To be sure, literally killing the other or the self is a desperate—albeit deplorably frequent—attempt to put an end to mutual acknowledging. But exclusive and complete affirmation is not the solution to this problem. Of course, I have the desire to define myself and to establish a stable and recognizable (*wiedererkennbar*) identity, but every such recognition also deals a blow. The very act that affirms my identity and self-sufficiency negates my status as a self-mediating, infinite, and free subject. It denies "the essence of self-consciousness, which is to be . . . immediately the opposite of the determinateness in which it is posited," that is, it denies my condition of being-outside-myself-in-another (§ 178). To receive recognition, in the sense of respect for what or who one is, is never entirely rewarding because it truncates the constitutive ambiguity and duplicity (*Doppelsinnigkeit*) of subjectivity. I might be recognized in my subject position, but not in my *ekstasis* in relation to this position. Respect might give me security, but it probably fails to give me my vulnerability. I am free only if I can abandon my present self in favor of an uncertain future, an uncontrollable other, or an unwanted past: "It is solely by staking one's life that freedom is realized and proven [*bewährt*]" (§ 187, trans. modified). Nevertheless, it is also important to remember that such staking of one's life does not require the literality and earnestness of dramatic life changes, but can happen in the lighthearted and unprestigious manner of everyday life.[20]

As self-reflective beings born into freedom and mutuality, we find ourselves torn between a desire for affirmation and a desire for negation. It is our responsibility to respond to both. Hegel dramatizes the strict ambiguity of freedom in the "life and death struggle [*Kampf auf Leben und Tod*]" (§ 187). This is not a struggle for survival or supremacy, but a struggle for the "and" between life and death. The struggle for life and death figures the forbiddingly difficult and at the same time pleasurably lighthearted effort to realize the mutuality of self-consciousness in all its duplicity.

Struggle for Mutuality

Mutuality must be wrested from the vigorous resistance of subjects against the destabilizing effects of acknowledging. In order to explore this struggle for mutuality—or, more precisely, the struggle to acknowledge the always transient mutuality of acknowledging—it is now time to turn to Hölderlin's poem "Andenken." I will read the blowing of the wind presented by "Andenken" as a conversation between lovers—indeed as the intersection of several conversations: between Friedrich Hölderlin and Susette Gontard, between the poet and the reader, between Hölderlin and Hegel, and even between the familiar and the foreign.

For Hegel, speculative thought is a form of self-mediation. It takes place in the mode of ac-knowledging, that is to say, as a coming-to-know-along-with-another the subject as in many ways doubled, ambiguous, and duplicitous. Speculative thought can be embarrassing, painful, and thoroughly troubling; it renders the subject emotional because consciousness has to respond to and negotiate its doubling, as well as the resulting ambiguity and duplicity. In the last chapter, we have discussed how speculative thinking takes the physical shape of a dance—of somebody dancing to her own heartbeat, affecting her pulse with her dance moves and adjusting her movements in turn to the new beat; or of different bodies bringing different rhythms to bear on one another with not one of these dancers leading. In the current context of acknowledging, speculative thought manifests physically as mutual self-penetration and mutual self-embrace. Here as well, whom one is coming to penetrate and embrace changes in the process. Self-consciousness has no stable identity. It transforms when it is grasped (through being grasped, indeed) and is transported when it penetrates. Hölderlin casts this shared movement as a conversation. But the conversation is no less physical—it takes place through trees, rivers, and winds. The medium of the self-mediation among lovers has its own materiality and subjectivity and thus opens the closed relation of self-consciousness onto a multiplicity of self-relating bodies. Any truth about the subject is negated in its affirmation; the conversation between the lovers thus keeps changing the subject and consciousness indeed has to juggle a multiplicity of selves. Such plasticity, multivalency, and uncertainty are hard to take. It is always easier to stabilize the scene of mutual acknowledging by establishing recognition. But such recognition, we will see, can also mean death.

Working with the enjambements *Doch gut / Ist ein Gespräch* (But good / Is converse) and *Mancher / Trägt Scheue* (Some / Bear shyness [my translation]) as the main coordinates of my reading, I will highlight the poem's efforts to facilitate a love that is mutual while interrupting and opening the dyad of the couple.

Andenken

Der Nordost wehet,
Der liebste unter den Winden
Mir, weil er feurigen Geist
Und gute Fahrt verheißet den Schiffern.
Geh aber nun und grüße
Die schöne Garonne,
Und die Gärten von Bourdeaux
Dort, wo am scharfen Ufer
Hingehet der Steg und in den Strom
Tief fällt der Bach, darüber aber
Hinschauet ein edel Paar
von Eichen und Silberpappeln;

Noch denket das mir wohl und wie
Die breiten Gipfel neiget
Der Ulmwald, über die Mühl',
Im Hofe aber wächset ein Feigenbaum.
An Feiertagen gehn
Die braunen Frauen daselbst
Auf seidnen Boden,
Zur Märzenzeit,
Wenn gleich ist Nacht und Tag,
Und über langsamen Stegen,
Von goldenen Träumen schwer,
Einwiegende Lüfte ziehen.

Es reiche aber,
Des dunkeln Lichtes voll,
Mir einer den duftenden Becher,
Damit ich ruhen möge; denn süß
Wär' unter Schatten der Schlummer.
Nicht ist es gut,
Seellos von sterblichen
Gedanken zu seyn. Doch gut
Ist ein Gespräch und zu sagen
Des Herzens Meinung, zu hören viel
Von Tagen der Lieb',
Und Thaten, welche geschehen.

Wo aber sind die Freunde? Bellarmin
Mit dem Gefährten? Mancher
Trägt Scheue, an die Quelle zu gehn;

Es beginnet nämlich der Reichtum
Im Meere. Sie,
Wie Mahler, bringen zusammen
Das Schöne der Erd' und verschmähn
Den geflügelten Krieg nicht, und
Zu wohnen einsam, jahrlang, unter
Dem entlaubten Mast, wo nicht die Nacht durchglänzen
Die Feiertage der Stadt,
Und Saitenspiel und eingeborener Tanz nicht.

Nun aber sind zu Indiern
Die Männer gegangen,
Dort an der luftigen Spiz'
An Traubenbergen, wo herab
Die Dordogne kommt,
Und zusammen mit der prächt'gen
Garonne meerbreit
Ausgehet der Strom. Es nehmet aber
Und giebt Gedächtniß die See
Und die Lieb' auch heftet fleißig die Augen,
Was bleibet aber, stiften die Dichter.
(Friedrich Hölderlin, 1803–05)[21]

"Andenken" is a wind poem. It initiates its own movement when it says in the first line that "the northeasterly blows" (*Der Nordost wehet*). Why the northeasterly? Why not any other wind? And precisely what direction does this northeasterly poem take? Most interpreters, among them most influentially Heidegger, take for granted that the act of "thinking-toward" (*Andenken*) follows the blowing of the wind from northeast to southwest.[22] Yet the first signifier of the opening verse orients us toward northeast. Since the geographic coordinates included in the descriptor of a particular wind do not indicate *into* which direction the wind blows but rather *from* which direction it is blowing, the line "the northeasterly blows" locates the lyrical I (as well as the writer and the reader) in the southwest facing northeast and feeling the wind (of the poem) blow in her face. As we have seen in the previous two chapters, Hegel would consider it an act of friendship to move against this wind poem and to twist and turn its lines. But a slight fear of headwind blows most readers away from the source of this wind and turns them toward southwest. "Many a man / Is shy of going to the source" (*Mancher / Trägt Scheue, an die Quelle zu gehn*). Hölderlin tries to be among the few, a *mancher,* who carries the burden of moving against the wind instead of being carried away by it.[23]

Hölderlin travels northeast from Bordeaux back to Frankfurt; he does so in real life, but also with the lines of this poem. In May 1802, Hölderlin sets out on his walk from Bordeaux, where he had assumed a position as tutor, to Frankfurt, the home of Susette Gontard. Drawn toward the impossible reunion with the forbidden love, this journey is marked by several detours and delays (in Paris, Stuttgart, Nürtingen, and again Stuttgart) until Hölderlin is struck by the news of Gontard's death. Written between one and three years after this agonizing (non-)experience, "Andenken" forms an attempt to reenact the journey in a way that keeps Gontard alive for him.

Admittedly, "Go now, go and greet / The beautiful Garonne" (*Geh aber nun und grüße / Die schöne Garonne*) seems at first to unequivocally address a greeting to the river Garonne, which flows through Bordeaux. This address would affirm the idea that the poem's *Andenken* turns from Germany to Bordeaux. But Baumann convincingly argues that the northeasterly is "of winds the dearest" (*der liebste unter den Winden*) because it tells "about the days of love" (*von Tagen der Lieb'*) and reminds Hölderlin of Gontard.[24] During his stay in Bordeaux, Hölderlin receives the northeasterly with special ardor. As this wind is a rare phenomenon in the region of Bordeaux, Hölderlin treasures it because, coming from the direction in which Gontard lives, it makes him hot with its promise of fiery spirit, *feurigen Geist . . . verheißet.*[25] If one understands the wind as a medium of communication between the lovers, the *schöne Garonne,* with its initials S.G., is to be read as an encoded evocation of Susette Gontard. With the line "Go now, go and greet / The beautiful Garonne," Hölderlin invites the northeasterly to move northeast, from Bordeaux to Frankfurt, to greet S.G., Susette Gontard.[26] He asks the wind to blow backward.

Geh aber nun then means something like: "You are the dearest among the winds to me because you give me fever, but now go back and greet S.G.; make her feel what I feel. . ." And, since Susette Gontard died of a pulmonary infection and, thus, literally had difficulties breathing, *geh aber nun* also suggests something like: "I love you because through you I get wind of the fever she suffers from, but now go and help her to get back her wind. . ." The movement of *Andenken* thus exceeds the word's sense of remembrance or recollection. It combines the retrospective thought process with the forward-oriented and open-ended activity of thinking-of or of thinking-toward, that is, *denken an.*

The accumulation of *f* and *s* sounds in "lieb*s*te," "*f*eurigen," "Gei*s*t," "*F*ahrt," "*v*erhei*ß*et," "*Schiff*ern," "grü*ß*e," and "*sch*öne" not only imitates the wind's blowing, but also transmits the initials of the two lovers, Friedrich and Susette. With the wind, the lovers whisper each other's names across time and space. Nevertheless, it is an overstatement when

Baumann writes that "the way Hölderlin takes it, the north-easterly *is* already conversation and exchange of ideas, that is to say, reciprocation" (Baumann 1997, 19). The northeasterly might be a medium for communication and a promise of mutuality between the lovers, but the realization of this "converse" (*Gespräch*) is far from being a given. It requires a constant battle against death.

As we have seen in our discussion of mutual acknowledging, *Gespräch* in its emphatic sense, as the double movement of mutual reflection between two free subjects, follows a logic that is hard to grasp and almost impossible to enable. The movement is constantly jeopardized by its arrest, and life is incessantly threatened by death. A *Weh* accompanies the *wehen* of "Andenken." *Gespräch,* as the realization of mutuality in the back-and-forth movement of thinking-of and thinking-toward, proves to be difficult and dangerous. It requires to be struggled for without respite. Even though it might be sweet to drowse amid shadows, it is not good as we can see in the fourth stanza: *süß / Wär' unter Schatten der Schlummer / Nicht ist es gut.* One might tire of the constant labor and yearn for a rest, but *gut / Ist ein Gespräch.* With the contrast that the poem establishes in the middle stanza between the sweetness of *Schlummer* and the value of *Gespräch,* it acknowledges the difficulty of keeping the conversation mutual. The work of love includes the almost impossible task of sending the wind in the other direction while the danger of losing the beloved lurks at the turn of every line.[27]

One-sidedness persistently threatens the conversation with arrest. Naturally, everything flows in one direction: the wind blows, the spirit is fiery, and the river Dordogne flows downward (*wo herab/ die Dordogne kommt*). Before long the movement is extinguished: *ausgehet der Strom.* Quickly, the poem gets effaced in its all too transparent message. When nothing is read between the lines, this nothing grinds the verses to sharp edges, *scharfe Ufer,* that speed up the reading and rush the water into the abyss where deep falls the brook, *tief fällt der Bach.*

But the words themselves fight against their death. *Darüber hinschauet* (look out above) stretches out its ambiguities allowing the "noble pair" (*edel Paar*) to overlook and look beyond the abyss, toward which the water races. *Der Steg* (footbridge) smoothes out the sharp edge when it nonchalantly "trails along" the bank (trans. Chadwick, *am scharfen Ufer / Hingehet*), distracting from the other, more gloomy meaning of *hingehet,* namely "to pass away."

The reader also contributes to the task of a loving conversation. She joins the lovers, thereby opening their potentially destructive tête-à-tête. The interpretation of the line *geh aber nun* is therefore not merely a question of right or wrong. For us to invest the *aber* with negating power is to rescue the poem's potential for love, its ability to move back and forth between the lovers. For us to understand this *aber* as initiating a turn of address between S.G. and F.H. means also to reverse the blowing of this wind poem that comes to us from the author, and to participate actively in the conversation that moves back and forth between author and reader.[28] It amounts to giving the poem some of what it means to offer—responding with love and friendship to the love that it gives by interrupting its flow and twisting its perspective.

Our difficulties with receiving the poem as a love letter and Friedrich's difficulties with receiving Susette's greetings are, in both cases, tied up with a frustration about the evasive character of the beloved. She is unreliable. I do not know what I have in her. I do not even know where she is, from where she sends her love, and if she will keep sending it. True, there is a promise. "The north-easterly promises me fiery spirit" (*Der Nordost verheißet feurigen Geist Mir*). Yet, how long can I wait for the promise to come true? Even if the promise is "now" (*nun*) fulfilled, I remain in the position of awaiting its (continued) realization since I cannot bear the thought of her love ever ending. Already, empty words are creeping up on me, habitual turns, without an individual address. But who am I to force her to speak to me? Doesn't the poem have the right to refuse to yield meaning if it needs to avoid the grasp of a reader who only pretends to be a lover?

To accept the *aber*'s refusal to signify might be intended as an act of chivalry but it hardly preserves anybody's freedom. Instead, it infects the poem with the reader's own helplessness. Abandoned by the reader amidst the beauty of the Garonne, Friedrich feels a sharp pain *am scharfen Ufer* and, struggling not to slide into the abyss of solitude, he tries to make sure that Susette will remember to greet him: *geh aber nun und grüße.* This might be an understandable desire, but the fact that he takes charge of the continuation of the loving discourse means that Friedrich stops to hear her voice in the wind. Susette disappears as an agent in the conversation. The imperative forms *geh* and *grüße* neglect to acknowledge that the wind already blows, and fail to recognize that S.G. in fact sends her love. The redundant imperative spreads its impotence to overshadow the promise of the wind. It catches up with the wind by apostrophizing and enclosing it in a "now" (*nun*) that interrupts the wind's movement, breaks the promise of *verheißet,* and acts as a brake on its futural drift. The imperative transforms the love for the wind into a suffocating clasp. It thrusts its will into the open flesh of the future and forecloses the adventing movement of futurity. In its final turn, this *aber nun* turns the loving conversation off.

Such a reading melancholically reenacts a loss of which the reader is barely aware: the immense and always frustrated desire to be smitten and completely overcome by the other's address. It projects onto the poem the reader's own refusal to receive the poem in its precariousness and unreliability. The chivalrous attempt at indifference is not really motivated by the wish to preserve the beloved intact in her difference, but by the desire to protect the self from the beloved's caprice. Within the parameters of this reading, loving and respecting the integrity of the other turns into a holding on to the other and anticipating her moves. The beloved thus loses the very qualities for which one loves her: her liveliness, her unforeseeability, or, in Hegelian terms, her negativity. We are left with no future, nothing that comes to us from the other. Nothing can move us. The result is stagnation, an empty repetition of nothing, an accumulation of a habitual *aber* that does not turn or move anything, but pitches the poem in a melancholy tone.[29] The insistence of a meaningless *aber* as a marker of indifference and distrust isolates the reader and encloses the poem in a circle of non-understanding and loneliness from which, at best, one cry emerges: "But where are the friends?" (*Wo aber sind die Freunde?*).

In a truly mutual relation, as Hegel conceives it, ac-knowledging (reading the other, coming to know the other) is intertwined with killing the other—but killing the other is not an autonomous act, its agency is shared with the other, since "the object of self-consciousness is equally self-sufficient in this negativity of itself" (§ 176). "For that reason, [self-consciousness] can do nothing on its own about that object if that object does not do to itself what the first self-consciousness does to it" (§ 182, trans. modified). Killing the other is killing self-consciousness and acknowledging oneself while doing it. Hegel is far from imagining mutual love as a peaceful and stable relationship: the two subjects move in a vertiginous struggle, ceaselessly negating each other and themselves. These negations can be blissful if they manage to realize a form of death that is moving without ending the encounter in definite destruction.

Hölderlin's poem models an ethics of reading that acknowledges this affirmative kind of negativity. "The north-easterly blows"; the poem speaks to us. But while Hölderlin writes this poem Susette is already dead, and when we read the poem the author is already dead. The wind may have come from the northeast, but by the time it hits Friedrich, Susette is somewhere else. Once we read the poem, we no longer know in what sense it was written. Even though Susette's death is a historical fact, "Andenken" demonstrates that Hölderlin did not experience her death as a fact, but struggled to stay in communication with Diotima Susette Gontard.[30] Her death figures as a trope for the experience of the negativity of the other. Because her freedom consists in being the subject of and subject to her own self-differentiality, the lover is always already somewhere else as soon as she presents herself for identification. In the very act of sending a loving message, the sender herself changes. The source is gone, and it does not make sense to search for it at the point of its departure unless one wants to arrest the greeting.

If Friedrich wants to communicate his love to Susette, it is not enough to simply reverse the direction of the greeting, and to give back what he received. Reciprocity does not realize mutuality. The wind would not reach the source even if it blew in the opposite direction. Friedrich has to speak without knowing where exactly to direct his words. He has to approach someone who is gone, dead, so to speak. Likewise, we have to communicate with the poem without knowing from where exactly it addresses us. To bear the embarrassment—*die Scheue zu tragen*—of articulating words against the wind, without any certainty as to where and how the other will receive the greeting, is the only way to recognize the other's negativity without killing her.

The lack of orientation resulting from the inability to locate the position of the beloved, combined with the strain of moving against the wind, provokes a wish for quiet that has strong suicidal undertones:

But someone pass me	*Es reiche aber,*
The fragrant cup	*Des dunkeln Lichtes voll,*
Full of dark light,	*Mir einer den duftenden Becher,*
So that I may rest now; for sweet	*Damit ich ruhen möge; denn süß*
It would be to drowse amid shadows.	*Wär' unter Schatten der Schlummer.*

The desire of the lover would be appeased—to put a different spin on *es reiche aber* (but it suffices)—if he could drink up her cup and rest in the beloved. Yet, since it is impossible to find quiet in S. who is alive with negativity, constantly moving and moved, F. wishes to rest with Susette's nonexistence. To put an end to their missed encounters, he is ready to go where she is clearly not, if only to secure the certainty of her full absence. He is ready to die. Like the reader who is tempted to give in to the lure of nothingness that threatens to collapse the poem into the one meaning of non-communication, F. is tempted to give himself over to destruction.

According to Baumann, the next line, *Nicht ist es gut* (It is not good), forms the heart of the poem (Baumann 1997, 38). Located at the exact midpoint of the poem, it marks its turning point—the point at which Hölderlin resolves to tear himself away from the temptation of actively or passively dying. The struggle for recognition in Hegel's *Phenomenology* initiates a similar turn when its protagonists realize that a dead opponent will not provide the desired recognition. Death is not good; so much might safely be said. But on which side are we to locate death: here or there, in this world or in the hereafter? The central line of the poem is so insignificant in its simplicity that we have to consult the neighboring verses to give it more substance. Like the other pivot with which we have been concerned—the potentially void *aber*—*Nicht ist es gut* reads like an empty heart until we widen our focus and attend to the blood of words that will have crossed in it:

It would be to drowse amid shadows.	*Wär' unter Schatten der Schlummer.*
It is not good	*Nicht ist es gut,*
To be soulless with mortal	*Seellos von sterblichen*

The preceding verse speaks of drowsing amid shadows. Shadows might refer to the underworld, the dominion of the dead and its shadowy inhabitants. Or, if we adhere to Platonic ideas, it might remind us of the fact that our empirical world consists of only shadows. Or the line might simply draw the picture of a nap in the shadows of the wooded homeland.[31] The next line reads *Seellos von sterblichen.* To be soulless would mean to be dead. More precisely—since the dead are often considered to be nothing but souls—it means to dwell in a death that entertains no relation to life. Those who have a soul are mortal; they are able to die or to live; they are affected by death, divided between death and life. But to be soulless would mean to be without death or life, to rest in an absolute beyond or a total immediacy. The line break between *sterblichen* and *Gedanken* isolates the adjective *sterblichen* from the term it is adjected to, so that it establishes its own substantiality and asks to be read as a substantive. Read on its own as *Seellos von Sterblichen* (soulless from mortals), the line evokes a state of soullessness caused by mortals, or rather, caused by the denial of mutual acknowledging—the refusal to acknowledge that F. shares the status of mortals, which consists in being with soul, or in being alive and affected by death, subject of and subject to one's negativity. He walks around on earth like a dead man amid shadows. The central line, *Nicht ist es gut,* is a light heart that flutters between the line before and the line after, which themselves are ambiguous in their relation to this world and the hereafter. *Nicht ist es gut* is itself one of the mortal thoughts (*sterblichen Gedanken*) that are interrupted by the line break and divided in themselves between life and death. The verse exchanges blood containing oxygen for blood that carries carbon dioxide and lightheartedly escapes identification as one or the other.

Lulling Breezes and Swaying Bridges

For Hegel, we will remember, coming to know is truly an ac-knowledging, something that subjects do together—not in loving peace and harmony, but wrangling with each other to keep the movement of thinking, grasping, penetrating, and embracing from fizzling out in mere negation or being stifled in mere affirmation. It is a struggle for mutuality that keeps changing the subject. Since subject/s are always beyond themselves, always subject to their own objectification, alienation, appropriation, and dissolution, they cannot be located or identified for very long. There is no *Wiederfinden* à la Goethe in Hölderlin's poem or in Hegel's *Phenomenology:* no recovery of the lost object, no reunion with an old lover, and no re-cognition even, that *trennt uns nicht zum zweitenmal.* Thinking one another (rather than thinking of one another), subject/s change.

This change has the advantage that the subjects multiply. In Hegel's text, we are treated to the panoply of different shapes of self-reflective life. Each shape emerges from a transformative act of ac-knowledging. Acknowledging entangles subjects in one another. It is an act of converse that exchanges and even confuses identities. Constitutively shared, the subjects or figures of spirit are thus not strictly separated from one another; they are not even always clearly distinguishable. Rather, they are imperfectly drawn into one another—figuring and standing in for one another while overlapping.

Again, Hölderlin's poem lends itself to elucidate the logic of this relation. Here as well, the couples keep multiplying. In the following, I will discuss how the human lovers are interlaced with the poem's several pairs of trees. A *Gespräch* emerges—not only in words, but also among words—a converse in the form of asymmetrical chiasms: of unfinished, non-reciprocal but nevertheless mutual exchanges.

The first stanza of "Andenken" names "a noble pair of oaks and white poplars [*ein edel Paar / Von Eichen und Silberpappeln*]." The lovers in this pair are quite different. White poplars are known to be fickle. They like to grow near the water so the liquid can flow in abundance through their supple stems. With the help of the water they grow silvery leaves that flicker in the wind. Oscillating between their two faces, these leaves enrapture with the music they sing in the breeze. The oak, on the other hand, is ancient and unfaltering. It was Jupiter's tree and gave honey to the Golden Age.[32] In the imagination of Hölderlin's time, in texts of German Romanticism and Idealism, it figures as *the* German tree. Big and steady, oaks lend themselves to mediate between gods and humans, or, as Hölderlin phrases it in another poem, to "stand beneath God's thunder-storms / To grasp the Father's ray . . . / And . . . offer it to the people" wrapped in the song of falling acorns.[33] Solitary, free, and wild, they attract the lightning, like Semele, and are likely to be burnt for their love.[34]

The obvious difference between these lovers could be a source of misunderstanding and death. But a certain shyness or shame earns the pair its attribute of ethical nobility (*ein edel Paar*).[35] They do not address each other directly. Their gaze is twice diverted. Overseeing together the gardens of Bordeaux, the river Garonne with its sharp bank, the falling brook, and the footbridge, they glance at each other across the entire world of their surroundings. But even this world is not the direct object of their gaze; they *hinschauet darüber* with a squinting look that looks at and looks beyond at the same time.[36] Acknowledging negativity, their gaze is attentive without identifying its object.

Hegel understands shame among lovers, quite counterintuitively, as a force against separation. To him, *Scham* is not a feeling that leads lovers to restore propriety and property, but he rather takes it as the expression of an aversion against the proper. In his 1797–98 fragment on love, Hegel writes: "Love is indignant over any remaining separation and property; this anger of love at individuality is called shame [*Scham*]." Reversing the common values of decency, he regards the messy entanglement of two bodies in love as an example of purity, whereas lovers who resist their intimacy trying to preserve some proper independence present to him an image of indecency: "A pure heart [*Gemüt*] is not ashamed of love; but it is ashamed of the fact that this love is not consummate [*vollkommen*]" (Hegel 1971, 306). Striving to overcome the obstacles that hinder love's culmination, shame is thus an agent in the service of love.

Hölderlin rephrases the role of *Scham* as *Scheue* (shyness). In his poem, shyness does the work of preserving dynamic differences within the pair. The stimulation of difference against the idea of an unqualified union is also part of Hegel's account of shame. Hamacher highlights the ambiguity of the work of shame in Hegel.[37] He shows that shame splits up the unity that it has produced in order to work toward a more inclusive unity. Shame relentlessly takes offense at the results of its own efforts because no union is radical enough to be absolutely pure.[38] The work of shame is unending. Its infinity can be frustrating when merely numerical, that is, when we presume separate countable entities. If we presuppose a clear-cut distinction between identity and difference, every newly achieved unity opposes the difference which it resolved and therefore adds to the series of terms to be reconciled. But a different logic gives rise to a pleasurable infinity. Such is the case when the lovers prevent their union from collapsing into an exclusive unity and make a love in which "the separate still exist, but not as separate, rather as united [*Einiges*]" (Hegel 1971, 305).[39] Then, like Hölderlin's noble pair, those who are ashamed of the fact that they are separated also take pleasure in letting more and more obstacles come between them. Rubbing against these hurdles, they actively enjoy their love: "This wealth of life love acquires . . . for it seeks out differences and devises unifications ad infinitum; it turns to the whole manifold of nature in order to drink love out of every life" (Hegel 1971, 307). The infinite work of shame opens the closed relationship between two individuals, their potentially violent tête-a-tête, and allows for more and more interference from the manifold riches of the outside world or, in Hölderlin's words, of the gardens of Bordeaux. As Hamacher puts it: "For shame being is given—its own not excepted—only in the plural" (Hamacher 1998, 89).

Indeed, the seemingly exclusive couple has always been a play of multiplicities in Hölderlin's poem: the pair does not consist of one oak and one white poplar, but oaks and white poplars in the plural: "A noble pair of oak*s* / and white poplar*s*" (*ein edel Paar / Von Eichen und Silberpappeln*). The couple has also always been interlaced with other pairs. Oaks and poplars are crossed with other trees. Indeed, the poem abounds with exchange, with *Gespräch,* with care, with confusion, with mutation, and with mutuality. There is care in the elm wood that protectively "bends its broad tops over the mill" (Chadwick; *neiget die breiten Gipfel . . . über die Mühl'*). The house takes the "fig tree" (*Feigenbaum*) into its courtyard and shelters it from storm and weather. *Der feige Baum,* the cowardly tree, needs protection. Yet, by its involvement in another pair, the fig gains a divine power to keep the house safe in return. When Hölderlin translates Euripides' *Bacchants,* he confuses fig tree (Greek: *sykon*) with sanctum (Greek: *saekon*).[40] The fig now offers protection precisely because it is *der Feigen Baum,* the holy tree of the cowards. In the context of love, cowardice turns into a special courage. It becomes the strength of not being afraid to let shyness show (*Scheue zu tragen*).[41] Hegel asserts that love "has no fear of its fear, but led by its fear, it relieves [*hebt auf*] separations" (Hegel 1971, 306–7, trans. modified). The lover bears (*trägt*) the brave timorousness of the fig tree in the same way that she wears (*trägt*) a fig leaf. The fig leaf "cancels separation" by denying the difference between lovers. Since neither of them can be sure that their love can tolerate their separation, they prefer to wear their shame. But the coy fig leaf also highlights the difference between them, if only as something that is impossible to pinpoint. The excessively shy love of the noble pair keeps differences moving.

The second stanza presents the movement of differences across the multiple interlacing pairs that form a noble pair. It begins with "there . . . / The brown women walk / On silken ground" (*Die braunen Frauen daselbst / Auf seidnen Boden*). The adjective *seidnen* is here used in the plural and is thus grammatically aligned with *Frauen* rather than *Boden.* But it would not exactly make sense to exchange the adjectives and to say: *Die seidnen Frauen daselbst auf braunem Boden* (The silken women there on brown ground). The exchange is not reversible; there is no identifiable point of origin. The *daselbst* functions as the eccentric pivot for an asymmetrically chiasmic exchange that never fully lines up and therefore never comes to rest.[42] Both sides are imperfectly drawn into the other so that both can neither be separated nor unified. Around the disempowered identity (*Selbigkeit*) of the *daselbst*, as the light heart of the chiasm, the verses keep insisting on the plural.

We find a similar structure in: "And over slow footbridges, / Heavy with golden dreams, / Lulling breezes drift" (*Und über langsamen Stegen, / Von goldenen Träumen schwer, / Einwiegende Lüfte ziehen*). Here, the converse explicitly engages more than two terms. The *Gespräch* moves in a round. Light and heavy at the same time, it is a slow dance over the abyss where deep down the river rages: *Über langsamen Stegen* (over slow footbridges)? One is tempted to correct this peculiar expression into *über einwiegenden Stegen* (over footbridges that give), and this sets the dance in motion: *von goldenen Träumen schwer, Lüfte ziehen langsam, langsam einwiegende Stege, Träume ziehen schwer, schwer einwiegende Lüfte ziehen langsam Stege, wiegen ein in goldene Träume, träumen goldene Stege . . .* (heavy with golden dreams, breezes drift slowly, slowly giving footbridges, dreams drift heavily, heavy swaying breezes slowly draw bridges, lull into golden dreams, dream golden bridges . . .).

What Hölderlin's poem discovers—a chiasmic exchange so eccentric and incomplete that it opens onto a round of different combinations and configurations itself inviting more and more transformations—is obviously very different from the model presented in Goethe's poem. There, we found mirror relations on several different yet neatly organized levels: between the two lovers, between the human and the cosmic couple, (more abstractly) between individuality and universality, and finally between the substance and the form of the poem. All of these mirrorings worked to substantiate the autonomy of the lyrical "I," thus granting the lyrical "I" recognition. This kind of recognition disallowed for any disturbing difference and prohibited multiplication, dispersal, and confusion. The result was a perfect poem, a poem satisfied with itself, as it were.

But it is Hölderlin's model that we encounter in the *Phenomenology*, as well. In the *Phenomenology*, we find no closed circuit of mirror images. Because of the imperfect entanglement of plural subject/s as they co-emerge in mutual acknowledging, the ostensible pair of the trope of mutual acknowledging has always already opened onto the multitude of the *Phenomenology*'s shapes of consciousness and shapes of spirit. All of the figures that the phenomenological narrative relates—from sense certainty to absolute knowing—share in this one movement of mutual acknowledging. Each presents another figuration of the subject/s that keep changing. But even the text as a whole is not closed. It needs us, the readers. The *Phenomenology* needs our acknowledging for any of these figures to come to life as acknowledged and thus to be transformed.[43] It needs us to join the struggle for mutuality.

Toward

I have relied on Hegel's signifier of "acknowledging"—with the prefix "ac" communicating a sense of togetherness—to support my argument for mutuality. I have argued that the acknowledgement of self-consciousness can only take place in the plural and is constitutively and structurally mutual. Nevertheless, this mutuality has to be struggled for because self-consciousness tends to want to settle for something less than mutual acknowledging, namely recognition, because recognition promises self-sufficiency and absorption. Hölderlin's lighthearted jumbling of grammar and predication suggests that the best strategy in the struggle for mutuality is often to abandon the struggle against it.

Before I draw my discussion of "mutual acknowledging" to a conclusion, we must consider another valence of the prefix *ac.* So far, I have read "ac" as the residue of "accord," which itself assimilates the Latin *ad* to the Latin *cor* (heart). It is the prefix *ad* (at, to, till) that will concern me now—especially since, while somewhat hidden in the English version of the signifier, it is in plain view on the surface of the German *Anerkennen.* As the prefix of a verb, *an* communicates the direction of the action that the verb expresses. Examples are *ansehen* (look at), *anschreien* (shout at), *anhören* (listen to), *ankleben* (glue on), or *anlehnen* (lean against). While most of the time the action is directed at an object, in some cases *an* marks a movement toward the action itself, as in *andiskutieren* (discuss briefly), *anblättern* (leaf through a little), *anlesen* (start reading), or *andeuten* (to incompletely explain or adumbrate). It then expresses the movement toward the action indicated by the verb; it suggests the incipience of this action and means "a little," "briefly," "incompletely," or "tentatively."

Hegel exploits this meaning of *an* in his discussion of the "unhappy consciousness":

> The unhappy consciousness does not conduct itself *towards its object* in a thinking manner. Rather, since it is just *in itself* pure thinking individuality, and since its object is itself precisely this pure thought, and since pure thought is not itself the *relation of each to the other,* it, so to speak, merely launches itself *in the direction* of thought [*geht es, so zu sagen, nur an das Denken hin*] and on that path it becomes *devotion* [*Andacht*]. (§ 217)

The unhappy consciousness moves toward thinking, but stops short of actually carrying it through. Hegel calls this figure of consciousness not *Denken* (thinking) and not even *Andenken* (remembrance, literally: "thinking at" or "incipient thinking") but *Andacht* (devotion). He does so because this figure of emerging thought skips the actual activity of thinking and jumps right away to a submissive devotion to ready-made thoughts, that is to say, to the posture of not needing to think anymore. Before it has even begun (*An-*), the thinking has already passed (*dacht* is the past tense of *denken*) and thus is *Andacht.*

Like the common reader of philosophical books, who enjoys reading the summaries of arguments in reviews or prefaces more than actually reading the books themselves, *Andacht* loves "having thought(s)" more than it loves to actually think. Yet Hegel's phenomenological philosophy insists that thinking (*denken*) and coming-to-know or realizing (*erkennen*) are movements that need to be carried out, journeyed through, or experienced even though they cause embarrassment and shame.

He famously claims that the task of phenomenology is "to bring [philosophy] nearer to the goal where it can lay aside the title of '*love of knowledge*' and be *actual knowledge*" (§ 5). The operative distinction in this claim is not one between love and knowledge, but between the mere inclination toward an activity and the actualization of that activity. Actual thinking (*Denken* or *Erkennen*) is mutual acknowledging: a reflexive movement of physical, intellectual, and emotional interchange of plural subjects who struggle with each other to acknowledge their freedom as well as their interdependence and vulnerability. When Hegel professes that "scientific cognition requires that [formal understanding] give itself over to the life of the object [*sich dem Leben des Gegenstandes zu übergeben*]," he clearly suggests that the philosopher must acknowledge that his so-called object is indeed, on a profound level, a self-reflective, free, and living subject, and he must acknowledge his interdependence with this subject if he is to actually think scientifically (§ 53). As the mutual embrace and mutual penetration of subjects in the plural, "actual knowing" is a form of love.

At the same time, the actualization of knowledge in experience does precisely not mean that absolute knowledge can be completed. Our discussion of Hölderlin's poem "Andenken" has shown the need for the struggle for mutuality. It is a struggle against the trap of self-sufficiency and against the rush to the finish line expressed in the word *An-dacht.* In Hölderlin's poem, we find this rush in a series of signifiers that figure *Andenken* in the rapid movements of going, running, blowing, and falling. "To think at" or "to think toward" is one of the first senses of *an-denken* that Hölderlin's poem suggests when he places *an* in the company of other directional prefixes, like *hin* in *hingehet* (go toward, go away) and *hinschauet* (look at), *herab* in *herabkommt* (come down), and *aus* in *ausgehet* (go out). Because the non-reflexive *Andenken* presses too fast and too decidedly in one direction, it overshoots the mark and kills the sense for the other direction. Because it rushes to the end this "thinking toward" remains incomplete.

While Hegel, like Hölderlin, certainly shows a predilection for slowness—even for viscosity—Hegel is not one to argue for infinite deferral. Instead, it is through closure (through definite but temporary accomplishments) that he opens "actual knowledge" to the advent of an unknown future. The movement of *Anerkennen* might—and indeed must repeatedly—be actualized in the form of a judgment—be it an epistemological judgment (in the mode of *Wiedererkennen*) or a value judgment (in the mode of *Anerkennung* or recognition)—but any such judgment will be called into question by precisely the reality that it actualizes. Neither the self nor the other is a stable thing in itself that could be known or recognized without that knowledge or recognition having a transformative effect on both. Knowledge—as a reified result of the movement of the concept—is of course possible, even required, but Hegel's journeys of thinking never end there. They always begin with knowledge (or certainty) and show how it disintegrates.[44] Similarly, everyone will at times ask to be recognized *as* something (or feel compelled to recognize others *as* something), but this very recognition will change the identity thus recognized.[45] Any act of recognition must therefore come to be viewed as misrecognition and will be outdated and updated by a new recognition. The completion of *Anerkennen* is itself transient. The process of acknowledging (and thus of thinking, of comprehending, of reading) is constitutively incipient, provisional, and unending.

With Hölderlin, we can extend Hegel's critique of *Andacht* to *Anerkennen. Anerkennen* also—and especially when it carries through the movement of *Erkennen*—remains constitutively incipient and incomplete. Yet, in this case, the incipience is the condition of possibility for mutuality. For both a deep understanding of Hegel's thought and a profound appreciation of ethical emotionality, it is of crucial importance, then, to keep in view the reflexive sense of incipience that is communicated by the prefix *An* and thus to read mutual *Anerkennen* as an unending process. In the ambiguous and ecstatic circulation of *Anerkennen,* we experience others across our frequent appropriations of them as not fully assimilable, and ourselves across our repeated insights as not completely intelligible. As the interminably repeated incipience of *Erkennen, Anerkennen* remains impossible to accomplish in a definitive way because it keeps changing the subject.

6

Tremble

> It felt the fear of death, the absolute master. In that feeling, it had internally fallen into dissolution, trembled inwardly in every fiber of its being, and all that was fixed within it had been shaken loose.
> —*Phenomenology*, § 194

Tremble becomes an explicit topic in the *Phenomenology* in a brief but memorable moment toward the end of the section on "Self-Sufficiency and Non-Self-Sufficiency of Self-Consciousness; Mastery and Servitude." In one of the *Phenomenology*'s frequent parabases, the phenomenologist communicates to the reader a truth about the protagonist of which the protagonist is unaware: whereas the servant's self-image is that of someone who is exclusively attached to and defined by his physical existence, the phenomenologist points out that the servant's true self encompasses absolute negativity—and its power:

> Servitude has this truth of pure negativity . . . *in fact in servitude itself,* for servitude has *experienced* this essence in servitude. This consciousness was not driven with anxiety about just this or that matter, nor did it have anxiety at just this or that moment; rather, it had anxiety about its entire essence. It felt the fear of death, the absolute master. In that feeling, it had internally fallen into dissolution, trembled inwardly in every fiber of its being, and all that was fixed within it had been shaken loose [*Es ist darin innerlich aufgelöst worden hat durchaus in sich selbst erzittert, und alles Fixe hat in ihm gebebt*]. However, this pure universal movement, this way in which all durable existence becomes absolutely fluid [*das absolute Flüssigwerden alles Bestehens*], is the simple essence of self-consciousness; it is absolute negativity, *pure being-for-itself,* which thereby exists in this consciousness. (§ 194, trans. modified)

In its fear of death, the enchained consciousness experiences its own essence as absolute negativity. It is not hard to imagine that chains would be unable to restrain a body that is thus spiritualized: trembles turn loose. The moment of absolute fear must be considered as the most precious moment of the protagonist's development so far. The shakes and trembles of absolute fear not only actualize the servant's being-for-himself, negate his mere being-for-others, and allow him to access his own power of negativity; they also shift the operative value of the dialectic of mastery and servitude from abstract negativity to absolute negativity.[1] Negation by fear exemplifies a non-abstract mode of negation, one that does not result in death or nothingness. Instead, the trembles dissolve the protagonist's inert being and set it in motion. Moved by fear, consciousness is able to apprehend and express itself "not merely as *substance* but also equally as *subject*" (§ 17).[2]

The feeling of absolute fear facilitates the shift in self-comprehension. Trembling is a mode of self-reflection. Not only will the servant have understood the true structure of his relation to the master; his embrace of absolute fear will also have changed his situation. Mastery and servitude are founded on the repression of absolute fear. Only the fear of absolute fear is able to arrest and enchain a consciousness that is capable of absolute fluidity. The actual experience of absolute fear destroys the fantasy of mastery and catapults consciousness out of servitude. As speculative negation, absolute fear is a productive force, an "instrument of progression," the motor for development (Cixous 1991, 255).[3]

Yet consciousness, the protagonist of the *Phenomenology*, is not able to experience absolute fear in the fullest sense of the word "experience." When Hegel, in the above-quoted passage, maintains that "servitude has . . . *experienced* this [truth of pure negativity] in servitude" (*die Knechtschaft . . . hat diese Wahrheit der reinen Negativität . . . an ihr erfahren*), the structure of the parabasis belies the phenomenologist's very observation. The fact that the phenomenologist here separates from the protagonist, who remains absorbed in the scene, and addresses the audience behind the servant's back, means that the servant cannot exactly benefit from the information. What is more, *an* ihr, of *an ihr erfahren*, indicates spatial contiguity but not conscious awareness; it means "in itself," not "for itself." The phenomenologist thus indicates that the servant underwent a fear that was unavailable for consciousness. To be precise, the servant cannot even have unconsciously lived through absolute fear, since he, strictly speaking, wasn't there (yet) to do so. The figure of the servant was only constituted as a reaction to the event of absolute fear. And this reaction consisted in the repression of the intense appreciation of life near death which is the experience of absolute fear. The servant qua servant did not undergo this experience and can have no recollection of the fear that led to his birth.

Therefore, when the phenomenologist retroactively establishes that absolute fear is indeed a factor in the life of this consciousness, this diagnosis can be read as an attempt to empathetically re-create an "experience" that in turn is only now and by this very diagnosis made available to the protagonist who might be shaken by the phenomenologist's statement. This is an example of Hegel pushing to an interesting emotional extreme the demand made in the preface, that the phenomenologist must surrender control to the self-unfolding of the protagonist's development. What is more—because the experience of absolute fear is, strictly speaking, unavailable to any one consciousness—we, as readers of the *Phenomenology,* cannot but tremble back and forth between the text's retroactive accounts on the one hand and the textual anticipations of fear on the other, both of which arrange themselves around the absence of any direct account of experienced fear. The missed experience of absolute fear cannot be claimed by any one figure of consciousness or even by the phenomenologist, but it does instead take shape in the textual trembling between and across various anticipations and recollections of spirit. The *Phenomenology of Spirit* inwardly trembles between the double genitive of its title—between spirit as the agent of the phenomenological inquiry and spirit as its subject matter, between spirit in the form of the protagonist and spirit in the form of the phenomenologist. At the same time, all that is fixed within these two characters—the different figures of the protagonist, the difference between author and various readers, which constitutes the phenomenologist—every fiber of this text shakes loose.

In the following, I will first explore the absence of an expression of fear when fear must have been felt. After an analysis of the retroactive and indirect account, given by the phenomenologist/s, of the servant's absolute fear, I will highlight the textual anticipations of absolute fear that precede the dialectic of mastery and servitude. Then, I will conclude the first part of this chapter by analyzing the retroactive attempts of the protagonist/s to realize and integrate the missed experience of absolute fear. Finally, in the second part of this chapter, I will explore the textual trembling that surrounds and traverses the chapter transitions of the *Phenomenology.*

Missed Experience

At the beginning of the chapter on mastery and servitude, at the moment when absolute fear must have assailed consciousness, the narrative does not acknowledge fear as the motivation for the formation of fixed subject positions. The protagonists' quest for mutual acknowledgment has turned into a struggle for life and death. Misunderstanding negativity as abstract nothingness, the individuals involved try to kill one another and themselves in order to gain status and recognition. It takes a near-death experience for consciousness to understand the simple fact that life is of the essence since a dead person can neither give nor receive recognition. Still, there is no mention of the protagonists' fear here at the beginning of the chapter. Absolute fear is identified only retroactively, at the end of the chapter, as a feeling the servant must have had. At the beginning of the chapter, master and servant are logically deduced from the struggle for life and death. The *Phenomenology* accounts for their emergence in a neutral tone without emotion or empathy:

> In this experience, self-consciousness learns that life is as essential to it as pure self-consciousness. . . . It is by way of that experience that a pure self-consciousness is posited, and a consciousness . . . is posited as an existing consciousness. . . . Both moments are essential. . . . One is self-sufficient; for it, its essence is being-for-itself. The other is non self-sufficient; for it, life, that is, being for an other, is the essence. The former is the *master,* the latter is the *servant.* (§ 189)

With this sober explanation, Hegel locates the necessity for the hierarchical division of consciousness in the protagonists' resistance to complexity. Consciousness refuses to accept contradictory values. For consciousness, either negation or life is of the essence, but not both. Therefore consciousness splits into two consciousnesses with opposed and hierarchically organized values.

The two consciousnesses hardly experience the lesson of the essentiality of life in the same way. The master never even sees the danger of death; he never assumes that negativity could harm him physically—since his body is precisely what he, as master, abstracts from. The master knows no fear. The servant, on the other hand, will have seen the danger clearly. He comes into being by virtue of his brush with death, but his very emergence is a turning away from absolute fear. He turns to the master to save his life. While both avoid the feeling of absolute fear, only one consciousness embraces the idea of life's value, which turns it into a servant; the other consciousness holds on to the idea of abstract negativity as the essence of consciousness, and becomes the master.

That the one who has developed further is subjected to the one who stubbornly refuses insight certainly offends the notion that the *Phenomenology* follows a logic of progression. The retrograde motion stems from the untimeliness of the servant's development. Not only the servant was unprepared for his encounter with death and his sudden appreciation of life. The spirit of his time is not ready to integrate the insight into the value of life either. As we have seen in the discussion of mutual acknowledging in our previous chapter, the "essence" or the main value that the entire chapter on "mastery and servitude" pursues is self-sufficiency. The servant might have already moved beyond the paradigm of self-sufficiency, and might be on the way toward reconciliation of being-for-self and being-for-another. Yet he is judged based on the standard of self-sufficient being-for-self and is thus enchained.[4]

Anticipation

The first anticipation of fear in the *Phenomenology*—before absolute fear is mentioned explicitly at the end of the chapter on mastery and servitude—can be found around the transition from the dialectic of perception to the dialectic of the understanding. Here, consciousness appears afraid of its own implication in the development of the other, its "object." Its fear takes the ironic form of an anxious avoidance of trembling. Already in the dialectic of perception, the protagonist realizes that he is implicated in the movement of the object which he thought to merely observe:

> For consciousness, it has thereby been determined just how its perceiving is essentially composed, namely, not as a simple, pure act of apprehending, but rather as *in its act of apprehending* at the same time taking a *reflective turn into itself from out* of the true. This return of consciousness into itself, which immediately *blends* itself into that pure apprehending . . . alters the true. (§ 118, trans. modified)

By way of acknowledging the mingling of subject and object, consciousness turns into a new figure of itself; it becomes the understanding.[5] But the insight does not carry through. The understanding loses access to the fleeting realization that it is entangled in the object because it is afraid of such entanglement: "*For us,* this object [the object of the understanding] has come to be through the movement of consciousness such that this consciousness is interwoven in the coming-to-be of the object. . . . However . . . consciousness itself is still withdrawing from what has come to be" (§ 132).

As a reader of the *Phenomenology,* one often wonders why the protagonists are so slow to develop. Consciousness often appears dumb and dense. Something has become more than obvious to us, but the protagonist still doesn't see it. This is because consciousness is afraid to discover new truths. It fears losing the stability of its current certainty when the alternative might be a world where "the truth is the bacchanalian revel where no member is not drunk" (§ 47, trans. modifed). Consciousness dreads to surrender to the dance of the speculative. The apprehensive anticipation of, and flight from, absolute fear slows down consciousness's development toward "absolute knowing."

The consciousness of the understanding insists on separating its own movement of explaining from the object's movement, which it describes here as a play of forces. The act of explaining is for the understanding a self-gratification that can do without touching and being touched by the object.

> It is precisely for that reason that there is so much self-satisfaction in explanation, because the consciousness involved in it is, to put it this way, in an immediate conversation with itself, enjoying only itself. While it undeniably seems to be pursuing something else, it is really just consorting with itself [*sich nur mit sich selbst herumtreibt*]. (§ 163)

Consciousness manages to reduce its immediate implication in the movement of the other to the distant relation of voyeurism. It pretends that it "has no part in [the object's] free realization but rather merely looks on that realization and purely apprehends it" (§ 133). Making the object exhibit itself, the protagonist withdraws into safety and masturbates.[6] Consciousness thereby escapes the erotic danger that Hegel mentions at the end of the dialectic of perception. It is the danger of being captured by the object, attracted by its force and pushed around in its whirl. This danger arises because the object is a manifestation of the self-reflecting concept, the concept in Hegel's emphatic sense. As such, the object does not exhibit a simple identity but comprises multiple "moments." Each moment of the concept is at once an abstraction of the whole and the whole. Thus, despite their status as abstractions, these moments can assume independent existence.[7] The object has multiplied, and consciousness is thrown from one embrace to the other, losing itself in an orgy of abstractions:

> Perceptual understanding, often called healthy common-sense . . . is, in the act of perceiving, merely the game played by *these abstractions*. . . . It is pushed around by these empty characters [*Wesen*] and thus thrown out of the arms of one abstraction into the arms of another. . . .

> Common-sense is the prey of these abstractions which spin it round and round in their whirling circle. (§ 131, trans. modified)

The pleasure that perception finds in merely observing the other might be without interest, in the Kantian sense, but here, by contrast with Kant's third *Critique*, the free play of forces (*Kräfte*) is located not only in the observer but also—and frighteningly so—in the observed. What consciousness here still calls "the object"—and doesn't yet acknowledge as another subject—has its own pleasure and draws the observer in.[8]

For now, fear is not felt as such, but avoided. The protagonist pays for this denial of fear with the impediment of his development. Consciousness, in the form of the understanding, is afraid to do what Hegel, in the preface to the *Phenomenology*, describes as the prerequisite for speculative thinking or true comprehension, that is, to "let [its] freedom descend into the content [of the 'object']" (§ 58). Consciousness is afraid to lose control.

Atremble with Freedom

The experience of absolute fear would open consciousness for the actualization of mutual acknowledging. The servant understands that recognition is possible only among living individuals (an insight that the master refused). But is he ready to embrace the fearful experience of mutual acknowledging?

In the beginning of the chapter on mastery and servitude, Hegel offers his account of mutual acknowledging. Mutual acknowledging creates an ecstatic relation where, in a circular movement of displacements, each consciousness finds and loses itself in the other. It is important to note that Hegel conceives of recognition not as a securing of one's position and dignity, but as an experience of mutual exposure and vulnerability. In the process of acknowledging, consciousness "does indeed get *outside of itself*" (*kommt es wohl außer sich,* § 184). What is more, the other cannot be expected to ground such a constitutively ecstatic self-consciousness. Why not? Because he is just as little in control and therefore cannot stabilize their relation either. The circular structure of mutual acknowledging shatters any attempt on the part of the individual to secure an identity. Instead, the process reaches its ideal shape when the parties involved become aware of the bottomless movement of their mutual acknowledging: when "they *acknowledge* themselves as *mutually acknowledging each other*" (§ 184, trans. modified). The experience thus draws the protagonist into the whirl of forces that the understanding consciousness had managed to avoid: "In this movement we see the process repeat itself which had been exhibited as the play of forces in consciousness" (ibid.). The fear that the understanding was able to repress now returns. It is the fear of losing control, of all too easily being carried away by an orgy of abstractions because one's own existence is not very substantive.

As in the dialectic of the understanding, the fear induced by the ecstatic movement of acknowledging is at first avoided. Instead of abandoning themselves to the bottomless process of "*acknowledging* themselves as *mutually acknowledging each other*," the two parties settle down in a stable relation where a firm hierarchy gives each one a solid identity: one is the master, the other the servant. These subject positions develop as strategic formations in the defense against the absolute fear that the bottomless movement of mutual acknowledging gives rise to. As such they prove effective: the master is indeed never afraid, and the servant gets away with merely being brushed by fear. The servant has the potential to turn fear into a resource, as Audre Lorde implies when she rearticulates Descartes' dictum as: "I feel therefore I can be free."[9] Instead of impeding the servant's development, "the fear of the master [could be] the beginning of wisdom" (§ 195, trans. modified). But the servant's fear of revisiting absolute fear enchains him now. Hegel's account reveals that the avoidance of absolute fear importantly motivates the constitution of repressive social and political structures.

The most important question—even beyond the specifics of the dialectic of master and servant—is then whether one is indeed capable of *experiencing* absolute fear. In the following, I will trace how this and subsequent figures of consciousness will try to recover the missed experience. It is crucial that fear be experienced as a physical affection (a tremble) rather than merely intellectually thematized. It is crucial that it be "absolute" fear rather than a particular, circumscribed fear. And it is important that consciousness find (its) pleasure in absolute fear. For, if consciousness "could not stand [*ausgestanden*] absolute fear but only a few anxieties, then the negative essence will have remained an externality in his eyes, and his substance will not have been infected all the way through by it. Because not each and every one of the ways in which his natural consciousness was brought to fruition has come to totter [*wankend geworden*], he is still attached *in himself* to determinate being" (§ 196, trans. modified).[10]

Only an unrestrained fear, an absolute fear, or a fear for fear's sake, so to speak, can emancipate the servant from the master because the master's power is lodged in the servant's investment in subsistence. Any circumscribed fear of something specific at a particular moment and for a certain aspect of consciousness's being, only reinforces consciousness's attachment to its particular reality. Only a fear that doesn't trigger a protective mechanism, but is experienced for its own sake—that is, for the sake of thoroughly melting away one's entire being—can set consciousness free. While Hegel positions freedom here clearly in opposition to determinism, he also avoids conflating freedom with autonomy. Rather, he points to the self-deluding character of autonomy when he underscores that, in self-determination, freedom and unfreedom are entangled: "having a mind of his own is merely *stubbornness* [*der eigne Sinn ist Eigensinn*], a freedom that remains bogged down within the bounds of servility" (§ 196).[11] It is true that the master can take advantage of the servant's belief in determinism in order to instrumentalize him. But if the servant seeks self-determination instead, he instrumentalizes himself. For Hegel, therefore, freedom speculatively integrates self-determination and self-abandon, self-investiture and self-dispossession.[12]

But how can consciousness not pursue its own will? Even if the servant selflessly labors to realize the desire of the master, he still does so in order to preserve himself. Naturally, with every fiber of its being, with every line of thought, consciousness tries to resist its own dissolution, tries to flee from absolute fear. How, under these circumstances, can consciousness *experience* absolute fear? The beginning of the answer to this question lies in the ambivalent pull of fear. On the one hand, consciousness is afraid of fear; on the other hand, it yearns to experience absolute fear in order to gain freedom as a subject.[13] Absolute fear pushes and pulls, repels and attracts consciousness. In repeatedly moving toward and away from fear, the subject enacts the experience of trembling.

To actualize fear—not in order to do away with it but to learn to cherish a living fear—will be the aim of consciousness's *Bildung* from now on. In his work, which he develops beyond the mere satisfaction of his master into an artful fashioning of things (*Bilden des Dinges*), the servant tries to acknowledge his trembling, tries to live it again or, rather, for the first time really (§ 196). In fashioning the thing, the servant actively uses the same power of negation that he passively succumbs to in fear: "this objective *negative* is precisely the alien essence before which he trembled" (§ 196). So far fear had been a traumatic event that could not be integrated into conscious experience: "without culturally formative activity [*ohne das Bilden*], fear remains inward and mute" (ibid., trans. modified). Now "in forming the thing, his own negativity, that is, his being-for-itself, . . . becomes an object in his own eyes" (ibid.).

In his work, the servant objectifies fear, turns it outward. Rather than fleeing fear, consciousness now expresses its fear. The servant's labor takes on a therapeutic aspect. He fashions objects in order to come to terms with the traumatic experience of the trembles of absolute life. Hegel is not uncritical of the therapeutic paradigm. On the one hand, trembles finally become real and objective through the labor of expression and the occupational therapy that the servant engages in. On the other hand, the therapeutic impetus of "coming to terms" with fear only allows for a domesticated version of fear. It does not enable the experience of the trembling life of absolute fear.

The activity of confronting fear by way of producing objects that bear the trace of one's fear holds a therapeutic promise. This promise relies on the power of the understanding, as it is described in the preface to the *Phenomenology*: "The act of parting [*die Tätigkeit des Scheidens*] is the force and labor of the *understanding*, the most astonishing and greatest of all the powers . . . spirit is this power only when it looks the negative *in the face* and lingers with it" (§ 32, my emphasis). To "face one's fear," to imagine standing before one (*vorstellen*), actually allows one to keep one's distance from the tremble and the infectious rhythm of fear's negativity. When it "keep[s] and hold[s] fast to [*festzuhalten*]" the negative, the understanding turns that negative into "*thoughts* which are themselves familiar and fixed . . . [and] motionless determinations" (§ 32). The understanding "start(s) with A as in ANT and give(s) to every terror a soothing name."[14] Abstract intelligence tames the negative and calms the fear by turning fluid, uncontrollable negativity into something that is known and can be labeled. "This lingering [with the negative] is the magical power that converts it into being" (§ 32). The fashioned object functions as a mirror for consciousness and as a tool for its self-fashioning. It reflects back to consciousness an image of itself as a stable being that has overcome negation and now remains "within the element of continuance" (§ 32).[15] Having thus liberated his work from the desires of the master and having developed it instead into a means for self-reflection, the working consciousness exceeds servitude proper. It has not, however, experienced the absolute transience epitomized in absolute fear.

Yet Hegel clarifies that work cannot overcome transience altogether; it is merely "vanishing *staved off*" (*aufgehaltenes Verschwinden*, § 195). The servant has enough time to see himself in his products, but these works nevertheless eventually disappear, and therefore reflect the servant's own mortality.[16] Similarly, Hegel pushes further his account of the understanding. For him the movement has not come to an end when rational "analysis arrives at *thoughts* which are themselves . . . fixed . . . determinations" (§ 32, trans. modified). The movement has only just begun, "for the concrete is self-moving only because it divides itself and turns itself into the non-actual" (ibid.). The understanding's power to make something out of nothing by separating what is inseparable sets things in motion. Fixity and fluidity overlap; and the rationality of the understanding is not as neatly opposed to the emotionality of absolute fear as one might assume.[17]

Consciousness, the protagonist of the *Phenomenology*, is certainly still afraid of absolute movement. At this stage of its *Bildung*—the therapeutic labor of expression—it is only willing to cope with one shift: from consciousness to the fashioned object. Consciousness is not (yet) able to negotiate the contradictions of speculative negation. Instead, the servant fashions the thing while clinging to a logic of non-contradiction where fixity excludes fluidity, self-will excludes another's will, and affirmation excludes negation. He envisions his *Bilden* as pure production, affirmation and self-immortalizing, while he views the master as purely negating and consuming. The servant and the master see themselves in a life-or-death struggle and not, as Hegel puts it, in a struggle for "life *and* death" (§ 187, my emphasis).

If absolute fear were felt, it would offer an experience of the overlap of negation and affirmation, of absolute rather than abstract negativity. Absolute fear dissolves the inert matter of consciousness, but this dissolution is itself material. It manifests itself as a trembling and shaking. Trembles and shakes are bodily modes of unsettling the body. Since the body is at the same time the object and the subject of the negation, it preserves itself in its supersession. Fear is not an abstract negation like death but a speculative negation, a dying within life that, instead of simply destroying the body, sets it in motion.

As a bodily negation of the body, absolute fear not only preserves the body in negation but actually produces the body. Throughout the first three chapters of the *Phenomenology*, consciousness occupies a naively disembodied position. Consciousness does not reflect on its own physical condition since the object is its only focus. Only when its object develops for it into another consciousness or an alter ego, is it confronted with its bodily condition. It immediately engages in the struggle for life and death to show that its body is inessential for its self-image. As a result of this struggle, it nevertheless becomes apparent that a living body is indispensable for consciousness. But even this insight remains at first disembodied. As I have shown here, the insight is not experienced by an embodied consciousness but is logically deduced. Only in the trembling of fear can the lesson of the body be experienced. As Cixous puts it, "one must almost die in order to take pleasure in being made of flesh."[18] The trembling of fear awakens a body for consciousness and, for the first time in the *Phenomenology*, it presents consciousness's insight as a bodily experience.

When the *Phenomenology* thus suggests that physical existence is not a simple given for consciousness, it actually—contrary to what one might assume at first—undoes, or speculatively reconciles, the traditional dichotomy of spirit and body. Hegel shows that the body is not to be *presumed* as a solid container for the movements of the soul (the interiority model of emotion) or as a stable matrix for feelings (the impression/expression model of emotion), but that absolute fear retroactively produces the body as trembling, precarious, and ecstatic matter. The servant has a body because he is afraid.

The trembling body *is* the actualization of absolute fear. As a trembling body, absolute fear is therefore not confined to interiority—it does not "remain inward and mute"—but is an experience in the full sense, in and for itself (§ 196). Trembling combines externalizing and inwardizing (*erinnern*), affirming and negating in a movement of self-reflection. This self-reflection does not need consciousness to take place. In fact, the figures of consciousness in the *Phenomenology* cannot quite claim absolute fear because they are still new to the speculative thinking of bodily experience. The structure of experience is paradoxical and highly precarious because it requires bodily involvement in order to produce the body by negating it. All this happens in the flash of an instant: the body needs to be engaged in order to be produced, and only in its negation will the body have been affirmed. The body is at the same time the subject and the object of its production. What is to come requires for its advent that it be already there. So how can it ever arrive? It is impossible—at least within a logic of non-contradiction. And so we might begin to understand why, for a consciousness that works with a relatively simple logic, absolute fear is so difficult to experience. Consciousness is utterly unprepared for the bodily thinking of speculative transports.

We have observed the rejection of embodiment in the figure of the master, who projects his bodily being onto the servant. The servant timidly misunderstands the lessons of the struggle for life and death, and of the fashioning of things. While he grasps the importance of saving his life, he misunderstands what life is, namely movement and interdependence. While he is attached to natural existence, he fails to understand that his body is not a simple given, but a speculative, self-reflecting subject. We have witnessed the anticipatory refusal of fear bound up with the rejection of the body in the first three chapters of the *Phenomenology*, where materiality was exclusively assigned to the realm of objectivity. We will now continue to see the protagonists' dismissal of bodily life when we discuss some of the configurations of consciousness after the dialectic of mastery and servitude.

Retroaction

In the further development of the *Phenomenology*, consciousness stubbornly clings to an idea of the self as constant and autonomous, or Stoic.[19] But consciousness cannot escape from its precarious body or from the trembling movement of fear. Even fear in its negative form, as the fearful flight from fear, produces the body as the focus of consciousness's, albeit negative, attention.[20] The unhappy consciousness—the protagonist of the next chapter after mastery and servitude—tries to detach from the body and to rise to the metaphysical sphere of "the unchangeable." But its flight from the body brings the body all the more into focus. The unhappy consciousness's obsession with its body, when it is "brooding" over its "animal functions," is rooted in its inability to experience absolute fear and to understand the logic of fear (§ 225). Because consciousness still thinks in abstract terms, because it still values the unchangeable instead of the absolute movement of speculative negation, it remains unhappily bound to its physical existence rather than taking pleasure in absolute fear. Inadvertently, the unhappy consciousness performs one speculative negation, that is to say, one bodily negation of the body, after the other. Yet, according to its timorously abstract logic, these negations don't count precisely because they preserve the body in its negation.[21]

The link between freedom and fear, which we have seen in our analysis of the dialectic of mastery and servitude, resurfaces when Hegel discusses the kind of spirit that drove the French Revolution.[22] It is a spirit that acknowledges negativity and absolute fluidity as the essence of freedom, but excludes any positive stance from its highly abstract notion of freedom. That is why this freedom spreads terror rather than enabling the experience of absolute fear. In a continuous revolutionary upheaval, which is an attack on fixed differences among subjects and on the value of unchangeability in general, the spirit of absolute freedom abolishes anything that tries to establish lasting existence. It cuts off the breath of any self-will. Misconceiving still the meaning of absolute negativity, it performs abstract negations or killings en masse. In this purely negative action, this "*fury* of disappearing" (*Furie des Verschwindens*) which it calls "absolute freedom," it remains cold and dry (§ 589). As a "simple, unbending cold universality," it performs an "arid destruction" (*trocknen Vertilgen*, § 590/§ 591). And as the "discrete, absolute and hard, unaccommodating and obstinate isolation [*eigensinnige Punktualität*] of actual self-consciousness," it refuses fear (§ 590). The attempt to actualize absolute freedom is, thus, in the last analysis, still directed against the body. The body is here still understood as inert matter, or "*abstract* existence as such," and not as a self-negating, moving, or trembling body (ibid.).

The consciousness of this revolutionary world has finally affirmed and realized what the consciousness of perception was so afraid of: the entanglement of subject and object. Yet the revolutionary consciousness both overshoots and undershoots the goal of acknowledging entanglement when it wants to see absolutely no difference between subject and object. As "pure *insightfulness*" (*reines Einsehen,* § 583), this shape of consciousness figures a penetrating gaze that knows neither interference nor limit. "This movement is thereby the interplay of consciousness with itself in which it lets nothing break loose so that it would come to be a free-standing object confronting it" (§ 588). Far from implying sympathy across difference, "insight" here means the direct "gazing of the self into the self" without the interference of any positive, meaningful, or objective difference (§ 583). The entanglement of "subject" and "object" has thus been reduced to a doubling of the same. In the mania of its "absolutely seeing-*itself*-as-doubled" (*das absolute sich selbst doppelt Sehen,* ibid.), the self gazes into the self and death stares back at it.

This sudden encounter with death is the terror of absolute freedom, its *Schrecken,* or fright. But I would not consider this sudden fright as an experience of absolute fear. All trembling is excluded from the terror of massive, uniform death: it is "the coldest, emptiest death of all" (§ 590). "The individuality of the universal will," by negating all inner difference, is reduced to the "banality of one syllable [*Plattheit dieser Silbe*]": death (*Tod*) (§ 591, trans. modified). The monosyllable remains mute because the flatness of its self-identity provides no volume—no interval for the song of death to resonate, and no leeway for the spiritualized body to tremble.[23] Instead of lingering with the negative, and trembling in fear, consciousness starts up in terror, turns around, and runs back to an earlier form of its life—or leaps "into another land" (§ 595).

The protagonist is still running when it becomes the *Phenomenology*'s final figure of consciousness, the beautiful soul, who despite or, rather, because of its "completely transparent" knowledge of itself, continues to live on the run, in suspicion, and in fear of absolute fear (§ 658):

> It lives with the anxiety that it will stain the glory of its inwardness by means of action and existence. Thus, to preserve the purity of its heart, it *flees* from contact with actuality, and it steadfastly perseveres in its obstinate powerlessness to renounce its own self, . . . to transform its thought into being and to *entrust* itself [*sich anzuvertrauen*] to absolute difference. (§ 658, trans. modified, my emphasis)

The beautiful soul—the last figure of consciousness and the pinnacle of self-knowledge and sensibility before "absolute knowledge"—

still exhibits the characteristic reluctance of the individual to abandon itself and to acknowledge the entanglement of thought and being, subject and object, and life and death, which the experience of absolute fear affords.[24]

There is thus no evidence in the *Phenomenology* that consciousness ever experiences absolute fear, or that the experience of absolute fear is even possible. Because consciousness is an abstraction, absolute fear simply destroys it.[25] As mere consciousnesses, the protagonists of the *Phenomenology* don't enjoy the elasticity to stand absolute fear.

So far, we have established that the fear of absolute fear at the same time impedes and facilitates consciousness's movement toward absolute knowing. By repeatedly averting the realization of absolute change, consciousness draws its path. In the next section of this chapter, I will discuss how this path—which twists and turns—performs precisely the movement of change and interdependence that consciousness is afraid of. In its turning back and forth—away from and toward fear—the text actualizes the oscillating movement, the absolute trembling of absolute fear. No single figure of consciousness experiences absolute fear, but in their arrangement or in their syntax the various figures of consciousness in the *Phenomenology* together realize fear's trembling motion.

I have argued that the development of the *Phenomenology* is driven by absolute fear, without that fear ever being experienced by any single consciousness. I will argue in the next part of this chapter that absolute fear occurs in between figures of consciousness, in the blanks between the chapters. If the experience of absolute fear is not possible for consciousness, it might be possible before consciousness, or after. It might be possible during the syncopes of consciousness, between consciousness and consciousness, during the impossible transition from one shape of consciousness to another.

In the following, I want to read the silences between the chapters of Hegel's *Phenomenology of Spirit* without filling them in and thereby losing them. Resisting the desire to explain how these chapters form a coherent line, I will interpret the leaps from one figure of consciousness to the next. The leap opens a space of negativity between the positive shapes of consciousness. This is the space of "absolute fear," an interval of trembling. The *Phenomenology* asks us to allow for the trembles of fear, to explore it, to find its joy, and its promise of freedom. In keeping with this demand, I propose a reading of Hegel's *Phenomenology of Spirit* in dialogue with Cixous' *L'ange au secret.* Cixous writes:

> And a child remembers the fear before being born, being born losing, before gaining in losing.
>
> But nobody there to tell the passion of birth, the expulsion and the

> joy, at the same time, the sudden fall and then the slow resurrection. Nobody there to tell the fairy tale. Not me either: the instant is too fragile to take into my hand. Yet behind my memory from before I knew how to speak I feel a very first instant glimmering, a trembling of fear. (Cixous 1991, 15)

My reading between Hegel and Cixous will attend to the birth of any new consciousness as a transport that trembles back and forth between where I am and where I am not, or between where I am and where I am differently.

Blank in Transition

In an essay on the chapter "Absolute Freedom and Terror," a frustrated reader of the *Phenomenology* notes that "transitions are not the Phenomenology's strong point."[26] This statement strikes me as a very accurate reenactment (not description) of the *Phenomenology*'s mode of operation. The critic implies that the transitions from one chapter to the next, or from one dialectic to the next, are not worth looking at because they don't make any sense. Exasperated, he turns away, and thereby imitates the attitude he accuses Hegel of, that is, of not being "strong," not being in control, not being present to clarify what happens.

The fact that Hegel's text does not satisfy the reader's desire for logical and narrative continuity is precisely its strength. Despite expectations to the contrary, the *Phenomenology* does not offer a continuous exposition and does not provide coherent logical derivations of each shape of consciousness out of the preceding one. As a result of these gaps or leaps in progression, it appears that the *Phenomenology* does not have one protagonist who develops to ever greater self-awareness, but many protagonists. This does not mean that the many figures of consciousness and spirit are unrelated, but (a) that their sequential relation is tenuous, and (b) that they form connections other than linear.

The movement between chapters differs from the movement within chapters. Every particular figure of consciousness—from sense certainty to the beautiful soul—follows its path according to a particular logic. Within this logic, one moment engenders the next. Just like the critic—whose statement "transitions are not the *Phenomenology*'s strong point" speaks of a wish for an unambiguous logic, for a continuous line as a railing to hold onto—consciousness needs to have a sense of where it is going: forward, of course; and the reader is happy to accompany the protagonist as long as she feels that she is taking a step up on the ladder toward absolute knowledge. Consciousness sets out with certainty and goes straight ahead to interpret the world or to create reality according to what it holds to be true. Yet, on its path of allegedly straightforward progress, consciousness has to twist and turn in order to keep hold of its certainty.[27] It does so eagerly, because it is absolutely defined by the particular "essence" or value or truth criterion of its certainty. To let go of what it holds to be true would mean to abandon its raison d'être.[28]

Over the course of many chapters it becomes clear that pure affirmation is impossible, that every affirmation is riddled with negation, that every actualizing of something held to be true also means abandoning that truth. Yet, for consciousness, because it is an abstraction lacking the elasticity of the full concept, such self-dispossession is impossible. What seemed to be a ladder to climb the heights of reason comes to lie crosswise in front of consciousness barring its way. No matter how often it turns, consciousness will always come up against the bars of its limited logic. They make up all sides of the cage in which each figure of consciousness circles while convincing itself of its own progress. To actually realize what it holds to be true would mean to put itself out there, would mean to cross the bar. Consciousness would have to go beyond the realm of its control. Suddenly it will be unclear what the next step could be. The future cannot be deduced; it can only be leaped or fallen into. As Lispector puts it in *Stream of Life* (1989)—a text Cixous is in dialogue with when she writes *L'ange au secret*: "I'm still afraid to depart from logic because I fall . . . into the future."[29]

Is consciousness alive? Does it feel absolute fear? "By the stiffness of my neck and of my members, and at the shock of my heart against the bars [*barreaux*], I can tell that it is fear" (Cixous 1991, 28). The protagonist hardens. If it paid attention, it could infer from the tension in its body and the paralysis of its mind that it must be afraid. But does it tremble? Is consciousness present during the transition? Does it experience absolute fear?

The interval of trembling, the moment when consciousness oscillates between two shapes or figures of itself, is a space of freedom. When the body is permeable to and the consciousness is open for the other, when the other shudders through the "I," speculative thought becomes reality. But consciousness doesn't quite understand speculative logic. The wind of fear "rattles until it falls" (*secoue jusqu'à tomber,* Cixous 1991, 9)—until the bar falls, until consciousness falls, until the wind falls.

Consciousness falls and faints. It loses consciousness so as not to witness its own dissolution. "'I fall' we say. Watch out! says Clarice breathlessly, I will die. It's the truth. We die. Sometimes a day, it can go up to four. Then she comes back. 'I'm back' she says to us. Without quite knowing yet who this *I* is" (Cixous 1991, 73). Consciousness turns and goes blank, the text with it, until it comes round on the other side of the transition as a new shape of consciousness. The new shape of consciousness opens its eyes not knowing what happened to it. "Ah if I only knew the score by heart, I would sing of fear" (Cixous 1991, 30). It doesn't know fear, not by heart. Its heart doesn't know it. It hasn't experienced it. It doesn't remember feeling its joy. Consciousness is always already the result of a transition; the transition has passed through it and has forgotten the liberating negativity of fear.

Transitions are moments of absolute fear. They are moments of death and of birth. They are frightful because there is no rule to go by. The railing, the ladder, the bars, everything that gives stability and security begins to tremble. "All that was fixed within it had been shaken loose" (§ 194). Absolute fear jeopardizes consciousness's entire being: "every fiber" of its body trembles; every certainty, every rung of the ladder consciousness sets its foot on, every sash bar that organizes its vision is seized by the wind of freedom (ibid.). "The free wind, the young one is getting to the bars [*barreaux*] and rattles" (Cixous 1991, 9).

As "this way in which all durable existence becomes absolutely fluid," absolute fear disappears as soon as it is thematized (§ 194). "The instant is too fragile to take into my hand" (Cixous 1991, 15).[30] Absolute fear is a moment of absolute negativity that can only be accounted for performatively. Spirit cannot grasp the transition from one figure of consciousness to the next; it goes through it. The wind blows through spirit, and consciousness goes blank. "Nobody there to tell the fairy tale." "Nobody there to tell the passion of birth" (Cixous 1991, 15). Fear escapes the narration of the *Phenomenology*.

Out of politeness, one might try to attenuate the rupture: "I think that now I'll have to ask for permission to die a little. Excuse me, will you? I won't be long. Thanks" (Lispector 1989, 53). But then one will have lost not only the experience of absolute fear, but also its negative presence as an unexpected break in expository coherence: "No. I couldn't die" (ibid.). It requires some strength to simply break with the demand for coherence:

> I'm going now.
>
> I'm back. Now I'll try to catch up again with what happens to me in the moment—and that way I'll create myself. (Lispector 1989, 69)

Transitions are in fact the *Phenomenology*'s strong point because they are the points where spirit shows that its movement is not a continuous progression. Consciousness dies and is reborn in a different incarnation, a different "*Gestalt*." The chapter transitions of the *Phenomenology*—albeit much wordier than Lispector's economic and elegant meditations on transport—enact the same break, the same death within life that she presents us with. The last few lines of the chapter on "absolute freedom and terror" offer an exemplary illustration of this (non-)transition: "Absolute freedom passes over [*geht über*] from its self-destroying actuality into another land of self-conscious spirit. . . . What has emerged is a new shape, that of the *moral spirit*" (§ 595). The so-called transition is effected as a leap across the border from revolutionary France to German moral philosophy à la Kant. Having led one shape of consciousness to the realization of its own destructiveness and destruction, the narrative turns away from it, leaves it to its own (ineffective, we know) devices, and turns to a new figure of consciousness. Rather than leading us, step by step, through a transition, Hegel presents us with a past event: "What has emerged is a new shape, that of the *moral spirit.*" The old shape of consciousness has passed on, the exact moment of the emergence of the new one has passed us by, and the protagonists are certainly not more actively engaged than we are in their death and birth. After a typographical blank space between the chapters, a newborn consciousness begins to slowly create itself. The next chapter (on morality) will meticulously describe this new figure's development; consciousness will catch up with what happens to it in the moment.

Again somewhat heavier than Lispector's lithe narration in the first person, Hegel regularly (at times explicitly, at others implicitly) interpolates a "we," the first-person plural of the phenomenologist, around the moments of transport. It might be Hegel's (somewhat awkward) way of being polite when he makes a bit of a fuss inserting explanations and excuses, anticipation and retrospection from the perspective of the phenomenologist/s right before and right after the break between chapters. Here is the end of the chapter on the understanding:

> In the inner division [*innern Unterschiede*], infinity indeed becomes itself the *object* of the understanding, but once again the understanding fails to notice it as such. . . . What is an object in sensuous covering for the understanding is now there for us in its essential shape as the pure concept. This apprehending of division [*Unterschied*] as it is *in truth,* that is, the apprehending of *infinity* as such, exists *for us,* that is, *in itself.* . . . However, consciousness as it *immediately* possesses this concept once again comes on the scene as its own form or as a new shape of consciousness that does not take cognizance of its essence in what has gone before but instead regards it as something completely other [*etwas ganz anderes*]. (§ 164, trans. modified)

The phenomenologist steps in to explain not so much how we get from one figure of consciousness to the next, but why there is no apparent connection between the two: each consciousness has a strong sense of its own individuality and considers its previous shape to be "something completely other."

After the transition from the figure of the unhappy consciousness to that of reason, the phenomenologist observes the same more or less active forgetting in consciousness: "Since self-consciousness is reason, what had so far been its negative relation to otherness is now converted [*schlägt um*] into a positive relation" (§ 232). It took one final twist and suddenly all the pain of the previous figure's attempts to negate and escape worldly existence is forgotten and reason is happy to embrace the world.

The phenomenologist lends support to each consciousness's sense of substance and separate individuality when he indicates that the old shape of consciousness does not transform into the new one, but continues to exist the same way it had before, even after the exposition has turned its attention away from this figure. Here the end of the dialectic of the unhappy consciousness:

> For on the one hand, surrendering one's own will is merely negative in terms of *its concept*, that is, *in itself*, but at the same time it is positive, specifically, it is the positing of the will . . . as universal, not as the will of an individual. . . . Hence, *for consciousness*, its will becomes universal will, a will existing *in itself*, although in its own eyes, it itself is not this will *in-itself*. . . . However, *for the consciousness itself*, activity continues, and its actual activity remains impoverished. Its enjoyment in consumption remains sorrowful, and the sublation of these in any positive sense continues to be postponed to an *otherworldly beyond*. (§ 230)

The unhappy consciousness remains unhappy. But that does not concern "us" anymore, since "within this object, the representational thought [*Vorstellung*] of *reason* has . . . come to be," and this is what interests "us" now (§ 230). Hegel's *Phenomenology* does not tell the story of *one* protagonist who consistently grows and continuously progresses toward absolute knowledge. It follows many protagonists observing each one faithfully until a new figure has "emerged," one knows not exactly how (§ 595).

Our Own Epoch

In addition to the performed transitions, that is, in addition to the blanks or the positive nothings between the chapters, Hegel offers two paradigmatic descriptions of transports. One of them can be found in the preface to the *Phenomenology*. On one hand, the preface is a methodological piece, which allows us to assume that what Hegel says there about the logic of transport is valid also for the transports in the text itself. On the other hand, Hegel explicitly refuses the notion of method; he refuses to offer us the railing that allows us to look down at the text without falling into it. Therefore, he gives no general theory of transport in the preface but simply an example. Or rather, *the* example: the transport we ideally experience as readers: "it is not difficult to see that our own epoch is a time of birth and a transition to a new period" (§ 11). What Hegel calls here "our own epoch" is not the historical time in which he lived. It should have become clear by now that transports do not take place within historical time; they are—or make up—the interstices in and between historical times.[31] "Our own epoch" is the textual time of the *Phenomenology*—that is, according to Hegel's system, the time of transition from historical time to the infinite (and, as we will see, itself interstitial) time of Hegel's philosophical science: the time it takes to transport the reader from one into the other:

> Besides, it is not difficult to see that our own epoch is a time of birth and a transition to a new period. Spirit has broken with the previous world of its existence and its ways of thinking; it is in the process of submerging them in the past [*in die Vergangenheit hinab zu versenken*] and working on its own transformation. To be sure, spirit is never at rest but rather always moving forward [*immer in fortschreitender Bewegung*]. However, just as with a child, who after a long silent period of nourishment draws his first breath and breaks with the gradualness of merely quantitative growth [*nur vermehrenden Fortgang*]—a qualitative leap—and as now the child is born so too, in bringing itself to cultural maturity, spirit ripens slowly and quietly into its new shape, dissolving bit by bit the structure of its previous world . . . This gradual crumbling [*Zerbröckeln*], which left unaltered the physiognomy of the whole, is interrupted by the ascent [*Aufgang*], which, a flash [*ein Blitz*], puts forth all at once the structure of the new world.
>
> Yet this newness is no more completely actual than is the newborn child, . . . so little is the reached concept of the whole the whole itself. . . . The actuality of this simple whole consists in those shapes which, having become moments of the whole, once again develop themselves anew and give themselves a shape, but this time within their new element, within the new meaning which itself has come to be. (§ 11–12, trans. modified)

Spirit is "never at rest," always growing and crumbling at the same time. Its transformations nevertheless leave "unaltered the physiognomy of the whole." Spirit moves without realizing it—or it realizes that it moves without showing it. It is moved but remains motionless, like a king in a sedan chair or a statue on a dolly. Spirit saves face and denies change until it breaks down. In this breakdown, a new world immediately replaces the old one. We leap from one world to the next. The interval of negativity or of trembling fails to become part of our experience; the time of infinity is reduced to virtually nothing. Transport appears as a flash or as lightning (*Blitz*).

The lightning destroys the old world and illuminates the new one. In the flash of an insight, we have been transported from a long and painful history of misrecognitions into the new reality of speculative science. The birth of speculative science should mean the end of history. Yet, surprisingly, Hegel insists here on a continuity between historical time and the non-linear time of speculative science. Just like the many figures of consciousness within the book, "we," the readers of the *Phenomenology*—even after we have grasped the logic of the infinite and leapt into the realm of the speculative—need to labor at giving spirit actuality and to "once again develop [its moments] anew and give them . . . a shape." Hegel insists that the labor of the concept is continuous and progressive, that "spirit is never at rest but rather always moving forward." Just like spirit, we can be "never at rest." And with this admonishment, Hegel has covered over the space of the blank, the lighthearted time of the leap, the rupture of the flash.

Hegel, who, as phenomenologist, shows the strength to frustrate the desire for continuity and to present transitions as leaps, succumbs to this desire in the moment when he thematizes the transition he himself undergoes when writing the *Phenomenology:* the transition from historical time to the non-historical time of speculative science. The dismissive "besides" and the boastful "it is not difficult to see" that introduce the passage are symptoms of his denial of fear. Refusing to show the strength to lose control together with his subject, Hegel remains a distant observer who claims to know better than to tremble with "our own epoch."

The *Phenomenology* keeps a record of what happens "behind the back of consciousness" (§ 87). It records the unconscious or unregistered experiences of the protagonists, and it archives the figures that the progressive development of the exposition leaves behind. The *Phenomenology,* as a text, functions as the archive or the "memory [that] still preserves the dead mode of spirit's previous shape as a passed history" (§ 545). As such, it is fundamentally torn within. On the one hand, this archive satisfies Hegel's anxious demand for continuous labor; on the other hand and by the same token it spoils his desire for the leap to the end of history and into a new, speculative world.[32] Despite Hegel's timorous reserve, the text syntactically (not thematically) cultivates the trembling movement of absolute fear that neither its authors nor its protagonists endure.[33] The *Phenomenology* as a text thus offers neither the (impossible) linear, continuous, and causal development from history to the end of history, nor the leap into the speculative via the erasure of the non-speculative. Rather, the text gives us to read a trembling-back-and-forth between the finite and the infinite, between the speculative and the non-speculative.

By insisting in the preface on his authority and superior knowledge, Hegel lends weight to a linear reading of the text. By describing the movement as a progression, he favors the next "higher" form of consciousness over the previous one. And by stressing that spirit's movement is continuous, he encourages the sense that the *Phenomenology* has only one protagonist and that the differences between the *Gestalten* indicate a development or growth of consciousness rather than an interaction between different consciousnesses. But in order to register the trembling of absolute fear, the different figures of consciousness in the *Phenomenology* need to be read neither as one consciousness in a linear development, nor as many strictly separate consciousnesses, but as a multiplicity of consciousnesses that are neither completely different nor strictly the same, that move through each other without collapsing into one, and that send each other into ecstasies.[34]

Hegel's weakness is to pretend that there is nothing to fear because Spirit always progresses. Thus, we need to modify the critic's remark: meta-discourse about transitions is not the *Phenomenology*'s strong point. Evidently, the phenomenologist (a narrative persona that includes the reader function) shows more strength than the author. Despite his strong overall argument for self-abandon and exposure, the preface to the *Phenomenology* shows that Hegel is afraid to abandon authority. We can take a breath: Hegel is no *Übermensch,* no absolute master of the speculative. Just like his protagonists, he avoids absolute fear.

Of course, Hegel's reserve in the preface will not prevent absolute fear from rising. According to his own account, saving face is an integral part of "the work [of self-] transformation" (§ 11). Avoiding the transition "to the other side of life," from where "the other side of me is calling," I "try to distract myself from [the] fear" that seizes us with a "pervading infection" (Lispector 1989, 12, 13; Hegel, § 545). Eventually, you cannot resist the onslaught any longer.[35] Suddenly your body jerks: you almost fall asleep; you almost fall into the future of speculative thought, but at the last moment you flinch and yank yourself back: "in the nightmare I finally in a sudden convulsion fall prostrate back onto this side" (Lispector 1989, 13). You wake up "*some fine morning*": "safe" (Hegel, § 545; Lispector 1989, 13). The lightning didn't strike, the scene is "bloodless," yet spirit crossed a line (§ 545). In a "sudden fall," he slipped through the bars, and the "kadump!" with which he hits the ground again jerks him out of his reverie (Cixous 1991, 15; Hegel, § 545). He will have been "on the other side of life," but any consciousness—and here Hegel is not different from his protagonists—considers where it is to be "this side," the *Diesseits*, or "this life" (Lispector 1989, 12). "Consciousness as such has never slept"; it has always been engaged in a continuous movement and does not conceive of its side as the other side (Nancy 1993, 16). While the nightmare of speculative thinking thus remains a well-kept secret, consciousness starts anew to set itself out as if nothing happened. It "has in this way painlessly shed merely its withered skin":

> Rather, now that it is an invisible and undetected spirit, [pure insight] thoroughly infiltrates [*durchschleicht*] all the nobler parts, and it has soon taken complete hold over all the fibers and members of the unaware idol. At that point, "*some fine morning* it gives its comrade a shove with the elbow, and thump! kadump! the idol is lying on the floor." —*Some fine morning*, the noon of which is bloodless if the infection has permeated every organ of spiritual life. Memory alone then still preserves the dead mode of spirit's previous shape as a passed history (passed one knows not how exactly), and the new serpent of wisdom, elevated for adoration, has in this way painlessly shed merely its withered skin. (§ 545, trans. modified)

This is the second exemplary description of a transition that I want to consider. It is located in the body of the text, not between chapters, but within the chapter on the enlightenment. While specifically describing consciousness's transformation from believer to enlightened subject, it also functions as an exemplary description of transitions in general and reflects on the *Phenomenology* as transition.

The account is torn between the perspective of the consciousness after the transition and that of the consciousness before the transition. From the perspective of the enlightened consciousness, the transition is painless. It didn't feel a thing. Consciousness wakes up to its new life without knowing what happened and, what is more, without knowing that it was indeed asleep or blacked-out. Emerging as a so-called enlightened and, thus, supposedly free consciousness, it did not experience absolute fear. Spirit's "work on its own transformation" (§ 11)—that is, the spreading of "pure insight" in the mind of the naively faithful consciousness—is identified as an unconscious work, a "pervading infection [that] is not noticeable beforehand" but "thoroughly infiltrates all the nobler parts" (§ 545).

Already in the dialectic of master and servant, the labor of fear was described as an infection. There we read that if consciousness "could not stand absolute fear . . . his substance will not have been infected [*angesteckt*] all the way through" by negativity (§ 196). Absolute fear produces self-consciousness by infecting substance with negativity. It performs its work quietly; we read in the above-quoted passage that insight "flows into" the believer and hollows out the idol.[36] This "way in which all durable existence becomes absolutely fluid" leaves "unaltered the physiognomy" of consciousness (§ 194; § 11). The change goes unnoticed until pure insight pushes the king from his sedan chair, and with a bang, it becomes apparent that the old shape of consciousness is already dead, and that the new one has already taken its place. The transition again happens in a trice; while in the passage from the preface it appears as a flash or lightning, here it is a sudden noise, a bang or thunder.

Again, the protagonist does not experience absolute fear. But somewhere the secret is kept. A trace of fear, a memory from before remains in the body after the leap: "And a child remembers the fear before being born" (Cixous 1991, 15). The young consciousness, "the newborn child" begins to tremble after the fact (§ 12). "It is only when the infection has become widespread that it is *for consciousness*" (§ 545). Then it flinches and yanks itself around, defends itself and struggles against its dissolution. Retroactively, consciousness fights against a fear it has never quite felt. In this struggle, which in our last example takes the form of a dispute between enlightenment and faith, the consciousness after the transition reenacts the consciousness before the transition. For itself, the enlightened consciousness is pure insight and pure intention, and its struggle "is directed against the impure intentions and perverse insights" of priests and believers (§ 537, trans. modified). But, in its fight against absolute fear, "pure insight . . . becomes the negative of pure insight; it becomes untruth and unreason, and as intention it becomes the negative of pure intention and grows into lies and dishonesty about its purpose" (§ 547).[37] The old idol, victim of an infection, comes back to haunt the new enlightened consciousness. Pure insight is infected with belief: it has faith in reason. So it indeed "fall[s] prostrate back onto this side," the side of the believer (Lispector 1989, 13). And the "noisy ruckus" of both figures' "violent struggle" echoes the wild roars of an even earlier figure of consciousness: the spiritual kingdom of animals and its deception (§ 546).[38]

Led by fear of absolute fear, we like to construe a firm separation between one life and another. That is why we tend to read the chapters of the *Phenomenology* separately. We pretend that each of these figures is stable and self-contained, and forget that they figure one another. One shape of spirit inadvertently replicates previous shapes of spirit and so the textual life of spirit retroactively makes up the experience of trembling it didn't have before.[39] The text keeps the secret. And that is why the newborn child, the new period of spirit can—if it is not too afraid of fear—rejoice in the replication of shapes across the lightning of the qualitative leap, and delight in hearing the echo through the thunder. The child might take pleasure in fright. Without a warning, the winds of fear and the shivers of birth rise again in its body. It does not avoid contact with the bars. Sitting on a climbing frame at the playground—with one leg in front of birth and one leg behind it—the child rocks back and forth. "On the spot we rode them, secretly, and we enjoyed ourselves on their backs. . . . On bars we traveled before all travel" (Cixous 1991, 9). Thus consciousness might remember the fear it has felt when it was someone other than it is now. The enlightened consciousness trembles, permeated by its previous shapes. "I'm still afraid. But my heart is beating. . . . You are a way of my being me, and I a way of you being you" (Lispector 1989, 54).

The memory and anticipation of one figure of consciousness in the other—as one figure shudders through the other—is the experience of absolute fear. The consciousness before the turn and the consciousness after the turn exchange shapes. The moments of impossible absolute fear function as turning points around which the movement of the *Phenomenology* pivots, oscillating between before and after. Fear keeps the different shapes of consciousness apart, and mediates between them at the same time. The moment of synthesis in Hegel's dialectic does not consist in the next higher form of consciousness, but precisely in this turning point, this blank, this flash of an instant that cannot be grasped because it is the concept itself that trembles and turns at this instant.[40]

If we linger a bit with the passing moment of reconciliation, we might, from this perspective, be able to register the trembles of the text that take place despite the author's call for steady work. Even the passage from the preface is several times torn and trembles across its multiple tears. Chiefly remarkable is the parenthesis "a flash" that completely interrupts the syntax of an otherwise well-organized sentence and thus performs the interruption that Hegel here thematizes: "This gradual crumbling, which left unaltered the physiognomy of the whole, is interrupted by the ascent, which, a flash, puts forth all at once the structure of the new world" (§ 11). Then one notices that the description cuts across spirit in transition and the authorial perspective that keeps a distance from such transport. It oscillates between modeling a moment within the *Phenomenology* and describing the moment *of* the *Phenomenology*. It moves back and forth between identifying gradual growth and gradual crumbling, or progress and dissolution. And finally one would be hard-pressed to precisely locate in time this account as it seems to shift with the transport it is describing. On the one hand, "spirit has broken with the previous world of its existence and its ways of thinking," which implies that the transition took place already (ibid.). On the other hand, the transition is about to occur, and spirit "is about to submerge them in the past" (ibid.). Moving between before and after, trembling across the limit line, the passage lingers in transition. It turns out that this description of transport is divided between calling it a leap and describing it as a continuous development.

Let's also look again at another one of the performative (not descriptive) accounts of transport. So far, we said that the blanks between the chapters mark the interruption of continuity and negatively present the experience of absolute fear. In the following, I will argue that the text trembles around these blanks. I want to consider again the transition from "Absolute Freedom and Terror" to "Spirit Certain of Itself: Morality." I have already mentioned that "absolute freedom passes over from its self-destroying actuality" and jumps the border "into another land of self-conscious spirit, . . . that of the *moral spirit*" (§ 595). For a moment, the phenomenologist follows not the line of progression but that of regress; he notes that the jump might as well take the shape of a similarly abrupt movement in the other direction—a being hurled back:

> In the way that it emerged from out of this tumult [of the revolution], spirit might have been hurled back to its starting-point, the ethical world and the real world of cultural maturation, which had only been refreshed and rejuvenated by the fear of the master, a fear which had once again entered into people's hearts. (§ 594)

We know that history could not benefit from the subjunctive Hegel employs here. A period of restoration did in fact follow the French Revolution. Hegel alludes to that historical fact:

> These individuals, who have felt the fear of their absolute master—death—now once again acquiesce in negation and divisions, put themselves into the various orderings of the social spheres and return to a divided and limited work. However, as a result, they return back to their substantial actuality. (§ 593, trans. modified)

In order to escape the terror of a meaningless death, society returns to stratification, discrimination, and servitude. As I have discussed in the first part of this chapter, terror does not afford an experience of absolute fear. It doesn't teach consciousness the pleasures of a living fear, but merely reminds it of its fear of death. The result repeats the outcome of the struggle for life and death: consciousness accepts a limited but secure position within a hierarchy.

But not only historically, also logically, spirit is bound to be thrown back to its starting point and to "run through this cycle of necessity all over again" (§ 594). The dialectic of absolute freedom and terror teaches a lesson in logic, namely that pure self-identity is impossible. When the universal will aspires to total self-identity and sets out to negate all difference within, it inadvertently negates itself. What is more, even death cheats the universal will out of the desired integrity: self-negation offers no relief from self-difference since self-negation only evinces self-difference: "As the *pure* parity-with-itself of the universal will, absolute freedom thus has the *negation* in it, and in turn it thereby has *the division* as such in it, and it develops this once again as *actual* division" (§ 593). The "actual division" here takes the shape of spheres or classes and apportioned tasks. Hegel makes it quite clear that the historical fact of a period of restoration following the revolution is only consistent with logical necessity.

In any case, the narrative development of Hegel's *Phenomenology* does not take its orders from history but from speculative necessity. Indeed, Hegel not only alludes here to historical events, but also refers to earlier chapters of the *Phenomenology*. "The ethical world and the real world of cultural maturation" to which "spirit might have been hurled back" (§ 594) refers to the preceding parts of the section on spirit: "True Spirit, Ethical Life" and "Spirit Alienated from Itself: Cultural Maturation." We are also, as I already indicated, thrown back even further, to the chapter on mastery and servitude with its preference for hierarchical yet stable relations over the uncertainty of mutual acknowledging. For the narrative of the *Phenomenology*, the only possibility to escape this eternal return is the leap into the next chapter.

The narrative trembles and turns on the meaninglessness of death. On one hand, the mass terror of senseless death throws the late consciousness of absolute freedom back to the beginning and into an endless cycle of repetitions. On the other hand, this same acknowledging of the absolute meaninglessness of death projects consciousness into the next dialectic. The massive negation is so abstract that it offers no recompense: "the *universal will* can give nothing in return for the sacrifice" (§ 594).[41] This means that no positive actuality can distract consciousness from acknowledging that its own essence is absolute negativity: "this negation in its actuality is not *alien*," but "is unmediated oneness with self-consciousness" (ibid.). With this acknowledgment, "the meaningless death, the unfilled negativity of the self, changes over suddenly into absolute positivity" (ibid.). We have reached here the point where the extremes of pure negativity and pure positivity touch one another across infinity and where we tremble back and forth from one to the other.

For a brief moment, the exposition reveals the pleasure in trembles that even the stern moral philosopher from Königsberg takes: "Spirit feasts [*sich labt*] on the thought of this truth" (§ 595, trans. modified). The truth here is that freedom consists in the sudden "changing-over" (*Umschlagen*) of pure positivity (universal will) into pure negativity (terror) and back into pure positivity (forms of experience that are transparent to knowledge) (§ 594). Morality, the next figure of consciousness, will quickly forget the pleasure of the "pure universal movement, this way in which all durable existence becomes absolutely fluid" (§ 194). But "we," as readers of the *Phenomenology*, can stand (*ausstehen*) or linger with death by trembling back to earlier parts of the text and forth to the following exposition.

If we read the *Phenomenology* forward and backward starting from its moments of transition, our reading could perform the trembles of fear. It will be no easy task; it takes a long time to unfold one instant. "We'll labor for months to copy the flash" (Cixous 1991, 70). Every figure of consciousness has to be read as permeated by many others. Every proposition of this book has to be read backward and forward. The entire development of the *Phenomenology* presents a meticulous actualization, and thereby multiplication, of *one* transport or instant of transition. The *Phenomenology* not only cuts across time periods and figures of consciousness, but, situated between history and philosophical science, it moves between time and non-time, or between linear time and the trembling of an infinite present. The linearity of its development as a whole is therefore broken up by a to and fro of different times echoing in each other. In the *Phenomenology*, time shudders with interlacing rhythms. Different times strike against one another, oppose each other, rub against one another, take each other's place in a trembling rhythm with the text's "heart beating wildly" (Lispector 1989, 54).

7

Broken

> It . . . has . . . the most painful feeling and the truest insight about itself—namely, the feeling of the dissolution of all of its self-assurances, the feeling that it has been rolled upon the wheel through all the stages of its existence and that every bone in its body has been broken.
>
> —*Phenomenology*, § 538

The twentieth century has read the *Phenomenology of Spirit* as a coherent narrative of progress. It has commonly accepted that "the *Phenomenology* raises empirical consciousness to absolute knowledge" while understanding this "raising" as an improvement and "absolute knowledge" as the final mastery of truth (Hyppolite 1974, 39). Fink, for example, describes the itinerary of the *Phenomenology* as a straightforward movement with "a definite point of departure and a definite end. The point of departure is the ordinary conception of being, in which we lodge, as it were, in a blind and ignorant fashion. . . . The end of the path is for Hegel the insight that is attained into what being is, that is, the truth of being or absolute knowledge" (Fink 1977, 42, my translation). Solomon spells out the common assumption that this passage is a progression from darkness to light when he suggests that "the 'root-metaphor' of the entire *Phenomenology* [is development understood as] growth and education. Hegel several times uses the image of a growing tree or a growing child to illustrate his model of philosophy, but perhaps the dominant philosophical image is Plato's metaphor of education, in which the philosopher leads the uneducated out of the shadows and into the light of truth" (Solomon 1983, 277).

The introduction to the *Phenomenology*, however, describes consciousness's path toward absolute knowledge as a "path of despair" (*Weg der Verzweiflung*, § 78). Quite contrary to the optimistic interpretations of many of its readers, "this path has a negative meaning" for the protagonist of this narrative of *Bildung* (ibid.).[1] The *Phenomenology* emphasizes repeatedly that the formation or *Bildung* of its protagonist means for this model subject "the loss of itself" (ibid.). Entwined with such self-loss is the loss of truth: "for it is on this path that it loses its truth" (ibid.). Consciousness starts its journey of formation as a righteous subject with a clear idea of the world. Then, not once, but many times, again and again, it loses itself and is forced to abandon the certainty of its knowledge until consciousness, "through a complete experience of itself, achieve[s] a cognitive acquaintance of what it is in itself": a consumed and shattered subject (§ 77).

The *Phenomenology* presents *Bildung* as a "path of despair," that is, as a path of spiritual and physical ruin. I will discuss over the course of this chapter how the subject in despair consumes and dismembers itself; how it loses its head, how its heart breaks, how its spirit is crushed but restless, how it loses a leg, and how its every bone is broken so that it feels like rubber. When we reach the part of the *Phenomenology* where consciousness begins to understand that it is not simply a natural given, but that it is the result of a long and ongoing path of formation—when we reach the self-alienated spirit of cultural maturation (*Bildung*)—the protagonist rather poignantly registers the despair of this journey: it has the "feeling that it has been rolled upon the wheel through all the stages of its existence and that every bone in its body has been broken" (*durch alle Momente ihres Daseins hindurch gerädert und an allen Knochen zerschlagen zu sein,* § 538, trans. modified). At that moment, it must dawn on the reader as well as the protagonist that *Bildung* is torture.

Yet the despair of the *Phenomenology* remains strangely impalpable. After the brief but powerful mention of it in the introduction, despair barely ever becomes a topic again. The feeling of despair is largely covered over by the teleological thrust of the narrative. Žižek points out that while subjectivity, in Hegel's sense of negativity, essentially creates self-disturbance, the stories we tell about the self have a stabilizing function. "The organization of the narrative history of 'what I am,'" (or of what spirit is) designates "the formation of a new, culturally created homeostasis which imposes itself as our 'second nature'" (Žižek 2006, 210). It is thus not surprising that spirit's autobiography—the bildungsroman of consciousness—creates a feeling of confidence and trust in automatic growth rather than communicating a sense of despair. Consciousness does not have the face of despair: every time it is crushed, it picks itself up and cheerfully starts anew. The introduction to the *Phenomenology* announces that what follows will be a text of despair but, once the story begins, this proclamation seems forgotten.

Nevertheless, despair affects the entire organization of the *Phenomenology.* It plays a syncopating and performative, rather than a thematic role. This is why it is important to read the *Phenomenology* not only for its narrative, but also for its theatrics and its rhythm. Attending to the significance of despair for the textual structure of the *Phenomenology*, I will follow a threefold approach. First, I will examine two of Hegel's rather curious and, in the traditional sense, non-philosophical mentions of despair: despair (*Verzweiflung*) as an etymological relative of doubt (*Zweifel*) and despair as an emotion of animals. Then I will discuss two examples of the breaking of a shape of consciousness: the judgment of phrenology and the hard heart of the beautiful soul. These last two sections will be bracketed by two explorations of textual performances of despair: the (dis)organization of rational thought, and the (dis)organization of the *Phenomenology*'s narrative. Throughout, I will move beyond an exegesis of Hegel toward an account of despair that I hope will be useful for emotion studies today. For this purpose, I will draw upon *The Passion According to G.H.* (1994), a novel by the Brazilian writer Clarice Lispector that describes an unexpected crisis in the life of an upper middle-class Brazilian woman: the encounter with a cockroach. An insignificant incident that is usually aborted by the quick killing of the cockroach takes greater, spiritually transformative dimensions for this woman who, for no particular reason, opens herself to the experience of the encounter. Without calling this experience by the name of despair, Lispector's text offers a poetic phenomenology of despair's (self-)shattering and (self-)consuming qualities. While called on the scene here to interrupt Hegel's narrative, *The Passion According to G.H.* thus resonates across a productive distance with the *Phenomenology of Spirit*—not least because they both offer de-Christianized, perhaps even parodistic, versions of the Passion.[2]

Wordplay

In the introduction to the *Phenomenology*, Hegel links the two conceptually rather disparate terms *Verzweiflung* (despair) and *Zweifel* (doubt, skepticism). As is often the case with Hegel, his attention to the linguistic material determines the thrust of his conceptual operation here. Added to the root *zweifel* are the prefix *ver-* (which can indicate the thorough accomplishment, but also the negation, of the action expressed in the verb it modifies) and the suffix *-ung* (English: "-ing," which is regularly used to turn verbs into nouns, and which emphasizes the continuous aspect of the action expressed). Hegel uses the resulting word (*ver-zweifl-ung*) to present despair as a thoroughgoing self-doubt or a "self-consummating skepticism" (*sich vollbringende Skeptizismus*, § 78). He thereby draws attention to three characteristics that make him validate despair over skepticism. First, with the use of the reflexive pronoun "self," Hegel affirms the self-reflexivity of despair. By contrast, he critiques the skeptic for directing his negativity solely toward the outside—that is, for being skeptical about everything except his own power to negate.[3] Second, Hegel considers despair to be more genuine and more effective than doubt. When skepticism pretends to negate accepted opinions and prejudices, it ends up reinforcing them.[4] Despair actually carries through what skepticism only claims to do. Finally, Hegel underscores the nature of despair as process: despite despair's effectiveness, the gerund "self-consummat*ing*" (*vollbring*end) presents despair as an ongoing movement that does not come to completion. Despair forms the self as constitutively incomplete, as torn between self-affirmation and self-negation without either one ever reaching its end.

As self-reflexive doubt or self-doubt, despair reveals that, while the essence of consciousness is negativity, this essence is only improperly called its nature. The self tends to want to claim a substantive essence for itself by protecting itself from its own negativity and employing its negativity solely against what is foreign to it. But consciousness cannot avoid becoming self-conscious. "*To think* does not mean to think as an *abstract I,* but as an I which at the same time signifies being-*in-itself* [*Ansichsein*], that is, it has the meaning of being as an object in its own eyes, or of conducting itself vis-à-vis the objective essence in such a way that its meaning is that of the *being-for-itself* of that consciousness for which it is" (§ 197). Thus, when consciousness negates the object, it cancels its own being-for-self as well. As soon as consciousness begins to genuinely think, it must realize that it truly is a self in despair.

In contrast to the genuine actuality and effectiveness of despair, Hegel describes doubt (*Zweifel*) as an incomplete despair (*Verzweiflung*). Descartes' skeptic philosophy asks consciousness to "advance but very little" because it is concerned about security, safety, and certainty (Descartes 1979, II.5). Hegel's *Verzweiflung,* on the other hand, leaps without falling back onto the originally presumed truth. According to Hegel's analysis, the skeptic's ineffective frenzy to denounce the vanity of all existence is driven by a "fear of truth." The skeptic masks this fear with a "fiery enthusiasm for the truth [*heiße Eifer für die Wahrheit*]" and a general scorn for all appearance (§ 80).[5] But in fact he even "hide(s) . . . behind the appearance" (*sich . . . hinter dem Scheine verbergen,* § 80, trans. modified). He needs illusions in order to demonstrate his scorn for them. Once he has abolished all untruth, he finds himself deprived of shelter. The skeptic then is on the verge of the abyss, exposed to the emptiness all around him. He freezes in terror until he manages to forget his situation and can begin anew: "Skepticism which ends with the abstraction of nothingness or emptiness cannot progress any further from this point but must instead wait to see whether something new will come along and wait to see what it will be if indeed it is then to toss it too into the same empty abyss" (§ 79). Oblivious to his predicament, the skeptic performs an unconscious version of self-negation: a self-negation that does not consummate genuine self-doubt, but takes the form of naive self-contradiction.[6]

Despair is an unending process. The subject in despair effectively negates itself and disarticulates the certainty of its own (positive or negative) opinions. Yet despair ruins the self without ever completely annihilating it. The self in despair will always contradict even its own negation; it will multiply, fly ahead of itself, and spoil the peace of its own death.[7] Mere negations are too simple for a hyperactive consciousness in despair. Despair does not lead into an abyss of nothingness because the desperate is too obsessively attentive not to find the trace of affirmation within negation that turns the entire operation around:

> This nothingness is determinately the nothingness of that *from which it has resulted*. . . . That nothingness is itself thereby *determinate* and thereby has a *content*. . . . When the result is grasped as *determinate* negation, that is, when it is grasped as it is in truth, then at that point a new form has immediately arisen. (§ 79, trans. modified)

Consciousness "can find no peace" (*keine Ruhe finden*, § 80). Because it reflects upon itself, it is always beyond itself: "Consciousness . . . is . . . its *concept*, and as a result it immediately goes beyond the restriction, and, since this restriction belongs to itself, it goes beyond itself too" (§ 80). Precisely because it grasps itself, the self will never grasp itself completely. Precisely because it negates itself, the self will never negate itself completely. It is always one step ahead of itself, and thereby one step behind. The subject can never catch up with itself. It doubles and therefore it doubts itself. It drives itself to despair. Torn within, it will never fall apart. There is a tension between its different sides that will always keep them from coinciding while always holding them together. "But as the self . . . [the 'I'] is the absolute elasticity" (*die absolute Elastizität*, § 517): a rubber subject.[8]

Consciousness moves by the elasticity of its rubber nature. Despairing, consciousness ruins its current existence, but this self-loss never keeps it down for long. It always bounces back. It neither stands nor falls: it does both at the same time. Like a Weeble, consciousness wobbles, but it doesn't fall down.[9] Even though it feels heavy with despair, it always flips up again. This is not its own freely exercised decision. Consciousness simply does not have the choice to find peace on the ground. While it keeps its head up high, it is ruled by its butt. And even though its butt is heavy, it touches the ground only ever so slightly, causing the head to always flip up again, without a purpose. Consciousness keeps staggering and bouncing back until, almost by accident, it realizes that it cannot stop. This does not mean that it has reached its goal. Despair is unending in the active sense; it undoes the internal teleology that some readers emphasize in the *Phenomenology*. When the protagonist realizes that it cannot stand still, all it has understood is that self-negation and being beside itself (*Außersichsein*) are part of what it is; they belong to its denaturalizing nature. On the path of despair, the protagonist "achieve[s] a cognitive acquaintance of what it is in itself"—a self in despair (§ 77).

Self-reflection leads into despair. But that is only the beginning. Doubtful, consciousness hesitates even to make one step—it is called to "advance but very little" (Descartes 1979, II.5). Desperate, the subject of the *Phenomenology* rolls on the wheel of determinate negations through its various shapes, on and on. At the end of the "path of despair" that is the *Phenomenology*, we fall even more thoroughly into a now utterly lighthearted despair. The movement of despair does not lead to the restoration of knowledge and self; it continues in the affirmation of restlessness and brokenness. The protagonist is crushed by the wheel, but it never falls apart completely. The self-reflexive energy of despair's determinate negations holds together the various shreds or shapes of the *Phenomenology*'s subject. The protagonist is both singular and plural, for it is "an 'I' that is genuinely self-dividing [*sich wahrhaft unterscheidendes*] in its simplicity, that is, an I remaining-in-parity with itself [*sich gleichbleibendes*] within this absolute division" (§ 197, trans. modified). There is one protagonist throughout, and yet there are different "shapes" or "figures" of this protagonist—different shreds of the broken subject. While despair ruins the original and final unity, it also prevents the shreds from settling into a shape completely of their own. Each figure speculatively relates to other broken figures and to the ruined whole. The subject of the *Phenomenology* is a subject in despair that keeps changing its form and does so to no end (no purpose, no limit).[10] Despair is unending (the self).

The desparate loses the legs that provide stability and begins to float slightly above ground; he self-divides and begins to hover lightly above himself.[11] Despair lets consciousness lo(o)se: it unleashes consciousness's (self-)destructive forces. This has its own pleasure: "a very difficult pleasure; but it *is* called pleasure" (Lispector 1994, i). When the path of despair opens onto the pleasure of despair, this pleasure consists in the difficult bliss of living the elastic tension between two irreconcilable yet unending pulls: to unify (without ever reaching complete unification) and to dismember (without ever reaching complete dissolution).

The word "despair" might carry too much pathos for the lighthearted despair that the *Phenomenology* produces. The term tends to leave us with our false imaginations of the worst. As an elastic transport—a "plastic" transport in Malabou's sense or a "speculative" transport in Hegel's sense—despair keeps its subject tumbling back and forth between its torturous and its pleasurable poles. The German word is perhaps more felicitous in that it draws us playfully into the double twist of *Verzwei* (two)*-fl-ung*. In the *Phenomenology*, despair doesn't take itself too seriously. It rather has an air of irony, with its simultaneously affirmative and negative gestures. Consciousness remains quite unpossessed by despair; it never experiences an absolute depth of nothingness, but always different degrees of a despair that is *aufgehoben* from the onset.

Animal Despair

Now that we have touched on the pleasurable aspect of despair, it might not be surprising that Hegel describes as despair something that we usually consider to be an enjoyment, namely eating. His first explicit example of a despairing act is the literal consumption—the eating up—of that which has no stable being. Sense certainty—the first and most immediate figure of consciousness—must, based on its own notion of truth, conclude that sensuous objects are unreal. For consciousness, true reality means unchangeable, everlasting being. Therefore, the figure of consciousness that has staked all its certainty on the reality of sensuous things will have to despair:

> What one can say to those who make assertions about the truth and reality of sensuous objects is that they should be sent back to the most elementary school of wisdom, namely, to the old Eleusinian mysteries of Ceres and Bacchus and that they have yet to learn the mystery of the eating of bread and the drinking of wine. This is so because the person who has been initiated into these secrets not merely comes to doubt the being of sensuous things. Rather, he is brought to despair of them. (§ 109)

Hegel in no way claims here that sensuous things are indeed unreal. Rather, he contends that a consciousness that views reality as everlasting being must come to the conclusion that sensuous things are not real.[12] This does not preclude the protagonist/s of the *Phenomenology* from changing their understanding of what counts as truth. In fact, over the course of a long process of self-education, consciousness will begin to appreciate the notion of a dynamic and transient truth. And then the status of sensuous things will be reevaluated.

This said, we can turn our attention to the puzzling fact that Hegel describes the consumption of sensuous objects—"the eating of bread and the drinking of wine," for example—as a way of despair. As discussed in the previous section, Hegel maintains in the introduction that despair genuinely negates what skepticism merely "resolves" to annihilate. In the first chapter of the *Phenomenology*, despair's actual negation takes the form of a physical destruction: the gobbling-up of the object. Such unmediated violence poses a problem for human taste. Therefore, those animals that are presumed to have no taste or culture or conscience are better at it:

> Nor are the animals excluded from this wisdom [of the Eleusinian Mysteries]. To an even greater degree, they prove themselves to be the most deeply initiated in such wisdom for they do not stand still in the face of sensuous things, as if those things existed in themselves. Despairing of the reality of those things in the total certainty of the nullity of those things, they, without any further ado, simply help themselves to them and consume them [*zehren sie auf*]. Just like the animals, all of nature celebrates these revealed mysteries which teach the truth about sensuous things. (§ 109)

Hegel considers animals to be able to despair but unable to doubt. In speculative circularity, a step forward is a step backward. And the abstract or merely "natural" negation that death is turns into a life-giving force. The reason animals don't doubt is that doubt requires a distancing from the object of doubt, a separation that creates the other as an object or *Gegenstand*—as something that *stands* stationary opposite to (*gegen*) the subject. But animals don't freeze the frame and "do not just stand idly in front of sensuous things." Instead, by eating the other, they affirm transience and interrelatedness. To eat the other means to abolish the separation between subject and object. Feuerbach will later coin the aphorism *Der Mensch ist, was er isst*—for Hegel, man is not the focus of this thought and the verb *sein* must be taken in the double (intransitive and transitive) sense: one is or becomes what one eats and one exists or brings to life what one eats.

Eating the other alive draws both parties into a mutual death-and-life-giving relation. Non-human animals can openly engage in a behavior that humans must keep a secret. They grasp the truth that remains a mystery to humans. Lispector suggests that the moral categories of victim and perpetrator do not exist in the animal realm because they presuppose a distance between subject and object: "The most profound of murders: one that is a mode of relating, a way of one being existing the other being, a way of our seeing each other and being each other and having each other, a murder where there is neither victim nor perpetrator but instead a link of mutual ferocity" (Lispector 1994, 74). Partaking in the cycle of eating and being eaten, animals consume in despair. "Without any further ado," they expose themselves to the whirl of consumption, and thus show that they not only grasp the truth of sensuous things, namely that sensuous beings (including animals) are transient, but that they also accept the higher, speculative notion of truth, namely that truth itself is dynamic. For these animals, transience does not mean unreality, and negation does not end in nothingness.

The element of self-reflexivity that distinguishes despair from doubt might not be immediately obvious in the context of the *Phenomenology*'s first chapter, on sense-certainty, but it becomes clearer against the background of Hegel's discussion of life at the beginning of the *Phenomenology*'s second part, on self-consciousness.[13] Here, Hegel describes the "cycle" (*Kreislauf*) of life as a "circulation" of (self-)consumption, where eating the other means eating oneself, and devouring means giving life (§ 171).[14]

Hegel first distinguishes between life in general and individual life. Organisms are individual forms of life, while life in general is unindividuated or de-individualized life matter (somewhat misleadingly, Hegel calls it "inorganic" to emphasize its opposition to the organism). Living organisms eat life matter. Here, consumption functions as separation: the organism "affirms itself . . . as preserving itself . . . by virtue both of its separation from its inorganic nature and by its consuming this inorganic nature" (§ 171). The organism defines and sustains itself as individual living being over and against life in general. But when the living being eats life, "what is consumed is the essence" (*was aufgezehrt wird, ist das Wesen,* § 171). The organism *isst, was es ist.* It negates its own essence. It incorporates that against which it means to stand out, and thereby undoes the separation. *Es ist, was es isst.* In other words, it is now life in general or unorganized life matter that consumes the living individual. The negation is mutual in the rigorous sense that the act of eating unorganized life matter makes it impossible for the organism to maintain its own separate and self-sufficient individuality. Consumption means both the destruction of the other, and the ruin of the self.

But consumption also restores the self and gives life to mere substance: "The sublating of individual durable existence is, conversely, equally its own engendering. . . . Since it posits the *other* as being within itself [*das Andre in sich setzt*], it in that way sublates its *simplicity*. . . , i.e., it estranges that simplicity. This estrangement of the undifferentiated fluidity is the very positing of individuality" (§ 171). When life eats up the living—that is, when undivided and unorganized matter literally swallows (*in sich setzt*) the individual—it introduces difference into the general fluidity, which in turn individuates life. The mutual (self-)negation is a mutual (self-re-)production. Each part of the cycle of life has its essence in the other. In the end, it becomes clear that the distinction between life in general and individual life doesn't hold: "The fluid element . . . is only *actual* as shape; and that it organizes itself [*sich gliedert*] is . . . once again a dissolution (§ 171, trans. modified). To say that the living eats life matter and that, in the same act, life consumes the living is, therefore, just another way of saying that the living eats itself. Animals eat themselves and each other alive. "Alive," then, has to be taken in both the attributive and the predicative sense. Animals eat living animals, and they make what they eat come alive.

Lispector offers a variation on this thought. The first-person narrator of *The Passion According to G.H.* has caught a cockroach between the two doors of a wardrobe. For G.H., the cockroach exemplifies eternal life, impersonal, unindividuated life matter that has survived millions of years on earth unchanged. Her description of the cockroach departs from the organicist, expressionist, and individualist paradigm: "A cockroach is an ugly, shiny being. The cockroach is inside out. No, no, I don't mean that it has an inside and an outside; I mean that [it] is what it is. What it has on the outside is what I hide inside myself" (Lispector 1994, 69). The cockroach is what it is: undivided, divine being. Its absolute nakedness reveals without revelation since it knows not even the trace of a secret. G.H. keeps many secrets; she is capable of lying.[15] In other words, G.H. has a heart. She is the proud proprietor of an interiority that allows her to "hide . . . behind the appearance" (§ 80).[16] And yet she begins to see herself—inverted—in the cockroach: "What it has on the outside is what I hide inside myself." Then G.H. watches how white pus slowly oozes out of the cockroach's cracked body: "The cockroach's pulp, which was its insides, raw matter that was whitish and thick and slow, was piling up on it" (Lispector 1994, 54). What was about to die is coming alive.

> Mother, I only pretend to want to kill, but just see what I have cracked: I have cracked a shell! Killing is also forbidden because you crack the hard husk and you are left with viscous life. From the inside of the husk, a heart that is thick and white and living, like pus, comes out, Mother, blessed be you among cockroaches, now and in the hour of this, *my death of yours*, cockroach and jewel. (Lispector 1994, 86, my emphasis)

The whitish pulp—life in general—slowly dissolves the boundaries of the individual—that is, of G.H. G.H. sees herself in the cockroach. She has projected her heart onto the cockroach that has no heart but wears its insides out. "A heart that is thick and white and living, like pus, comes out" of the first-person narrator G.H.—Georg Hegel, perhaps—who abandons the attachment to interiority: "As if saying the word 'Mother' had released a thick, white part in me, . . . like after a violent attack of vomiting, my forehead was relieved" (Lispector 1994, 86). Cockroach and G.H. are each other. They eat each other and they vomit each other into existence—each one the mother of the other. G.H. has been swallowed by the neutral, non-individual eyes of the cockroach, and she tastes the white pus, the thick matter of life. G.H. despairs of the cockroach's reality and, without any further ado, consumes it. Despair lets her lo(o)se. She abandons the defining traits of her persona, the adornments of her ego, the initials that mark her property.[17] "My death of yours" is a resurrection to "a life that at last is not eluding me" (Lispector 1994, 57). The "suitcases with the engraved initials" of the narrator and the "hard husk" of the cockroach are but different pieces of dried surface from the same continuous fluidity of life (Lispector 1994, 107, 86). G.H.: two pieces from the alphabet, nothing behind it. And the cockroach has become an "I." Like G and H, I is a letter to be exchanged. "I, neutral cockroach body, I with a life that at last is not eluding me because I finally see it outside myself—I am the cockroach" (Lispector 1994, 57). I am the external interior; I "remains the same," I has survived millions of years on earth unchanged because it is empty—"the proper empty core of subjectivity" (Žižek 2006, 227).

Desperate Analysis

By eating each other and themselves alive, animals grasp and share (in) some truth of sensuous beings. For Hegel, eating is a way of thinking.[18] "All of nature, like the animals, celebrates these open Mysteries" (Hegel), this "link of mutual ferocity" (Lispector). But man likes to part from the feast. While animals "prove themselves to be the most deeply initiated in [the] wisdom" of the mysteries of despair, man emerges from the revel of mutually consuming reflection by way of a peculiar kind of stupidity (§ 109). He fixes his gaze, wherever he looks, on the dull but stable opacity of self-identity.

Identification is a unilateral reflection that interrupts the circle of mutual reflection. It relies on the rational work of the understanding: "The act of parting [*Scheiden*] is the force and labor of the *under-*

standing, the most astonishing and the greatest of all the powers, rather, which is the absolute power" (§ 32, trans. modified). Men—including Hegel—take great pride in this rational faculty, which nevertheless stops short of the speculative movement of reflection that animals are capable of. By cultivating the power of distance and analysis, man protects himself against the destabilizing effect of despair's "being-of-itself-outside-itself-in-the-other" (Nancy 2002, 35). He refuses to join the round, go in circles, and lose his head in despair.

The rational withdrawal from and dissection of the whirl of life has a deadly ring to it (*Scheiden* also means "to depart this life," "to die"): "It is the tremendous power of the negative; it is the energy . . . of the pure I. Death, if that is what we wish to call that non-actuality, is the most fearful thing of all, and to keep and hold fast to what is dead requires only the greatest force" (§ 32). The source of man's power is his ability to analyze, that is, to detach elements from the fluidity of life and to assign object status to these elements that as such really don't exist. "That . . . what is bound to other actualities and only exists in their context should attain an isolated freedom and its own proper existence is the effect of the tremendous power of the negative, of the energy . . . of the pure I" (§ 32, trans. modified). By virtue of hypnotic fixation—facing death or "look[ing] the negative in the face"—man gives this non-actuality a face in the first place (ibid.). By fixing his gaze on abstractions, he confers upon them an objective identity: "This lingering is the magical power that converts it into being" (ibid.). The same prosopopoeial operation is also applied to the one who uses it: the "pure I" is itself an abstraction with no actuality. It comes into being by way of a concentrated self-contemplation, a form of autosuggestion. Through the magic of the understanding, the rational "I" generates itself. That is to say, this epigenetic operation of man takes the shape not so much of a self-birth as of a suicide. By giving itself its own, authentic, Heideggerian death—and thus by actively resisting "my death of yours"—the "I" posits itself. Facing death, man gives himself a face.

With the declaration, "to keep and hold fast to what is dead requires only the greatest force," Hegel contributes to the human conceits of grandeur. Man likes to see himself as the superior animal and Hegel locates this superiority in the ability to keep a cool head. For the sake of maintaining his self-conceit, man abhors nothing more than to "roam about as a throng of madly rapturous women, the untamed revel [*ungebändigte Taumel*] of nature in self-conscious shape" (§ 723, trans. modified). Hegel here combines women, animals (via the adjective "untamed"), and gods (Dionysus, Demeter) in one dizzying semantic field of bodies in ecstasy that threaten the authority of the rational "I." Lispector helps us to reclaim this potentially misogynous combination for a phenomenology of the intensity of neutral life that is declined in the feminine: "Living life instead of living one's own life is forbidden. It is a sin to go into divine matter. And that sin has an inexorable punishment: the person who dares go into that secret, in losing her individual life, disorganizes the human world" (Lispector 1994, 136). Neutral life or life in general, which is indifferent to the individual's life and death, cannot be owned; its ecstasy is improper and unpossessed. Lispector calls this impropriety of living neutral life "immund" (*immundo* in Brazilian Portuguese).[19] With this word she retrieves connotations of "unclean" (in the sense that some religions place a ban on eating certain animals), but also of "unadorned" (the Latin adjective *mundus* can refer to a woman's elegant dress and jewelry), and of "chaotic" (the Latin noun *mundus* means "world"; it translates the Greek *cosmos,* which represents the world as an orderly arrangement; the antithesis of *cosmos* is *chaos*). To "go into" the unclean nakedness of chaotic life is a sin that can neither be attributed to nor borne by an individual, because the individual life gets lost in the process. The punishment for this sin therefore strikes not the individual, but human society as a whole: it "disorganizes the human world." Living neutral life instead of living one's own life ruins the intelligibility of the anthropocentric world. The cosmos becomes unpredictable. We begin to stagger and fall into despair.

In order to prevent such stagger and remain in control as best as possible, man parts and analyzes. And yet, it is precisely this rational analysis that produces the fragmentation and despair of the whole. Lingering with the negative, the understanding gives separate existence to what in itself exists only as a passing moment in a fluid movement. The analysis was meant as an intellectual exercise, a rational self-discipline, and a kind of self-cultivation (*Bildung*). But here, epigenesis does not enable a claim to absoluteness; rather, it ruins the absolute.[20] Here, the stabilizing effect of rationality speculatively joins the shattering effect of rationality. Against its intention, the understanding creates despair by scattering the dynamic whole. And this is precisely the reason why Hegel praises the work of the understanding. Rational analysis brings about the disruption and dismemberment that keep moving speculative, despairing self-reflection. The locus of agency in man's "act of parting" thus turns out to be rather uncertain (§ 32). As doer, man is done. Avoiding despair, he falls into despair. Pentheus, who keeps his distance from Dionysian revelry, will have his head torn off by his mother. Like him, every king will lose his head on the *Phenomenology*'s path of despair: Hegel will break anyone who "asks for a royal road to science" (§ 70).

Of course, the reader rejects such violence. Similarly, the protagonists of the *Phenomenology* resist despair's unending movement. They do not lightheartedly give themselves over to be transported by despair. Instead, each figure of consciousness develops a "tremendous power" (*ungeheure Macht,* § 32) to hold fast to the abstraction that it is (compared to the whole). In the face of these resistances and since, according to his own diagnosis, "it is much more difficult to set fixed thoughts into fluid motion than it is to bring sensuous existence into such fluidity," Hegel has developed complex strategies to break shapes of consciousness and shatter readers' expectations (§ 33). In the following, I will discuss two of them—the breaking of the phrenologist's judgment and the breaking of the hard heart.

Lacerating Judgment

Phrenology, which is the attempt to scientifically determine a person's character based on the shape of her skull, emerges within the sphere of reason—more specifically, of "observing reason." The sphere of reason is animated by the assumption that the objective, material world is not foreign to the world of the mind: "It is the concept of this entire sphere . . . that thinghood is the *being-for-itself* of spirit itself" (§ 359). This not only means that the mind has access to the external world and that it finds its own rules of intelligibility confirmed in nature. It also means that it is perfectly rational to regard spirit—and by consequence any individual consciousness—as a thing, for example, a bone.

How does the phrenologist model of observing and classifying human subjects emerge? Despite the fact that "observing reason" is happily reconciled with external reality, reason develops a strong introversion.[21] For its own epistemic purposes, it creates a stable opposition and law-governed relation between an inner world and an outer world. That is to say, it "creates the law that says *the outer is the expression of the inner*" (§ 262). The law of expression arrests the self-moving concept and relegates it to interiority. Reason here clings to an inwardness that it has inherited from the dialectic of the understanding. When the understanding noticed the transience of the empirical world, it developed the image (*Vorstellung*) of a supersensible "*inner* of things" (§ 142). At that time, self-consciousness identified with this interiority, and now reason, still beholden to the understanding, cannot quite live up to its own idea that the (external) real is rational and the rational is (externally) real. Instead, it takes external reality as an *expression* of internal reality. The demand for expression perpetuates, within the anti-metaphysical perspective of reason, the metaphysical stance of the understanding—the "image [*Vorstellung*] of appearance and appearance's inner" (§ 165, trans. modified).

The theory of rational existence—that the rational exists in objective form—governs all of reason's assumptions, including its assumption of an inner life. The law of expression dictates that there can be no inwardness that is not linked to outwardness. So reason ends up with a rather problematic, even at times downright silly, and yet extremely influential image of interiority. Rational consciousness imagines the internal as coming in a solid and fixed, that is to say, essentially external shape: "the inner as such must have an outer being and a shape just like the outer as such, for the inner . . . is itself posited as existing and as available for observation" (§ 264). This reification of inner life makes reason less spiritual than spirit because the "inner being of spirit" remains "spiritless" when it is "interpreted as a fixed . . . being" (§ 340). In the sphere of reason, the truth criterion of unchangeability or timelessness, which has governed all previous shapes of consciousness from sense certainty to the unhappy consciousness, is once again used as the measure to test certainty, and once again it will fail this protagonist.

The proper response when one finds oneself evaluated based on phrenology would be to bash in the critic's head: "the retort here would really have to go as far as smashing the skull of the person who makes a statement like that" (§ 339). This would be appropriate in the sense that it would respond to the allegations on the phrenologist's terms. Somebody who has reduced the dynamic life of spirit to something as rigid and random as a boss of the skull might not be able to understand otherwise than through hard evidence that his skull is not as solid as he thought. One would have to break his skull "in order to demonstrate to him in a manner as palpable as his wisdom that for a person a bone is nothing in-itself and is even less *his* true actuality" (§ 339).

And yet this mimetic identification—responding to the phrenologist on his own terms—is not sophisticated enough to set the phrenologist on the path of despair. Doing violence to his body will not move his thoughts. As mentioned earlier, "it is much more difficult to set fixed thoughts into fluid motion than it is to bring sensuous existence into such fluidity" (§ 33). I have suggested that Hegel beat in many a head and broke many a bone with his *Phenomenology of Spirit*. The text certainly registers that spirit's self-knowledge comes at the expense of the bone health of its protagonist, who, in a moment of "truest insight about itself," has the "feeling that it has been rolled upon the wheel through all the stages of its existence and that every bone in its body has been broken" (§ 538, trans. modified). At this point, it is time to attend again to the self-reflexivity of despair, that is to say, to the fact that there is no transitive sense of despair. In the case of the phrenologist, while smashing his head might be warranted by his own logic, he would still experience this negation as coming from the outside and therefore it would not bring about the self-doubt that is despair. And indeed, Hegel doesn't quite break the phrenologist's skull.

Instead, Hegel sympathizes with the phrenologist and takes his judgments seriously. There is of course a certain irony in Hegel's sympathy, but that is nothing new.[22] A mix of sincere identification and ironic distance characterizes all the discussions of the various shapes of consciousness/spirit. As I have suggested in the introduction, the *Phenomenology* presents the philosophems of its protagonist/s in free indirect discourse—oscillating often imperceptibly between the protagonist's voice and the phenomenologist's voice. Hegel uses the freedom afforded by this style of thought representation in order to gain and communicate an intimate knowledge of perspectives. Such intimacy would be precluded by a more straightforward approach. Hegel points out that "the raw instinct of self-conscious reason will reject out of hand [*unbesehen verwerfen*] such a science" as phrenology (§ 340; trans. modified). But the Hegelian phenomenologist refrains from crude reasoning and outright rejection and, instead, approaches the phrenologist in a more cultivated manner: he takes the perspective of phrenology, he speaks its language, he ventriloquizes its thoughts.[23] And after he has done so in detail, he introduces a referential shift when he declares that, even though this is not what observing reason in the shape of phrenology *means* to say, "what in truth [it] has been saying is expressed in the statement that the *being of spirit is a bone*" (§ 343, trans. modified). Here Hegel doesn't speak directly with the voice of phrenology anymore, but takes the liberty to reflect on the phrenologist position and to distill it down to one tangible verdict. Hegel won't be trapped by the intentional fallacy. It doesn't matter what the phrenologist *means* to say; his pedestrian ideas have already disqualified him. What matters is what his position actually comes down to, namely "that the *being of spirit is a bone.*" In keeping with his rejection of expressionism, Hegel detaches the judgment from the person who pronounced it. He separates thought and mind. As soon as the thought is no longer taken as an expression of a mind, he can treat both—the judgment and the phrenologist—as things, to be broken.[24] Rather than literally bashing in his head, Hegel demonstrates that the phrenologist doesn't know what he is saying, that he is indeed the bonehead he idiotically claims he is, that he is indeed an abstract thing without self-awareness.

Then again, Hegel's use of free indirect discourse gives him the liberty to swing all the way back to a sympathizing identification with the phrenologist. Hegel gives him credit, suggesting that the future of spirit harkens back to the phrenologist when he feels some embarrassment about his position. The thing that is the phrenologist's mind knows embarrassment—a promising fact, one would think: "Out of a kind of natural honesty which lies at a deeper level of self-conscious spirit," the phrenologist "conceals from [him]self the shamefulness of the naked, conceptless thought [*begrifflosen, nackten Gedankens*]" that underlies his position (§ 345, trans. modified). And yet, the phrenologist's sheepishness only drives his mind further into the traps of un-self-reflection. Toning down "the crudeness [*das Grelle*] of the proposition," that the being of spirit is a bone, he inadvertently obscures the significance of his stance (§ 345, trans. modified).

Since the phrenologist either doesn't know what he is saying or is too embarrassed to state the naked truth, the phenomenologist has to carve out the actual shape of the phrenologist position: "what in truth the foregoing has been saying is expressed in the statement that the *being of spirit is a bone.*" Now Hegel can begin to break this thing. First its referent: what, a bone?!—In order to tear the statement to shreds, the phenomenologist simply needs to point out "that for a person a bone is nothing in-itself." A bone is nothing essential and certainly not the true expression of a mind—"even less *his* true actuality" (§ 339). That was easy.

But let's not get carried away by the "raw instinct of self-conscious reason"! Let's linger a while longer with the most dazzling verdict, "that the *being of spirit is a bone.*" The sphere of reason is animated by two contradicting premises, that of rational existence and that of interiority. Hegel's attack on phrenology is leveled not so much against the idea that spirit could be a thing as against reason's investment in interiority. The discussion of phrenology serves to show that reason remains utterly spiritless when it seeks to satisfy its desire for unchanging and solid reality by looking inward. To project interiority as the abstract opposite of exteriority means to reify it, to turn it into a dead thing and thus—against the intention of the discourse of interiority—to turn it into something external. The idea of an "inner being of spirit" renders spirit "as a fixed spiritless being"—and that is why thinkers belonging to the sphere of reason are faced with the conundrum that, to put it bluntly, there seems to be no such thing as inner life: whenever we can put our finger on it, it is already dead.[25]

But this is not the end of Hegel's discussion of phrenology. Given the paradoxical, or rather, the speculative workings of Hegel's *Aufhebung*, his attack on the (inner) thing is not a destruction, but a spiritualization of the (outer) thing. The speculative reading of the proposition "that the *being of spirit is a bone*" reveals that even "externality . . . in the sense of a dead thing" is indeed spiritually animated and presents "the outer immediate actuality of spirit" (§ 343). Not just the organism, not just language—where one might expect a certain impersonal capacity for self-reflection and self-negation—but any simple object, even a bone, has a kind of mind of its own. Rational self-consciousness's declared "certainty of being all reality" may seem egocentric (§ 230), but the flip side of this worldview is the contention that all reality is self-conscious, including such utterly objectifiable and seemingly inert matter as the boss of a bone: "The concept of this image [*Vorstellung*] is that reason is to itself *all thinghood,* even *purely objective thinghood*" (§ 346, trans. modified). In the distilled verdict of phrenology, we have thus found the most concrete and spiritual actualization of reason's governing premise of rational existence.

The spiritualization of things completely depends on the reading of the judgment "that the *being of spirit is a bone.*" If read at face value, it turns the reader into a spiritless bonehead who pisses away his capacities for self-reflection.[26] But read speculatively, the judgment negates and spiritualizes itself. When, in her discussion of defenses against hate speech, Riley quotes Hegel saying that the aim is to "have done with the thing altogether," she knows that treating the thing as a thing or the other as an object does not present an effective strategy, especially if the goal is destruction (Riley 2005, 25). The *Phenomenology* famously demonstrates that the object must negate itself in order for the subject to be able to have done with it: "on account of the self-sufficiency of the object [I] can only achieve satisfaction if the object itself effects the negation in it" (§ 175).

The proper response when one finds oneself evaluated by phrenology is, then, to make room for and respect the freedom of the judgment to negate itself. This can be accomplished by a not-quite-straightforward reading of the judgment. It is therefore absolutely no accident that Hegel renders the phrenologist judgment about spirit in indirect speech. From the slightly removed and oblique vantage point of indirect discourse, the phenomenologist allows the thought of phrenology to develop its peculiar form so that it can appear as "the *infinite judgment* that the self is a thing—a judgment which sublates itself" (§ 344). Read categorically or crudely as positive judgments, the propositions "the self is a thing" or "spirit is a bone" are easily rejected. But read as infinite judgments, they are actually true.[27] It is true that underdeveloped forms of reason (like phrenology) have an ossifying notion of interiority. At the same time, this very insight sublates the factual truth—the infinite judgment negates itself—and transports us to a more sophisticated conception of spirit.

The larger truth of this infinite judgment is that spirit is indeed a thing in space and time, but a speaking and self-reflecting thing—or rather, an infinite number of things that communicate (with) and reflect each other and themselves. This truth can barely be conveyed in the propositional form of a judgment. The infinite judgment presents a borderline judgment. It hovers precariously and emotionally at the edge of its own self-negation by adjoining two terms that cannot be logically related. Spirit and Bone are like apples and oranges. There is no expressive continuity between them but simply a gap of negativity. They are so unrelated that the identity posited by the copula cannot be achieved via subordination (which is the usual procedure by which the judgment identifies what appears different).[28] Instead, the infinite judgment says that the abstract is the abstract: spirit, understood abstractly as substance, is a bone, understood abstractly as a solid being. In this very judgment—"the abstract is the abstract"—each abstract thing or term reflects itself in the other abstract thing or term. Through this self-reflection, they become "concrete." We are witnessing the process of mutual acknowledging between bone and spirit. Passing through the infinite judgment, one term becomes affected by the other: Spirit emerges as ossified and Bone as spiritualized. It is hard to tell them apart at this point. One is entangled in the other. Neither being nor self-consciousness can be taken as a fixed term anymore; instead one must juggle both as dynamic subjects constantly in the process of self-dissolution and self-generation. The entanglement of spirit and bone, ideality and materiality, inwardness and outwardness forms an emotional thought—the self-reflective emotionality of the Bacchanalian revel "where no member is not drunk" (§ 47, trans. modified).

Come Break My Heart

While on the one hand the protagonist breaks bone after bone in the course of the *Phenomenology*, on the other hand it hardens more and more. Consciousness is scarred and scared. Its scars are traces of a loss that it is afraid to endure again, traces of a fear that it hasn't really felt (because it was unbearable) but of which it becomes more and more afraid. Its fear grows with every new scar pulling it together tighter and tighter until the rubbery pulsating mass petrifies, and consciousness takes the shape of a "hard heart." The "hard heart" is the last figure of consciousness in the *Phenomenology*. It dialectically emerged from the figure of the "beautiful soul," which had no substance to speak of.

The very impossibility of experiencing despair is one of the main characteristics of despair. Despair quite literally breaks the subject by dividing it from its own experience: "unendurable is the measureless interval separating me from suffering. Suffering such that I cannot bear it *is* this interval, this gaping void dividing me from suffering" (Smock 2003, 8). The inability to despair drives one to despair. "I whom pain has liquidated before I even begin to undergo it, have always yet to endure it" (ibid.). What Smock formulates here so poignantly in dialogue with Blanchot, helps us to understand the paradox that the despairing protagonist of the *Phenomenology* faces. As a result of its missed encounter with despair, consciousness learns to fear despair. It fights despair toward the end of its journey even more than in the beginning. The final figure of consciousness in the *Phenomenology* displays the toughest resistance to the self-negation of despair.

With the glue of an extreme self-will, the hard heart keeps itself together. Unwilling to open, it "rejects any continuity with the other" (§ 667). As if it were casting pearls before swine, it "refus[es] to throw itself away against another" (*sich gegen einen andern wegzuwerfen*) and, "mutely keeping itself within itself," it throws but stinging predicates (not even full judgments) at the other (§ 667, trans. modified). "In crying out 'base,' 'vile,' and so on against the hypocrisy" of the other, it keeps the other at a distance, and "repels this community" (§ 663, trans. modified; § 667). The verbal projectiles allow the hard heart to remain firm in its position. While the arrows are flying, it doesn't budge an inch. "Stiff-necked," it insists on its judgment about the other and resists any turn the judgment might take when the other receives and interprets it (§ 667). "This was not what was meant by the judgment—Quite the contrary!" is the response implied by the hard heart's posture when the other allows the judgment to enter its own flesh and then returns it, expecting the hard heart to touch the blood-smeared dart again (§ 667). The fact that the other accepts the accusation instead of fending it off cannot move the hard heart: "Following on the admission of the one who is evil—*I am so*—there is no reciprocation of the same confession" (§ 667, trans. modified). Stubbornly and self-righteously, the beautiful soul turned hard heart holds its head high where the air is thin but pure, and where it doesn't have to smell the baseness of the other.

Opposite the hard heart Hegel positions a consciousness that, in full knowledge of the contingency of all standards, nevertheless finds it important to answer a call to action. This figure of consciousness is clearly the wisest, freest (in both senses of freedom, as self-determination and as self-abandon), and most plastic single manifestation of spirit in the entire *Phenomenology*.

The acting consciousness acknowledges the judging consciousness by pronouncing the other half of its judgment; it finishes the other's speech act. While the beautiful soul only throws predicates around, the other completes its sentences by saying, "I am so" (*Ich bins,* § 667, trans. modified). Together, they form statements such as "'bad!' . . . 'I am so'" or "'vile!' . . . 'I am so.'" Hegel presents us here with a dance of shared speech. The judgment (*Urteil*) is literally divided (*geteilt*) between the two figures. The bits of judgment and their corresponding configurations of consciousness enjoy a certain kind of independence, but each also reaches out to the other and complements the other. *Ich bins*—which can also be translated as "it's me"—can be heard then as a sign of familiarity. One answers the question "who is it?" with "it's me" only within the horizon of a trusted intimacy. These two know each other so well that one can complete the other's sentences. One can mirror the other's steps as they move across the dance floor. One is the protagonist of the *Phenomenology* and the other the phenomenologist. They have moved together through so many life stages of spirit at this point that they know each other inside out. Along the path, the phenomenologist has again and again furnished the predicates for the protagonist's naive propositions of being, and the protagonist has ever anew realized in action what the phenomenologist could only abstractly posit.

Now it is as if the judging consciousness does not hear the pronouncements of intimacy. It does not react. It never receives the love letters that the acting consciousness sends. It is too set on denying (itself) pleasure, too judgmental.[29] When the other says "it's me; I am so," the judging consciousness hears a self-deprecating admission of guilt. It sees a slobbering dog that gets so excited at the slightest attention that it is unable to differentiate between love and maltreatment. "This was not what was meant by the judgment"; it's not love, "quite the contrary!"—it's hatred and disgust, says the hard-hearted judge (§ 667). Meanwhile the drooling puppy eagerly acknowledges, "I am base" and "I am vile," because any interpellation—no matter how degrading—offers at least a minimal amount of recognition.

Of course, the acting consciousness doesn't mean its admission of guilt as a definitive and final account of its character. It means it as a contextual response.—"Yes, I can see why you think that I am vile and, yes, I think it is true that I am vile, but that is not all that I am, plus, we all have vile aspects or moments." Here, the beautiful soul refuses to follow. But the other has just outed himself as a Romantic ironist.[30] When he says, "I am base" and "I am vile," he means what he says and does not mean it at the same time. He states a passing truth. He simultaneously affirms and negates that he is base or vile. That is to say, he puts the emphasis on the subject when he says *Ich bins* (I am so). Within the coercive parameters of interpellation, the "I" insists on its right to bind or unbind the pieces that make these sentences. In no way does it submit to an essentializing character statement.

But whether we see ourselves as drooling puppies or, more flatteringly, as Romantic ironists—how can we get the hard heart to admit a mistake and to ask for forgiveness? How do we facilitate another's despair? Perhaps the one who resists despair is precisely not the other. "We"—that is probably the phenomenologist/s. But if these last two figures of consciousness in the *Phenomenology* figure the relation between phenomenologist and protagonist, the acting consciousness (the wisest and freest figure) would be the protagonist—it is the one involved in the action. And the phenomenologist is revealed here to be the judgmental hard heart who since the beginning of the story has done nothing but "cry out 'base,' 'vile,' and so on against" each and every incarnation of natural consciousness. Such phenomenologists, it turns out, do not learn much because they resist transport; they miss the love letters because they refuse to ac-knowledge (to think-along-with).

A pure heart can hardly love. In order to reach out to another, it must "let go of its own simplicity and rigid unchangeableness" (§ 786). If nothing else helps, it will need to be broken: "its one-sided unacknowledged [*nicht anerkanntes*] judgment must be broken in a way that for the former, its one-sided, unacknowledged [*nicht anerkanntes*] existence of particular being-for-itself had to be broken" (§ 669, trans. modified).[31] Mutual acknowledging means the death of the solitary, unmoved being-for-self: "The former dies back from its being-for-itself and empties itself [*entäußert sich*] and confesses; the latter disavows the rigidity of its abstract universality and thereby dies back from its lifeless self and its unmoved universality" (§ 796). But—just as with the phrenologist—force won't produce lovers. Since its hard-heartedness is an effect of its denial of its broken-heartedness, all one can do is to show that the beautiful soul is not as "lifeless" as it appears, that there is a crack that runs through the hard heart and that this crack makes transport possible, and finally that the judgment is in fact already doubled and broken in half and thus shared and moving, and that this is where the beauty lies.

At this late point in the phenomenological game, consciousness knows itself as continuously changing. This knowledge is its power: "conscience is this power because it knows the moments of consciousness to be *moments*, and as their negative essence, it rules over them" (§ 641). Through self-knowledge, consciousness rises above its ever-changing manifestations to find a lasting self-identity in the ethereal essence of its ever-changing forms. Whatever material reality consciousness gives itself, either in acting or in speaking, has no importance for it. For itself, it has its essence in spirit—but it understands spirit in a non-speculative, un-Hegelian way as the distilled negativity of the "I" that is devoid of any material impurities. The beautiful soul grounds itself in its conscience. Conscience defines itself as the "assurance [that] assures that consciousness is convinced that its conviction is the essence" (§ 653, trans. modified). "This absolute *certainty* into which substance has been dissolved" is consciousness's last bastion against despair (§ 657).

And yet the bastion is obviously on the verge of falling apart. The self-reflexivity that guarantees the absoluteness of the certainty of conscience on the one hand, disintegrates it on the other hand. The verbal doublings of an "assurance [*Versicherung*] [that] assures [*versichert*]" and a being "convinced [*überzeugt*] [of] its conviction [*Überzeugung*]" can sidetrack the tight-knit circle of conscience. Each doubling forms two lips ready to open and to eat conscience alive. Absolute certainty is self-consuming: the "absolute *self-consciousness* within which *consciousness* drowns [*versinkt*]" because "substance has been dissolved," this absolute self-consciousness will not be able to remain pure (§ 657, trans. modified).

Holding on to its clear conscience, the beautiful soul inhabits the zone in between figurations. It refuses to take shape and thus becomes a figure for the phenomenologist who, of course, doesn't take shape in the text, either, but emerges in the form of the first-person plural around the transitions from one figure of the protagonist to another, that is, around the zones in between figurations. As if it knew that it is the last figure of consciousness in the *Phenomenology*, and therefore has no new life to escape to but can only fall apart, the beautiful soul refuses to "commit itself to the absolute division [*Unterschied*]" and to expose itself to the alienating forces of reality (§ 658, trans. modified). And yet its spirituality overlaps with materiality. The utterly beautiful transparency of this soul takes shape as the absolute impenetrability of a heart of glass. Not only is the hard heart a thing, but it is a broken thing—glued together with its last reserves of clotted, rubbery blood. The crack is still noticeable and threatens to open any time. Only the softness of a *d* holds the pieces of the hard heart together. A *d* so hard to pronounce, so easily rendered as a *t* (at least for me), that it betrays the latent doubletalk. It doubles the heart and makes it fall apart. One who heard the crack at the heart of the hard could give it a start. Unexpectedly, the beautiful soul turned hard heart might "let go of its own simplicity and rigid unchangeableness," forgive evil, and begin to move out of its cardiac arrest (§ 786). It's in the cards that, sooner or later, the heart won't be able to ward off its breaking. Yet how this break comes about will be decided only by accident.

Unexpectedly, "acknowledgment [*Erkennen*] bursts forth as the *Yes* between these extreme terms" (§ 786, trans. modified). Acknowledgment is not foreseeable.[32] There is no guarantee that it will be reciprocated. When the other "repels this community," the rejection certainly arouses "the utmost outrage [*höchste Empörung*] of the self-certain spirit" (§ 667, trans. modified). Even so, acknowledgment responds to no demand. Acknowledging is structurally mutual but, from the perspective of one, it can happen only accidentally. Using violence to break the hard heart won't turn glass into flesh, and the blood that might flow will only be spent. Instead, in an instant of lightheartedness, a moment off guard, the hard heart falls apart and a *Yes* escapes the shell. Consciousness affirms the other, ac-knowledges the other, and feels an unexpected pleasure. It falls in love. And the scar opens.

Narrative (Dis)organization

We encounter the shattering force of despair also on the narrative level of the *Phenomenology of Spirit*. The narrative of the *Phenomenology* can be described as a path of despair because despair—in this case the text's despair—breaks the dynamic "whole" that is "the true" into separate chapters, shapes of consciousness, or "stations" (*Stationen*).[33]

None of the *Phenomenology*'s chapters or figures of consciousness alone speaks the truth in an absolute sense that transcends all conditions. Their truth and reality are relative and, in the end, none of them can stand on their own. And yet each shape of consciousness does present an iteration or instantiation of spirit and as such can claim a certain station and level of independence.[34] This relative self-sufficiency of the different shapes produces a range of different activities undertaken in the interest of self-preservation. Not one shape of consciousness wants to change. Rather, each shape reacts to any potentially life-changing experience with an effort to integrate this experience into its existing set of ontological insights.[35] The result is a narrative extension of each shape and of each chapter that makes it extremely hard for the reader to keep in view the whole of spirit's story of formation.

From the perspective of the protagonist, survival would be guaranteed if it were the consciousness of a transcendent and stable truth. That is to say, consciousness resists not only its own despair but also spirit's despair: it fears the truth that is self-negating: "The fear of truth may lead consciousness to hide both from itself and from others behind the appearance" (§ 80, trans. modified). Or, as the narrator of *The Passion According to G.H.* puts it, "I'm terrified of that profound disorganization. . . . I know that I can walk only when I have two legs. But I sense the irrelevant loss of the third one, and it horrifies me, it was that leg that made me able to find myself, and without even having to look" (Lispector 1994, 3–4). As we have seen in our discussion of fear in the previous chapter, whenever a figure of consciousness has reached a point where it cannot integrate its experiences any further, it loses consciousness and slips into oblivion. On the other side of this death, a new figure emerges. The resulting gaps in the narrative tear the body of the text apart. We might want to call it the cunning of spirit (as opposed to the cunning of reason) that the protagonist/s' efforts to resist despair and to preserve themselves intact—through post-traumatic amnesia if necessary—effectuate despair on the larger level of spirit's self-lacerations.

From the perspective of spirit, none of the figures of consciousness can lay claim to absolute knowledge, since "the truth is the whole. However, the whole is only the essence completing itself through its own development" (§ 20). Truth is, thus, achieved only in the narrative exposition of spirit, which exposes spirit:

> This exposition [*Darstellung*] . . . can be taken to be the path of natural consciousness which presses forward towards true knowledge, or it can be taken to be the path of the soul as it wanders through the series of the ways it takes shape, as if those shapes were stations laid out for it by its own nature so that it . . . might purify itself into spirit. (§ 77, trans. modified)

The word "stations" certainly echoes the Stations of the Cross. The quote, then, figures the *Phenomenology* as the passion of the Christ: the suffering of the phenomenal aspect of God as he goes through the drawn-out and torturous process of purifying physical existence into the Holy Spirit. This is the Passion according to G. W. F. Hegel—according to most of his readers. But the description of the *Phenomenology*'s path as purifying the soul into the life of the spirit also resonates with Hegel's description of the rites of the Eleusinian mysteries: "This cultus . . . is based on cheerfulness or serenity. The path of purification is one that is traveled physically [*durchwandert*]. . . . The physical traveling [*Durchwanderung*] of the road [counts] as an actually accomplished purification of the soul, an absolution" (Hegel 1987, 180). The cult of Demeter and Dionysus taught its followers the secrets of death, resurrection, and life.[36] Traveling through a series of stations on the road to Eleusis, the Mystai were effectively absolved from the terror or panic (Pan is a companion of, and at times another name for, Dionysus) that death induces.

The myths of Dionysus's double birth and repeated dismemberment, and of Persephone's rape-rapture-capture by the underworld and periodic reemergence from it remind Hegel of spirit's despairing mediation with itself:[37]

> The chief basis of the representations of Ceres and Proserpine, Bacchus and his train, was the universal principle of Nature; representations mainly bearing on the vital force and its metamorphoses. An analogous process to that of Nature, Spirit has also to undergo; for it must be twice-born, i.e. abnegate itself [*sich in sich selbst negieren*]; and thus the representations given in the mysteries called attention . . . to the nature of Spirit. (Hegel 1956, 248)

In the *Phenomenology*, spirit is not just born twice, but with each transition to a new chapter and a new figure of consciousness, spirit is born anew. This parceling out of spirit's truth "may readily induce the traveler to lose sight of the road altogether in the course of . . . its bends and distracting stations [*zerstreuende Stationen*]" (Hegel 1971, 79, trans. modified).

Since Hegel superimposes the path of the *Phenomenology of Spirit*, the passion of Christ, and the initiation rites of the Eleusinian mysteries, I take the liberty to add *The Passion According to G.H.* In all four cases, some body will have been dismembered and consumed. Christ breaks the bread that is his body and gives it to his disciples to eat. Dionysus is torn to shreds by the Titans and Zeus asks Semele to drink his heart. G.H. cracks and tastes the cockroach. The readers of the *Phenomenology* are supposed to digest and re-collect the stations of this book. It's always us, the mortals who are to swallow the pieces. But can we make them whole?

According to one topos of our cultural imaginary, true love can heal fragmentation: "To reconstruct 'this shipwreck of fragments, these echoes, these shards . . .' needs a special love. . . . 'Break a vase,' says Walcott, 'and the love that reassembles the fragments is stronger than the love that took its symmetry for granted when it was whole'" (Hartman 1996, 111–12).[38] This statement modulates the deep-seated idea that desire is fed by lack, that love grows with labor, and that we therefore love the imperfect more than the perfect. But it also presupposes the idea of a proper shape (genuine and symmetrical) and bespeaks a strong investment in its restoration. Because the commitments to lack and to integrity are equally strong, this topos presents love as the desire to heal (in both the transitive and the intransitive sense) that never ends because it constantly reproduces the wound as the condition of its own continued possibility. Such love puts the burden again on us, asking us to unify emotional energies and to focus them exclusively on the one god, the one person, or the one work of philosophy.

While Hegel's earlier theological writings call upon love—in particular the love of Jesus—to unify and reconcile what is disrupted, the *Phenomenology* invites us to disperse emotional energy in the negativity-sharing movement of a lighthearted despair. With a laconic note in his wastebook of the time when he writes the *Phenomenology*, Hegel clarifies that repair can be counterproductive: "a mended sock is better than a torn one; not so with self-consciousness" (Hegel 2002, 251). The narrative of the *Phenomenology*, thus, draws more on the pleasure of Dionysian dismemberment than on the healing power of Christian love. Here is the beginning of the entry on Dionysus in Hederich's *Gründliches Lexikon der Mythologie*, the authoritative source on Greek mythology during Hegel's time:

> DIONYSUS. . . . A common epithet of Bacchus, which according to some accounts is supposed to mean *dionyzos*, the one who opens and reveals [*der Eröffnende*], according to others, *dianysos*, the one who sweetly penetrates us [*der lieblich in uns hinein geht*], and according to yet other accounts, *dialysos*, the one who dissolves us [*der uns auflöset*]. (my translation)

Bacchus's epithet speaks of mutual penetration. Like Dionysus, the *Phenomenology*'s narrative spreads open for its readers and penetrates them. The mutuality of this double movement dissolves the boundaries between remembering (or "inwardizing") and dismembering. Or, to put it in slightly different terms, it has the effect that thesis and antithesis don't complement one another in a synthesis, but share the same negativity.[39] Hegelian-Dionysian negativity propels other configurations of consciousness to enter the scene and to play their part. It is the negativity of emotionality, or the power of transport, that doesn't congeal into a fixed lack or a terrifying nothingness, but gives pleasure: "Thrice happy they of men that have looked upon these rites ere they go to Hades' house" (Sophocles).[40] Like the myths of Demeter and Dionysus, the *Phenomenology* explores the overlap of finitude and infinity, and thereby initiates the reader into an affirmation of despair.[41]

Spirit—the subject of the *Phenomenology*—is broken and scattered; truth is offered up in morsels. This has its sex appeal, as Butler points out:

> We begin the *Phenomenology* with a sense that the main character has not yet arrived. . . . Our immediate impulse is to look more closely to discern this absent subject in the wings; we are poised for his arrival. As the narrative progresses beyond . . . the various deceptions of immediate truth, we realize slowly that this subject will not arrive all at once, but will offer choice morsels of himself, gestures, shadows, garments strewn along the way, and that this "waiting for the subject," much like attending Godot, is the comic, even burlesque, dimension of Hegel's *Phenomenology*. (Butler 1999, 20)

Butler sketches the sexiness of the *Phenomenology*'s textual despair. We can linger on each part of the textual body. While reading, we disjoint the body of this truth that is often figured as an "organic unity" (§ 2). The sex act has a dismembering effect.[42] Some might be disappointed in the end. Those who were not distracted enough by the activity of taking the narrative apart and tasting its bits might actually realize that Godot never came, that the grand subject never arrived, that their love for absolute knowledge was never consummated. Or was it? The sexiness and pleasure of this text, if it exists, lies not in deferred gratification, but in the orgiastic transport of every bit at any bend of the road: "The truth is the bacchanalian revel where no member is not drunk" (§ 47).

There is no reason for us to feel obliged to indulge the desire to heal when we read Hegel. Rather than labor to restore a presumed (w)holiness, we can join his text's lighthearted despair. And yet, like the protagonist, most readers of the *Phenomenology* have their own resistance to despair. The *Phenomenology* has never been read as what it claims to be—a path of despair. There are two ways of resisting the *Phenomenology*'s despair, or rather, two despairs to be resisted: the protagonist's despair and the text's despair. The reader can escape the protagonist's despair by distancing herself from the protagonist and instead identifying with the narrator—the phenomenologist. She can avoid the text's despair by reading the text as a triumphant narrative of progress.

Rather than attending to the existential quality of the protagonist/s' suffering, some readers sense the comedy in these desperate attempts and foreground the protagonist/s' less-than-concrete existence, describing it as cartoonish. These readers notice that, while consciousness repeatedly gets knocked down, it always gets up again. As soon as it is back on its feet (however many) or its four wheels (for those who grew up in the U.S. of the 1950s and '60s), the protagonist seems happier than ever:

> For Hegel, tragic events are never decisive. . . . What seems like tragic blindness turns out to be more like the comic myopia of Mr. Magoo whose automobile careening through the neighbor's chicken coop always seems to land on all four wheels. Like such miraculously resilient characters of the Saturday morning cartoon, Hegel's protagonists always reassemble themselves, prepare a new scene, enter the stage armed with a new set of ontological insights—and fail again. (Butler 1999, 21)

This non-identificatory absence of sympathy makes sense: after all, "consciousness" is not a real person, and it is rather delightful to follow the display of such magic resilience. Of course the resilience is purchased with oblivion. After each crisis, a new shape of consciousness sets out with the confidence that it has found the truth that will last forever. This confidence is possible only because it has forgotten its history of many painful failures to find such truth. Consciousness's resilience stems from its myopia, from the fact that it doesn't see the whole, but simply universalizes its own particular moment. And yet it is precisely its blindness that will be each consciousness's downfall. Amnesia produces resilience, but it also consumes the self; it is a way of despair. Similarly, the protagonist/s' lack of awareness about their historical determinateness fragments the whole; it breaks the text apart into a series of positive shapes without much coherence. Because consciousness does not remember its previous life and does not recollect the many torturous self-negations that have led to where it is, the protagonist of the *Phenomenology* falls apart into many protagonists. And just as the protagonists' turning away from despair generates despair—their own as well as the text's—so the reader who dis-identifies with the protagonist/s and remains oblivious to their suffering produces a cartoonishness and lightheartedness that in fact overlaps with Hegelian despair.

The more common strategy to avoid the textual despair of the *Phenomenology* is to read for the happy ending. Such a reading assumes that spirit's self-formation (*Bildung*) concludes in absolute knowledge. Instead of on oblivion, this strategy stakes its bets on recollection. Rather than giving in to the distraction of the various stations, this reader keeps in view the whole, relates all the shreds of experience, and thus unifies the many protagonists into the one: spirit. And yet—as Hegelian as it sounds—this kind of reading actually doesn't take seriously Hegel's speculative notion of *Erinnerung*. Inwardizing never produces a whole. It expropriates the one who appropriates. We have seen earlier in this chapter that consumption consumes the self. "Spirit only wins its truth when it finds its feet within its absolute disruption"—when it has lost the third foot, the foot of synthesis, and finds its feet within absolute disruption, not after the disruption has been repaired (§ 32). Relying on remembrance to produce a coherent story of progress leaves the reader with empty hands. In chapter 3 ("Release"), I have discussed how the final chapter of the *Phenomenology* (on "Absolute Knowledge") yields nothing in the sense of stable and positive knowledge. It rather leaves us with a feeling of disappointment: remembering dismembers.

There is yet another way of neutralizing the threat of this path of despair; it consists in containing despair. Many have read Hegel's dialectic as an economy of drama, where each conflict is brought to a head in order to provoke a solution. This solution inevitably takes the form of destruction and new beginning.[43] Despair, then, appears not as an avoidable breakdown—along the lines of "don't despair now, we are almost there"—but as a necessary stage, because, without despairing, we would never get there. Each section of the road springs from the protagonist's despair. This story has two problems. First, it integrates suffering into an economy of sacrifice in the service of absolute knowledge. But the solution does not follow in any necessary way from the sacrifice. It is only by accident that the heart opens.[44] Second, this scheme is complemented by the logic of *Aufhebung* understood in such a way that the repetition of the dialectic process can be read as progress. Obviously, this understanding of *Aufhebung* relies on a notion of recollection that again does not do justice to the speculative character of Hegel's *Erinnerung*. I agree with Rajan who sees in the repetitions and returns of the phenomenological narrative a suspension and even an undoing of teleology—what she calls "Hegel's self-consuming narrative" (Rajan 1995, 164). If we take seriously the double vector of the movement of inwardizing, it becomes very hard to construct a teleology, and we ultimately have to accept that there is no use for and no redemption of despair other than the pleasure of despair itself.

The pathbreaking sentence of the *Phenomenology*'s preface—"spirit . . . wins its truth only when it finds itself in absolute disruption [*in der absoluten Zerrissenheit sich selbst findet*]"—does not mean that tears (teardrops) heal the tears (cracks) (§ 32, trans. modified). It does not mean that finding oneself in disruption or registering inner conflict undoes such incoherence. It means that self-remembrance is self-dismembering. I thus take issue with the dramatic reading of the *Phenomenology* that relies on a simple notion of memory in its interpretation of *Aufhebung*, and argue instead that *Aufhebung* works to slightly dissociate emotionality from itself and to produce not drama, but lightheartedness. The logic of lighthearted despair relies on the overlap of remembering and dismembering. To remember (to incorporate—to consume—to join and hold together—to learn by heart—to keep secret) and to dismember (to break—to shatter—to scatter and become scattered—to distract and get distracted—to forget—to open—to reveal) play each other and echo one another. "Dismembering" literalizes "remembering," and "remembering" spiritualizes "dismembering." Despair is fragmentation *and* stickiness.[45] For the rubber subject of the *Phenomenology*, falling and getting up are one and the same movement. The elastic self stretches until it tears; and when it tears, its pieces still stick together, without pathos or ambition. The cracks of the cockroach heal without leaving scars. This healing is just as little triumphant as the cracking is dramatic. And yet a humble and unexcited emotionality pervades and propels all of these movements.

Epilogue: Against Emotional Violence

Appadurai locates the reasons for the increase in global violence in the spread of specific emotional conditions. In *Fear of Small Numbers: An Essay on the Geography of Anger,* he argues that the ethnic cleansings of the early 1990s in eastern Europe, Rwanda, and India, as well as the terror that has come to dominate the beginning of the new millennium, are the effects of a "geography of anger." By this he means that global, regional, national, and local spaces are interwoven to replicate hatreds that are fueled by "social uncertainties" and ideological fears, such as the "anxiety of incompleteness" (Appadurai 2006, 8–10). Understandably, Appadurai doesn't make it his job to thoroughly theorize the emotional conditions that he features so prominently in the title of his illuminating book, namely fear and anger. But the recent wealth of political analysis, such as his, that takes emotion, affect, or feeling into account while investigating specific political issues, makes a thorough theory of emotional phenomena all the more necessary.

Reemtsma argues as part of his wide-ranging critique of why modernity's excesses of violence have not destroyed modern faith in modern institutions that the civilized taboo on violence makes us more sensitive and more susceptible to trauma (Reemtsma 2008, 136). In response to Reemtsma's diagnosis, one might want to propose homeopathic doses of violence to raise the threshold for trauma again. It was perhaps in this spirit of remedying easy bourgeois traumatization that Fisher has made his case for what he calls the "vehement passions." And it seems to me that much of modernity's characteristic cultivation of sexual passion has been serving exactly this function of a homeopathic cure against epidemic trauma. But Reemtsma has a more mediated form of homeopathy in mind when he argues that the social and personal fragmentations so typical of modernity are the kind of violence that also provides the mechanisms to cope with trauma. Modern rationality—in the form of social and mental operations that distinguish, separate, and even split off parts of the self—can protect the person from being seized completely and broken irremediably by violence (Reemtsma 2008, 137). I have shown throughout this book, and in particular in the last chapter ("Broken"), that such anti-totalizing gestures and self-differentiating mechanisms do not exclusively, and not even primarily, belong to rationality but are, rather, the domain of emotionality.

I subsume rationality under emotionality—in counter-distinction to cognitivist accounts of emotion, where emotions are shown to serve rational processes. I do so in the hope that a better awareness of the workings of emotionality will change what we accept as rationality, or, to put it more concisely, that emotionality will affect logic. I thus pursue a strategy slightly different from those accounts of affect that demand a radical separation of affect and cognition (because they want to foreground the values of emotion as irreducible to those of reason). In this conclusion, I will address two representatives of the separatist anti-cognitivist camp in emotion theory: one I disagree with—that is Fisher's *The Vehement Passions*—and one I have a lot of affinities with, Altieri's *The Particulars of Rapture*. Their book titles already indicate that they both favor emotional figures of complete seizure (passion for Fisher and rapture for Altieri). But one reinforces the bluntness of such seizure by insisting on vehemence while the other implies internal differentiation by promising the particulars.

My argument for the self-differentiating force of emotionality brings me into almost complete disagreement with Fisher's case for premodern passion. Fisher wants to rehabilitate the passions that have been ostracized, as it were, by a long history of civilization. Beginning with Stoicism and continuing with the Enlightenment and the establishment of modern bourgeois society, Western culture has spent enormous disciplining energy to moderate and privatize passionate experiences. Fisher is interested in the passions over and against modern "emotions" or "moods," not because the term "passion" vacillates fruitfully between passivity and activity (or because the term is tied to a rhetorical culture of affectation and self-affectation), but—quite to the contrary—because passion, in his view, propels to "immediate action" (Fisher 2002, 14).

He identifies two strands in the history of the discourse on the passions: one that models all passions on fear (the strand inaugurated by Stoicism) and one that describes their characteristics using the template of anger. Fisher himself praises the advantages of focusing on anger. "The inner material of anger is . . . the will," he maintains, while "where fear is used as a template, as it was in Stoicism, the passions are taken as disturbances of the self, rather than internal material of the self" (Fisher 2002, 14). "No one," he contends, "thinking of the passions by means of the template of anger could ever think of the passions as passive or opposed to actions" (ibid.). This is a rash claim, and I have shown in my chapter on pathos that impassioned action must, from the perspective of even only a slight remove, indeed be deemed at least somewhat compulsive and unfree. The fact that Fisher brushes away any concerns about unfreedom within action leaves me wondering whether he equates anger with activity and fear with passivity simply because the object of fear might attack us while we might attack others in anger. He thus confuses emotion with behavior. By insisting that passion is "internal material" rather than a disturbance from the outside, Fisher assumes a substantive inner core (the will) and doesn't get into view that the self disturbs itself. Not to mention that fear and anger are much closer connected than Fisher's forced separation of two strands of passion theory wants to make us believe. The entanglement of anger and fear is evident everywhere in the work of Appadurai, who sees anger and hatred grow out of fear and anxiety as well as spur fear in return. But most importantly, Fisher's celebration of sheer activism seems rather dangerous in light of Appadurai's diagnosis of a global geography of anger.

What, then, are the values that drive Fisher's account? Why does he want this truth about the passions and not another one? Fisher provides a bold answer to such questions when he suggests that "the template of anger . . . sponsors a fundamental claim for a model of human worth and dignity, inseparable from the passions and nearly equal to the worth and dignity of reason" (Fisher 2002, 15). This statement has two parts. He wants equal respect for passion and for reason. In addition, he claims to be invested in "human worth and dignity." Let's turn again to his descriptions of anger to see what such apparent humanism might entail: "In anger an outward-streaming energy, active, fully engaging the will and demonstrating the most explosive self-centered claims on the world and on others, makes clear the relation of the passions to spiritedness or to high-spiritedness, to motion, to confidence, and to self-expression in the world" (Fisher 2002, 13). When he speaks of "human worth and dignity," Fisher, thus, clearly means that of the self—over and against the worth and dignity of the other. Indeed, he endorses "the most explosive self-centered claims . . . on others." "The passions," he argues, "assert a world in which there is only a single person over against all others" (Fisher 2002, 64). The vehement passions he wants to rehabilitate are impervious to arguments. They have a "fixed and immobile quality, a stubborn indiscussable intensity" (Fisher 2002, 67). And the passionate person is asocial and tyrannical; he creates in one swoop "a kinglike or godlike world where only the reality of his anger . . . has any importance"—that is to say, "a world in which there is only one center and all others exist as circumference" (Fisher 2002, 69).

But there are indeed also values to the passions. According to

Fisher, passions center the self and show who we truly are. "In a moment of extreme [passion], the self is completely given" (Fisher 2002, 54). Such centering is achieved by the "absorbing concentration on one present-time object." Fisher observes that "instead of diversified investment," passion "solidifies attention in the direction of one monopolizing fact" (Fisher 2002, 62). He underscores that such focus creates a sense of unity and intensity: "In the moment of extreme [passion] . . . full momentary unity of the self is achieved, and it is a unity in which each part is pitched at a peak of activity" (Fisher 2002, 54). Typically modern frustrations, such as the mind-body split or the hierarchy among the personal faculties, are overcome in the state of passion: "All the parts of the self . . . —the body . . . , the mind . . . , the soul or spirit . . . —can . . . be demonstrated in an impassioned state not merely to be connected but to pervade one another so as to be capable of being fully and simultaneously present" (Fisher 2002, 55). From this sense of "living life to the fullest" stems the tremendous attraction of passionate states: "within the passions lies the most potent experience of our own individual reality of which we are capable" (Fisher 2002, 60).

The separate values of the passions, in Fisher's account, are authenticity and absorption, unity of self and full presence. These are values that are not commonly associated with the antisocial and anti-democratic ethos that Fisher exhibits. But the brashness of Fisher's argument has the advantage that it clearly and unmistakably reveals the indeed inherent link between the desire for authenticity and the need for violence.[1] Fisher's account privileges passion over less vehement emotional states such as mood, emotion, or feeling because his appreciation of authenticity and fullness of life creates a strong need for vehement states. But such fullness is short-lived and doesn't happen very frequently. The transient experience of passion creates a longing desire for passionate states. Similarly, once we are in a state of heightened passion, Fisher admits, "we are protecting [its vehemence] from interruption by other moods or other claims" (Fisher 2002, 67). Here we get a hint of the actual fragility of vehemence. It requires a lot of energy to boost and protect the supposedly "natural" states of high passion. And sometimes, it simply requires violence.

The feeling of absorption that the passions afford comes at the expense of the reality of others: "With extreme fear, we seem to enter a world where no other person any longer exists" (Fisher 2002, 60). The intensity of high passion is also bought at the expense of other realities of the self. Vehemence lies in "the most uncompromising experience of the present moment of time. That moment of pure present time stands uninflected and uncompromised by any secondary feeling for claims of other times past or future in which, under other circumstances, we might imagine our identity invested" (ibid.). Intersubjective and intrasubjective differences suffer equally in moments of great passion. Passionate states deny inner difference, that is to say, the fact that we are both more and less than one person and that we are invested in various different versions of ourselves. They also deny outer difference, that is to say, the friction that the various claims of others provide. The monopolizing attention of vehement passion does not care about the destruction of any of the things and values—and in extremis even people—which at that moment do not fall within its focus. Fisher's example of Achilles—who, in his extreme anger, "withdraws into a solitude from which he can watch the destruction of his own social world"—supports what we have seen in chapter 2, namely that the self-destructive stubbornness of the tragic hero provides evidence for the peculiar indifference of single-minded passion to the complexities of life and the subtleties of transport (Fisher 2002, 64). That the passionate hero doesn't have the energy and mind to rescue his world makes sense because his passion has already (if subjectively and temporarily) annihilated that world: significant others, as well as all previous and future realities of the self, have become utterly irrelevant.

Transport

I have cast emotionality not as passion, but as transport. While passion singularizes, transport pluralizes—it pluralizes both the subject who "has" the emotion and the subject that the emotion is. My account therefore does not explain all emotionality through one paradigmatic transport (it belongs neither to Fisher's anger strand nor to the fear strand he identifies as governing the discourse on emotion). Instead, it brings out the internal differences of transports. For example, I have shown how the orgasmic quality of release that indeed seems to bring the *Phenomenology* to a passionately heroic end is offset by its sorrowful quality: the grief about the many figures of consciousness that were former selves and that have been negated along the way. Through this grief, the subject of the *Phenomenology* (spirit) connects with its former selves. It might seem contradictory, but release relates. Transports are modes of self-relation that both project future selves and remember past selves. The ejaculatory valence of release projects the *Phenomenology* into the future, while the sustained process of relinquishing, that is part of release, involves remembrance.

The transports that are thus divided also divide or pluralize the subject. The characteristic ambivalence of transports unsettles those who try their best to experience them. They constantly need to renegotiate the specific valences and internal distributions of that ambivalence. I thus describe transports as driven by Hegelian dialectic, which is precisely not a regulated process of calm resolution through mediation of in themselves stable terms, but a messy dynamic where each pole is folded into its opposite so that both continually and internally modify one another, and where recognition (*Erkennen*) doesn't follow with necessity but "bursts forth" as if by accident (§ 786).

Transports transform and they create a multiplicity of selves along the way. Altieri has argued that feelings can activate and advance processes of transformation, especially if we adopt the right attitude toward them. In a wonderful reading of "The Dead," the last story in Joyce's *Dubliners,* Altieri shows that expanding one's capacities to both express and read feelings (that is to say, cultivating an aesthetic approach to affective states) enables change (Altieri 2003, 220–30). Using Hegel against Butler here, Altieri appreciates that such change of self be achieved not through a re-signification of the codes that interpellate the subject but through "recontextualization." He attributes more agency to the subject than Butler does. At the same time, his seemingly introspective approach (self-transformation via thorough explorations of feelings) is indeed aesthetic and outward-oriented. It transforms the world. The self must change by creating a new world, a new context for itself. The affinities with the procedure of Hegel's *Phenomenology of Spirit* are evident. Here, the protagonist/s are transported with reflective emotion to make existential shifts in perspective: with the transition to a new worldview, a whole new world emerges.

The emotional subject is never an individual. It is divided or multiplied within by the history of its previous figurations that are *aufgehoben* or folded into the story of its future unfoldings. The boundaries of the emotional subject are troubled; it is not a self-centered but an ek-static subject, or better, a subject in transport. Altieri foregrounds this interstitial character of emotional transport when he observes that Gabriel, the main character of Joyce's "The Dead," "does not so much create new meaning as learn to dwell more attentively at the edges of meaning, where he can begin to see why his sense of self-importance cannot suffice" (Altieri 2003, 228). Transports take place at the edges of meaning, at the margins of worlds, or, as Cixous puts it, "at the corner, at the angle" between states (Cixous 1997, 42).

Plasticity

Emotional subjectivity is plastic. In the last chapter, I have used the term "rubber subject" to describe the plasticity of emotionality. My discussion of the rubber subject of despair has shown the positive aspects of ambivalence and dividedness, namely that emotionality conceived as transport never seizes the person as a whole. Altieri also underscores the satisfaction that plasticity affords. He describes plasticity as "the capacity of a psyche or a work of art to establish satisfaction in holding together without collapsing diverse aspects of experience which all have substantial claims upon us" (Altieri 2003, 205). For him, plasticity thus means the flexible negotiation of ambivalence and complexity. Even though he appreciates the capacity to "hold together without collapsing," Altieri, rather haphazardly, rejects dialectical mediation (ibid.).[2] In contrast, I consider Hegelian dialectic as a great tool not for reconciling what is torn, but for reconciling oneself to tears. Speculative plasticity thus strengthens us precisely for, as Altieri puts it, "dwelling emotionally within what the oppositions help unfold" (Altieri 2003, 206).

But wherein exactly lies the satisfaction that complexity, ambivalence, and plasticity afford? Transports set us free despite, or precisely because of, the intensity of their call. They "eat us alive" (they consume us and make us come alive). Their intensity and vitality stems not from force or weight but from the diversity of their address. With Hegel—who of course famously sponsors "the whole"—we can say that transports foster a version of the whole that is not unified, solid, and consistent but internally differentiated, articulated, and unfolding.[3] Even though it might be difficult to respond to contradictory claims, the interstices between the different aspects of the experience of transport always leave us space to breathe. The transported self never goes all out, so to speak. Transports are differentiated forms of emotionality that self-augment and self-attenuate through reflection and that mobilize the self's resources to reflect and save itself. Put differently, the emotional subject or the subject in transport doesn't have to die for its passion.

As we have seen when analyzing Fisher's account of vehement passion, the topic of emotion is often used to buttress an unelastic first-person perspective and a blunt narcissism. Yet, the plasticity of emotional subjectivity includes the capacity to switch from my first-person to other first-person perspectives and to appreciate other singularities without losing my own (see chapter 4, "Juggle"). One of the greatest values of plasticity lies in its encompassing both intra- and intersubjective relations while intertwining them. Altieri distinguishes between plasticity and "involvedness," another major advantage of affective life. By "involvedness" he means the appreciation for the affective lives of others. To me, such involvedness is part of plasticity precisely because the plastic subject of emotionality relates to itself as another, and feels the other as itself. It can sympathize with others because it has learned to sympathize with itself. Interpersonal emotional relations are formed by way of a complex interplay of "sympathy and distance . . . fully conjoined" (Altieri 2003, 223). And not only does "using self-awareness [in affective matters] as a means of appreciating what creates significance and shapes dispositions in other lives" show the identificatory aspect of sympathy, but it also reveals that without such appreciation self-transformation would not be possible (Altieri 2003, 195). Every seemingly independent individual that forms emotional relations to others is itself already mediated, that is to say, it is the result of a history of emotional self-transformations that, each time, involve the mediation through or identification with others and that also, each time, deposit a remainder of otherness within the self.

Alternately, one can view the different selves that develop along the way of emotional self-transformation not so much as different articulations of one and the same subject, but indeed as different subjects with independent existences that then can relate to one another as if through sympathy across distance. Emotional plasticity is able to hold both perspectives together.

The discourse on emotion often serves the self-congratulatory celebration of humanity, but the most stunning and rewarding achievement of plasticity lies in its impersonal sympathy. To offer an example, I would like to turn briefly to Altieri's reading of the concluding stanza of Wallace Stevens's "Sunday Morning." Altieri shows a fine sense for the other-than-human quality of emotionality when he observes that "the poem's final reflections try to expand the affective field into an elastic space" (Altieri 2003, 206):

> And in the isolation of the sky,
> At evening, casual flocks of pigeons make
> Ambiguous undulations as they sink
> Downward to darkness, on extended wings. (quoted in Altieri 2003, 206)

Even though Altieri locates the agency of this plasticity at first in an actant that can be readily identified as the expression of human agency, namely the poem ("the poem's final reflections try to expand"), he quickly shifts to the non-human agency of pigeons: "The pigeons stretch out this isolated sky . . . and their 'ambiguous undulations' also slow down the time framed by that sky" (Altieri 2003, 207). The plastic capacities of pigeons stretch human worries about mortality into the elastic space of a sky. As if contagioned with the undulating ambiguity of the pigeons' motions, the vital materiality of the literary language follows suit: "Sound and syntax also work to slow down the sentence by suspending clauses and by playing long vowels and lush n and d sounds against the temporal flow of the sentence" (ibid.). And here the specific reward of this plasticity comes to the fore: "At first, the poem could not reconcile in one space the idea of religious value and the fact of mortality. But now we can see that . . . resolution may be possible if we can simply approach consciousness as if it could treat its own embodiment as closely allied to the force of these extended wings" (ibid.). A subtle and calm—perhaps "casual"—satisfaction lies in the practice of consciousness—be it that of the poet, the speaker, or the reader—to treat itself as "closely allied" with the elastic movements of other bodies and to get a plastic afterfeeling (*nachempfinden*) for the ambiguity of the pigeons' casual fall (see chapter 4).

Syntax

Such plasticity that extends into the impersonal calls into question—and here I differ from Altieri's account—the "experience" character of emotional transports. Rather than somehow merely providing the raw stuff for human experience and representation, emotionality articulates itself. It has a syntax of its own.

Using the example of trembling, I have elaborated that consciousness can never fully experience a transport (i.e., it is not capable of the experience of absolute fear) but gets eclipsed in the transition from one version of self to another and can therefore relate to the actual transport only indirectly. Nancy submits that "the subject is—or makes up—the experience of its being affected" (Nancy 2002, 42). "To make up" means "to form" but also "to fabricate."[4] As experience, transport always has a fabricated quality to it. The human subject "has" the experience of absolute fear (for example) only in the future perfect, that is to say, it has to make up the experience retrospectively and in anticipation.

Nevertheless, subject and emotionality are synonymous in Nancy's statement ("the subject is—or makes up—the experience of its being affected"). Transports are self-relations. But by this I mean that emotionality relates to itself. Highlighting the impersonality of transport must overlap with the inverse strategy, namely, to personify emotionality itself. Emotionality is fundamentally performative. That is to say, emotionality constitutes herself as a subject in transport in response to her dividedness, a dividedness which always also has the character of an interpellation—before other (witnessing) subjects who are thereby equally transported (compare the contagion of "Moi" with the emotionality of Rameau's nephew that I have discussed in the introduction). No human subject is necessary for this emotional self-relation or performative interpellation to take place. Human subjects can be involved, but the whole dynamic is never quite a personal "experience." If transports can be called "experiences" at all, this term would refer to emotionality's experience of itself; but in any case it would be a mediated, articulated, and indirect experience—the experience of a plural, syntactic, and ambiguous subjectivity.

As made-up experiences, transports do not take place in time, but they shape—and even constitute—time. I thus agree with Fisher when he argues, building on Hume's account of relative measure, that "by means of the passions, time undergoes granulation and is given units other than the mechanical and identical units of seconds, minutes, hours, days, and years" (Fisher 2002, 76). His focus on the vehement passions frames Fisher's consideration of temporality and makes him describe the passionate subject as exclusively concerned with the pressing quality of nearby time (the immediate past and the imminent future). Such urgency does not at all belong to the temporal features of transports. In chapter 5, I have explored how the transport of mutual acknowledging (which crosses mutual embrace with mutual penetration) makes time flow or blow in reverse. The winds and rivers of Hölderlin's poem "Andenken" there gave evidence to the ambivalent pulls of such cross-vectored time. The mutual reflections among and between the moments of transport add a spatial character to time—rendering it extremely slow and thick.[5] Hegel shows not only that knowledge (*Erkennen*) is inherent in emotionality but also that this part of the transport of acknowledging is unending—mutual acknowledging is the trope of the repeated incipience of knowledge (*Anerkennen*). We have encountered another example of the decelerating, cross-vectored time of emotionality in the "ambiguous undulations" of Stevens's pigeons. An image of mutual embrace and penetration, the casual flocks of pigeons both embrace and stretch the sky with their extended wings while being held by the sky and pierced with its darkness so that they sink down. Chapter 7 has shown that transports break and multiply the subject, and in chapter 6 I discussed how the breaks within/between the subject/s reorient time. Time trembles back and forth across these cracks and, as a result, those subjects who would be distant from one another on a linear time continuum come to overlap here, in the broken temporality of transport.

Throughout this book, I have pursued different genre considerations, describing Hegel's *Phenomenology* as a narrative, as a theatrical piece, and as a poem, as well as making an argument about emotionality as constitutively theatrical (it needs a scene in order to transport one; see chapter 3, "Release") and about the experience of transport as essentially narrative (it becomes available only via anticipation or retrospection; see chapter 6, "Tremble"). At this point, I want to underscore again that the mediated structure and specific temporality of emotionality resonates most thoroughly with poetry. This is so not so much because of the characteristic subjectivity of lyric poetry but because of its rhythm. Poetic rhythm generates a different kind of syntax than that of logical sequence and rule-bound subordination.

Lyric poetry, says Hegel, "allows particular ideas to subsist alongside one another . . . whereas thinking demands and produces dependence of things on one another, reciprocal relations, logical judgments, syllogisms, etc."[6] Things and ideas (and voices and sounds and fonts, among other things) subsist alongside one another in the poem, without a clear hierarchy. Different versions of the same poem (one that foregrounds a sound structure, one that highlights a certain meaning, one that focuses on the visual line breaks, for example) are layered one upon the other. These versions are certainly not unrelated. Their distinction and connection, their affinities and frictions, their reflections across their incongruences build an emotional syntax.

Lightheartedness

The more the emotional subject wants to experience sincere and substantive emotion, the more it becomes palpable (first of all to the emotional subject itself) that such emotional substance must be produced (that experience must be made) by a rather tenuous operation of intensification through reflection and cross-identification—the concentration of emotional energy through a play of mirrors. The (non-)experience of the sublime, Pfau has shown convincingly, means the death of natural feeling (see the end of chapter 1). From hence on feeling has something fictional about it.

On the other hand, even a cynic would not be able to deny her impotence to fabricate transports completely at will. That we need to make up the experience of transport does not give us a fully constructionist version of emotion. Malabou's "*voir venir*"—which she devised to "represent that interplay, within Hegelian philosophy, of teleological necessity and surprise"—also brilliantly captures the (un)anticipatory structure of transport: we are sure of what is coming and yet we don't know what is coming (Malabou 2005, 13). Feelings surface when we least suspect them and fail to come about when we think we should feel something. In their fleetingness they escape our control even though we participate in their production. Even if it is very slight, a transport always bursts. Transports form a language that evades us in a way that is similar to ironic language. Indeed, the awareness of the intrinsically ironic character of language in general (the fact that we cannot with final certainty prevent our utterances from turning against us, or others from twisting our words) facilitates the acceptance of the ambiguity of transports, of the fact that we are both subjects of emotion and subject to emotion. Instead of suffering from this condition, one might playfully embrace it.

In the first two chapters, I have discussed Hegel's critique of naturalizing accounts of emotion. The second part of the book (on emotional syntax) has therefore explored Hegelian emotionality as largely synonymous with negativity. It has emphasized the tears (in both pronunciations), the blanks, the syncopes, and the brokenness of subjectivity, as well as the unending quality of the labor of the negative. As a result, my discussion has featured quite a few primarily negative emotions (grief, shame, fear, despair). But Hegel also offers the element of levity, improvisation, and playfulness that lifts the weight and earnestness from the Hegelian "labor of the negative." Loosely quoting Goethe's translation of Diderot's *Rameau's Nephew,* Hegel notes with regard to the performative quality of transports that "a strain of the ridiculous will be blended in . . . , which denatures [feelings] [*ihnen ihre Natur benimmt*]" (§ 521). Rameau's nephew exemplifies the emotional subjectivity operative throughout the *Phenomenology,* and this emotional subjectivity is not characterized by consistency and integrity but instead slides through a whole scale of tones and feelings. The range and speed of the nephew's performances turns up the ludicrous and silly aspect of emotionality. It undoes the idea that feelings are natural and therefore can and must be frankly expressed and respected.

Brushing aside the usual scholarly insistence on Hegel's supposed scorn for irony, Trilling contends that "Hegel in his *Phenomenology* goes far towards explaining the intellectual value that irony may be supposed to have" (Trilling 1972, 12). Clearly, there is also an emotional value to irony that we can read off the *Phenomenology*. Rather than suffering from its inability to achieve a fundamental unity of self and to safeguard the sincerity of natural feeling, spirit takes its tears lightly. It mocks itself. The very articulation of disruption that Rameau's nephew accomplishes "is" in turn "the derisive laughter about the disorientation of the whole and about itself" (§ 524). The phrase "disorientation of the whole" must remind us of Hegel's description of truth in the preface: "The truth is the whole. However, the whole is only the essence completing itself through its own unfolding [*Entwicklung*]" (§ 20, trans. modified). Through the figure of the nephew, spirit explicitly acknowledges that its journey of formation—this whole, which is the truth—is indeed confusing and confused. Trilling concludes that "if 'the whole' is seen as 'confused' rather than as orderly and rational . . . the human relation to it need not be fixed and categorical; it can be mercurial and improvisational" (Trilling 1972, 121). Spirit's laughter about itself liberates its readers and its various conscious manifestations (or figures of consciousness) from the weight of the "labor of the negative."

I share Trilling's appreciation for contingency, improvisation, and levity in Hegel. But I am not exclusively concerned with "the human relation" to spirit. I consider irony to be not just a rhetorical device, but also a constitutive factor of emotionality itself. Trilling's wonderfully simple description of irony as an instrument to establish a disconnection, detachment, or reflective distance "between the speaker and his interlocutor, or between the speaker and that which is being spoken about, or even between the speaker and himself," nevertheless does not get into view the non-instrumental and non-anthropogenic forms of irony (Trilling 1972, 120). While Ngai has argued that a particular group of emotions—she calls them "ugly feelings"—have a special relationship to irony, it seems to me that it is rather a certain understanding of emotion that brings the ironic quality of emotionality to the fore.[7] The account that I have offered here—of emotionality as a relation to alterity that is internally mediated—clearly relies on the slight and volatile distance that irony provides. Irony is part of emotionality. The tremendous energy that naturalizing accounts of emotion have to spend in the attempt to keep irony out of the emotional picture (by locking feeling into the heart or by dramatizing the weight of passion) only proves this point.

Irony ruins pathos and breaks hearts. Yet there is no need to get overly invested in the pathos of distance, either. The "generous irony" that Altieri envisions overlays, in my view, self-differing with the inverse operation, namely excessive presencing (Altieri 2003, 228). The heart breaks but one doesn't suffer in earnest because what "bursts forth" is the "Yes" of affirmation (§ 786). The heart bursts into laughter. If all goes well, the ironic account of emotion proposed in this book encourages hearts to stop laboring at dramatizing passion and to embrace lightheartedness instead. Such lightheartedness may well take the form of excessive sentimentality.

If the experience of transport is that "I is an other," then "I" cannot fully live up to my feelings. The dishonesty lies not only in the linguistic expression. To be certain, I cannot mean what I say when I say "I love you." In the final analysis, I will be unable to prove or even justify this declaration (see Smock 2003). But the hypocrisy of declarative language comes from the fact that transport itself is performative; it cannot provide a substantive referent for linguistic description. My discussion of fear in chapter 6 has shown that one can never fully experience fear because the experience divides the self. In love and in fear, to remain with these examples, we are unable to be serious. A certain kind of lightheartedness always slips into the experience of emotionality. We are incapable of owning up to our self-descriptions when we say that we fear or that we love, because transports keep changing the subject. Emotions are a joke, and we are laughable when emotional.

But in its very impotence lies also the innocence of emotionality. Most accounts of feeling since the eighteenth century construct innocence as naive and natural feeling as uncontaminated by reflection, while knowledge is seen as bringing about the fall from natural grace and thus as guilty. Yet, in a speculative account of emotionality innocence and guilt, reflection and feeling are maintained one within the other. Innocence might then be described as the practice of bearing "the unbearable remoteness of incessant pain," or love, or shame, or fear, or any other unjustifiable feeling that is irretrievable yet inescapable in its remoteness from itself (Smock 1984, 61). Bearing the lightheartedness of emotionality then coincides with protecting emotionality from our urge to mean it. Such practice could reduce the need for violence that stems from our terror of being nothing but a joke.

Of course, sooner or later we will fail this innocence, the trope of transport will add one more spin and innocence will turn into guilt, love into hate, and the remoteness of pain into the immediacy of a blow (see Smock's discussion of Melville's "Billy Budd" in Smock 2003). But, despite such turns for the worse, we have now caught a glimpse of the turn from pretense to innocence. We might want to linger for a while and join this revel of valences in which no member is not drunk. The turn from pretense to innocence can also be described as a return from modern emotionality to an eighteenth-century sentimentality now conceived differently. If emotionality turns back into sentimentality, this return displaces the trope of the heart: sentimentality now can be understood not as an investment in sincerity but as a hyperpresence, a playful relation to lack. To the self-reflexive staging of emotionality this sentimentality responds with an excess of sincerity, the very excessive character of which, Sokolsky argues, mocks any sincere investment in sincerity.[8]

The heart breaks and breaks and breaks and each breaking heals without leaving scars, mocking the impossible verdict of self-expression with lightheartedness. "Unabashed sentimentality would be understood not as a search for an encompassing substantial unity, but instead as an attempt to render unintelligible both this search and the counterargument that one must fail to be adequate to oneself" (Sokolsky 1987, 83). Instead of naively denying alienation or forcefully prohibiting unity, sentimentality in this sense takes the heterogeneity of the self so excessively and unreasonably seriously that, together with the allegedly natural unity of the "I," it loses also the "conceptual means to describe this loss as loss" (ibid.). Among her excessive tears such a sentimentalist suffers no sense of loss. If emotionality all too often turns either into the violent negation of the vulnerability that runs through the condition of self-differentiality (as in the turn from impossible love to a very possible hate) or else into the self-punishing prohibition of unity, excessive sentimentality offers over-presence or being "too much oneself" as a playful yet critical alternative. This ludic relation to lack challenges the self-tormenting obsession with lack as both too serious and not serious enough. Compared with unabashed sentimentality, the melodrama of self-denial still subscribes, despite its own declarations to the contrary, to a logic of noncontradiction that is unable to conceive of negativity, alienation, and reflection as embroiled with presence, innocence, and naïveté.[9] It is the distinction of Hegel's speculative philosophy that it affirms the overlap between the mediated and the immediate, between irony and sincerity, and between the fervent and the cool.

Notes

Introduction

1. Among them most importantly are Judith Butler, Rebecca Comay, Eva Geulen, Frederic Jameson, Catherine Malabou, John McCumber, Jean-Luc Nancy, Terry Pinkard, Tilottama Rajan, and Slavoj Žižek. Rebecca Comay's *Mourning Sickness: Hegel and the French Revolution* was published after this book had been submitted to Northwestern Press. Comay puts behind us the topos of Hegel as grand unifier focusing on "nonrecognition, nonproductivity, noncommemoration, nonredemption" (80) and analyzing "absolute knowledge" as the exposition of the constitutive yet traumatic untimeliness of consciousness (5–6). The book is a brilliant reading of the "Spirit" section of the *Phenomenology* that foregrounds the role of emotion in Hegel and thoroughly thickens our understanding of this text by applying the tools of literary criticism (in addition to exploring the historical context of the French Revolution and situating Hegel in the history of ideas as close to Nietzsche and Freud). Comay offers an example for the constitutive self-reflection of emotion that I explore in this book, when she describes how "the bad infinite of suspicion makes terror both reflexive . . . and in turn self-reflective" (82).

2. I quote from Pinkard's new translation of the *Phenomenology of Spirit*, available online at http://web.mac.com/titpaul/Site/Phenomenology_of_Spirit_page.html. From here on this translation of the *Phenomenology of Spirit* is referred to by paragraph numbers only (using the section sign). When referring to a specific figure of the protagonist/s I use the neuter pronoun, unless Hegel gives this figure a masculine designation. In this case, I follow Hegel in the use of masculine pronouns. In doing so, I don't mean to suggest that the positions of master and servant, for example, or of any other figure of consciousness he renders masculine, cannot be occupied by female subjects.

3. For an argument for the use of "emotionality" as the term of art for emotion studies, see Pahl, "Emotionality: A Brief Introduction."

4. Compare Pinkard, "Symbolic, Classical, and Romantic Art," 19: "In modern . . . art, the characters . . . not only worry about what they in fact feel, but also worry if what they feel is real, worry about how they *should* feel, and constantly offer explanations to each other about all these things in an effort to determine what it is that is going on 'within' themselves."

5. Compare Illouz, who argues in *Cold Intimacies* that we currently participate to an unprecedented degree in the staging of personal authenticity, a highly

paradoxical and embattled practice that extends into the spheres of corporate business and politics.

6. The term "transport" safeguards against conceiving of emotions as "states." Compare Pippin, *Hegel's Practical Philosophy,* 53: "Feelings thus in Hegel's language are also said to be 'modes of negativity'—or non-identity, where this means a mode of self-relation within an experience, not merely . . . just being in . . . a state."

7. Speight accurately describes the *Phenomenology* as "quasi-literary" in his cogent analysis of the essentially literary shape of Hegel's philosophy of agency.

8. On the *Phenomenology* as bildungsroman, see Royce, *Lectures on Modern Idealism,* 147–56; and Abrams, *Natural Supernaturalism,* 225–37. Even though Speight addresses how the different literary genres of tragedy, comedy, and the novel inform Hegel's philosophy of agency (by modeling the practices of retrospectivity, theatricality, and forgiveness), he reduces the differences between these genres to the one overarching notion of "narrative" and describes the *Phenomenology* as "Hegel's novel."

9. I agree with Altieri's preference for adverbial over adjectival treatments of the emotions (*The Particulars of Rapture,* 9–16). See also Pfau, *Romantic Moods,* 31: "Emotions thus are not 'owned' by an individual as some discrete representation but, instead, are experienced as a dynamic or mood by which the quotidian practice of representation and cognition is suffused."

10. I use "sympathy" as the translation of the German *Nachempfindung* rather than of *Einfühlung,* because the latter (literally: "feeling oneself into") reinscribes interiority and because I appreciate the temporal lag and supplementarity of *Nachempfindung* ("having an afterfeeling" or "imitating a feeling"). For more on sympathy, see chapter 4.

11. Nussbaum seems to appreciate disruption when she describes emotions as "acknowledgements of neediness and lack of self-sufficiency" (Nussbaum, *Upheavals,* 22). Unfortunately, this aspect of emotional ethics gets lost in her overall normative treatment that differentiates between ethical and unethical, good and bad, or healthy and sick emotions. See also Altieri's critique of Nussbaum in *The Particulars of Rapture,* 153–80.

12. The quotation marks are in Hegel's text and indicate quotations from Goethe's translation of *Le neveu de Rameau.* Hegel at times condenses vastly disparate parts of the dialogue and he does not always quote correctly.

13. Hegel combines here a quote from "Moi" reacting to "Lui" with a quote from another performance of the nephew.

14. Taylor has addressed some of the asocial and apolitical effects of being absorbed in the quest for individual authenticity in *The Ethics of Authenticity.* Trilling ends his discussion of sincerity and authenticity in a strong critique of the intellectual tendency to see the ultimate promise of authenticity in madness. He finds the "belief that human existence is made authentic by the possession of a power, or the persuasion of its possession, which is not to be qualified or restricted by the co-ordinate existence of any fellow man" "appalling" precisely because it exalts "ultimate isolatedness" at the expense of social relations (Trilling, *Sincerity and Authenticity,* 171).

15. Discourse ethics could help to de-dramatize and to externalize emotion, but its proceduralism paints a rather fragile picture of democracy. Proceduralists see democracy "founder" if rational agents do not adhere to the sincerity principle. See Anderson's paraphrase of Rawls: "If citizens do not undertake to present their views sincerely, and if those in power do not sincerely believe in the reasons they themselves offer for their actions, then the entire project of political liberalism founders" (Anderson, *The Way We Argue Now,* 168). Given the highly paradoxical character of sincerity (not to mention the tricks that language plays on us) and the various possible ways to conceive of truthfulness, the sincerity principle seems a rather tall order. In light of these difficulties, proceduralism must define the rules of communicative action with such exaggerated strictness that making everybody adhere to its rules verges itself on the unethical.

16. Compare Hamacher on philology as affection for language as affection (Hamacher, *Für—Die Philologie*).

17. Trilling, *Sincerity and Authenticity,* 16.

18. Compare Altieri on plasticity (*The Particulars of Rapture,* 205–7). Altieri identifies three aspects of affective states that bring satisfaction as ends in themselves: intensity, involvedness, and plasticity. He insists that these are "conative," not ethical, values, but qualifies this statement, announcing that he is "most interested in the possibility of demonstrating how an emphasis on conative states is compatible with immediate and sustained attention to the situations of other human beings" (182).

19. To take Hegel's disparagements at face value is often misleading and only gets one trapped in resentful stupidity. Geulen's brilliant reading of the Hegelian verdict of the end of art is an excellent case in point. She shows that when Hegel draws the line around ancient Greek art as the consummation of the aesthetic ideal, he does, in fact, not ring the death knell for art in general, but both points to the dubious and ambivalent ending of the prehistory of classical art and opens the floor for the specific vitality of modern art. See Geulen, "Hegel ohne Ende."

Chapter 1

1. Compare Redding, *Logic of Affect,* 130: "Hegel was rather concerned that a wedge not be driven between feeling and concept in mental life such that feeling would thereby become sequestered in an inaccessibly private subjective realm."

2. Schleiermacher, *Über die Religion: Reden an die Gebildeten unter ihren Verächtern,* 22–74 (my translation).

3. See § 9: "Whoever seeks mere edification, who wants to surround the diversity of his existence and thought in a kind of fog, and who then demands an indeterminate enjoyment of this indeterminate divinity, may look wherever he pleases to find it. . . . However, philosophy must keep up its guard against the desire to be edifying."

4. See Nietzsche, "Ecce Homo," 777: "In the history of the quest for knowl-

edge the Germans are inscribed with nothing but ambiguous names; they have always brought forth only 'unconscious' counterfeiters (Fichte, Schelling, Schopenhauer, Hegel, and Schleiermacher deserve the epithet as well as Kant and Leibniz: they are all mere veil makers [*alles blosse Schleiermacher*])."

5. Hegel mocks the rejection of rationality as a misplaced frugality that results in spiritual impoverishment rather than philosophical superiority: "Even to a lesser extent must this kind of science-renouncing self-satisfaction [*Genügsamkeit*] claim that such enthusiasm and obscurantism is itself a bit higher than science" (§ 10).

6. For example, by the politically influential Rosenkreuz Orden.

7. Compare Pfau, *Romantic Moods*, 12: "Kant had shown . . . the essentially nonpropositional status of feeling."

8. See, for example, Rousseau, "Origins of Inequality," 202: "The imagination which causes such ravages among us, never speaks to the heart of savages, who quietly await the impulses of nature, yield to them involuntarily, with more pleasure than ardor, and, their wants once satisfied, lose the desire." Rousseau's valorization of natural needs and feelings hinges upon their involuntary character; they are unaffected by the will and the imagination, and thus escape the perils of reflection.

9. Among the wealth of cognitive philosophy on emotion that emphasize the world-structuring and salience-giving faculty of the emotions, the most significant are perhaps De Sousa's *The Rationality of Emotions* and Nussbaum's *Upheavals of Thought*.

10. Another worry with Enlightenment rationality stems from a more jaded reaction to the rule of reason as generating not so much a crisis of values and beliefs but a cold objectivity that levels first-person experiences and investments. This position also seeks recourse in emotion but usually requires more heat for emotion than those who battle disorientation and undecidability with "the intelligence of emotions" (subtitle to Nussbaum's *Upheavals of Thought*). Compare Fisher, *The Vehement Passions*, 248–49: "The passions, as I have tried to define them . . . insist on . . . the differential reality of life in time. Time's distinct parts . . . are details not to be surrendered or blended somehow into any objective, larger abstraction of time. . . . The passions are evidence in us for the prior importance of *my own* world over *the* world." Even though Fisher mentions "the guiding Kantian ideals of reciprocity and universality" in his conclusion as one of several important victories of objectification, he spends the bulk of his book dismantling these Kantian ideals (246).

11. Chapter 7 circles back to the question of how to respond to skepticism. There, I discuss despair as a transport that, rather than protecting against skepticism, radicalizes it, exposing the self to its negativity from which it emerges lightheartedly.

12. Compare Hegel, *Encyclopedia*, § 438: "The essential and actual truth which reason is, lies in the simple identity of the subjectivity of the concept with its objectivity. . . . The universality of reason, therefore, whilst it signifies that the object . . . is now itself universal, permeating and encompassing [*das Ich durchdringend und befassend*] the 'I,' also signifies that the pure 'I' is the pure form

which overlaps the object and encompasses [*über das Objekt übergreifend und es in sich befassend*] it" (trans. modified).

13. Compare Hegel, *Philosophy of Right,* 14.

14. They deplore the fact that "humanity . . . does not live in the gratifying unity of the law and the heart. Rather, it either lives in dreadful separation and suffering, or it at least lives as being deprived in taking pleasure in *itself* when it *obeys* the law" (*Phenomenology,* § 371).

15. Russo discusses how the French philosophes of the late Enlightenment, despite their taste for the serious and the sublime, inadvertently fall into the frivolity and irony of the *goût moderne* they so despise. Hegel certainly makes a similar argument when he claims that the proponents of the "law of the heart" are simply unaware to what extent they reproduce the pleasure principle that ruled the previous dialectic. I agree with Russo when she points to the political suspiciousness of conceiving of feeling as a unifying force: "Emotion became a weapon in the philosophical struggle, applied in order to control and unify an audience that until then had been insubordinate, scattered and unresponsive to truth" (Russo, *Styles of Enlightenment,* 12).

16. Compare Žižek, *Parallax,* 206: "Hegel's thesis that 'subject is not substance' has thus to be taken quite literally: subject . . . is *something that exists only insofar as it appears to itself.* This is why it is wrong to search behind the appearance for the 'true core' of subjectivity: behind it there is, precisely, nothing. . . . A Self is precisely an entity without any substantial density, without any hard kernel that would guarantee its consistency."

17. See the next section for a more detailed discussion of the alienating experience of self-realization.

18. Against this organicism of self-expression, Žižek argues that the self emerges as "a violent rupture of organic homeostasis" (Žižek, *Parallax,* 210).

19. "Instead of attaining *its own being,* it therefore attains within being the alienation [*Entfremdung*] *of itself from itself*" (§ 374, trans. modified).

20. We might be more familiar today with the more recent critiques of sentimentality offered by Berlant (in *The Female Complaint*), by Baldwin (who contends that "sentimentality . . . is always . . . the signal of secret and violent inhumanity" ["Everybody's Protest Novel," quoted in Berlant, 33]), and by Trilling (who traces the convoluted itinerary from Rousseau's sentimental idealization of the savage to Conrad's story of civilization's paradoxical embrace and contempt for the "heart of darkness" [Trilling, *Sincerity and Authenticity*]). But Hegel was one of the first to articulate this critique, and despite the differences between eighteenth-century and twentieth-century forms of sentimentalism, the gist of his critique still holds.

21. Speight follows Royce and Hyppolite in exploring this allusion (*Hegel, Literature and the Problem of Agency,* 27–31).

22. The figure of the "heartless rebel" is rather common in late eighteenth-century German literature. In addition to Schiller's *The Robbers,* see, for example, Hölderlin's *Hyperion,* second vol., book 1. Hyperion participates in the Greek war of liberation against Turkey in hopes of establishing the reign of the law of the heart: "wo einst in unser Gesetzbuch eingeschrieben werden die Gesetze der

Natur, und wo das Leben selbst, wo sie, die göttliche Natur, die in kein Buch geschrieben werden kann, im Herz der Gemeinde seyn wird" (Hölderlin, *Sämtliche Werke,* 3:116). But he soon realizes that his companions in battle are less than excellent: "Es ist aus, Diotima! Unsere Leute haben geplündert, gemordet, ohne Unterschied . . . es war ein außerordentliches Project, durch eine Räuberbande mein Elysium zu pflanzen" (ibid., 3:117).

23. Berlant, *The Female Complaint.*

24. In the *Encyclopedia,* Hegel describes madness (*Verrücktheit*) as a situation where the subject "remains fast in a *particularity* of its self-feeling [*in einer Besonderheit seines Selbstgefühls beharren bleibt*]" (§ 408).

25. As is necessarily the case, according to Hegel, since "individuality, which entrusts itself to the objective element, makes itself vulnerable (*gibt preis*) to being altered and turned topsy-turvy" (§ 322).

26. Schiller, "Sprache," published in *Musenalmanach 1797* under the title "Tabulae Votivae." The full text is: "Warum kann der lebendige Geist dem Geist nicht erscheinen? / *Spricht* die Seele, so spricht ach! schon die *Seele* nicht mehr" (Why does the living spirit fail to appear to the spirit? / When the soul *speaks,* alas, it is no longer the *soul* that speaks). My translation.

27. Schiller's distich is of course set in verse, but he mangles the rhythm; instead of maintaining the trochaic meter he opts for the cursive. The trochaic version—"Spricht die Seele, so spricht ach! die Seele schon nicht mehr"—would have kept the phrase "spricht die Seele" intact, with the exception of the then even more dramatic interjection "ach!" while the rules of meter would have put the stress on *Seele.*

28. Indeed, the expressionist premise shows a lack of spirit. See § 340: "it has spiritlessly [*auf diese geistlose Weise*] grasped cognition as 'The outer is supposed to be an expression of the inner.'"

29. Taylor ties back to Herder the idea of (holistic) expression that he finds in Hegel (see *Hegel and Modern Society*). Taylor describes German Romanticism as driven by attempts to reconcile the expressive unity emphasized by Herder with the philosophy of radical autonomy developed by Kant. In his view, it is Hegel who eventually solved the problem. Pippin draws on Kant to make an argument for spirit's self-legislation. He calls this model of self-actualization an "expressive" one, in distinction to the "causal" model of natural self-making that is derived from Aristotelian teleology. See Pippin, *Hegel's Practical Philosophy,* 17: "The key and very controversial point to be defended is: Hegel's self-making model is not derived from Aristotelian notions of natural growth and maturation into some flourishing state, but from a claim about the self-legislated character of all normativity." Menke pursues a very interesting program. He argues for a rejuvenation of the tragic (in the strictly Hegelian sense of two irreconcilable but equal values) where self-expression and justice are recognized as equal yet conflicting values.

30. The foremost example of spirit's textual relation to itself is of course the *Phenomenology of Spirit* itself. Within the *Phenomenology,* it is the chapter on spirit, in particular, that both thematizes and performs the text model of self-realization. Speight has convincingly made the important argument that the *Phe-*

nomenology takes a "literary turn" in the transition from the chapter on "Reason" to that on "Spirit" and that the three sections of the "Spirit" chapter together offer a complex account of the textual character of action and agency that is intrinsically tied to this chapter's engagement with literary works (*Hegel, Literature and the Problem of Agency,* 18).

31. Compare Taylor, "The Expressivist Turn," 368–90.

32. Compare Müller-Sievers, *Self-Generation,* 4: "'Organic' indeed became the ultimate praise in philosophical and aesthetic judgment in the period of the epigenetic turn [around 1800], a status the word has not lost since."

33. Moyar argues the same in his article on "Self-Completing Alienation." While Moyar establishes (self-)transparency as a necessary condition for non-alienated life, he concludes with the strong claim that "alienation is not simply an enemy to be stamped out, but rather the very background tension that maintains modern societies in their imperfect freedom" (172).

34. Pinkard proposes "emptying oneself" as a translation of *Entäußerung.* He points out that Hegel quotes with this term Luther's German translation of the Greek *kenosis*—"God's becoming flesh by virtue of renouncing large parts of his own divinity" (Pinkard, "Shape of Spirit," 120).

35. Pippin comes close to understanding actualization as utterance when he compares agency with being a speaker of a natural language. But he doesn't have a textual notion of language. For him, the comparison with natural language serves to evince the collective social construction of rational agency, that is to say, he relies on the idea of a transparency of language. His argument is that one can function as a rational agent only if one adds another thread to the safety net of mutual recognition, just as "vocalizations count as speaking the language only within a language community" (Pippin, *Hegel's Practical Philosophy,* 197). Hegel's conception of action as exposure, on the other hand, emphasizes the *Verkehrung, Verfremdung,* and transformation of any deed by others, rather than a collective construction of mutual transparency.

36. In fact, *Äußerung* is not the privilege of the human subject. Any force—including those of the natural world—is bound to exert itself (*sich äußern*). See the chapter in the *Phenomenology* on "Force and the Understanding."

37. With *The Inoperative Community* Nancy had not yet embarked on his extraordinarily interesting and novel reading of Hegel that he offered in *Hegel: The Restlessness of the Negative.* In the earlier work, Nancy still treats Hegel as a thinker of the state—and even equates Hegelian philosophy somewhat flippantly with the state (see Nancy, *Inoperative Community,* 32: "it is no longer Hegel. It is no longer the State"). Because of the consistency of his thought of the community's unworking with his reading of the restlessness of the negative, I find it nevertheless useful to also draw on Nancy's earlier work to illuminate Hegel's model of textual utterance.

38. See § 62: "thought, instead of getting any farther with the transition from subject to predicate . . . finds the subject also to be immediately present in the predicate." For a more detailed discussion of the speculative proposition, see chapter 4 ("Juggle").

39. I agree with Terada's conclusion of the impersonal textuality of emo-

tion and fully endorse her project to dislocate emotion from the human subject. But, with Hegel, I describe textual (self-)reference as (non-human) subjectivity. Thus foregrounding impersonal subjectivity in Hegel, I agree with Nancy's notion of the subject: "the self is what does not posses itself" (Nancy, *Hegel,* 36).

40. "What will later come to be for consciousness will be the experience of what spirit is, that is, this absolute substance which constitutes the unity of its oppositions in their complete freedom and self-sufficiency, namely, in the oppositions of the various self-consciousnesses existing for themselves: The *I* that is *we* and the *we* that is *I*" (§ 177).

41. Following Žižek, Egginton correctly identifies the operative fiction of absolute knowledge as one of Hegel's most important lessons. See Egginton, *The Philosopher's Desire,* 103.

42. The passage I just analyzed is a good example of "the complicated footwork" of the *Phenomenology* that Jameson appreciates because it allows the *Phenomenology* "to avoid taking positions at the same time that it expounds them" (Jameson, *Hegel Variations,* 7). Not only the "heterogeneity of the book" has prevented its various themes and textual passages from being transformed "into pure or coherent philosophical positions, into identifiable ideas or concepts, . . . about which we can say that they represent Hegel's official thoughts," as Jameson has recently observed, but also, and more specifically, Hegel's use of free indirect discourse has done so (ibid.).

43. Pfau identifies this kind of epistemological paranoia as one of the three moods constitutive of Romanticism.

44. See again Hegel's discussion of the power of the understanding in the preface to the *Phenomenology,* § 32: "Spirit only wins its truth when it finds its feet [*sich selbst findet*] within its absolute disruption [*Zerrissenheit*]." For further discussion of the understanding as the self-lacerating mode of spirit, see chapter 7 ("Broken").

45. See § 32: "to keep and hold fast to what is dead requires only the greatest force"—it requires the strength and the labor of the understanding.

46. Arguing against my reading, one might propose that when Hegel writes "it turns out that behind the so-called curtain, which is supposed to hide what is inner, there is nothing to be seen unless *we* ourselves go behind it," the "we" refers to the phenomenologist/s who can fill the empty space with their superior knowledge. The phenomenologist/s—such objection would suggest—play the role of Goethe's *Turmgesellschaft* in *Wilhelm Meisters Lehrjahre,* who providently guides the protagonist on its path of *Bildung.* It is true that the "we" is ambiguous here; it can refer to both the phenomenologist/s over and against the protagonist/s, as well as to a narrative identification with the protagonist. In the following, I will make the case for the latter.

47. See § 303: "Observational psychology . . . discovers all sorts of faculties, inclinations, and passions, and since in its recounting of this collection, the recollection of the unity of self-consciousness does not allow itself to be suppressed, it follows that observational psychology must at least get to the point of being astonished that in spirit so many sorts of things and such heterogeneous things

without connection can exist alongside one another in the way they would in a sack [*wie in einem Sacke*]."

48. Around 1800, the pit is widely used as a metaphor for interiority. One particularly interesting example is to be found in Schiller's *Wallensteins Tod* (*Werke* II, 3): "Des Menschen Thaten und Gedanken, wiszt! / Sind nicht wie Meeres blind bewegte Wellen. / Die innre Welt, sein Microcosmus, ist / der tiefe Schacht, aus dem sie ewig quellen." Quoted after *Deutsches Wörterbuch von Jacob und Wilhelm Grimm*, s.v. "Schacht." Schiller's use of the metaphor shows particularly well what its function was and wherein its appeal lay, namely to stabilize emotional and mental life against the unpredictable fluidity of "blindly stirred waves" (*blind bewegte Wellen*).

49. See Hegel, *Encyclopedia*, § 453: the "inability to grasp a universal [as] intrinsically concrete [yet] *simple*, is what has led people to talk about special fibres and areas as receptacles of particular ideas."

50. Of course any perceptual image can serve as a sign, and perhaps even a kind of writing. But this is not Hegel's concern here.

51. Derrida shows that Hegel cannot maintain this distinction. See "The Pit and the Pyramid: Introduction to the Semiology of Hegel."

52. "Acquired habit subsequently effaces the peculiarity by which alphabetic writing appears . . . , it makes them a sort of hieroglyphic to us" (*Encyclopedia*, § 459, *Zusatz*). The note suggests that Hegel considers reciting by heart as writing in Derrida's sense. Derrida doesn't use this passage for his argument.

53. Compare Nancy, *Hegel*, 34–35: "To penetrate negativity demands 'another language' than the language of representation. The latter is the language of separation: the language of concepts in their fixity, of propositions and their copulas; it is the language of signification. . . . The language of philosophy is language itself spoken in its infinity; which is to say, at each instant, at each word, at each signification, language is put outside itself, insignificant or more-than-significant, interrupted and strained toward its own negativity—toward the 'vitality' of 'the self.'"

54. About the "*an sich*" as an ingredient in experience, see McCumber, "The Temporal Turn," 44–59.

55. In the context of agency, this double movement takes the form of internalized habits that form a second nature. For a brilliant discussion of "second nature" in Hegel, see Malabou, *The Future of Hegel*, part 1.

56. The beautiful soul appears in literary texts usually as feminine (see "Bekenntnisse einer schönen Seele" in Goethe's *Wilhelm Meister* and Henriette in Jacobi's *Woldemar*). On the other hand and quite predictably, this female figure is used to treat questions of male friendship (in particular the friendship between Jacobi and Goethe themselves). Hegel, as usual, uses the neuter or a strictly grammatical gender (in this case: *die Seele* is feminine).

57. "This created world is its *speech*, which it has likewise immediately heard and whose echo returns only to it [*deren Echo nur zu ihm zurückkommt*]" (§ 658; trans. modified).

58. See chapter 3 ("Release") for a discussion of speculative friendship, i.e., of the idea that friendship includes aggression, enmity, difference, and negativity.

59. One of the principal literary examples of the beautiful soul, Jacobi's *Woldemar,* has drawn criticism by others than Hegel for its generalization of personal experiences and its lack of awareness for differences. Schopenhauer, for example, in his preface to *Die Welt als Wille und Vorstellung,* mockingly describes Jacobi as a great philosopher "welcher wahrhaft rührende Bücher geschrieben und nur die kleine Schwachheit hat, Alles, was er vor seinem fünfzehnten Jahre gelernt und approbiert hat, für angeborene Grundgedanken des menschlichen Geistes zu halten."

60. "The content that language has acquired here is no longer the inverted and inverting, disrupted self of the world of cultural maturation [*Welt der Bildung*]. Rather, it is spirit which has returned into itself, is certain of itself, certain within itself of its truth, that is, certain of its recognition and certain as the spirit which is recognized as this knowledge" (§ 653). This certainty (*Gewissheit*) that constitutes *conscience* (*Gewissen*)—the certain knowledge of recognition accomplished or guaranteed, rather than incipient (*An-erkennen*) as a process requiring struggle—is the last unbroken bone, as it were, in the *Phenomenology*'s otherwise completely broken protagonist. It is the most solid bastion against alienation and tears (*Zerrissenheit*). But the hard heart will break without violence (more on that in chapter 7, "Broken").

61. "The articulation of this assurance sublates the form of its particularity, and it therein recognizes the *necessary universality of the self.* In that it calls itself 'conscience,' it calls itself pure self-knowledge and pure abstract will, i.e., it calls itself the universal knowledge and willing" (§ 654).

62. Kant seems to evoke a kind of *conatus* of aesthetic pleasure when he insists that "this pleasure is in no way practical. . . . But yet it involves causality, viz. of *maintaining* without further design the state of the representation itself and the occupation of the cognitive powers. We *linger* over the contemplation of the beautiful because this contemplation strengthens and reproduces itself" (*Critique of Judgment,* § 12).

63. Sokolsky has argued that sentimentalism might subscribe less (and more) than usually assumed to the values of honesty, purity, naïveté, natural feeling, and (self-)transparency. In her reading, the sentimental mocks the declaration of sincerity by being more than sincere. She thus uncovers an irony through excess in sentimentalism. See also epilogue.

64. Despite using "virtual" and "notional" here, Pfau more precisely argues that, after Kant's account of the sublime, feelings become essentially literary. That is to say, from then on we need literature—especially its most complex configurations (Pfau's examples are Novalis's *Bildungsroman* and Hölderlin's triadic hymns)—to produce feelings and to communicate them to ourselves and to others.

Chapter 2

1. See Nietzsche, *Gay Science,* section 317: "Retrospection.—While we are living each phase of our lives we rarely recognize its true pathos, but always see

it as the only state that is now possible for us and reasonable and—to use some words and a distinction of the Greeks—thoroughly an *ethos* and not a *pathos*."

2. Wahl, *Le Malheur de la conscience.*

3. I draw on Malabou's notion of "plasticity" to bring out the layered quality of theatrical pathos and to spatialize *Aufhebung.*

4. Large and influential traditions of moral philosophy have thought of the passions as by definition immoral. For the Stoa, for example, *páthe* are not only "alogical," but against nature and by the same token unethical.

5. Hegel does not explicitly reference Aristotle in the *Phenomenology,* but he studied Aristotle intensely for his first course on the history of philosophy in 1805. Ferrarin has demonstrated the influence of Aristotle on Hegel's substantial changes in his systematic conceptions around 1805, especially on the changes in his concepts of subjectivity and self-realization (Ferrarin, *Hegel and Aristotle,* esp. 408–11). I think that it is safe to assume that Aristotle's critique of Socratic intellectualist moral philosophy had already informed Hegel's notion of ethics by the time he was writing the *Phenomenology* (around 1806). It allowed him to project his own critique of Kant's intellectualist moral philosophy on a different screen.

6. Here I quote from the 1817 version of the lectures on the history of philosophy (*Heidelberger Niederschrift*). An English translation of the 1825–26 version has been published. Where the two versions overlap, I quote the published translation; otherwise the translations are my own and the page numbers in parentheses refer to the German original.

7. "Passion (love, ambition, thirst for glory) is the universal not in the realm of insight, but in the realm of agency and . . . as self-actualizing" (Hegel, *Geschichte der Philosophie,* 474, my translation).

8. These two views are only different sides of the same coin: the acknowledgment that personal intentions are subjected to ironic reversal.

9. Hegel often uses both terms interchangeably. Yet, in contexts where he wants to draw a distinction between self-serving passions and passions for a cause of ethical substance, he uses *Leidenschaft* for the former and reserves *Pathos* for the latter.

10. With the emergence of tragedy in the history of Athenian theater, the number of characters a play featured was extended from one to two.

11. With this link that Hegel draws between ethics and tragedy, we are reminded of Aristotle's *Poetics.* In the *Poetics,* Aristotle uses the word *páthos* to refer to the grave suffering that the tragic heroes experience. Aristotle mentions "death on stage, severe pain, and injuries" (chapter 11). The qualification "onstage" *páthos* here refers to physical suffering in the presence of spectators.

12. See chapter 1 ("Heart").

13. The heroes of Greek tragedies often insist on the existential weight of their pathos and resist the attempts of the chorus or of other characters to diffuse the crisis. See Butler on Antigone's refusal to dissociate the deed from her person (Butler, *Antigone's Claim,* 8); and Menke on the excessive self-judgment of Oedipus in Menke, *Gegenwart der Tragödie,* 13–101, in particular 40–46.

14. In line with Hegel's own merging of the ethical and the theatrical realms, Speight draws attention to the fact that the actors of Athenian tragedy

wear masks (*Hegel, Literature and the Problem of Agency*, 64). The character of their persona is thus fixed in advance.

15. We have recently witnessed a renaissance of arguments in favor of a tragic worldview. For the best among them, see Connolly and Menke. I appreciate the humbling effect of the tragic worldview on notions of human agency and autonomy (Connolly) as much as I appreciate the argument in favor of sustaining the fundamental conflict between different normative perspectives (Menke). My contribution to this discussion on the tragic lies in drawing attention to the fact that tragedy creates pathos as much as pathos creates tragedy. This cannot be good news since pathos in the dramatic sense, as Hegel defines it, does not do much to humble human agents or to make them appreciate the equal relevance of irreconcilable normative values.

16. Hegel clarifies that the genre of tragedy requires that the law that is violated must be apparent to the one who violates it. The fault of the tragic hero lies in not taking seriously what, in principle, is known to him.

17. Hegel discusses tragic pathos twice in the *Phenomenology;* first in the context of issues regarding communal life and ethical conduct ("Spirit" section), and then again as part of his discussion of the religious worldview of the Greeks ("Religion" section). His later *Lectures on the Philosophy of Art* expand on the second perspective. Hegel never published his lectures on art and aesthetics. At this point, there are three editions of the lecture notes: (1) Hotho's 1835 compilation of notes taken by various students from the four different times Hegel gave the lecture in Berlin—this text is widely used and has been translated into English (and is referred to as "Hegel 1975" in this study), (2) the critical edition of Hotho's notes from the 1823 lecture (referred to as "Hegel 1998" in this study), and (3) the critical edition of Pfordten's notes from the 1826 lecture (referred to as "Hegel 2005" in this study). Because of the dubious authorship of Hotho's compilation, I have, whenever possible, avoided using this text.

18. Hegel quotes Sophocles, *Antigone,* verse 926, probably in his own translation (see the editor's notes to the Meiner edition of the *Phenomenology*). Willige and Bayer translate: *So muß ich duldend wohl gestehn: ich frevelte* (München: Artemis, 1995). Kuchenmüller translates: *Dann seh ich ein: ich leide, weil ich fehlte* (Stuttgart: Reclam, 1955). Wyckoff's translation into English reads, "In suffering I'll see my error clear" (Chicago: University of Chicago Press, 1954). Franklin and Harrison translate "When I have suffered, I will understand that I have sinned" (Cambridge, Eng.: Cambridge University Press, 2003)

19. I translate *Anerkennen* as "acknowledging," rather than "recognition." For the reasons, see chapter 5 ("Acknowledging").

20. The auxiliary verb *sollen* ("should") makes all the difference. Hegel does not say that *Leidenschaft* is base, but that "'passion' carries the connotation of something that should be . . . base."

21. He speaks of the "depopulation of heaven" (*Entvölkerung des Himmels,* § 741).

22. Compare Menke, "Learning from Suffering," in *Tragic Play.*

23. Speight describes Antigone's acknowledgment of error as an expression of *amor fati* (*Hegel, Literature and the Problem of Agency,* 64–67). In his view, she

accepts the partitiveness of ethical action as necessary, rather than relativizing her pathos.

24. In Antigone's and Oedipus's insistence on their guilt we can see the auto-aggressive and suicidal streak bound up with the self-important streak of *Pathos.* See note 13.

25. See Pinkard, *Sociality of Reason,* 146: "Because the Greeks (or at the least the adulated, idealized Greeks) conceived of their ethical life as quasi-natural, as something that naturally restored itself to a happy and just equilibrium, they could not understand that their success depended not so much on a *naturally* self-restoring form of life as on their own actions."

26. Nobody since Jean Wahl has analyzed this structure of Hegel's dialectic as an emotional economy.

27. It is important to note that Hegel doesn't find this comparison very productive. See § 66: "It would . . . be expedient to avoid the name, 'God,' because this word is not immediately the concept but is rather . . . the fixed point of rest of the underlying subject. . . . Even when speculative truths are stated about that subject, their content lacks the immanent concept because that content is only present as a motionless subject, and in these circumstances, speculative truths easily take on the form of mere edification."

28. Without us, the readers, spirit would have comprehended itself only once: in Hegel's mind, one would assume. But an unacknowledged singularity doesn't count in Hegel's world.

29. For a more extensive discussion of *Bildung* as torture, see chapter 7 ("Broken").

30. I have already discussed that the world of "ethical order" doesn't learn from the tragic crisis, but considers justice done when the initial calm is restored. Another example is the "unhappy consciousness" who, even though it hears from the "mediator" the true meaning of action and agency, insists that "*for itself,* action and its actual activity remain impoverished, its enjoyment in consumption remains sorrowful, and the sublation of these in any positive sense continues to be postponed to an *other-worldly beyond*" (§ 230, trans. modified).

31. The *Phenomenology* has its moments of authorial boasting as well. I discuss one of them in chapter 6 ("Tremble").

32. I discuss Hegel's strategies to draw the reader into the textual process in chapter 4 ("Juggle"). They are rather complicated and sometimes counterproductive.

33. Hegel would chastise such repudiation as spiritless: "Spirit is not this power which . . . avoids looking at the negative, as is the case when we say of something that it is nothing or that it is false, and then, being done with it, go off on our own way on to something else" (§ 32).

34. While Žižek (*On Belief,* chapter 4) and Malabou (*The Future of Hegel,* 91–94 and chapter 7) have shown the importance of *kenosis* in Hegel's thought, they have not discussed God's suffering as an instance of *Pathos.*

35. Hegel's critique of Schlegel's notion of irony is certainly motivated by Hegel's strong position in favor of actual self-abandonment. For his critique of irony, see *Philosophy of Right,* 147–49, and *Aesthetics: Lectures on Fine Art,* 64–68. The

passage on irony is part of Hotho's compilation of the lecture notes of various students of Hegel's various lectures on aesthetics; it is not part of his own notes taken during Hegel's 1823 lecture on fine art. Due to Hotho's compilation, we might thus have a skewed sense of the actual importance for Hegel of the critique of Romantic irony. The same holds for the *Philosophy of Right,* where some of the more derogatory discussion of irony is to be found in the "additions" (lecture notes of questionable origin). It is important to note that Hegel did not dismiss all forms of irony. As part of the lectures on aesthetics, he speaks positively of the irony of the Greek gods. He also appreciates Solger's notion of irony (see his "Review of Solger's *Posthumous Writings and Correspondence*"). In fact, I will use the remainder of this chapter to argue that Hegel's speculative philosophy embraces irony.

36. De Boer offers a very interesting version of the argument that "Hegel's conception of tragic conflicts is not bound to his analysis of Greek culture, but constitutes the very heart of his philosophical method," because she foregrounds and appreciates the "entanglement" of the terms in conflict, rather than the conflict's resolution (De Boer, *On Hegel: The Sway of the Negative,* 180).

37. I want to thank Rüdiger Campe for the opportunity to co-teach two sessions on Hegel's theory of tragedy at Johns Hopkins University. During these sessions, he drew my attention to the word *Handlung.*

38. For Speight's worry about theatricality, see, for example, 70: "If desire and motivation . . . have instead a socially mediated or 'theatrical' character, is there a notion of self that can escape the alternation between hypocritical imitation or role playing on the one hand and reflection about it on the other?" For his discussion of forgiveness, see his chapter 4 ("Forgiveness and the Romantic Novel: Contesting the Beautiful Soul"). For Pinkard's stipulations for free agency, see *Sociality of Reason,* 188.

39. Antigone refers to her pathos as the gods' "unwritten and unchanging laws" (v. 554). Creon has the positive laws of the polis to draw on.

40. See § 467 (trans. modified): "In universal ethical life . . . it is not *this individual* who acts and is guilty, for as *this* self . . . he exists merely as the universal self. Individuality is purely the *formal* moment of *doing* anything at all, and the content of action are the laws and mores, and those are determined for the individual by his station in life. . . . As part of a people, self-consciousness descends from the universal only down to the point of particularity; it does not get as far as the point of individuality."

41. See Aristotle, *Poetics,* chapter 19.

42. Derrida offers *relever* as the equivalent in French (not the French translation) of *aufheben.* He thereby displaces *aufheben* and introduces a shift within the logic of *Aufhebung* to the logic of *différance.* Expanding on one of the meanings of *relever* (to lift again), Nancy presents *Aufhebung* as a repetitive plasticity (in the sense that the product of *Aufhebung* precedes its own production) rather than a linear progression. According to Nancy's analysis, *Aufhebung,* thus, both has already passed and is still to be performed (through the work of reading). The reader finds herself in the midst of an ongoing procedure without knowing its rules: "we must—à la commedia dell'arte—improvise, and without know-

ing our lines we must make progress through the plot" (Nancy 2001, 18). Coming from a different theoretical perspective but also with a sense for the paradoxes of Hegelian logic, Redding offers an evolutionary account of *Aufhebung* and proposes "bootstrapping" as a synonym (*Logic of Affect,* 150–58). Even though they dispute the reductionism of linear time, all of these accounts still envisage *Aufhebung* as temporal.

43. See my discussion of the chapter transitions in chapter 6.

44. For the logic of this identity of identity and difference, see Hegel on division (*Unterschied*) at the end of the chapter on the understanding in the *Phenomenology,* the section on "Contradiction" in "Book Two: The Doctrine of Essence" in the *Science of Logic,* and sections 115–22 of the *Encyclopedia.*

45. In chapter 7 ("Broken") and chapter 6 ("Tremble"), respectively.

46. Female irony takes the form of intrigue because women are not supposed to act. "The feminine has its pleasure" in the "brave youth" (*tapfre Jüngling*) because he is ready for action (§ 474). This gendered distribution of action and inaction is rather heteronormative. Hegel queers Spirit when he calls for dissolving (*aufheben*) the pathos of natural gender in transgender performances: "ethical *action* has the moment of crime in itself because it does not sublate [*aufhebt*] the *natural* allocation of the two laws to the two sexes[, but] rather [persists] within *natural immediacy*" (§ 467). I don't agree with Jagentowicz Mills's reading that Hegel "confin[es] women to the family" ("Hegel's Antigone," 84) or with Lydia Rainford's statement that "Hegel's portraits of the position of 'woman' place her firmly within the lower strata of being and consciousness" (Rainford, *She Changes by Intrigue,* 87).

47. See § 730: "the invincible elasticity of its unity extinguishes the point-like singleness of the actor and his figurations."

48. See Benhabib, "On Hegel, Women, and Irony," 40–41.

49. See § 746: "The force of dialectical knowledge . . . puts weapons of deception into the hands of preoccupied and anxiety-ridden old age." Creon belongs to the category of "old age"; he positions himself in opposition to Haemon's youth (see Sophocles, *Antigone,* v. 725ff.).

50. See § 747: "Rather, the genuine self of the actor coincides with the persona he plays, just as the spectator is perfectly at home in what is represented to him and sees himself playing a role therein . . . It is the return of everything universal into the certainty of itself, which . . . is, on the part of consciousness, well-being and letting-oneself-be-well [*Sich-wohlsein-lassen*], which is no longer to be found outside of this comedy."

51. I am referring here to the pit (*Schacht*) of the intellect in which memory deposits its images. See the previous chapter.

52. Among the several descriptions of irony Hutcheon offers, the following is particularly useful for the context of my concern with an emotional ethics: "[Irony] undermines stated meaning by removing the semantic security of 'one signifier: one signified' and by revealing the complex and inclusive, relational and differential nature of ironic meaning-making" (Hutcheon, *Irony's Edge,* 13). I'd like to rephrase this description for my context as: the plasticity of emotion in Hegel undermines the substance of pathos and the security of "one individual:

one god/law" by revealing the complex and inclusive, relational and differential theatricality of emotional meaning-making.

53. See Altieri's "A Plea for 'Generous Irony' in Interpreting Affective Experience" (*Particulars of Rapture,* 228–30), in particular, p. 229: "We do not have to repudiate all . . . intimacies . . . in order to approximate the forms of freedom provided by more bitter ironic stances."

Chapter 3

1. Pfau argues the same. He locates the historical emergence of this conception of feeling with Kant's third *Critique* (in particular, with Kant's analysis of the sublime). See my discussion at the end of chapter 1 ("Heart"). Terada encounters the idea that emotions require theatricality already in Rousseau (read through Derrida). In fact, one can move back further in time. Medievalists submit that feelings were commonly authenticated theatrically in the Middle Ages (see, for example, Eming, "On Stage: Ritualized Emotions and Theatricality in Isolde's Trial," 555–71). And scholars of rhetoric argue that the practice of affection and auto-affection common in Greek and Roman rhetoric relied on a notion of theatrically produced affect (see Campe, *Affekt und Ausdruck*).

2. Cixous, *Rootprints,* 31.

3. See also Agamben, *Language and Death,* 78: "The metrical-musical element demonstrates first of all the verse as a place of memory and a repetition. The verse (*versus,* from *verto,* the act of turning, to return, as opposed to *prorsus,* to proceed directly, as in prose) signals for a reader that these words have always already come to be, that they will return again, and that the instance of the word that takes place in a poem is, for this reason, ungraspable" (ibid.).

4. Even after correcting the reading from a parallel to a chiasmic syntax, the very chiasm of the stanza's third and fourth line gives *Verzweiflung* a prominence that counteracts the explicit mood of the poem.

5. Both Miller and Pinkard shift to the masculine pronoun in the last two lines (Miller even capitalizes "Him"), after referring to spirit by the neuter personal pronoun throughout their translation of the *Phenomenology.* This decision unnecessarily forces the entire passage into a Christian horizon of meaning.

6. To my knowledge, Hegel uses the word *Schädelstätte* in only two other passages; both are to be found in his lectures on aesthetics. In the first instance, *Schädelstätte* refers to the passion of Christ; in the second, it signifies lifeless, non-self-reflective matter. See Hegel, *Werke in zwanzig Bänden,* 14:152: "Der eigentliche Wendepunkt in diesem Leben Gottes ist das Abtun seiner einzelnen Existenz als *dieses* Menschen . . . , die Schädelstätte des Geistes, die Pein des Todes"; Hegel, *Werke in zwanzig Bänden,* 14:370 (on the beautiful form of sculpture): "Freilich darf dabei nicht in der Weise Galls verfahren werden, der den Geist zu einer bloßen Schädelstätte macht." Note the questionable authorship of the compilation of lecture notes published as Hegel's aesthetics.

7. See *Meyers,* s.v. "Golgatha" ("schädelförmiger Hügel bei Jerusalem").

8. See *Brockhaus,* s.v. "Golgatha" ("Der Name Golgatha wurde später mit dem Schädel Adams in Verbindung gebracht, der nach der Legende hier begraben sein soll. Dahinter steht wohl der Gedanke, daß Christus als zweiter Adam die Schuld Adams sühne").

9. *Grimms Wörterbuch* defines "Schädelstätte" as "stätte, wo schädel liegen" and cites Jean Paul's *Dämmerungen* with an example of this general and non-religious use of the word: "Wir hätten von Glück im Unglück zu sagen, . . . hätte man für die gefüllte Schädelstätte eines Schlachtfeldes stets einen groszen Kopf erkauft."

10. Scarry, *The Body in Pain,* introduction.

11. Emily Dickinson, "The Mystery of Pain."

12. Note the challengers of Scarry's understanding of pain. Ahmed, for example, explores the mediatedness and the sociality of pain in *The Cultural Politics of Emotion,* 23–31. Lethen identifies an inability to even feel pain in the face of the absolute lack of an (ideological, cultural, or religious) superstructure (*Überwölbung*) serving as a sound board ("Die Evidenz des Schmerzes").

13. See Terada, *Feeling in Theory,* 47.

14. One can also describe this emotionality as an aesthetic relationality where the parties and/or states inaccurately replicate one another. Such a description would draw on Bersani's work with Dutoit in *Forms of Being* and with Phillips in *Intimacies.*

15. See Cixous, *Déluge,* 14: "As soon as the dark song starts, nobody can resist drinking. . . . We are all ancient children dying of thirst / Ah! I was thirsty! Let's cry / For dozens of years, I so felt like crying!" (my translation).

16. This is not the only instance where the *Phenomenology* breaks into verse. Hegel quotes four lines from Goethe's *Faust* at the beginning of "Pleasure and Necessity" (§ 360), and two lines, in Hegel's own translation, from Sophocles' *Antigone* in the section on "Ethical Life" (§ 436). In both cases Hegel does not quote verbatim, and these two other insertions of verse can also be read as performances of personal friendship. His reference to *Faust* easily gives away Hegel's regard for Goethe, while the lines from *Antigone* hide the interlocutor more thoroughly. It is in dialogue with Hölderlin—beginning when they were both students at the Tübinger Stift—that Hegel reads, translates, and even attempts a metrical rendering of *Antigone.*

17. McCumber observes that "the lonely Master of Worlds, independent of his creation, is gone: absolute Spirit, Spirit which knows itself, is result *only.* And what it results from, the series of shapes of consciousness which 'foams forth' to it, is not the set of all possible shapes—the *ganze* realm of shapes of consciousness. It is merely *this* realm . . . Its self-determining unity is not infinitude itself, *die Unendlichkeit,* but the infinitude immanently determined by that specific whole: *seine Unendlichkeit*" (McCumber 2000, 56–57).

18. See Schiller, "Die Freundschaft," line 27: "Nur in dir bestaun' ich mich."

19. See, for example, § 795: "the knowing of pure knowledge not as abstract *essence* . . . , but the knowing of *this* pure knowledge as an essence which is *this* knowing, *this* individual pure self-consciousness."

20. See Blanchot, *The Infinite Conversation,* 75: "The fact that speech needs to pass from one interlocutor to the other in order to be confirmed, contradicted, or developed shows the necessity of interval."

21. Blanchot distinguishes three overlapping modes of interruption: "to interrupt oneself for the sake of understanding," "to understand in order to speak," and "speaking . . . only to interrupt oneself and to render possible the impossible interruption" (Blanchot, *The Infinite Conversation,* 79).

22. *Nur* is anticipated and echoed by the *ohne* (without) in the previous phrase.

23. In chapter 4, I will analyze in more detail what it means that Hegel considers his philosophical prose to be affected by verse. Specifically, I argue there that he wants the philosophical proposition to be read not only in one direction, but forward and backward, as it were.

24. See § 95: "In order to put the truth of sense-certainty to the test, a simple experiment will suffice. We write down this truth; a truth cannot be lost by being written down no more than it can be lost by our preserving it, and if *now, this midday,* we look at this truth which has been written down, we will have to say that it has become rather stale."

25. Chase notes that "it is as material occurrences not amenable to conceptualization that history may have to be conceived once the concept of progression or regression has been dissolved" (Chase, "Getting Versed," 136). When spirit gets versed, the concept of progression or regression does indeed dissolve, and what Chase claims here for history counts also for Hegel's future.

Chapter 4

1. As in Mikhail Baryshnikov's performance *HeartBeat: mb.*

2. For literature on Hegel's thought on language, see Surber (ed.), *Hegel and Language;* McCumber, *The Company of Words: Hegel, Language, and Systematic Philosophy;* and Simon, *Der Begriff der Sprache bei Hegel.*

3. Derrida, *Glas,* 1a: "Those who still pronounce his name like the French (there are some) are ludicrous only up to a certain point: the restitution (semantically infallible for those who have read him a little—but only a little) of magisterial coldness and imperturbable seriousness, the eagle caught in ice and frost, glass and gel."

4. Derrida offers *hérisson* or *istrice* as answers to the question of an Italian poetry journal: "Che cos'è la poesia?"—"What kind of thing is poetry?" He found this answer in the work of Friedrich Schlegel, who uses the hedgehog as simile for his favorite incarnation of Romantic poetry: the fragment. Athenäum Fragment 206: "Ein Fragment muß gleich einem kleinen Kunstwerke von der umgebenden Welt ganz abgesondert und in sich selbst vollendet sein wie ein Igel."

5. I wish to clarify that I don't defend an idealistic notion of poetry that sees in poetry a particularly personal and emotional mode of expression. I rather agree with Chase when she shows the disconcerting and decomposing effects of

Hegel's notion of language, especially his understanding of the sign. I also agree with Riley, who introduces us to impersonal passions, as well as with Terada, who argues that "we would have no emotions if we *were* subjects" (Terada, *Feeling in Theory*, 4).

6. This as a nod to John McCumber, who writes in the introduction to his superb book on Hegel's philosophy of language: "The most forgotten need, the one that cuts us open and makes us human, cries at us unspoken from the pages of . . . Hegel. It is the need for a company of words" (McCumber, *Company of Words*, xv).

7. Through exemplary readings, Nägele has shown how attention to echoes and echolalia (over and against the syntax of logical meaning) productively "breaks up the integrity of the individual text" (Nägele, *Echoes of Translation*, 16).

8. *Hegel's Aesthetics*, 1035, quoted in Mieszkowski, "Derrida, Hegel, and the Language of Finitude," § 22.

9. Versions of this argument can be found in such different accounts of emotion as Nussbaum, "Emotions as Judgments of Value and Importance"; De Sousa, *The Rationality of Emotion;* and Sartre, *Esquisse d'une théorie des emotions.*

10. See also Nussbaum, "Emotions as Judgments," 237: "What, then, makes the emotions in my example unlike the thoughtless natural energies I have described? First of all, they are *about* something; they have an object."

11. This is why Hegel usually uses "concept" in the singular. Since the logic of the concept turns fixed separations into permeable differences, it creates an ontological immanence where all differences can be viewed as differences within the concept and not between distinct concepts. While this singular doesn't exclude the plural (the singular actually pluralizes), the use of the phrase "the concept" certainly lends itself to (mis)understandings of the concept as a metaphysical entity.

12. "This disruption of the concept into the difference of its constituent functions [*Momente*]—a disruption imposed by the concept's own activity—is the judgment" (*Encyclopedia*, §166 *Zusatz*, trans. modified).

13. Compare McCumber on bivalence and degrees of truth in *Reshaping Reason*, 40–49.

14. The predicative judgment belongs to what Hegel calls "the old science [*die alte Wissenschaft*]" (*Hegel's Science of Logic*, 92, trans. modified). Hegel does not offer a full-fledged theory of the speculative proposition. As Nancy notes, "the yet necessary speculative theory of syntax is dispersed and is disarticulated from text to text; it goes absent where one was expecting it, and it is brought out in unpredictable contexts—never in the pure style of theory" (Nancy, *Speculative Remark*, 75–76). Further explanations of the relation between speculative syntax and predicative judgment are to be found in *Hegel's Science of Logic*, 90–92.

15. For a more detailed explanation of the logic of the predicative judgment, see *Hegel's Science of Logic*, 622–30.

16. The pejorative word *Räsonnieren* connotes superficiality in combination with a know-all attitude.

17. See *Hegel's Science of Logic,* 630: "What the judgment enunciates to start with is that *the subject is the predicate;* but since the predicate is supposed *not* to be what the subject is, we are faced with a *contradiction.*"

18. The German language makes it clear that in order to speak about (*über*) something, one has to be above (*über*) it. The fact that the predicate, as the more general term, gives meaning to the particular or individual and thus undefined subject distinguishes the logical judgment from any other grammatical sentence. See *Hegel's Science of Logic,* 625: "We may take this opportunity of remarking, too, that though a *proposition* has a subject and predicate in the grammatical sense, this does not make it a *judgment.* The latter requires that the predicate be related to the subject . . . as a universal to a particular or individual."

19. See Plato, *Symposium,* 176e (Eryximachus): "I would like now to make a further motion: let us dispense with the flute-girl . . . ; let her play for herself or, if she prefers, for the women in the house. Let us instead spend our evening in conversation."

20. The manifesto continues: "mythology must become philosophical in order to make the people rational, and philosophy must become mythological in order to make the philosophers sensible [*sinnlich zu machen*]." Note that the text uses the same phrase with respect to the philosophers that we find in Kant's *Critique of Pure Reason* with respect to the abstract concept, the object of Hegel's critique: *einen abgesonderten Begriff sinnlich zu machen* (*Critique of Pure Reason,* B299).

21. Nancy perceptively observes a sort of tai chi move in Hegel when Hegel takes his leave from "clever argumentation" by yielding to rather than opposing attacks that come in the form of complaints about the unintelligibility of philosophical writing: "Through the singular logic of a reply that does not answer, Hegel has already subtracted his text from the logic of argumentation, from the play of the *Gegenreden,* of discourses of opposition" (Nancy, *Speculative Remark,* 11).

22. For further explanation of why the speculative doesn't agree with the demand for expression, see chapter 1.

23. Marking and remarking (on) the language that is available to him in order to let resonate the speculative through juggle and syncopation, Hegel thus pursues something akin to what Derrida has explored in *Monolingualism of the Other.*

24. Pinkard aptly translates *spekulativer Satz* as "speculative judgment," thus underlining that Hegel does not invent a new syntax but rhythmizes the existent syntax of the judgment by accentuating its internal contradictions.

25. Malabou elaborates the double meaning and thus speculative character of the word "plastic" (*Future of Hegel,* 5–12). When something is said to be plastic, this can mean that it easily receives form or that it gives form. Plasticity moves between the complete fixity of form (in sculpture) and malleability to the point of formlessness.

26. Lecturing on art, Hegel observes in Greek sculpture an "air of lifelessness, an aloofness from feeling, and that tranquil trait of mourning." Quoted from Pinkard, "Symbolic, Classical, and Romantic Art," fn. 28.

27. Jameson has recently argued with similar exasperation against the three-step scheme. See *Hegel Variations,* 18: "We need to . . . forestall one of the

most notorious and inveterate stereotypes of Hegel discussion, namely the thesis-antithesis-synthesis formula. . . . For even if the tripartite rhythm happens to do justice to this or that local Hegelian insight, it still reifies that insight in advance and translates its language into purely systemic terms."

28. Nancy notes that the word *aufheben* appears in the *Science of Logic* first as part of the expression *ein Aufhebens machen*, "to make a fuss" (Nancy, *Speculative Remark*, 34).

29. "Since the predicate itself has been articulated as a subject . . . as the *essence* which exhausts the nature of the subject, [thought] finds the subject also to be immediately present in the predicate. Now, instead of having returned into itself in the predicate [*im Prädikate in sich gegangen*], and instead of having preserved the free status of clever argumentation [*des Räsonnierens*], it is still absorbed in the content, or at least the demand to be so absorbed is present" (§ 62, trans. modified).

30. The same shift happens in the other example Hegel offers: "In that way when it is said, 'The *actual* is the *universal*,' the actual, as subject, vanishes into its predicate. The universal is not supposed to [*soll nicht*] have merely the meaning of a predicate such that the proposition would state that the actual is universal; rather, the universal ought to express the essence of the actual" (§ 62, trans. modified). Note the use of the modal auxiliary *soll* ("is supposed to") in both examples. It implies that the speculative reading of these propositions is not the only reading possible. The proposition can always be read as an abstract judgment.

31. Compare § 58: "To deny oneself the right to insert one's own views into the immanent rhythm of the concept [*sich des eignen Einfallens entschlagen*] and not to interfere arbitrarily with that rhythm by means of wisdom acquired elsewhere, this abstinence is an essential moment of attentiveness to the concept" (trans. modified).

32. Compare § 57: "[An assertion to the contrary] is usually the first reaction on the part of knowledge when something unfamiliar appears to it. It usually resists it in order to save both its freedom and its own insight and its own authority against alien authority, since that is the shape in which what is now apprehended for the first time appears: as alien—knowledge also stages its resistance in order to rid itself . . . of the kind of shame which supposedly lies in something's having been learned" (trans. modified).

33. In the next chapter, I will more closely discuss Hegel's (and Hölderlin's) thoughts on "bearing shame" as part of the process of "acknowledging," which is the mode of knowing that is characteristic of the phenomenological approach.

34. Compare § 58: "It is supposed to let . . . [it] move itself by its own nature, which is to say, to let it move itself by means of the self as its own self and to observe this movement" (trans. modified).

35. The current discussion about empathy is carried on within and sometimes across many disciplines, including psychology (simulation theory), neuroscience (mirror neurons), psychotherapy, moral philosophy, feminist philosophy, political theory, philosophy of law, and literary studies. For a helpful critique of empathy from the perspective of rhetoric, see Rüdiger Campe, "An Outline for

a Critical History of *Fürsprache:* Synegoria and Advocacy." An example for the modernist literary tradition's strong resentment toward calls for empathy provides Rainer Nägele's somewhat undertheorized comment: "Neither writing nor political analysis can emerge from empathy and public concern. The latter are the sites of a misplaced moralization that blocks analysis on every level and provides the fertile ground for any rhetorical seduction that appeals to resentment" (*Echoes of Translation,* 4). Wendy Brown (*States of Injury*) and Lauren Berlant ("The Subject of True Feeling") have provided much more thorough and informed critiques of the politics of compassion. Another scholar of literary modernism, Charles Altieri, advocates a version of "feeling one's way in" that relies on reflective judgment (*Particulars of Rapture*). Stanley Cavell emphasizes the reality and everyday experience of our "mutual attunement" (*The Claim of Reason*).

36. David Depew's "Empathy, Psychology, and Aesthetics" helpfully distinguishes the different historical valences of the concept of empathy.

37. In fact, as Campe points out, Theodor Lipps was the pivotal figure not only in that he gave rise to the discourse on empathy as we know it today, but also in that his own work pivoted from "the broader—and older—notion of perceptual Einfühlung in the world and, with it, the aesthetics of empathy" to "the narrower—and new—concept of empathy with the human body and the other" (Campe, "An Outline for a Critical History of *Fürsprache,*" 356). Depew focuses on Lipps's early work in aesthetics when he strengthens the critical (anti-idealist and anti-Romanticist) gist of Lipps's theory of *Einfühlung.* Depew clarifies that Lipps was then not concerned with the possibility to feel somebody else's feeling, but rather understood *Einfühlung* as akin to animation: as a projection of one's own feelings into external objects. In this context, *Einfühlung* is very closely related to expression (if I find that the weeping willow expresses my sadness, this is an example of *Einfühlung*). This notion of *Einfühlung* maintains a radical difference in experience between subject and object (the willow does not feel sad). In that way, it is very different from the kind of sympathy Hegel propagates. Hegel's epistemological sympathy can be traced back to Herder, who makes the—then novel—argument that peoples of different historical periods and cultures have radically different concepts, beliefs, perceptions, and so forth. He uses the phrase *sich einfühlen* (feeling one's way in) in an unsystematic way to elaborate his hermeneutics that consist in an arduous process of historical-philological inquiry.

38. Literary scholars tend to be suspicious of empathy because it psychologizes textual relations. My aim here is to propose a textual (and non-psychological) notion of sympathy.

39. Only a retrospective assessment, an afterfeeling, or a reflective judgment can establish—but also only in a transitory way—a sense of the self in transport. Here Altieri's use of Kant's reflective judgment meets with Pippin's notion of agency as retroactive credit. See Altieri, *The Particulars of Rapture,* 14: "For example, where determinative judgment would conclude that Othello is jealous because his behavior is governed by particular traits, reflexive judgment can attend to Othello as bringing together a set of traits that in the future would have to be considered part of our model for what jealousy might be."

40. Throughout this book, I discuss examples of such word twists—from Schiller's verses that end the *Phenomenology* to Hegel's ventriloquizing of phrenology.

41. § 57: "That is the shape in which what is now apprehended for the first time appears: as alien" (see note 31).

42. The verb *übersieht* means "overlooks" in the double sense of "surveys" and "ignores."

43. Compare Ahmed, *The Cultural Politics of Emotion,* 31: "The ungraspability of my own pain is brought to the surface by the ungraspability of the pain of others."

44. Gertrude Stein, "Sacred Emily," 395.

45. Consider Hegel's aphorism, "The questions which philosophy does not answer are answered in that they should not be so posed" ("Aphorisms from the Wastebook," 248).

46. I agree with Hirt when he suggests that Hegel "fut avec Platon, du point de vue de la visée de la constitution d'un discours proprement philosophique, à la fois le plus grand ennemi de la poésie et le plus grand poète de la philosophie" (Hirt, *Versus: Hegel et la philosophie à l'épreuve de la poésie,* 15). Chase offers a similar argument when she insists that for Hegel the philosophical idea appears only in a language "susceptible of memorization and inscription," that is, in verse (Chase, "Getting Versed," 135).

47. See § 61: "The nature of judgment . . . which includes within itself [*in sich schließt*] the distinction of subject and predicate."

48. For clarification about how logic is bound up with ontology, and for an argument in favor of transforming logic by accommodating the flexible and contextual use of different ontologies, see McCumber, *Reshaping Reason.*

49. Mieszkowski argues that Hegel views language as "a dynamic whose transgressive potential paradoxically depends precisely on its essentially finite character" (Mieszkowski, "Derrida, Hegel, and the Language of Finitude," § 2).

Chapter 5

1. After the somewhat extradiegetic description of the ideal movement of mutual acknowledging, the protagonist/s of the *Phenomenology* do fall back to treating each other and themselves as objects. In the dialectic of lordship and bondage, the bondsman does not acknowledge and is not acknowledged but "retrieves" (*wiederfinden*) himself in the objects of his labor (§ 196). *Anerkennen* has here regressed into *Wiederfinden.* See my discussion of *Wiederfinden* in the next section.

2. Compare Butler, *Account of Oneself,* 44: "Recognition cannot be reduced to making and delivering judgments about others."

3. There is only one mention of *Anerkennung* in the *Phenomenology:* in the spirit chapter when Hegel discusses Antigone's relation to her brother (§ 456).

4. Hegel apparently liked this poem. Hotho's compilation of different students' lecture notes, published under the title *Vorlesungen über die Ästhetik,* includes

the following assessment: "Besonders unterscheiden sich Goethes Gedichte im *Divan* wesentlich von seinen früheren. In 'Willkommen und Abschied' z. B. ist die Sprache, die Schilderung zwar schön, die Empfindung innig, aber sonst die Situation ganz gewöhnlich, der Ausgang trivial, und die Phantasie und ihre Freiheit hat nichts weiter hinzugetan. Ganz anders ist das Gedicht im *West-östlichen Divan,* 'Wiederfinden' überschrieben. Hier ist die Liebe ganz in die Phantasie, deren Bewegung, Glück, Seligkeit herübergestellt. Überhaupt haben wir in den ähnlichen Produktionen dieser Art keine subjektive Sehnsucht, kein Verliebtsein, keine Begierde vor uns, sondern ein reines Gefallen an den Gegenständen, ein unerschöpfliches Sich-Ergehen der Phantasie, ein harmloses Spielen, eine Freiheit in den Tändeleien auch der Reime und künstlichen Versmaße, und dabei eine Innigkeit und Froheit des sich in sich selber bewegenden Gemütes, welche durch die Heiterkeit des Gestaltens die Seele hoch über alle peinliche Verflechtung in die Beschränkung der Wirklichkeit hinausheben" (Hegel, *Werke in zwanzig Bänden,* 14:241). Since this is not one of Hegel's published texts, I don't want to make too much of the wording—but the use of "peinlich" here ("peinliche Verflechtung in die . . . Wirklichkeit"), in contrast to Goethe's "Freiheit" and "Heiterkeit des Gestaltens," is certainly an interesting echo to Hegel's description of his own writing style and of the labor of the concept (see my discussion in the next section).

5. The phrase "a reading of love" is borrowed from Hamacher, *Pleroma,* 89. Hamacher uses the phrase to describe a mode of reading that seeks to maintain a movement of multiple differences within the unity of the text.

6. Ormiston argues that the knowledge of love (even though at first dim and subconscious) drives the development of the *Phenomenology.* She intends only the genitive of the object in the phrase "knowledge of love." Throughout her study, she perpetuates the dichotomy between a supposedly unifying love and what she calls reflective consciousness. See, especially, Ormiston, *Love and Politics,* 36.

7. In his review of Clark Butler's and Christiane Seiler's English edition of Hegel's letters, John McCumber calls to our attention that we have, to this day, avoided penetrating the depths of Hegel's text: "We have not yet learned how to read Hegel closely; doing so will require, not merely logic and common sense, but appropriating the still foreign techniques of deconstruction and hermeneutics. It will take time" (McCumber, "Hegel: Life, Letters and System," 641).

8. Clark Butler points out in his commentary to Hegel's letters that "by the time he replied on November 2, Schelling had read only the Preface. This reply was the last recorded correspondence between the two philosophers. In his letter, Schelling exposes his refusal to grasp Hegel's basic concern when he writes: 'Thus I confess I do not yet understand your sense in opposing "concept" to intuition'" (*Hegel: The Letters,* 80).

9. For evidence of rage, see Hegel's wastebook: "Der *Effekt* am Publikum ist ein absoluter Maßstab, über den das Subjekt wohl rasend werden kann. Es hat alles getan; aber seiner *Einsicht* steht eben der bewußtlose *Instinkt* entgegen" (Hegel, *Werke in zwanzig Bänden,* 2:558).

10. Hegel's mention of a "multi-sided and multi-meaning intertwining" (*vielseitige und vieldeutige Verschränkung*) shows that what he reduced here, for ana-

lytic purposes, to a double relation really expands into a multitude (*Phenomenology*, § 178).

11. In chapter 2 ("Pathos"), we have discussed that knowledge in the mode of acknowledging can come at the expense of great physical suffering, even death.

12. Hegel dramatizes duplicity throughout the *Phenomenology* by using free indirect discourse and by having different sections of the narrative figure other sections while slipping in and out of explicit distinctions. One section might render as inner difference what another section has described as a difference between subjects (the internalized lordship and bondage of the unhappy consciousness, for example), or one section makes a difference explicit that was implicit in the previous one (conscience splits into various configurations of the beautiful soul, for example).

13. I am not as convinced as most commentators on the hard heart seem to be that a final reconciliation of the two final figures of spirit does indeed take place.

14. This is Pinkard's argument in "Reason, Recognition, and Historicity," 47–66.

15. Goethe surely knows a thing or two about *Begierde* (appetite, animal desire, or hunger). His *Faust* immortalizes the image of man who can get no satisfaction. In the *Phenomenology*'s section on "Pleasure and Necessity," Hegel offers his own version of a Faust-like figure bent on proving that he is bound to nothing in his pursuit of pleasure. He comes to realize that he is bound to his own actions.

16. See Taylor, "The Need for Recognition" and "The Politics of Recognition."

17. Taylor insists that recognition has become a problem in modernity. While in premodern cultures recognition was built into the socially derived identity by virtue of the very fact that it was based on social categories that everyone took for granted, moderns value authenticity in the sense of an inwardly derived, personal, and original identity. The authentic qua original identity does not enjoy recognition a priori but has to win it, and the attempt to win recognition for one's authentic self can fail (Taylor, "The Politics of Recognition," 34–35).

18. See Pippin on agency, in *Hegel's Practical Philosophy*.

19. Pinkard argues as much in "Symbolic, Classical, and Romantic Art," 8. I am sympathetic to the solution he identifies in Hegel, which, abstractly put, consists in everyone being *both* master and slave to one another. This would be one version of the mutuality of acknowledging.

20. Kojève comes too close for my taste to glorifying death.

21. Here and in the following, I quote Hamburger's translation in Hölderlin, *Selected Poems and Fragments*, 251–53. Other translation consulted: Vernon Chadwick in Haverkamp, *Leaves of Mourning: Hölderlin's Later Work*, 58–59.

22. See my article on "Andenken" for a brief synopsis of the perspectives taken and the directions identified in the most influential readings of this poem ("A Reading of Love in Hölderlin's 'Andenken,'" 194).

23. *Mancher* can mean both "many" and "some." Chadwick translates: Some / are reluctant to go to the source.

24. See Baumann, *Das Geheimnis wird Licht*, 17.

25. About the rarity of the northeasterly in the region of Bordeaux, see Baumann, *Das Geheimnis wird Licht*, 17–18.

26. Baumann extends the cryptonym to D.S.G. (*Die schöne Garonne*).

27. Compare Butler, *Account of Oneself*, 43–44. Butler also warns of the potentially deadly violence of recognition: "As we ask to know the other, or ask that the other say, finally or definitely, who he or she is, it will be important not to expect an answer that will ever satisfy. By not pursuing satisfaction and by letting the question remain open, even enduring, we let the other live, since life might be understood as precisely that which exceeds any account we may try to give of it." I don't see the problem in the satisfaction of desire. On the contrary, satisfaction keeps desire alive because, as Hegel shows, it can never be final. Rather, I see the problem in the aim of this desire. The desire for self-sufficiency and the correlating desire to be completely captured by the other's address destroy the fragile life of mutuality.

28. In "Sober Recollections: Hölderlin's De-Idealizations of Memory in 'Andenken,'" Santner affirms the additive rather than adversative use of the conjunction *aber* as liberating and as a sign of Hölderlin's new, more relaxed style. See esp. 19.

29. Heidegger reads a sense of melancholy into the series of *aber*. See Heidegger, "Remembrance."

30. In his letter from June 30, 1802, informing Hölderlin of Gontard's death, Sinclair tries to remind Hölderlin that she survives her death: "Du glaubtest an Unsterblichkeit, da sie noch lebte, Du wirst gewiß itzt mehr denn vorher glauben . . . Und was ist größer und edler, als ein Herz, das seine Welt überlebt" (Hölderlin, *Sämtliche Werke*, 7:170).

31. See Heidegger, "Remembrance."

32. See Ovid, *Metamorphoses*, v. 9–11: "And men, content with food which came from no one's seeking, gathered . . . acorns fallen from the spreading tree of Jove. . . . and yellow honey was distilled from the verdant oak."

33. Hölderlin, "As on a holiday. . ."/ "*Wie wenn am Feiertage*. . .," v. 56–60 (trans. Hamburger).

34. In "The Oak Trees" ("Die Eichbäume"), Hölderlin, mobilizing anti-French sentiments, describes oak trees as Titans who refuse to subject themselves to the cultivated garden of society (*gesellige Leben*). Hölderlin uses the Semele myth in the sixth stanza of "As on a holiday. . . ." Semele, the mortal mother of Dionysus, asked her lover Zeus to show his true shape. When he appeared to her as the god of thunder, she was struck by lightning and died.

35. Hölderlin uses the word *Scheue* while Hegel opts for *Scham*. Hegel often prefers the more carnal term to the more refined connotation Hölderlin chooses.

36. *Darüber hinschauen* extravagantly extends the basic phrase *überschauen*, which by itself already carries a similar ambiguity as "to overlook" in English, meaning both to survey and to fail to notice. The *hin-* of *hinschauen* accentuates the focusing aspect of looking, while *darüber* emphasizes the movement beyond such focus.

37. I am not as confident as Hamacher is that we can neatly distinguish between Hegel's intention (which is supposedly to give shame the task of work-

ing in the service of unity) and the way he presents his ideas (which Hamacher sees as undermining Hegel's intention). In any case, it is the presentation that counts, also and especially for Hegel.

38. See Hamacher, *Pleroma*, 89.

39. In the same fragment, Hegel calls this identity of love that preserves its difference within, a "vollendete Einigkeit" as opposed to the "unentwickelte Einigkeit" which is only the seed of life but not life itself. The unity of love is mature precisely because it preserves difference between the lovers while eliminating "allen Charakter eines Fremden." That love does not kill otherness in favor of an abstract identity is of foremost importance to Hegel already in the early writings.

40. Beissner notes: "In der Übersetzung aus den Bacchantinnen des Euripides steht er (der Feigenbaum) für saekon (Heiligtum), verwechselt mit sykon (Feige)" (Hölderlin, *Sämtliche Werke*, 2:803).

41. In "Secluded Laurel—Andenken," Haverkamp traces a rhetorical tradition from the New Testament through Augustine and Petrarch to Hölderlin that uses the fig tree as a figure for conversion. As the figure of conversion, the fig tree also figures the vacillation and anxiety involved in such a turning, as well as the brave cowardice that is open to and endures such fear.

42. While in the prose form of the phrase the word *daselbst* stands in the middle between the two terms *die braunen Frauen* and *auf seidnen Boden*, the layout of the poem invites the reader to draw the chiasmic exchange between the parallel structures:

braunen Frauen
seidnen Boden

with *daselbst* standing off center at the upper right corner of this imaginary X.

43. See Butler, *Subjects of Desire*, 20: "We do not merely witness the journey of some other philosophical agent, but we ourselves are invited on stage to perform the crucial scene changes."

44. Compare Butler et al., *Contingency*, 19–20: "Hegel's own persistent references to 'losing oneself' and 'giving oneself over' only confirm the point that the knowing subject cannot be understood as one who imposes ready-made categories on a pregiven world. . . . We do not remain the same, and neither do our cognitive categories, as we enter into a knowing encounter with the world. Both the knowing subject and the world are undone and redone by the act of knowledge."

45. Appiah argues for the importance of continuous transformation (i.e., determinate negation) of identity over the protection of identities in the interest of their survival in "Identity, Authenticity, Survival: Multicultural Societies and Social Reproduction."

Chapter 6

1. In Hegelian terminology, "abstract" means exclusive of the opposite, while "absolute" means encompassing the opposite. "Abstract negation" thus merely negates whereas "absolute negation" negates and affirms.

2. "Everything hangs on apprehending and expressing the truth not merely as *substance* but also equally as *subject*" (§ 17).

3. This and all the following quotations from Cixous' *L'ange au secret* are my translations.

4. The servant is subordinated to the master because, in his rapid development, he has learned the lessons of the value of life and of the essentiality of the body much quicker than the master has. The step that he seems to have skipped is the realization of the pure negativity of the "I." This negativity will have been realized in absolute fear. The judgment on the servant is passed from the perspective of the master, that is, from the perspective of the consciousness that went through the life-and-death struggle untouched and unshaken by any experience. The master does not learn the lesson of life's essential value, and that is why he considers the insight of the servant to be a failure. Only at the very end of the chapter does the phenomenological account turn to an examination of the servant according to the logic of the servant's own experience: "We only saw what servitude is in relation to mastery. However, servitude is self-consciousness, and thus what it is in and for itself is now up for examination" (§ 194).

5. See Gadamer, *Hegel's Dialectic: Five Hermeneutical Studies*, 35–53.

6. I am not making an argument against masturbation or for coital intercourse here. Nor do I think that this part of Hegel's text can be used to make a sexual argument along normative lines. We will see in a moment that the valorized term in this dialectic—the practice that is being avoided through masturbation—is the orgy.

7. For further clarification about Hegel's notion of the concept, see chapter 4 ("Juggle").

8. The perceptual consciousness's fear of the other's pleasure prefigures the hunger (*Begierde*) for objects that arises when consciousness develops into self-consciousness (in the dialectic of master and slave). This hunger, which Hegel describes as the desire to incorporate all objects and to thereby destroy objecthood in general, is symptomatic of a categorical paranoia vis-à-vis the object, the first traces of which we have caught here.

9. Lorde, "Poetry Is Not a Luxury," 38. See also Žižek, *Parallax*, 210: "A free Self not only integrates disturbances, it *creates* them, it explodes any given form or stasis. This is . . . the ultimate traumatic Thing the Self encounters in the Self itself."

10. I draw here on the ambiguity of *ausstehen*, meaning both "to withstand" and "to like."

11. See chapter 2 for a discussion of the proximity of stubbornness and pathos and its role in Hegel's examination of tragedy.

12. Here I disagree with Nancy who, in "Identity and Trembling," an essay that continues to importantly inform my work, writes: "The freedom that speculative spirit grasps is self-determined, and so sublates all determination. . . . Speculative spirit prefers not to think [that freedom could be given by another]. It designates heteronomy as pathology" (21).

13. Cixous explores the ambivalent pull of fear with *L'ange au secret:* "The wind that never abates in this book, the spirit that whispers without interruption,

it's her: My fear, who is my mystery, the force that pushes me to take to my heels, in what direction? In her direction" (73). I will discuss Cixous' exploration of fear in more detail in the next part of this chapter.

14. Erica Hunt; quoted in Trinh and Kirby, *Nothing But Ways*, installation at the Yerba Buena Center for the Arts, San Francisco, June 5–August 15, 1999.

15. Butler has shown that the servant's attachment to the stability of the fashioned thing is based on an illusion. What she calls the "bondage contract" supports the illusions and denials of both parties. It allows the master to deny his bodily existence; and it allows the servant to forget that what he reads as his own signature on his works is always only the proxy of the master's signature. See Butler, "Stubborn Attachment, Bodily Subjection: Rereading Hegel on the Unhappy Consciousness," 31–62.

16. Later in the course of the *Phenomenology*, when *Bildung* has become a self-alienating rather than self-immortalizing process, we encounter a notion of work as work of art (*Werk*), which operates with a greater awareness of the overlap of negation and affirmation: "The work *is*, i.e. it exists for other individualities, . . . *their* interest in the work . . . is something different from this work's *own* peculiar interest, and the work is thereby transformed into something different. The work is thus something utterly transitory which is effaced by the counter-play [*Widerspiel*] of other forces and interests and which exhibits the reality of individuality itself to an even greater degree to be something transitory rather than something achieved" (§ 404, trans. modified). Rather than immortalizing the artist, the work of art gives rise to the artist's experience of finitude, non-mastery, and interdependence with others. The author's signature is perverted by those who receive the work and make it their own. Their affirmation of the artwork is the negation of the artist's intention. While pursuing its own will, the authorial consciousness is co-opted by the will of others. The self-alienated spirit of the world of culture or *Bildung* knows that self-will is negated precisely in its realization.

17. For a more extended discussion of how rational analysis furthers emotionality, see chapter 7, the section on "Desperate Analysis."

18. Cixous, *Stigmata*, 62.

19. Stoic consciousness is the figure immediately following the dialectic of master and servant.

20. For an excellent discussion of the unhappy consciousness's self-subjection as a defense against absolute fear, see Butler, "Stubborn Attachment, Bodily Subjection," 31–62.

21. I am referring here to the self-negation of consciousness by way of working, giving thanks, sacrificing, fasting, and castigating (§ 222–28). In all these forms of self-negation, the unhappy consciousness continues to cultivate the pleasures of the body.

22. The *Phenomenology* has six major parts ("Consciousness," "Self-Consciousness," "Reason," "Spirit," "Religion," and "Absolute Knowledge"). They vary in length, with "Reason" and "Spirit" being the longest and "Absolute Knowledge" the shortest. In our discussion of absolute fear, we have skipped the entire section on "Reason" and are now analyzing the dialectic of "Absolute Freedom and Terror" at the end of the second third of the part on "Spirit."

23. In the first chapter of *Déluge*, entitled "Cétait l'entre deux," Cixous stresses our disappearing ability to live the moments of the *entre-deux*. For her, as I will show in the next part of this chapter, transitions are intervals of fear and grief whose claim on us for voice and volume is fading: "Bientôt on pourra naître sans crier, ensuite ce sera sans crier faire l'amour, perdre un enfant, mourir. Non, je ne suis pas folle. On va vers le silence. . . . Nous allons vers le *Monde sans Transition.* Autrefois à la strophe 988 l'époux de Kriemhild s'éffondrait parmi les fleurs, on voyait le sang s'écouler à flots de sa blessure. . . . Sigfrid ne voulait pas mourir sans avoir dit tout ce qu'il pensait. Le mourant parlait tour à tour aux amis at aux traîtres et à chacun, mortellement blessé, le mourant dit ce qu'il avait à dire. A la strophe 999 les fleurs à la ronde étaient mouillées de sang. A la fin le mourant prenait encore la peine de souffrir à la place de son père, de sa mère et de ses barons. N'ayant plus la force de parler il repoussait à la fin une terrible strophe encore. Il avait une si furieuse pitié de ceux qui attendaient longtemps son retour. C'était l'agonie de ceux qui l'attendraient en vain qu'il voulait pleurer avant de mourir. Maintenant dès que Sigfrid s'effondrera, ils vont couper, paraît-il. On ne va plus laisser aux gens le temps de crier, l'heure du violoncelle, c'est terminé. / Je ne veut pas qu'il arrive, ce meurt-petit, - moi dont la moitié de vivre est mourir, je vis de vivre et mourir enchevêtrés en sonate. / Je ne veux pas le monde à un oeil et une seule dimension, non, notre vie n'est pas sèche et plane, mais au moins cinq fois accidentée, torte, convulsée." Cixous, *Déluge,* 15–16.

24. Throughout the sections on "Consciousness," "Self-Consciousness," "Reason," and "Spirit," the *Phenomenology* traces various figures of finite consciousness. Hegel treats the same subject matter, but from the perspective of the divine substance, in the chapter on "Religion," and he addresses the synthesis of both perspectives (finite consciousness and divine substance) in the chapter on "Absolute Knowledge."

25. See § 439: "Spirit is . . . the self-supporting, absolute, real essence. All the previous shapes of consciousness are abstractions from it; they are just this, that spirit analyses itself, distinguishes its moments, and lingers at each individual moment. . . . As so isolated, these moments seem as if they *were to exist* as isolated. However, their advance and retreat into their ground and essence points to the way in which they are merely moments or vanishing magnitudes, and this essence is this very movement and dissolution of those moments."

26. Schmidt, "Cabbage Heads and Gulps of Water: Hegel on Terror," 23. Even though instrumental for his subsidiary argument that the Hegel of the *Phenomenology* found no solution to the problem that drove the French Revolution into terror, the quoted statement does not play a central role in Schmidt's essay as a whole. Schmidt offers an illuminating analysis of the historical changes in Hegel's thought on the Terror from his earliest notes on the subject to his lectures on the philosophy of history.

27. Hegel's use of the term "certainty" is counterintuitive to a modern scientific understanding. In Hegel's text, certainty is not what consciousness arrives at after a process of verifying a hypothesis, but it is what consciousness starts out with and loses in the process of verifying or actualizing what it holds to be

true. The loss of one certainty immediately produces a new one, which will have to be verified again. Certainty, thus, corresponds to a subjective need, rather than an objective reality.

28. As I discussed in chapter 2 ("Pathos"), the pathos of each figure in the *Phenomenology* is to live and die for its certainty.

29. Lispector, *The Stream of Life,* 11.

30. Compare Nancy, *Hegel,* 42: "Self-knowing in negativity and as negativity is therefore no more a knowing than it is a victory that would subdue or domesticate pain, death, the other, or joy. It is not knowing of an object; it is self-knowing—but only to the extent that, in this knowing, self does not become its own object. . . . The subject is—or makes up—the experience of its being-affected as the ordeal of what dissolves its subsistence."

31. See Nancy, *Hegel,* 44: "It is always the trembling of the finite seized by the infinite: it is the sensibility of the infinite in the finite."

32. This explains the melancholy tone of the *Phenomenology*'s last chapter. See chapter 3 ("Release").

33. I use "authors" in the plural because of the ambivalence within the authorial position between insisting on continuity and marking the transitions as leaps.

34. Compare Nancy, *Hegel,* 42: "The subject does not reappropriate its other and its contradiction: that it knows this contradiction to be its own, and that this knowing is exactly what constitutes it as subject, does not make its own contradiction become its subsistence. It remains its contradiction, just as my pain, my death, and my other, or my joy, remain outside of me: outside of me—what, being *mine,* makes me go out of myself."

35. By switching pronouns in this paragraph I mimic and thus foreground how Hegel's text moves fluidly and often ambiguously between its different subjects (consciousness, spirit, author, readers).

36. See § 545: "the communication between them [the enlightener and the naive believer] is *immediate,* and their giving and receiving is an undisturbed flow [*ungestörtes Ineinanderfließen*] of the one into the other."

37. "It is thereby entangled in this contradiction as a result of having both let itself get into this quarrel and thinking of itself as doing battle with something *other*" (§ 548).

38. "This world [of the enlightenment] still contains in it the aspect of the spiritual kingdom of animals [*geistiges Tierreich*], where in mutual violence and disarray, they fight and deceive each other over the essence of the real world" (§ 536, trans. modified).

39. Nancy plays on the French phrase *faire une experience,* which also exists in German (*eine Erfahrung machen*) and which means "to have an experience" but also, literally, to create an experience (Nancy, *Hegel,* 42).

40. See Nancy, *Hegel,* 41: "Reconciliation is in the point, or in passage."

41. Note that it was the problem of the unhappy consciousness that it gained from each mortification.

Chapter 7

1. Chase foregrounds the "disarticulation of the figure of progression" in her rapprochement of Hegel with Baudelaire in "Getting Versed," 113–38.

2. Ngai suggests that Lispector's *Passion According to G.H.* could be read as a religious parody (Ngai, *Ugly Feelings,* 346). If parody consists in an act of mimetic repetition that draws on the need for iteration of a power configuration (in this case Christian dogma) to introduce a shift in meaning, then I don't see why we couldn't extend her suggestion to Hegel's *Phenomenology of Spirit.*

3. "Throughout the changing flux of everything which would be secure for it, skeptical self-consciousness thus experiences its own freedom . . . the unchangeable and *genuine certainty of its own self*" (§ 205).

4. Skepticism engages only in a "shaking of this or that alleged truth which is then followed by the disappearance of the doubt, and which in turn then returns to the former truth in such a way that what is at stake is taken to be exactly what it was in the first place" (§ 78, trans. modified).

5. "The fear of truth may lead consciousness to conceal itself both from itself and from others and to take refuge behind the appearance that holds that its fiery enthusiasm for the truth itself makes it more difficult or even impossible to find some truth other than the individual truth of vanity itself—that of being at any rate cleverer than any of the thoughts one might get from oneself or from others" (§ 80, trans. modified).

6. *Zweifel* is etymologically related to *Zwiefalt* (twofold) and thus signifies a doubling. In its vanity, the skeptic doesn't hesitate to assume contradictory positions for the sake of always negating its opposite party: "If *parity* [*Gleichheit*] is pointed out to it, it points out *disparity* [*Ungleichheit*], and if it is reproached with the latter (about which it had just spoken), it quickly shifts over into pointing out *parity.* Its talk is indeed like that of a squabble among stubborn children, one of whom says A when the other says B, and says B when the other says A. By being in contradiction *with himself,* each of them purchases the delight of remaining in contradiction *with each other*" (§ 205). Enacting these contradictory roles, the skeptic can scarcely go on pretending to be a pure self-identical being-for-self. It must realize that, instead of one, it is (at least) two: "In skepticism, [self-consciousness] . . . it doubles *itself* to an even greater degree, and is in its own eyes now something twofold [*ein Zweifaches*]" (§ 206). Skepticism (*Zweifel*) splits consciousness in two (*zwei*) and thereby initiates the absolute movement of despair (*Verzweiflung*). The prefix *ver,* in that it means both consummation and negation, adds an additional speculative twist to the word.

7. Compare this restless consciousness in despair to the stoic consciousness who "maintain[s] the lifelessness which consistently *withdraws* from the movement of existence, *withdraws* from actual activity as well as from suffering" (§ 199).

8. Malabou has developed the concept of "plasticity" that aptly captures both the power to shape and the capacity to self-differentiate, self-negate, or self-distance (see Malabou, *The Future of Hegel*). With my notion of a rubber subject or a rubber tumbler subject I take her concept to a playful extreme.

9. Its wobbling motion (which would be *Taumeln* in German) is an effect of the bacchanalian revel (*Bacchantischer Taumel*) of truth. See § 47: "The truth is the bacchanalian revel where no member is not drunk."

10. While "absolute knowledge" might be considered the end, it has no positive content beyond its function to ruin the natural certainty of each shred, figure, or shape of the whole.

11. For my spatial interpretation of *Aufhebung*, see chapter 2 ("Pathos").

12. For the importance of deriving the concept of truth from the consciousness one observes, instead of judging that consciousness based on an external standard of truth, see § 81–85.

13. § 168–76.

14. Hamacher, Bahti, and Clark find Hegel eating flesh to be ethically, epistemologically, politically, and aesthetically appalling. See Hamacher, *Pleroma*, 230–95; Bahti, *Allegories of History*, 80 and 109ff.; and Clark, "Hegel, Eating," 124–30. I see eating in Hegel instead as a physical form of communication that engages with the other at the cost of (also) ruining the self. I thus agree with Rajan when she argues that "in Hegel's lurid figuration of nature as spirit and thus of mind as (human) nature or psyche, such organisms also consume themselves" ("(In)digestible Material," 222). Rajan considers the physiological details of Hegel's discussion of digestion and illness in the *Encyclopedia*'s "Philosophy of Nature" as "the logical organism's rethinking of its subjectivity" as "inability to digest nature" (ibid., 220, 218).

15. For Lacan, non-human animals are incapable of lying (Lacan, *Seminar II*, 244–45).

16. See chapter 1 ("Heart") and the beginning of this chapter's section on "Narrative (Dis)organization."

17. Lispector, *The Passion According to G.H.*, 64: "Eating of living matter would expel me from a paradise of adornments"; and 107: "learn from this one who has had to be laid completely bare and lose all her suitcases with the engraved initials."

18. So much attention has been paid to the all-devouring character of Hegelian thought that the inverse relation between eating and thinking has been overlooked.

19. "I had committed the forbidden act of touching something impure [*immundo*]" (Lispector, *The Passion*, 64).

20. Müller-Sievers's vehement critique of epigenesis is based on the premise that "epigenesis is . . . the condition of the possibility of any claim to absoluteness, be this a philosophical or literary absolute" (*Self-Generation*, 4). Hegel shows how epigenesis undoes the absolute.

21. See my discussion of the interiority of reason in chapter 1 ("Heart").

22. See my discussion of Hegel's half-sympathetic speech acts in chapter 4 ("Juggle").

23. See, for example, the following passage where the phenomenologist moves from observing the phrenologist's stance to identifying with his position to speaking in his voice: "However, the observing consciousness is not concerned with how to determine this relation. This is so because, in any event, it is not the

brain that stands on one side of the relation as an *animal* part. Rather, it is the brain as the *being* of *self-conscious* individuality. This individuality, as settled character and self-moving conscious activity, exists *for itself* and *within itself.* Its actuality and its existence for others stand in opposition to being-for-and-within-itself. This being-for-and-within- itself is the essence and subject, which has a being in the brain, but this being, the brain, is *subsumed under the former,* and it receives its value merely by way of the indwelling meaning. However, the other side of self-conscious individuality, namely, that of its existence, is *being* as self-sufficient and as subject, that is, as a thing, namely, a bone. The *actuality and existence of man is his skull-bone*" (§ 331; trans. modified).

24. This is an example of Hegel performing what Riley calls "hate's work" (Riley, *Impersonal Passion,* 24). By "hate's work," she means the long and laborious process of neutralizing hateful speech. See *Impersonal Passion,* 9–27, in particular p. 22: "I'll ignore the utterer, the better to dissect the utterance. To isolate the word as thing, to inspect it and refuse it, demands a confident capacity to act unnaturally toward language, which normally functions as an energetic means of exchange."

25. Compare Žižek, *Parallax,* 206: "If we penetrate the surface of an organism, and look deeper and deeper into it, we never encounter some central controlling element that would be its Self, secretly pulling the strings of its organs. The consistency of the Self is thus purely virtual; it is as if it were an Inside which appears only when viewed from the Outside, on the interface-screen—the moment we penetrate the interface and endeavor to grasp the Self 'substantially,' as it is 'in itself,' it disappears like sand between our fingers. Thus materialist reductionists who claim that 'there really is no self' are right, but they nonetheless miss the point." Žižek offers these thoughts in the context of a discussion of neuroscience. Brain science is the twenty-first-century version of "observing reason." That is to say, the infinite judgment that Hegel distilled from the phrenologist stance must be reformulated today as "the mental is the neuronal" or "the being of spirit is 'the piece of meat' that is the brain" (*Parallax,* 211).

26. See § 346: "The infinite judgment as infinite would be the fulfillment of self-comprehending life, whereas the consciousness of the infinite judgment which remains trapped within representational thought conducts itself like pissing" (trans. modified).

27. The infinite judgment is the one judgment of existence that can be called true in a reasonable kind of way. The other judgments of existence are the positive and the negative judgment (The rose is red. The rose is not red.) They can be correct statements of facts, but not *Vernunftwahrheiten.* See Hegel, *Hegel's Science of Logic,* 630–43.

28. In the case of "The rose is a plant," the rose, as the particular term, is subordinated to the general category of plant. In the case of "The rose is red," the general characteristic of color is subordinated to the individual rose, which combines many characteristics in addition to color.

29. For my discussion of the beautiful soul as a figure that refuses pleasure, see chapter 1.

30. Pinkard identifies the acting consciousness as a Romantic ironist. See Pinkard, *The Sociality of Reason,* 214–20.

31. If it is confusing that Hegel here claims that existence and judgment are not acknowledged, let me add that acknowledging always comprises a negative element. Acknowledging is always split into affirmation and negation. When the acting consciousness says *Ich bins,* it both agrees with the other's judgment and reveals the inherent hypocrisy of this judgment.

32. Malabou argues that there is an anticipatory structure to subjectivity as Hegel conceived it. Her speculative notion of this structure—which she calls *le 'voir venir'*—actually enables us to say that consciousness can anticipate its future while specifying that this anticipation consists in an openness to surprise. See Malabou, *The Future of Hegel,* 13: "It is an expression that can thus refer at one and the same time to the state of 'being sure of what is coming' and of 'not knowing what is coming.' It is on this account that the 'voir venir,' 'to see (what is) coming,' can represent that interplay, within Hegelian philosophy, of teleological necessity and surprise."

33. "The truth is the whole. However, the whole is only the essence completing itself through its own development" (*das Wahre ist das Ganze. Das Ganze aber ist nur das durch seine Entwicklung sich vollendende Wesen,* § 20).

34. Malabou articulates the tension between the relativity and the independence of the figures of consciousness as one between two notions of time that are both put to work in Hegel's narrative: a Greek sense of time that emphasizes synthesis and a modern sense of time that emphasizes the independence of moments along the line of Kantian hypotyposis (translation of the concept into the form of the sensuous). See *Future of Hegel,* 18 and 125–30.

35. Compare Pinkard, *Sociality of Reason,* 11: "When confronted with self-generated skepticism, a reflective form of life seeks reassurance in the accounts that it gives itself of what is authoritative for it. One of two things happens: either the reassurance is successful, and there is a renewal of that form of life; or it fails, and a new conception of what is authoritative—and thereby a new form of life—is required." "Self-generated skepticism" is Pinkard's paraphrase for "self-negation." He thus attends to the double pull of self-affirmation or self-reassurance and self-negation or self-doubt that consciousness experiences.

36. Hegel is well aware of the historical link of Christianity to the Greek cults of Demeter and Dionysus.

37. According to Greek myth, Dionysus was taken out of the burnt body of his mother Semele (first birth) and inserted into his father Zeus's thigh, out of which he was born again once fully developed. (See Hederich, *Gründliches Mythologisches Lexikon,* s.v. "Bacchus." Hederich's lexicon was the authoritative source on Greek mythology during Hegel's time.) According to an Orphic version of the myth, Dionysus was the child of Zeus and Persephone. Zeus's jealous wife, Hera, incited the Titans to lacerate the child. Athena saved his pulsating heart and brought it to Zeus, who made a potion of it and gave it to Semele to drink. From this, she became pregnant with Dionysus (second birth) (see Tripp, *Crowell's Handbook of Classical Mythology,* s.v. "Dionysos"). Under the entry

"Dithyrambus," Hederich explains that one epithet of Dionysus was Dithyrambus ("double door" or "twice-born") because he was torn apart by the Titans and then put back together by Ceres. Dionysus's dismemberment as a child is repeated in the stories of raving female followers (Maenads) who lacerate those who refuse to worship Dionysus.

Like all her siblings, Ceres was eaten by her father Kronos, but he vomited her out again after Metis had given him an emetic (see *Gründliches Mythologisches Lexikon*, s.v. "Ceres"). During the time of her grief for Persephone, Ceres hides in a cave. According to Hederich, this was meant to symbolize the seed in the earth, before it sprouts or comes to light (symbolized by Pan's disclosure of Ceres' dwelling place to Jupiter). Persephone spends part of the year in the underworld and part of the year with her mother Ceres above ground. Her name has been taken to mean "concealed fruit," which can refer to the seed in the ground or to the harvest stored in the barn during winter (see *Gründliches Mythologisches Lexikon*, s.v. "Proserpina").

38. Hartman quotes Derek Walcott.

39. See Žižek, *Tarrying with the Negative*, 122–24, for an excellent explanation of why the Hegelian synthesis is not based on complementarity.

40. Fragment 719 (Dind.), quoted from Lawson, *Modern Greek Folklore and Ancient Greek Religion*, 563.

41. Each piece of Dionysus is Dionysus himself.

42. Compare Grosz, "Animal Sex."

43. Nobody since Wahl has analyzed this structure of Hegel's dialectic as an emotional economy.

44. See the previous section, "Come Break My Heart."

45. Compare Ahmed's concern for "what sticks?" in *Cultural Politics of Emotion*.

Epilogue

1. By violence, I mean here the unambiguous destruction or forceful eclipse of other realities. Determinate negation—even in its most bodily form, that is, as "eating alive"—is a different animal altogether. The ambiguity of eating alive—the fact that it gives life to the extent that it gives death (or takes death to the extent that it takes life)—creates interdependence.

2. Altieri prefers it when "dialectical reconciliation seems impossible because there is no mediating principle" (*Particulars of Rapture*, 206).

3. "The truth is the whole. However, the whole is only the essence completing itself through its own unfolding [*Entwicklung*]" (§ 20).

4. The French original perhaps even more clearly highlights the fabricated quality of experience: "Le sujet est, c'est-à-dire fait, l'experience de son être affecté" (Nancy 1997, 63). Nancy dismantles here the phrase *faire l'experience* ("to have an experience," literally: "make an experience"), which also exists in German (*eine Erfahrung machen*).

5. Transports both propel and slow down the development of the *Phenomenology*.

6. *Hegel's Aesthetics,* 1035; for complete reference, see chapter 4.

7. Ngai, *Ugly Feelings,* 10.

8. Sokolsky, "The Resistance to Sentimentality," 83: "The sentimental may be described as something more which subtly mocks the declaration of sincerity by being more than sincere."

9. Most of the more interesting French readings of Hegel in the twentieth century have read his work through the paradigm of the unhappy consciousness. See Baugh 2003. That is to say, they didn't get the levity of taking tears excessively seriously.

Bibliography

Abrams, M. H. 1971. *Natural Supernaturalism: Tradition and Revolution in Romantic Literature.* New York: Norton.

Adorno, Theodor W. 1995. *Studien zum autoritären Charakter.* Frankfurt am Main: Suhrkamp.

Agamben, Giorgio. 1991. *Language and Death: The Place of Negativity.* Translated by Karen E. Pinkus and Michael Hardt. Minneapolis: University of Minnesota Press.

Ahmed, Sara. 2004. *The Cultural Politics of Emotion.* New York: Routledge.

Altieri, Charles. 2003. *The Particulars of Rapture: An Aesthetics of the Affects.* Ithaca, N.Y.: Cornell University Press.

Anderson, Amanda. 2006. *The Way We Argue Now.* Princeton, N.J.: Princeton University Press.

Appadurai, Arjun. 2006. *Fear of Small Numbers: An Essay on the Geography of Anger.* Durham, N.C.: Duke University Press.

Appiah, K. Anthony. 1994. "Identity, Authenticity, Survival: Multicultural Societies and Social Reproduction." In *Multiculturalism: Examining the Politics of Recognition,* edited by Amy Gutmann, 149–63. Princeton, N.J.: Princeton University Press.

Aristotle. 1991. *On Rhetoric: A Theory of Civic Discourse.* Translated by George A. Kennedy. Oxford and New York: Oxford University Press.

———. 1977. "Magna Moralia." In Aristotle, *Metaphysics,* books 10–14. *Oeconomica. Magna Moralia.* Loeb Classical Library, vol. 287. Translated by Hugh Tredennick and G. Cyril Armstrong. Cambridge, Mass.: Harvard University Press.

———. 1961. *Poetics.* Translated by S. H. Butcher. New York: Hill and Wang.

Bahti, Timothy. 1992. *Allegories of History: Literary Historiography After Hegel.* Baltimore, Md.: Johns Hopkins University Press.

Baldwin, James. 1985. "Everybody's Protest Novel." In *The Price of the Ticket: Collected Nonfiction, 1948–1985,* 27–34. New York: Saint Martin's.

Baugh, Bruce. 2003. *French Hegel: From Surrealism to Postmodernism.* London: Routledge.

Baumann, Eberhard. 1997. *Das Geheimnis wird Licht.* Essen: Blaue Eule.

Benhabib, Seyla. 1996. "On Hegel, Women, and Irony." In *Feminist Interpretations of G. W. F. Hegel,* edited by Patricia Jagentowicz Mills, 25–43. University Park: Pennsylvania State University Press.

Berlant, Lauren. 2008. *The Female Complaint: The Unfinished Business of Sentimentality in American Culture.* Durham, N.C.: Duke University Press.

———. 1998. "The Subject of True Feeling: Pain, Privacy, and Politics." In *Cultural Pluralism, Identity Politics, and the Law,* edited by Austin Sarat and Thomas Kearns, 49–84. Ann Arbor: University of Michigan Press.

Bersani, Leo, and Ulysee Dutoit. 2004. *Forms of Being: Cinema, Aesthetics, Subjectivity.* London: British Film Institute.

Bersani, Leo, and Adam Phillips. 2008. *Intimacies.* Chicago: University of Chicago Press.

Blanchot, Maurice. 1993. *The Infinite Conversation.* Translated by Susan Hanson. Minneapolis: University of Minnesota Press.

Boer, Karin de. 2010. *On Hegel: The Sway of the Negative.* Basingstoke, Eng.: Palgrave Macmillan.

Brockhaus, F. A. 1996. *Brockhaus, Die Enzyklopädie: In Vierundzwanzig Bänden.* 20th revised and updated edition. Leipzig: F.A. Brockhaus.

Brown, Alison L. 1996. "Hegelian Silences and the Politics of Communication: A Feminist Appropriation." In *Feminist Interpretations of G. W .F. Hegel,* edited by Patricia Jagentowicz Mills, 299–319. University Park: Pennsylvania State University Press.

Brown, Wendy. 1995. *States of Injury: Power and Freedom in Late Modernity.* Princeton, N.J.: Princeton University Press.

Butler, Judith. 2005. *Giving an Account of Oneself.* New York: Fordham University Press.

———. 2004. *Precarious Life: The Powers of Mourning and Violence.* London: Verso.

———. 2000. *Antigone's Claim.* New York: Columbia University Press.

———. 1999. *Subjects of Desire: Hegelian Reflections in Twentieth-Century France.* New York: Columbia University Press.

———. 1997. "Stubborn Attachment, Bodily Subjection: Rereading Hegel on the Unhappy Consciousness." In *The Psychic Life of Power: Theories in Subjection,* 31–62. Stanford, Calif.: Stanford University Press.

Butler, Judith, Ernesto Laclau, and Slavoj Žižek. 2000. *Contingency, Hegemony, Universality: Contemporary Dialogues on the Left.* London: Verso.

Campe, Rüdiger. 2008. "An Outline for a Critical History of *Fürsprache:* Synegoria and Advocacy." *Deutsche Vierteljahrsschrift für Literaturwissenschaft und Geistesgeschichte* 83, no. 3 (September): 355–81.

———. 1990. *Affekt und Ausdruck : Zur Umwandlung Der Literarischen Rede Im 17. und 18. Jahrhundert.* Studien Zur Deutschen Literatur, Vol. 107. Tübingen: M. Niemeyer.

Cavell, Stanley. 1999. *The Claim of Reason: Wittgenstein, Skepticism, Morality, and Tragedy.* New York: Oxford University Press.

Chase, Cynthia. 1986. "Getting Versed: Reading Hegel with Baudelaire." In *Decomposing Figures: Rhetorical Readings in the Romantic Tradition,* 113–38. Baltimore, Md.: Johns Hopkins University Press.

Cixous, Hélène. 1998. *Stigmata: Escaping Texts.* Translated by Catherine A. F. MacGillivary. London: Routledge.

———. 1997. *Rootprints.* Translated by Eric Prenowitz. New York: Routledge.

———. 1992. *Déluge.* Paris: Des femmes.

———. 1991. *L'ange au secret.* Paris: Des femmes.

———. 1989. "Vivre l'Orange: To Live the Orange." In *L'heure de Clarice Lispector,* 6–113. Paris: Des femmes.

Clark, David L. 2004. "Hegel, Eating: Schelling and the Carnivorous Virility of Philosophy." In *Cultures of Taste/Theories of Appetite: Eating Romanticism,* edited by Timothy Morton, 115–40. New York: Palgrave Macmillan.

Comay, Rebecca. 2011. *Mourning Sickness: Hegel and the French Revolution.* Stanford, Calif.: Stanford University Press.

Connolly, William. 2008. "Christianity, Capitalism, and the Tragic." In *Capitalism and Christianity, American Style.* Durham, N.C.: Duke University Press.

Corngold, Stanley. 1998. *Complex Pleasure: Forms of Feeling in German Literature.* Stanford, Calif.: Stanford University Press.

Deleuze, Gilles, and Félix Guattari. 1987. *A Thousand Plateaus: Capitalism and Schizophrenia.* Minneapolis: University of Minnesota Press.

Depew, David. 2005. "Empathy, Psychology, and Aesthetics: Reflections on a Repair Concept." *Poroi* 4, no. 1: 99–107.

Derrida, Jacques. 1998. *Monolingualism of the Other: or, The Prosthesis of Origin.* Translated by Patrick Mensah. Stanford, Calif.: Stanford University Press.

———. 1991. "Che cos'è la poesia?" Translated by Peggy Kamuf. In *A Derrida Reader: Between the Blinds,* edited by Peggy Kamuf, 221–37. New York: Columbia University Press.

———. 1986. *Glas.* Translated by John Leavey, Jr., and Richard Rand. Lincoln: University of Nebraska Press.

———. 1982. "The Pit and the Pyramid: Introduction to Hegel's Semiology." In *Margins of Philosophy,* translated by Alan Bass, 69–108. Chicago: University of Chicago Press.

Descartes, René. 1979. *Discourse on Method and the Meditations.* Translated by F. E. Sutcliffe. Harmondsworth, Eng.: Penguin.

De Sousa, Ronald. 1990. *The Rationality of Emotion.* Cambridge, Mass.: MIT Press.

Deutsches Wörterbuch von Jacob und Wilhelm Grimm. 1893. Leipzig: Hirzel.

Dickinson, Emily. 1891. "The Mystery of Pain." In *Poems,* edited by Mabel Loomis Todd and T. W. Higginson. Boston: Roberts Brothers.

Easton, Susan M. 1987. "Hegel and Feminism." In *Hegel and Modern Philosophy,* edited by David Lamb, 30–55. New York: Croom Helm.

Egginton, William. 2007. *The Philosopher's Desire: Psychoanalysis, Interpretation, and Truth.* Stanford, Calif.: Stanford University Press.

Eming, Jutta. 2009. "On Stage: Ritualized Emotions and Theatricality in Isolde's Trial." *Modern Language Notes* 124, no. 3: 555–71.

Ferrarin, Alfredo. 2001. *Hegel and Aristotle.* Cambridge, Eng.: Cambridge University Press.

Fink, Eugen. 1977. *Hegel: Phänomenologische Interpretationen der Phänomenologie des Geistes.* Frankfurt am Main: Vittorio Klostermann.

Fink-Eitel, Hinrich, and Georg Lohmann. 1993. *Zur Philosophie der Gefühle.* Frankfurt am Main: Suhrkamp.

Fisher, Philip. 2002. *The Vehement Passions.* New Jersey: Princeton University Press.

Gadamer, Hans-Georg. 1976. *Hegel's Dialectic: Five Hermeneutical Studies.* Translated by P. Christopher Smith. New Haven, Conn.: Yale University Press.

Gauthier, Jeffrey A. 1997. *Hegel and Feminist Social Criticism.* Albany: State University of New York Press.

Geulen, Eva. 2002. "Hegel ohne Ende." In *Das Ende der Kunst: Lesarten eines Gerüchts nach Hegel,* 36–60. Frankfurt am Main: Suhrkamp.

Goethe, Johann Wolfgang von. 1994. "Wiederfinden/Reunion." Translated by Christopher Middleton. In *Selected Poems,* 213–14. Princeton, N.J.: Princeton University Press.

Grosz, Elizabeth. 1995. "Animal Sex." In *Space, Time and Perversion: Essays on the Politics of Bodies.* New York: Routledge.

Hamacher, Werner. 2009. *Für—Die Philologie.* Basel: Roughbooks.

———. 1998. *Pleroma—Reading in Hegel.* Translated by Nicholas Walker and Simon Jarvis. Stanford, Calif.: Stanford University Press.

Hartman, Geoffrey. 1996. "Public Memory and Its Discontents." In *The Longest Shadow,* 99–115. Bloomington: Indiana University Press.

Haverkamp, Anselm. 1996. "Secluded Laurel—Andenken." In *Leaves of Mourning: Hölderlin's Later Work,* 56–77, translated by Vernon Chadwick. Albany: State University of New York Press.

HeartBeat: mb. 1998. Dance performance by Mikhail Baryshnikov. Choreography directed by Sara Rudner. Project conception and sound score by Christopher Janney. Zellerbach Hall, Berkeley, Calif., May 8.

Hederich, Benjamin. 1996. *Gründliches Mythologisches Lexikon.* Reprographic reprint of the 1st edition. Darmstadt: Wissenschaftliche Buchgesellschaft.

Hegel, Georg Wilhelm Friedrich. *Phenomenology of Spirit.* Translated by Terry Pinkard. http://web.mac.com/titpaul/Site/Phenomenology_of_Spirit_page.html. This translation of the *Phenomenology of Spirit* is cited by paragraph numbers only (using the section sign).

———. 2008. *Outlines of the Philosophy of Right.* Translated by T. M. Knox. Edited by Stephen Houlgate. Oxford: Oxford University Press.

———. 2006. *Lectures on the History of Philosophy 1825-6.* Translated by R. F. Brown. Edited by R. F. Brown and J. M. Stewart. Oxford: Oxford University Press.

———. 2005. *Philosophie der Kunst: Vorlesung von 1826: Nachschrift von P. von der Pfordten.* Edited by Annemarie Gethmann-Siefert, Jeong-Im Kwon, and Karsten Berr. Frankfurt am Main: Suhrkamp.

———. 2002. "Aphorisms from the Wastebook." Translated by Susanne Klein, David L. Roochnik, and George Elliot Tucker. In *Miscellaneous Writings of G. W. F. Hegel,* edited by Jon Stewart, 245–55. Evanston, Ill.: Northwestern University Press.

———. 2002a. "Review of Solger's *Posthumous Writings and Correspondence.*" Translated by Diana I. Behler. In *Miscellaneous Writings of G. W. F. Hegel,* edited by Jon Stewart, 354–400. Evanston, Ill.: Northwestern University Press.

———. 1998. "Vorlesung über die Philosophie der Kunst (1823): Nachschrift von H.G. Hotho." In *Vorlesungen: Ausgewählte Nachschriften und Manuskripte.* Vol. 2. Edited by Annemarie Gethmann-Siefert. Hamburg: Meiner.

———. 1989. *Hegel's Science of Logic.* Translated by A. V. Miller. Atlantic Highlands, N.J.: Humanities.

———. 1988. *Phänomenologie des Geistes*. Hamburg: Felix Meiner.

———. 1987. *Lectures on the Philosophy of Religion: Volume II: Determinate Religion*. Translated by R. F. Brown, P. C. Hodgson, and J. M. Stewart. Berkeley: University of California Press.

———. 1986. *Vorlesungen über die Geschichte der Philosophie (Heidelberger Niederschrift): Teil 2*. Edited by Eva Moldenhauer and Karl Markus Michel. Frankfurt am Main: Suhrkamp.

———. 1986a. *Werke in zwanzig Bänden*. Frankfurt am Main: Suhrkamp.

———. 1984. *Hegel: The Letters*. Translated by Clark Butler and Christiane Seiler. Bloomington: Indiana University Press.

———. 1975. *Aesthetics: Lectures on Fine Art by G. W. F. Hegel*. Translated by T. M. Knox. Oxford: Clarendon.

———. 1975a. *Hegel's Logic: Being Part One of the Encyclopedia of the Philosophical Sciences (1830)*. Translated by William Wallace. Oxford: Oxford University Press.

———. 1971. *Early Theological Writings*. Translated by T. M. Knox and Richard Kroner. Philadelphia: University of Pennsylvania Press.

———. 1971a. *Hegel's Philosophy of Mind: Part Three of the Encyclopedia of the Philosophical Sciences (1830)*. Translated by William Wallace. Oxford: Oxford University Press.

———. 1956. *Philosophy of History*. Translated by J. Sibree. New York: Dover.

Hegel, G. W. F., Friedrich Hölderlin, and F. W. J. Schelling. 2002. "The Earliest System-Program of German Idealism." Translated by H. S. Harris. In *Miscellaneous Writings of G. W. F. Hegel*, 110–12. Evanston, Ill.: Northwestern University Press.

Heidegger, Martin. 2000. "Remembrance." In *Elucidations of Hölderlin's Poetry*. Translated by Keith Hoeller. Amherst, N.Y.: Humanity Books.

Hirt, André. 1999. *Versus: Hegel et la philosophie à l'épreuve de la poésie*. Paris: Éditions Kimé.

Hölderlin, Friedrich. 1998. *Selected Poems and Fragments*. Translated by Michael Hamburger. London: Penguin.

———. 1988. *Essays and Letters on Theory*. Edited by Thomas Pfau. Albany: State University of New York Press.

———. 1943–77. *Sämtliche Werke. Große Stuttgarter Ausgabe*. Vol. 1–5 edited by Friedrich Beissner; vol. 6–7 edited by Adolf Beck. Stuttgart: Kohlhammer, Cotta.

Homer. 1976. "Hymn to Demeter." Translated by Apostolos N. Athanassakis. In *The Homeric Hymns*, 1–15. Baltimore, Md.: Johns Hopkins University Press.

Hutcheon, Linda. 1994. *Irony's Edge: The Theory and Politics of Irony*. London: Routledge.

Hutchings, Kimberly. 2003. *Hegel and Feminist Philosophy*. Malden, Mass.: Polity.

Hyppolite, Jean. 1974. *Genesis and Structure of Hegel's Phenomenology of Spirit*. Translated by Samuel Cherniak and John Heckman. Evanston, Ill.: Northwestern University Press.

Illouz, Eva. 2007. *Cold Intimacies: The Making of Emotional Capitalism*. Malden, Mass.: Polity.

Jacobi, Friedrich Heinrich. 1969. *Woldemar.* Stuttgart: Metzler.

Jagentowicz Mills, Patricia. 1996. "Hegel's Antigone." In *Feminist Interpretations of G. W. F. Hegel,* 59–88. University Park: Pennsylvania State University Press.

Jameson, Frederic. 2010. *The Hegel Variations: On the Phenomenology of Spirit.* London: Verso.

Kant, Immanuel. 1996. "An Answer to the Question: What Is Enlightenment?" In *What Is Enlightenment? Eighteenth-Century Answers to Twentieth-Century Questions,* edited by James Schmidt, 58–64. Berkeley: University of California Press.

———. 1990. *Critique of Pure Reason.* Translated by J. M. D. Meiklejohn. Buffalo, N.Y.: Prometheus Books.

———. 1951. *Critique of Judgment.* Translated by J. H. Bernard. New York: Hafner Press.

Kojève, Alexandre. 1947. "L'idée de la mort dans la philosophie de Hegel." In *Introduction à la lecture de Hegel,* edited by Raymond Queneau, 529–75. Paris: Gallimard.

Kontje, Todd. 1998. *Women, the Novel, and the German Nation 1771–1871: Domestic Fiction in the Fatherland.* Cambridge, Eng.: Cambridge University Press.

Lacan, Jacques. 1988. *Seminar II: The Ego in Freud's Theory and in the Technique of Psychoanalysis, 1954–1955.* Translated by Sylvana Tomaselli. New York: W.W. Norton.

Lacoue-Labarthe, Philippe. 1989. *Typography: Mimesis, Philosophy, Politics.* Cambridge, Mass.: Harvard University Press.

Lawson, John Cuthbert. 1964. *Modern Greek Folklore and Ancient Greek Religion.* New York: University Books.

Lethen, Helmut. 2005. "Die Evidenz des Schmerzes." *Merkur* 59, no. 674 (June): 491–503.

Levine, Michael G. 1997. "Writing Anxiety: Christa Wolf's Kinheitsmuster." *Diacritics* 27, no. 2 (Summer): 106–23.

Lispector, Clarice. 1994. *The Passion According to G.H.* Translated by Ronald W. Sousa. Minneapolis: University of Minnesota Press.

———. 1989. *The Stream of Life.* Translated by Elizabeth Lowe and Earl Fitz. Minneapolis: University of Minnesota Press.

Lonzi, Carla. 1996. "Let's Spit on Hegel." Translated by Giovanna Bellesia and Elaine Maclachlan. In *Feminist Interpretations of G. W. F. Hegel,* edited by Patricia Jagentowicz Mills, 275–98. University Park: Pennsylvania State University Press.

Lorde, Audre. 1984. "Poetry Is Not a Luxury." In *Sister Outsider: Essays and Speeches,* 36–39. Trumansburg, N.Y.: Crossing.

Malabou, Catherine. 2005. *The Future of Hegel: Plasticity, Temporality, and Dialectic.* New York: Routledge.

McCumber, John. 2005. *Reshaping Reason: Toward a New Philosophy.* Bloomington: Indiana University Press.

———. 2002. "The Temporal Turn in German Idealism: Hegel and After." *Research in Phenomenology* 32, no. 1: 44–59.

———. 2000. "Writing Down (Up) the Truth: Hegel and Schiller at the End of the *Phenomenology of Spirit*." In *The Spirit of Poesy: Essays on Jewish and German Literature and Thought in Honor of Géza von Molnár*, edited by Richard Block and Peter Fenves, 47–59. Evanston, Ill.: Northwestern University Press.

———. 1993. *The Company of Words. Hegel, Language, and Systematic Philosophy*. Evanston, Ill.: Northwestern University Press.

———. 1986. "Hegel: Life, Letters and System." *Queen's Quarterly* 93, no. 3: 637–44.

Menke, Christoph. 2009. *Tragic Play: Irony and Theater from Sophocles to Beckett*. New York: Columbia University Press.

———. 2005. *Die Gegenwart der Tragödie: Versuch über Urteil und Spiel*. Frankfurt am Main: Suhrkamp.

———. 1996. *Tragödie im Sittlichen: Gerechtigkeit und Freiheit nach Hegel*. Frankfurt am Main: Suhrkamp.

Meyers Neues Lexikon. 1973. 2nd edition. Bibliographisches Institut Leipzig.

Mieszkowski, Jan. 2009. "Who's Afraid of Anacoluthon?" *Modern Language Notes* 123, no. 4: 648–65.

———. 2005. "Derrida, Hegel, and the Language of Finitude." *Postmodern Culture* 15, no. 3 (May).

Moyar, Dean. 2008. "Self-Completing Alienation: Hegel's Argument for Transparent Condition of Free Agency." In *Hegel's Phenomenology of Spirit: A Critical Guide*, edited by Dean Moyar and Michael Quante. Cambridge, Eng.: Cambridge University Press.

Müller-Sievers, Helmut. 1997. *Self-Generation: Biology, Philosophy, and Literature Around 1800*. Stanford, Calif.: Stanford University Press.

Nägele, Rainer. 1997. *Echoes of Translation: Reading Between Texts*. Baltimore, Md.: Johns Hopkins University Press.

Nancy, Jean-Luc. 2002. *Hegel: The Restlessness of the Negative*. Translated by Jason Smith and Steven Miller. Minneapolis: University of Minnesota Press.

———. 2001. *The Speculative Remark: One of Hegel's Bons Mots*. Translated by Céline Surprenant. Stanford, Calif.: Stanford University Press.

———. 1997. *Hegel: L'inquiétude du négatif*. Paris: Hachette.

———. 1993. "Identity and Trembling." Translated by Brian Holmes. In *The Birth to Presence*, 9–35. Stanford, Calif.: Stanford University Press.

———. 1991. *The Inoperative Community*. Translated by Peter Connor, Lisa Garbus, Michael Holland, and Simona Sawhney. Edited by Peter Connor. Minneapolis: University of Minnesota Press.

Ngai, Sianne. 2005. *Ugly Feelings*. Cambridge, Mass.: Harvard University Press.

Nietzsche, Friedrich. 2001. *The Gay Science*. Translated by Josefine Nauckhoff. Edited by Bernard Williams. Cambridge, Eng.: Cambridge University Press.

———. 2000. "Ecce Homo." Translated by Walter Kaufmann. In *Basic Writings of Nietzsche*, 655–800. New York: Random House.

Nussbaum, Martha. 2001. *Upheavals of Thought: The Intelligence of the Emotions*. New York: Cambridge University Press.

———. 1997. "Emotions as Judgements of Value and Importance." In *Relativism, Suffering, and Beyond,* edited by P. Bilimoria and J. N. Mohanty. Oxford: Oxford University Press.

Olaso, Ezequiel de. 1988. "The Two Skepticisms of the Savoyard Vicar." In *The Sceptical Mode in Modern Philosophy: Essays in Honor of Richard H. Popkin,* edited by Richard A. Watson and James E. Force, 43–59. Dordrecht: Martinus Nijhoff.

Ormiston, Alice. 2004. *Love and Politics: Re-Interpreting Hegel.* Albany: State University of New York Press.

Ovid. *Metamorphoses.* 1984. Translated by Frank Justus Miller. Cambridge, Mass.: Harvard University Press.

Pahl, Katrin. 2009. "Emotionality: A Brief Introduction." *Modern Language Notes* 123, no. 4: 547–54.

———. 2005. "A Reading of Love in Hölderlin's 'Andenken.'" *German Quarterly* 78, no. 2: 192–206.

Pfau, Thomas. 2005. *Romantic Moods: Paranoia, Trauma, and Melancholy, 1790–1840.* Baltimore, Md.: Johns Hopkins University Press.

Pinkard, Terry. 2008. "What Is a 'Shape of Spirit?'" In *Hegel's Phenomenology of Spirit: A Critical Guide,* edited by Dean Moyar and Michael Quante. Cambridge, Eng.: Cambridge University Press.

———. 2007. "Symbolic, Classical, and Romantic Art." In *Hegel and the Arts,* edited by Steven Houlgate. Evanston, Ill.: Northwestern University Press.

———. 2004. "Reason, Recognition, and Historicity." In *Subjektivität und Anerkennung,* edited by Barbara Merker, Georg Mohr, and Michael Quante, 47–66. Paderborn: Mentis.

———. 1994. *Hegel's Phenomenology: The Sociality of Reason.* Cambridge, Eng.: Cambridge University Press.

Pippin, Robert P. 2008. *Hegel's Practical Philosophy: Rational Agency and Ethical Life.* Cambridge, Eng.: Cambridge University Press.

Popkin, Richard H. 1992. "New Views on the Role of Skepticism in the Enlightenment." *Modern Language Quarterly* 53, no. 3: 279–97.

Rainford, Lydia. 2005. *She Changes by Intrigue.* Amsterdam: Rodopi.

Rajan, Tilottama. 2004. "(In)digestible Material: Illness and Dialectic in Hegel's Philosophy of Nature." In *Cultures of Taste / Theories of Appetite: Eating Romanticism,* edited by Timothy Morton, 217–36. New York: Palgrave Macmillan.

———. 1995. "Phenomenology and Romantic Theory: Hegel and the Subversion of Aesthetics." In *Questioning Romanticism,* edited by John Beer, 155–78. Baltimore, Md.: Johns Hopkins University Press.

Ravven, Heidi M. 1996. "Has Hegel Anything to Say to Feminists?" In *Feminist Interpretations of G. W. F. Hegel,* edited by Patricia Jagentowicz Mills, 225–52. University Park: Pennsylvania State University Press.

Redding, Paul. 1999. *The Logic of Affect.* Ithaca, N.Y.: Cornell University Press.

Reemtsma, Jan Philipp. 2008. *Vertrauen und Gewalt: Versuch über eine besondere Konstellation der Moderne.* Hamburg: Hamburger Edition.

Riesman, David. 1961. *The Lonely Crowd: A Study of the Changing American Character.* New Haven, Conn.: Yale University Press.

Riley, Denise. 2005. *Impersonal Passion: Language as Affect.* Durham, N.C.: Duke University Press.

Rousseau, Jean-Jacques. 1992. *The Reveries of the Solitary Walker.* Translated by Charles E. Butterworth. Indianapolis, Ind.: Hackett.

———. 1979. *Emile, or On Education.* Translated by Allan Bloom. New York: Basic Books.

———. 1920. "A Discourse on the Origins of Inequality." Translated by G. D. H. Cole. In *The Social Contract and Disourses,* 155–255. London: J.M. Dent.

Royce, Josiah. 1919. *Lectures on Modern Idealism.* New Haven, Conn.: Yale University Press.

Russo, Elena. 2007. *Styles of Enlightenment: Taste, Politics and Authorship in Eighteenth-Century France.* Baltimore, Md.: Johns Hopkins University Press.

Santner, Eric L. 1985. "Sober Recollections: Hölderlin's De-Idealizations of Memory in Andenken." *Germanic Review* 60, no. 1: 16–22.

Sartre, Jean-Paul. 1995. *Esquisse d'une théorie des émotions.* Paris: Hermann.

Scarry, Elaine. 1997. *The Body in Pain: The Making and Unmaking of the World.* Oxford: Oxford University Press.

Schiller, Friedrich. 1983. *Schillers Werke: Nationalausgabe.* Edited by Norbert Oellers. Weimar: Hermann Böhlaus Nachfolger.

———. 1982. *On the Aesthetic Education of Man in a Series of Letters.* Translated by Elizabeth M. Wilkinson and L. A. Willoughby. Oxford: Clarendon.

———. 1902. *The Poems of Schiller.* Translated by E. P. Arnold-Forster. New York: Henry Holt.

Schlegel, Friedrich. 1967. "Athenäum Fragment 206." In *Kritische Friedrich-Schlegel-Ausgabe,* vol. 2, edited by Ernst Behler, Jean-Jacques Anstett, and Hans Eichner. Paderborn: Schöningh.

Schleiermacher, Friedrich. 2004. "Über das Wesen der Religion." In *Über die Religion: Reden an die Gebildeten unter ihren Verächtern,* 22–74. Hamburg: Meiner.

Schmidt, James. 1998. "Cabbage Heads and Gulps of Water: Hegel on Terror." *Political Theory* 26, no. 1: 4–32.

Schopenhauer, Arthur. 1988. "Die Welt als Wille und Vorstellung." In *Arthur Schopenhauers Werke in fünf Bänden.* Zürich: Haffmans Verlag.

Simon, Josef. 1966. *Der Begriff der Sprache bei Hegel.* Stuttgart: Kohlhammer.

Smock, Ann. 2003. *What Is There to Say?* Lincoln: University of Nebraska Press.

———. 1984. "Disastrous Responsibility." *L'esprit créateur* 24, no. 3: 5–20.

Sokolsky, Anita. 1987. "The Resistance to Sentimentality: Yeats, de Man, and the Aesthetic Education." *Yale Journal of Criticism* 1, no. 1: 67–86.

Solomon, Robert E. 1983. *In the Spirit of Hegel: A Study of G. W. F. Hegel's Phenomenology of Spirit.* Oxford: Oxford University Press.

Sophocles. 2003. "Antigone." In *Sophokles: Antigone.* Translated by David Franklin and John Harrison. Cambridge and New York: Cambridge University Press.

———. 1996. "Fragments." In *Sophocles,* vol. 3, translated by Hugh Lloyd-Jones. Cambridge, Mass.: Harvard University Press.

———. 1995. "Antigone." In Sophokles, *Dramen: Griechisch und deutsch,* translated by W. Willige and K. Bayer. Munich: Artemis.

———. 1955. "Antigone." In *Sophokles: Antigone: Tragödie,* translated by Wilhelm Kuchenmüller. Stuttgart: Reclam.

———. 1954. "Antigone." In *Sophocles I,* translated by Elizabeth Wyckoff, edited by David Grene and Richmond Lattimore, 157–204. Chicago: University of Chicago Press.

Speight, Allen. 2001. *Hegel, Literature and the Problem of Agency.* Cambridge, Eng.: Cambridge University Press.

Stein, Gertrude. 1999. "Sacred Emily." In *Stein: Writings 1903–1932,* 387–96. New York: Library of America.

Surber, Jere, ed. 2006. *Hegel and Language.* Albany: State University of New York Press.

Szondi, Peter. 2002. "Hegel." Translated by Paul Fleming. In *An Essay on the Tragic,* 15–22. Stanford, Calif.: Stanford University Press.

Taylor, Charles. 1994. "The Politics of Recognition." In *Multiculturalism: Examining the Politics of Recognition,* edited by Amy Gutmann, 25–73. Princeton, N.J.: Princeton University Press.

———. 1992. "The Expressivist Turn." In *Sources of the Self: The Making of the Modern Identity,* 368–90. Cambridge, Eng.: Cambridge University Press.

———. 1991. "The Need for Recognition." In *The Ethics of Authenticity,* 43–53. Cambridge, Mass.: Harvard University Press.

———. 1979. *Hegel and Modern Society.* Cambridge, Eng.: Cambridge University Press.

Taylor, Mark C. 1990. *Tears.* Albany: State University of New York Press.

Terada, Rei. 2001. *Feeling in Theory: Emotion after the Death of the Subject.* Cambridge, Mass.: Harvard University Press.

Trilling, Lionel. 1972. *Sincerity and Authenticity.* Cambridge, Mass.: Harvard University Press.

Trinh T. Minh-ha. 1999. *Cinema Interval.* New York: Routledge.

———. 1989. *Woman Native Other.* Bloomington: Indiana University Press.

Trinh T. Minh-ha and Lynn Marie Kirby. 1999. *Nothing But Ways.* Installation at the Yerba Buena Center for the Arts, San Francisco, June 5–August 15.

Tripp, Edward. 1970. *Crowell's Handbook of Classical Mythology.* New York: Crowell.

Wahl, Jean. 1929. *Le malheur de la conscience dans la philosophie de Hegel.* Paris: Rieder.

Warminski, Andrzej. 1987. *Readings in Interpretation: Hölderlin, Hegel, Heidegger.* Minneapolis: University of Minnesota Press.

Žižek, Slavoj. 2009. "Discipline Between Two Freedoms: Madness and Habit in German Idealism." In *Mythology, Madness, and Laughter: Subjectivity in German Idealism,* edited by Markus Gabriel and Slavoj Žižek, 95–121. London: Continuum.

———. 2006. *The Parallax View.* Cambridge, Mass.: MIT Press.

———. 2005. "The Act and Its Vicissitudes." In *The Symptom: Online Journal for Lacan* 6, Spring (May 26).

———. 2001. *On Belief.* London: Routledge.

———. 1993. *Tarrying with the Negative: Kant, Hegel, and the Critique of Ideology.* Durham, N.C.: Duke University Press.

Index

Katrin Pahl is an assistant professor of German at the Johns Hopkins University.